Palgrave Studies of Marketing in Emerging Economies

This book series focuses on contemporary themes in marketing and marketing management research in emerging markets and developing economies. Books in the series cover the BRICS (Brazil, Russia, India, China and South Africa), MINT (Mexico, Indonesia, Nigeria and Turkey), CIVETS (Colombia, Indonesia, Vietnam, Egypt, Turkey, and South Africa); EAGLE economies (those which are expected to lead growth in the next ten years, such as Brazil, China, India, Indonesia, South Korea, Mexico, Russia, Taiwan, and Turkey) and all other African countries (classified under developing countries), taking into consideration the demographic, socio-cultural and macro-economic factors influencing consumer choices in these markets. The series synthesizes key subject areas in marketing, discuss marketing issues, processes, procedures and strategies across communities, regions and continents, and also the way digital innovation is changing the business landscape in emerging economies.

Palgrave Studies of Marketing in Emerging Economies presents a unique opportunity to examine and discuss marketing strategy and its implications in emerging economies, thereby filling a gap in current marketing literature.

All chapter submissions to the series will undergo a double blind peer review and all book proposals will undergo a single blind peer review.

More information about this series at
https://link.springer.com/bookseries/16591

Ogechi Adeola · Jude N. Edeh ·
Robert E. Hinson · Fulufhelo Netswera
Editors

Digital Service Delivery in Africa

Platforms and Practices

palgrave
macmillan

Editors
Ogechi Adeola
Lagos Business School
Lagos, Nigeria

Robert E. Hinson
University of Ghana Business School
University of Ghana
Accra, Ghana

Jude N. Edeh
Kedge Business School
Marseilles, France

Fulufhelo Netswera
Durban University of Technology
Durban, South Africa

ISSN 2730-5554 ISSN 2730-5562 (electronic)
Palgrave Studies of Marketing in Emerging Economies
ISBN 978-3-030-83908-6 ISBN 978-3-030-83909-3 (eBook)
https://doi.org/10.1007/978-3-030-83909-3

This Palgrave Macmillan imprint is published by the registered company Springer Nature Switzerland AG
The registered company address is: Gewerbestrasse 11, 6330 Cham, Switzerland

Preface

Digitalisation is transforming value chains, ecosystems and operation dynamism. The adoption of digital technologies is increasingly becoming an imperative for enterprises irrespective of their size, age, location, or industry. By utilising digital technologies, governments and enterprises across the globe are creating value, sustaining competitive advantage and improving the delivery of services to citizens and customers. In developing economies such as Africa, digitalisation holds huge opportunities. It enables enterprises to develop innovative business models, create stronger interactive loops with clients, engage and manage relationships with customers better. Against this background, this book aims to enhance our knowledge of how enterprises and governments in Africa leverage various digital technologies and digital platforms in their service delivery.

In Africa, digitalisation has led to the creation of new ventures, the transformation of existing businesses and the rise in digital entrepreneurship. It is a success factor for doing business in today's world, hence it is no longer an option but a survival and growth strategic tool. By effectively leveraging digital technologies, organisations can create value, enhance service delivery, gain competitive advantage and achieve sustainable performance. This book examines how African enterprises and governments are re-thinking, developing and implementing digital technologies in service delivery by leveraging platforms, and adopting new practices. As digital business transformation requires that organisations develop core competencies that allow them to exploit digital business opportunities, the book places special focus on skills that enable organisations to create value in digital business. These skills are even more critical in the present time, as the Covid-19 pandemic has revealed, with its disruptions of traditional ways of doing business.

The book is novel in its approach because it moves the discourse beyond the mere application of digital tools to examine how African enterprises in private and public sectors utilise digital technologies to engage, retain and manage their relationships with citizens, customers and other stakeholders. Finally, it brings together insights from both scholars and practitioners and as a result, covers a broader readership, ranging from a general audience and students to academics and practitioners who desire to gain a deeper understanding of digital service delivery in Africa.

Lagos, Nigeria — Ogechi Adeola
Marseilles, France — Jude N. Edeh
Accra, Ghana — Robert E. Hinson
Durban, South Africa — Fulufhelo Netswera

Contents

Part I Digital Service Delivery - The African Context

1 **Digital Service Delivery in Africa: An Introduction** 3
Ogechi Adeola, Jude N. Edeh, Robert E. Hinson, and Fulufhelo Netswera

2 **Digital Channels Catalysing Businesses in Fast-Expanding African Markets** 17
Esi A. Elliot, Robert E. Hinson, Anthony Annan, and Martin J. Eppler

3 **The Role of African Founded Firms in the Growth of the Digital Economy** 53
Ebimo Amungo

4 **Customer Relationship Management and Business Performance: Do Digital Platform Capabilities Matter?** 81
Jude N. Edeh

5 **Digital Supply Chain in Sub-Saharan Africa: A Multi-Country Study** 107
Marvel Ogah and Raymond Onuoha

Part II Country- Based Themes and Practices

6 **Digital Entrepreneurship in Africa: Case Studies of Nigeria and South Sudan** 135
Itoro Emembolu, Charles Emembolu, Olumide Aderinwale, and Emmanuel Lobijo

7 **Digital Informal Credit System for Student Entrepreneurship Promotion in Higher Learning - The Case of South Africa** 163
Ishmael Obaeko Iwara

8 **Banking the Cocoa Farmer in Ghana: The Role of Mobile Technology** 187
Robert E. Hinson and Louis Numelio Tettey

9 **Strategy in Digital Business—The East African Perspective** 205
Paul Katuse

10 **Digitalisation and Public Sector Service Delivery in Kenya** 229
Abel Kinoti Meru and Mary Wanjiru Kinoti

Part III Recommendations for Skills Development in Digital Service Delivery

11 **Digital Skills and Strategic Postures: Insights from African Digital Entrepreneurs** 251
Nasiru Taura

12 **Developing and Managing Skills and Competencies for Digital Business in Africa** 281
Isaiah Adisa and Ogechi Adeola

13 **Virtual Teams: The New Work Norm for the Post Covid-19 Era** 305
Abdullah Promise Opute

14 **NETIQUETTE: Towards Digital Etiquette in Africa** 327
J. N. Halm

Index 351

Notes on Contributors

Ogechi Adeola is an Associate Professor of Marketing and Head of Department of Operations, Marketing and Information Systems at the Lagos Business School, Pan-Atlantic University, Nigeria. She is 2016 Visiting International Fellow, Open University Business School, UK and a 2017 Paul R. Lawrence Fellow, USA. She has published academic papers in top peer-reviewed journals, and her co-authored articles won Best Paper Awards at international conferences in 2016–2019, consecutively. She is the founder of *Digital Business Tutelage for Women Empowerment in Africa Initiative*.

Olumide Aderinwale is the Operations Manager at TechQuest STEM Academy. He is skilled in agile project management, non-profit leadership and education technology. He is a Project Management Professional PMP® with the Project Management Institute, and holds a certificate course in Operations Management from the Kellogg School of Management, Northwestern University. Olumide, a Microsoft Innovative Educator Expert, is passionate about social impact and development in Nigeria. He is driven by a personal mantra that Africa's problems would be solved by Africans. At TechQuest, he manages the design, implementation and evaluation of TechQuest's programmes and strategic initiatives across Nigeria.

Isaiah Adisa is a management researcher and consultant based in Nigeria. He holds a MSc degree in Industrial Relations & Human Resource Management from the Olabisi Onabanjo University, Ago-Iwoye, Nigeria. Isaiah has co-edited book(s) on green marketing and green people management. He has co-authored book chapters and journal articles to his name. His research interest cut across human resources management, organisational behaviour, marketing and gender studies.

Ebimo Amungo is Managing Partner of Amungo Consulting. He has had a career as a journalist and an academic. He is presently an independent researcher with a strong interest in international business, African diaspora studies and determinants of Africa's development path. He is the author of "The Rise of the African Multinational Enterprise: The Lions accelerating the development of Africa."

Anthony Annan is an Assistant Professor of Finance at Caldwell University. He received his Doctorate in Business Administration from the Georgia State University, and Master of Business Administration (M.B.A.) from The Wharton School (University of Pennsylvania). He is a Research Associate at the Centre for Engaged Business Research, Georgia State University. His broad areas of research interest include development finance, corporate finance and strategic management. Dr. Annan's has held senior management roles at the International Monetary Fund (IMF), Citigroup Inc., Standard Bank Group and Ecobank Transnational. He is a certified business valuation analyst.

Jude N. Edeh is a postdoctoral researcher with the Chair of Business as Unusual: Innovative Practices and New Business Models at the Kedge Business School Marseille, France. He received his Ph.D. from the Faculty of Economics and Business Sciences, University of Sevilla, Spain. His research is at the intersection of innovation, global strategy, international business and digitalisation in the context of organisational transformation. He has published in several academic journals and won Best Paper Award.

Esi A. Elliot is a professor of International Business at the University of Texas at Rio Grande Valley. She has extensive teaching experience at various universities including George Washington University and the University of Illinois at Chicago. Her academic achievements as a global innovation educator has won her an award from Marquis who is who Industry leadership as well as millennium award. Dr. Elliot has published her works in many scholarly Marketing and International Business journals and has contributed articles to scientific journals and chapters to multicultural books as well as authored a novel.

Charles Emembolu is an IT professional with 2 decades of cognate experience in IT Strategy, Business Transformation, Innovation and Entrepreneurship. He is a serial entrepreneur and an information technology systems architect. He holds an Engineering degree from the University of Nigeria, has attended Management programmes at Lagos Business School, Harvard University and obtained a diploma in entrepreneurship and innovation from Lund University Sweden. Besides founding Crestsage Limited, he founded TechQuest STEM Academy, a not-for-profit STEM education organisation, (http://www.tqstem.org/), co-founded Roar Nigeria Hub (www.roarnigeria.org), Nigeria's 1st University embedded business/technology incubator.

Itoro Emembolu is a Director at TechQuest STEM Academy, a technology education hub in Nigeria, and a Researcher at Northumbria University, UK. She is a STEM advocate, a digital access and technology adoption enthusiast and a TedX speaker. She has a B.Eng. in Mechanical Engineering, An MSc in International Business, Energy & Petroleum, an M.Phil. in Management and a Ph.D. in Computer Networks & Security. Itoro was recently recognised by AfriLabs SHEROES of Africa for her leadership role in improving education and providing decent work through EdTech Innovation and she is the Principal Lead on the Female Entrepreneurship Support Programme initiative.

Martin J. Eppler is a Swiss communication and management scholar, Professor of Media and Communication Management at the University of St. Gallen and director of its Institute for Media and Communication Management, known for his contributions in the field of knowledge management, specifically information overload and Information Quality Management, Collaboration and Knowledge Visualisation. Dr. Eppler has teaching experience in various universities including the University of Geneva, Georgiatech, Simon Fraser University in the United States and Cambridge University. In the United Kingdom.

J. N. Halm is an entrepreneur, author, speaker and business consultant specialising in *Service Excellence.* He has a decade of experience from Ghana's banking industry. He holds an M.Phil. in Communications from School of Communication Studies, University of Ghana and a BSc in Agriculture from Kwame Nkrumah University of Science and Technology. Halm is a weekly columnist with a full-page column in Ghana's leading business newsprint, *Business & Financial Times.* He is also the author of two award-winning books, *CUSTOMER ROMANCE* and *SERVICE SINS.* He was adjudged the Service Excellence Leader Award at the 2019 Global Brands Awards.

Robert E. Hinson is a marketing communications practitioner, turned scholar. He holds a D.Phil. in Marketing from the University of Ghana and a Ph.D. in International Business from the Aalborg University Business School. Since turning scholar in 2003, Robert has served as Rector of the Perez University College, Acting Director of Institutional Advancement at the University of Ghana and twice as Head of the Department of Marketing of Entrepreneurship at the University of Ghana Business School. In 2019, Prof Hinson was listed as one of the top 100 speakers in Ghana by the Speakers Bureau Africa (https://speakersafrica.com/top100-3/).

Ishmael Obaeko Iwara has received his Ph.D. and Master's degree in Rural Development with a focus in Entrepreneurship and Economics from the University of Venda, where he is a Research Fellow. Over the years, his research agenda has evolved in the pursuit of distilling traditional African models for entrepreneurship promotion on the continent. His research leadership history among others includes Manager, NRF funded project on Social Innovation and Entrepreneurship and Co-principal Investigator, Buddy programme for social cohesion, both at the University of Venda.

Paul Katuse is an Associate Professor of Strategic Management. He teaches and trains on Strategy and Change Management. He has consulted with several organisations both public and private and has been an external examiner and a visiting faculty for several Universities in Africa, Asia and the Middle East. He is interested in globalisation and its impact on society advances made by organisations to acclimatise with their dynamic environments and the role of strategic leadership.

Mary Wanjiru Kinoti is an Associate Professor of Marketing and acting Director, Intellectual Property Management Office and the Associate Dean, Graduate Studies, School of Business, University of Nairobi. Her research interests are mainstreaming green marketing and customer care in public institutions and among micro, small and medium enterprises in sub-Saharan Africa.

Emmanuel Lobijo is a South Sudanese social entrepreneur and an activist. He studied Entrepreneurship and Innovation at HTC and has an Advanced Certificate in Peace Building and Conflict Resolution from Whitaker Peace and Development Initiatives. He is the Cofounder of Elite Security and Concierge Services, a private security firm in South Sudan, founder and Executive Director at Junub Open Space, a technology information and innovation hub, Team54project international coordinator, a group of youth driving Climate Action, an ambassador for Youth for Planet and a volunteer at EatBCH SS.

Abel Kinoti Meru is an Associate Professor of Business Management, acting Deputy Vice-Chancellor, Academic Affairs and Dean, Riara School of Business, Riara University, Kenya and first Chair of Academy of International Business Africa—Chapter. His research interests are in social innovation and business incubation, entrepreneurship and marketing.

Fulufhelo Netswera holds a D.Phil. Sociology of Development from the University of Stellenbosch. He is the former director of the North West University Business School and Philanthropy fellow of the City University of New York. Currently dean of the Faculty of Management Sciences at the Durban University of Technology (DUT). He writes in the areas of entrepreneurship, governance and higher education management and policy.

Marvel Ogah is a full-time faculty member and Alternate Director, M.B.A. programmes at Lagos Business School, Pan-Atlantic University where he facilitates sessions in operations and supply chain management; his research interests include lean and behavioural operations. Before transiting to academia, Marvel had worked as a management executive in various operational roles spanning over two decades. Among his publications, he recently co-authored a book titled "Work-Life Integration in Africa: A Multidimensional Approach to Achieve Balance" which was published by Palgrave in 2021.

Raymond Onuoha is a Technology Policy Fellow at the Lagos Business School (LBS), where his research focuses on the institutional and policy challenges in the evolution of the digital economy and technology innovation in developing countries, with a focus on sub-Saharan Africa. Raymond is a Doctoral Fellow of the IDRC Award (2018) which aims to build emerging leaders in communications policy in the Global South and is currently a doctoral candidate at the Nelson Mandela School of Public Governance (NMSPG), University of Cape Town (UCT), South Africa where his thesis interrogates competition policy in developing countries' telecommunications market.

Abdullah Promise Opute is a researcher and freelance academic and management consultant with over 15years professional experience in the academic industry. Dr. Abdullah Promise Opute is Visiting Professor (Lecturer, Ph.D. (D.B.A.) Supervisor and Examiner) in several Management fields at UK and African Universities. He won "Best Paper" award at the AM-Conference in 2007. Dr. Abdullah Promise Opute is a reviewer, and has published in top Journals. His research interest includes inter-functional integration, relationship management, cross-cultural management, consumer behaviour, entrepreneurship and SMEs, strategic management accounting, etc.

Louis Numelio Tettey holds a degree in Bachelor of Science in Marketing from the University of Professional Studies, Accra where he obtained a First-Class Honour, an M.Phil. in Marketing from the

University of Ghana and a Certificate in Business Accounting from the Chartered Institute of Management Accounting (CIMA). Currently, He is a Senior Research Assistant and the Head of Marketing and Communications at the Office of Institutional Advancement, University of Ghana. He is passionate about research.

Nasiru Taura is a Senior Lecturer in Entrepreneurship at Bournemouth University, UK. He is a seasoned academic, international consultant on innovation management, digital entrepreneur and social innovator. With over 10 years' experience, his research and professional expertise cover aspects of Entrepreneurship, innovation in hostile environments and design management. He was the acting programme coordinator for M.Sc. Innovation Management & Entrepreneurship (IME) at Bournemouth University, UK (2019–2020), and also served as an academic lead to the Bournemouth University's Small Business Charter accreditation team. He is a visiting lecturer at Southampton University, UK, and an External Examiner at Bath Spa University, UK. He is currently an Associate Editor of the Journal of the International Council for Small Business (Washington DC).

List of Figures

Fig. 3.1	Individuals using internets in Sub-Saharan Africa (*Source* World Bank Development Indicators)	62
Fig. 3.2	Map showing the various submarine cables in Africa (*Source* Steven Song: Many possibilities)	63
Fig. 6.1	Ability to use of business development resources	147
Fig. 6.2	Ability to use of collaborative tools	148
Fig. 6.3	Ability to leverage technology for business	148
Fig. 7.1	Motivation for involvement in E-Stokvel consolidated by the author	173
Fig. 8.1	Cocoa farmer access to mobile banking technology benefit (CFAMBTB) model (*Source* Authors)	192
Fig. 11.1	The Digital Entrepreneurs Skills Matrix (*Source* Author's Diagram)	272
Fig. 12.1	Process of developing digital skills and competencies (*Source* Authors)	295
Fig. 12.2	Steps to managing digital skills and competencies in Africa (*Source* Authors)	296
Fig. 13.1	Optimising Virtual Team Working: A Leadership Strategy underpinned on HRM, Infrastructural and Psychological Foundations (*Source* Author)	317

List of Tables

Table 2.1	Demographic profile of participants—microenterprise customers in Ghana and Kenya	25
Table 2.2	Demographic profile of participants—financial services firms in Ghana	26
Table 2.3	Social media and outcomes of digital social networks	38
Table 2.4	Upscaling of social media ecosystems	40
Table 2.5	Table of participant narrations	42
Table 2.6	Social ecosystems illustrations with indirect network effects	45
Table 3.1	Some of the largest Fintechs in Africa	71
Table 4.1	Convergent validity results	92
Table 4.2	Discriminant validity (Fornell-Larcker criterion) (Heterotrait-Monotrait Ratio)	93
Table 4.3	Results of the structural equation model test	94
Table 6.1	Identified challenges of digital entrepreneurship in Africa	150
Table 6.2	Identified opportunities for digital entrepreneurship in Africa	154

Table 7.1 Nature of student enterprises at the university 170
Table 12.1 Skills needed for digital businesses transformation 287
Table 13.1 Level of Use of Virtual Working Teams in Organisations (including Estimates of Use) 310

Part I

Digital Service Delivery - The African Context

1

Digital Service Delivery in Africa: An Introduction

Ogechi Adeola, Jude N. Edeh, Robert E. Hinson, and Fulufhelo Netswera

1.1 Digital Transformation in Today's Global Economy

Today's globalised world is characterised by pervasive digital technologies. These technologies permeate the core of the way we live, work and do business (Makridakis, 2017; Pirola et al., 2020; Roundy & Fayard, 2019). Increasingly, business operations and processes are driven

O. Adeola (✉)
Lagos Business School, Pan-Atlantic University, Lagos, Nigeria
e-mail: oadeola@lbs.edu.ng

J. N. Edeh
Kedge Business School, Marseille, France
e-mail: jude.edeh@kedgebs.com

R. E. Hinson
University of Ghana Business School, Accra, Ghana
e-mail: rhinson@ug.edu.gh

O. Adeola et al. (eds.), *Digital Service Delivery in Africa*, Palgrave Studies of Marketing in Emerging Economies,
https://doi.org/10.1007/978-3-030-83909-3_1

by digital and knowledge-based resources. Digital reality is facilitating a new form of organisational change, namely; digital transformation (Tekic & Koroteev, 2019). Digitalisation is the adoption or integration of digital technologies into business to enhance processes and services (Liu et al., 2011; Van Veldhoven & Vanthienen, 2021). It creates, among other things, new market opportunities and unparalleled consumer choice (Kopalle et al., 2020). Companies utilising the potentials of digital technologies can develop new products and services. Besides, they can integrate these emerging technologies into their organisation as well as functional structures (Hinterhuber & Nilles, 2021; Vial, 2019). Certainly, digitalisation offers a wide range of growth opportunities because it expands the customer base beyond the traditional physical reach. For example, high performing enterprises such as Amazon, Alphabet, Jumia, Tesla, Mpesa, Flutterwave, etc. have a common success factor, namely, the use of new digital technologies. Expectedly, scholars are beginning to describe digital technology as a 'general-purpose technology' because of its ability to continually self-transform, branch out and increase productivity across all sectors and industries (Brynjolfsson & McAfee, 2014; Mühleisen, 2018).

However, these digital trends and advancement are accelerating the speed of change in the business environment as well as shifting the foundations of competition (Ghezzi & Cavallo, 2020). These developments, among other things, imply that enterprises failing to integrate digital technologies into their strategy and operations will struggle to attract new customers and retain existing ones as well as survive in today's changing marketplace. Digitalisation is becoming inevitable for sustainable competitiveness and the growth of enterprises of all sizes. Despite its potential, the adoption of digital technologies is to a large extent shaped by the availability of resources and capabilities, which in turn creates a digital divide. For example, there is a significant digital technology adoption gap between small and large companies (Denicolai et al., 2021;

F. Netswera
Durban University of Technology, Durban, South Africa
e-mail: fulufheloN@dut.ac.za

Van Deursen & Van Dijk, 2011). Similarly, enterprises from developed economies have much higher rates of digital technology adoption than their counterparts in developing economies such as Africa (Cariolle, 2021; Mignamissi & Djijo, 2021). However, this is not surprising due to the presence of certain barriers (e.g. access to electricity, digital literacy, financial constraints, adequate policy frameworks) prevalent in these regions (Apulu & Ige, 2011; Melia, 2020; Yoon, 2020). As a result of these factors, enterprises in these regions are yet to fully reap the numerous opportunities linked to digitalisation (Counted & Arawole, 2016).

While there are burgeoning studies proffering recommendations on how this digital divide can be bridged (Albiman & Sulong, 2016; Myovella et al., 2020), our knowledge of how African enterprises adopt and leverage digital technologies is still limited (Badran, 2021; Steel, 2021). Against this backdrop, this book fills this gap by exploring the various digital technologies and digital platforms that enterprises in Africa deploy to enhance efficiency in service delivery.

1.2 Africa and Digital Opportunities

Africa is not immune to the impact of the digital revolution (Solomon & van Klyton, 2020). Research shows that the dynamics of digital technologies in transforming industries across Africa and enabling enterprises in the region to create sustainable competitive advantage and value for customers and clients is undisputed (Odularu & Adekunle, 2020). Notably, the barrier-breaking effect of digital technologies has brought about a 'new space' where the existing geographical location is rapidly becoming less relevant for doing business today (Ritter & Pedersen, 2020). This has important growth implications for Africa (Myovella et al., 2020). With more than 1.3 billion inhabitants, more than 40% below the age of 16, and three of the top five fastest-growing economies in the world, digitalisation has enormous opportunities for African enterprises (The Africa Report, 2020). Hence, to exploit the full potential of the current digital marketplace, African enterprises, especially companies in the service delivery sector, need to adopt new structures, processes and business models that will enable them to respond and satisfy customers' demands (Sjödin et al., 2020). In other words, enterprises that fail to strategically integrate digital technologies into their service delivery process stand a higher risk of failure and exit (Bouwman et al., 2019).

The current Coronavirus (COVID-19) pandemic has shown that the adoption of digital technologies is now a business imperative. COVID-19 crisis, though a health tragedy, has significant adverse impact on the global economy (Hossain, 2021). In Africa, for example, economic growth declined by 2.1% in 2020 (African Development Bank, 2021). In terms of economic growth, the South African region was the hardest hit by the Covid-19 pandemic in 2020, followed by the Central African, West African, North African regions, respectively (Anyanwu & Salami, 2021). COVID-19 crisis continues to change the way enterprises of all sizes and in all sectors do business in Africa. Despite the efforts of the private sector and governments across the region, many private and public enterprises in Africa are still struggling to survive and navigate the effects of the COVID-19 crisis. To overcome these challenges, these enterprises are re-thinking and deploying innovative ways of serving their customers. In other words, the disruption caused by the COVID-19 pandemic requires a digital-embedded strategy that ensures not only the survival but also enhances the productivity of African enterprises.

Digitalisation has been identified as a major driver of value creation and service delivery, especially during this crisis (Priyono et al., 2020; Richter, 2020). The McKinsey Global Survey conducted in 2020 shows that responses to COVID-19 have accelerated the integration of digital technologies into customer and supply-chain interactions by several years. If properly utilised it 'contains the seeds of a large-scale reimagination of Africa's economic structure, service delivery systems and social contract' (McKinsey & Company, 2020: 4). Digitalisation can immensely contribute to the recovery and growth of African enterprises, as digital platforms and other related tools enable them to leverage opportunities (Bharadwaj, 2000; De Reuver et al., 2018). According to Hänninen et al., (2018: 155), digital platforms are 'dynamic and purposive inter- or intra-dependent networks where participants co-create value, and to which participants attach supplementary products, services, or technologies'. One example of firms utilising these opportunities is *Kobo360*, a freight logistics company that uses digital platforms to connect truck owners and fleet operators with customers across Kenya, Uganda, Togo and Ghana, thereby making delivery fast, efficient, affordable and transparent. Similarly, *Greenage Energy* is integrating a vast range of digital tools in its delivery of renewable energy services to homeowners, schools, businesses and government institutions across sub-Saharan Africa. Digital technologies hold great potential for African enterprises, especially in the service sector. In other words, these enterprises can transform their operations, develop new capabilities and serve their customers/clients more efficiently by leveraging digital technologies.

1.3 Digital Service Delivery in Africa

This book focuses on how digitalisation is shaping service delivery in Africa. The concept of service delivery is an essential aspect of management and marketing (Goodwin & Radford, 1993; Spurrell et al., 2019). It includes how enterprises design, process, and deliver value propositions to customers, clients and users (Ponsignon et al., 2011; Seyitoğlu & Ivanov, 2020). The digitalisation of service delivery can be beneficial to customers, users and organisations in several ways (Chowdhury et al., 2021). For example, it enables enterprises to explore and understand customers' needs as well as improve service quality (Chan & Tung, 2019). In this book, Digital Service Delivery (DSD) is conceptualised as the utilisation of digital technologies in the design, process, and actual delivery of services to customers or clients for increased effectiveness and efficiency. Enterprises in Africa can use digital technologies to gather and share data to enhance their organisational systems, structures and processes. Besides, enterprises can leverage digital platforms to interact and respond to customers' needs efficiently (Fernández-Rovira et al., 2021), and in turn, sustain competitive advantage and productivity (Ibarra et al., 2019). Moreover, digital technologies create new business opportunities, drive and diversify service offerings and delivery, especially in today's changing environment (Berman, 2012; Zaki, 2019).

Although research is expanding and offering insights into the opportunities, drivers, and models of digital service delivery (Coreynen et al., 2020), surprisingly there is still a paucity of studies in the African market. Significantly, the notion of DSD in Africa remains largely unclear. This lack of clarity may lead to ambiguous perceptions of DSD. Additionally, there is insufficient research examining the emergence and evolution of DSD business models in developing countries, particularly Africa. This book addresses these gaps. Beyond the mere application of digital tools, it considers how African enterprises both in the private and public sectors utilise digital technologies to attract, engage, retain, and manage their relationships with their customers.

1.4 Overview and Contributions of the Book

This book brings together different approaches and insights from scholars and practitioners on how digitalisation shapes various aspects of service delivery in Africa. The fourteen chapters contained in this book are not only conceptually focused but also based on the multi-country experience of digital service delivery, especially in the sub-Saharan African region. This book is structured in three parts. The first part covers the concept of digital service delivery in the African context; whereas the second part focuses on digital service delivery in various African countries. Finally, part three recommends skills and norms for effective digital service delivery in Africa.

Chapter 2, 'Digital Channels Catalysing Businesses in Fast-Expanding African markets' by Esi Elliot, Robert E. Hinson, Anthony Annan and Martin J. Eppler, addresses how digitalisation promotes profitability and social impact across the continent. Advances in social media and novel business models are increasingly creating dynamic platforms for social interactions and the formation of commercial social networks. The authors explain how digitalisation is shaping new markets that emerge at individual, industry and business levels with robust, and fast-growing economies. The chapter contributes to the literature by extending Hoffman and Novak's (2012) model on how digitalisation evolves into a unique social medium for communication, information and commerce. Finally, the chapter discusses how digitalisation, especially social media, promotes the interaction between Microenterprises and Financial Services Firms.

The COVID-19 pandemic has created unprecedented socio-economic challenges with widespread lockdowns that led to the closure of schools and businesses in Africa. However, digital technologies have helped many countries in Africa respond to the disruptions caused by this pandemic. In Chapter 3 titled 'The Role of African Founded Businesses in Growth of the Digital Economy', Ebimo Amungo, argues that African Founded Firms (AFF) contributed significantly in developing the digital infrastructure that increased access to the internet and digital services in Africa. The chapter also examines the policies and investments that enabled the emergence and expansion of the digital economy in Africa.

Moreover, digital transformation is motivating firms of all sizes to integrate digital platforms into their strategy to attract new customers, manage customer relationships, create new value and achieve greater performance. In Chapter 4, 'Customer Relationship Management and Business Performance: Do Digital Platform Capabilities Matter?' Jude N. Edeh draws on the dynamic capability view to examine how two forms of capabilities, namely, customer relationship management capability and digital platform capability, interact to affect the business performance. Using data from Nigerian small and medium-sized enterprises, the author shows that digital platform capability has a mediating effect on the relationship between customer relationship management capability and business performance. Therefore, the chapter suggests that developing relevant capabilities in today's digitalised business environments is critical to achieving superior performance.

The emergence of digital supply chain management continues to redefine current processes as well as enabling innovative solutions to evolve business needs in Africa. In Chapter 5, 'Digital Supply Chain in Sub-Saharan Africa: A Multi-country Study,' Marvel Ogah and Raymond Onuoha examine digital supply chain framework, transformative aspects of the digital supply chain, opportunities and barriers to sustainable digital supply in Nigeria, South Africa, Kenya and Tanzania.

In Chapter 6, 'Digital Entrepreneurship in Africa: Case Studies of Nigeria and South Sudan', Itoro Emembolu, Charles Emembolu,

Olumide Aderinwale and Emmanuel Lobijo, focus on how digital technologies are enabling African entrepreneurs to overcome the traditional constraints of engagement. The authors outline the emergence of digital entrepreneurship in Africa, highlighting the importance of innovation and organisational skills. Besides, they point out the opportunities and challenges faced by digital enterprises in Africa. Based on surveys and case studies from Nigeria and South Sudan, the authors examine how female entrepreneurs interact with digital technologies. Finally, the authors provide recommendations on how entrepreneurs can secure competitive advantages as well as develop dynamic digital skills and capabilities required for successful entrepreneurship.

Furthermore, informal credit systems, often referred to as Rotating Savings and Credit Associations or Accumulating Savings and Credit Associations, compensate for the lack of access to finance as well as limitations of the formal financial systems in many countries in Africa. In Chapter 7, 'Digital Informal Credit System for Student Entrepreneurship Promotion in Higher Learning', Ishmael Iwara focuses on how digitalisation is shaping the informal credit system in South Africa. Using qualitative data collected from 31 rural-based university students, the author examines the formation, function, motivation, merit and demerit of the digital Stokvel system. The chapter concludes by providing policy and structural arrangement recommendations that can aid in formalising the operations of student digital informal credit initiative for entrepreneurship promotion.

Africans are increasingly connected to the digital space especially through smartphones and other mobile devices. For example, mobile phone adoption and ownership have surged remarkably over the last decade across the continent, presenting a wide range of opportunities to both individuals and enterprises. In Chapter 8, 'Banking the Cocoa Farmers in Ghana: The Role of Mobile Technology', Robert Ebo Hinson and Louis Numelio Tettey highlight the importance of integrating mobile banking technology into the Ghanaian cocoa value chain. They argue that notwithstanding the development of mobile technology, for example, mobile money, and its usage among rural farmers, particularly cocoa farmers in Ghana, it is mainly for personal money transfer purposes. Against this backdrop, the authors suggest how adopting and utilising these technologies for business purposes can promote financial inclusion.

In Chapter 9, 'Strategy in Digital Business: The East African Perspective', Paul Katuse discusses the emergence of digitisation as well as the barriers to digitalisation in the East African region. Drawing on the concept of platformisation, the author explores the impact of digitalisation on the East African marketing sector, marketing activities and competitive landscape. The chapter provides some recommendations on how the integration of digitalisation into the McKinsey model can help enterprises in Africa optimise their service delivery.

Kenya is one of the leading countries in sub-Saharan Africa in terms of the implementation of digital initiatives in the 4th industrial revolution. In Chapter 10, 'Digitalisation and Public Sector Service Delivery in Kenya,' Abel Kinoti Meru and Mary Wanjiru Kinoti argue that a citizen-centric digital public service is important to address the specific needs and wants of the citizens. The authors examine six main elements of digital public service delivery in Kenya. They also discuss how the Kenyan government is digitalising its public services, especially in the areas of essential citizen services, social protection services, health, energy, digital learning, tax administration, judiciary, and land registry. Despite these efforts, the authors made recommendations on how the Kenyan government can enhance service delivery through digitalisation.

Although enterprises and governments in Africa are rapidly embracing digitalisation, they are yet to fully utilise their learning and growth opportunities due to factors such as the scarcity of personnel with the right digital skills and competencies. In Chapter 11, 'Digital Skills and Strategic Postures: Insights from African Digital Entrepreneurs', Nasiru Taura argues that many African digital entrepreneurs engaging in digital skills development do so without a clear strategy. As a result, they end up amassing a wide 'hodgepodge' of a largely fragmented portfolio of digital skills, which do not create and capture local and global values. The author suggests that digital skill development is shaped by a context where an entrepreneur operates. Then, the author discusses the nature of variations, leading to some African entrepreneurs prospering in skill and competency development while others either stagnate or retrogress. Accordingly, the author developed four baseline propositions, namely digital bricolage, passion and learning from failure, breadth and depth of digital skills, and co-evolution of digital competencies.

Isaiah Adisa and Ogechi Adeola, in Chapter 12, 'Developing and Managing Skills and Competencies for Digital Business in Africa', draw on resource-based theory to identify the process of developing and managing digital skills and competencies by businesses. More precisely, the authors argue that digital security, mobile technologies, big data analytics, artificial intelligence are critical to the success of digital business in Africa. The chapter highlights the role of government and businesses in supporting digital capacity building in Africa.

Chapter 13, 'Virtual Teams: The New Work Norm for the Post Covid-19 Era' by Abdullah Promise Opute proposes a theoretical framework that emphasises the role of leadership strategy on effective management of virtual teams working towards optimal symbiotic interrelation, and organisational outcomes of virtual teams. The author outlines psychological factors, human resource management, and infrastructural facilities as the critical factors for managing virtual teams, especially in the post-COVID-19 phase. The chapter concludes by providing recommendations on how organisations in Africa can optimise virtual team experience.

Finally, Chapter 14 'Netiquette: Recommendations for Africa' by J. N. Halm, explores how digital platforms enable social interactions and engenders digital citizenship. The author examines the normative implications of the increased use of digital social platforms. The chapter highlights the main factors driving Netiquette, particularly among internet users in Africa.

References

African Development Bank. (2021). *African Economic Outlook 2021—From debt resolution to growth: The road ahead for Africa.* African Development Bank, Abidjan.

Albiman, M. M., & Sulong, Z. (2016). The role of ICT use to the economic growth in Sub Saharan African region (SSA). *Journal of Science and Technology Policy Management, 7*(3), 306–329.

Anyanwu, J. C., & Salami, A. O. (2021). The impact of COVID-19 on African economies: An introduction. *African Development Review*. https://doi.org/10.1111/1467-8268.12531

Apulu, I., & Ige, E. (2011). Are Nigeria SMEs effectively utilizing ICT? *International Journal of Business and Management, 6*(6), 207–214.

Badran, M. F. (2021). Digital platforms in Africa: A case-study of Jumia Egypt's digital platform. *Telecommunications Policy, 45*(3). https://doi.org/10.1016/j.telpol.2020.102077

Berman, S. J. (2012). Digital transformation: Opportunities to create new business models. *Strategy & Leadership, 40*(2), 16–24.

Bharadwaj, A. S. (2000). A resource-based perspective on information technology capability and firm performance: An empirical investigation. *MIS Quarterly, 24*(1), 169–196.

Bouwman, H., Nikou, S., & de Reuver, M. (2019). Digitalisation, business models, and SMEs: How do business model innovation practices improve performance of digitalising SMEs? *Telecommunications Policy, 43*(9). https://doi.org/10.1016/j.telpol.2019.101828

Brynjolfsson, E., & McAfee, A. (2014). *The second machine age: Work, progress, and prosperity in a time of brilliant technologies*. W. W. Norton.

Cariolle, J. (2021). International connectivity and the digital divide in Sub-Saharan Africa. *Information Economics and Policy, 55*. https://doi.org/10.1016/j.infoecopol.2020.100901

Chan, A. P. H., & Tung, V. W. S. (2019). Examining the effects of robotic service on brand experience: The moderating role of hotel segment. *Journal of Travel & Tourism Marketing, 36*(4), 458–468.

Chowdhury, S., Åkesson, M., & Thomsen, M. (2021). Service innovation in digitalized product platforms: An illustration of the implications of generativity on remote diagnostics of public transport buses. *Technology in Society, 65*. https://doi.org/10.1016/j.techsoc.2021.101589

Counted, A. V., & Arawole, J. O. (2016). 'We are connected, but constrained': Internet inequality and the challenges of millennials in Africa as actors in innovation. *Journal of Innovation and Entrepreneurship, 5*(1), 3. https://doi.org/10.1186/s13731-015-0029-1

Coreynen, W., Matthyssens, P., Vanderstraeten, J., & van Witteloostuijn, A. (2020). Unravelling the internal and external drivers of digital servitisation:

A dynamic capabilities and contingency perspective on firm strategy. *Industrial Marketing Management*. https://doi.org/10.1016/j.indmarman.2020.02.014

De Reuver, M., Sørensen, C., & Basole, R. C. (2018). The digital platform: A research agenda. *Journal of Information Technology, 33*, 124–135.

Denicolai, S., Zucchella, A., & Magnani, G. (2021). Internationalization, digitalization, and sustainability: Are SMEs ready? A survey on synergies and substituting effects among growth paths. *Technological Forecasting and Social Change, 166*. https://doi.org/10.1016/j.techfore.2021.120650

Fernández-Rovira, C., Valdés, J. A. Molleví, G., & Nicolas-Sans, R. (2021). The digital transformation of business. Towards the datafication of the relationship with customers. *Technological Forecasting and Social Change, 162*. https://doi.org/10.1016/j.techfore.2020.120339

Ghezzi, A., & Cavallo, A. (2020). Agile business model innovation in digital entrepreneurship: Lean startup approaches. *Journal of Business Research, 110*, 519–537.

Goodwin, C., & Radford, R. (1993). Models of service delivery: An integrative perspective. In T. A. Swartz, D. E. Bowen, & S. W. Brown (Eds.), *Advances in services marketing and management* (Vol. 2, pp. 231–252). JAI Press.

Hänninen, M., Smedlund, A., & Mitronen, L. (2018). Digitalization in retailing: Multisided platforms as drivers of industry transformation. *Baltic Journal of Management, 13*(2), 152–168.

Hinterhuber, A., & Nilles, M. (2021). DIGITAL transformation, the HOLY GRAIL and the disruption of business models. *Business Horizons*. https://doi.org/10.1016/j.bushor.2021.02.042

Hoffman, D. L., & Novak, T. P. (2012). Social media strategy. In S. Venkatesh & G. S. Carpenter (Eds.), *Handbook of marketing strategy* (pp. 198–214). Cheltenham: Edward Elgar Publishing Limited. ISBN 978-1-84980-098-3.

Hossain, M. (2021). The effect of the Covid-19 on sharing economy activities. *Journal of Cleaner Production, 280*, Part 1. https://doi.org/10.1016/j.jclepro.2020.124782

Ibarra, D., Igartua, J. I., & Ganzarain, J. (2019). Business model innovation from a technology perspective: A review. In Á. Ortiz, C. Andrés Romano, R. Poler, & J. P. García-Sabater (Eds.), *Engineering digital transformation*. Lecture Notes in Management and Industrial Engineering. Springer.

Liu, D., Chen, S., & Chou, T. (2011). Resource fit in digital transformation: Lessons learned from the CBC Bank global e-banking project. *Management Decision, 49*(10), 1728–1742.

Kopalle, P. K., Kumar, V., & Subramaniam, M. (2020). How legacy firms can embrace the digital ecosystem via digital customer orientation. *Journal of the Academy of Marketing Science, 48*, 114–131.

Makridakis, S. (2017). The forthcoming Artificial Intelligence (AI) revolution: Its impact on society and firms. *Futures, 90*, 46–60.

McKinsey & Company. (2020, May 29). *Reopening and reimagining Africa—How the COVID-19 crisis can catalyze change.*

Melia, E. (2020). *African jobs in the digital era: Export options with a focus on online labour* (Working Paper No. 3/2020. Discussion Paper). https://doi.org/10.23661/dp3.2020

Mignamissi, D., &. Djijo T. A. J. (2021). Digital divide and financial development in Africa. *Telecommunications Policy, 45*(9). https://doi.org/10.1016/j.telpol.2021.102199.

Mühleisen, M. (2018). The long and short of the digital revolution. *Finance & Development, 55*(2), 4–8.

Myovella, G., Karacuka, M., & Haucap, J. (2020). Digitalization and economic growth: A comparative analysis of Sub-Saharan Africa and OECD economies. *Telecommunications Policy, 44*(2), 101856. https://doi.org/10.1016/j.telpol.2019.101856

Odularu, G., & Adekunle, B. (2020). Understanding digitalization in the African context. *Journal of African Development, 21*(1), 1–13.

Pirola, F., Cimini, C., & Pinto, R. (2020). Digital readiness assessment of Italian SMEs: A case-study research. *Journal of Manufacturing Technology Management, 31*(5), 1045–1083.

Priyono, A., Moin, A., & Putri, V. N. A. O. (2020). Identifying digital transformation paths in the business model of SMEs during the COVID-19 pandemic. *Journal of Open Innovation: Technology, Market, and Complexity, 6*(4), 104. MDPI AG.

Richter, A. (2020). Locked-down digital work. *International Journal of Information Management, 55*. https://doi.org/10.1016/j.ijinfomgt.2020.102157

Ponsignon, F., Smart, P. A., & Maull, R. S. (2011). Service delivery system design: Characteristics and contingencies. *International Journal of Operations & Production Management, 31*(3), 324–349.

Ritter, T., & Carsten Lund Pedersen, C. L. (2020). Analyzing the impact of the coronavirus crisis on business models. *Industrial Marketing Management, 88*, 214–224.

Roundy, P. T., & Fayard, D. (2019). Dynamic capabilities and entrepreneurial ecosystems: The micro-foundations of regional entrepreneurship. *The Journal of Entrepreneurship, 28*(1), 94–120.

Seyitoğlu, F., & Ivanov, S. (2020). A conceptual framework of the service delivery system design for hospitality firms in the (post-)viral world: The role of service robots. *International Journal of Hospitality Management, 91*. https://doi.org/10.1016/j.ijhm.2020.102661

Sjödin, D., Parida, V., Kohtamäki, M., & Wincent, J. (2020). An agile co-creation process for digital servitisation: A micro-service innovation approach. *Journal of Business Research, 112*, 478–491.

Solomon, E. M., & van Klyton, A. (2020). The impact of digital technology usage on economic growth in Africa. *Utilities Policy, 67*. https://doi.org/10.1016/j.jup.2020.101104

Spurrell, M., Araujo, L., & Proudlove, N. (2019). Capturing context: An exploration of service delivery networks in complex case management. *Industrial Marketing Management, 76*, 1–11.

Steel, G. (2021). Going global—Going digital. Diaspora networks and female online entrepreneurship in Khartoum, Sudan. *Geoforum, 120*, 22–29.

Tekic, Z., & Koroteev, D. (2019). From disruptively digital to proudly analog: A holistic typology of digital transformation strategies. *Business Horizons, 62*(6), 683–693.

The Africa Report. (2020). *Jack Ma: Today's Africa is the China of 20 years ago!* Retrieved January 11, 2020, from https://www.theafricareport.com/22056/jack-ma-todays-africa-is-the-china-of-20-years-ago/

Van Deursen, A., & Van Dijk, J. (2011). Internet skills and the digital divide. *New Media & Society, 13*(6), 893–911.

Van Veldhoven, Z., & Vanthienen, J. (2021). Digital transformation as an interaction-driven perspective between business, society, and technology. *Electronic Markets*. https://doi.org/10.1007/s12525-021-00464-5

Vial, G. (2019). Understanding digital transformation: A review and a research agenda. *The Journal of Strategic Information Systems, 28*(2), 118–144.

Yoon, C. (2020). Digital Africa: An analysis of digital trends in Africa and their driving factors. In A. Froehlich (Ed.), *Space fostering African societies: Developing the African continent through space* (Vol. 1, pp. 109–133). Springer.

Zaki, M. (2019). Digital transformation: Harnessing digital technologies for the next generation of services. *Journal of Services Marketing, 33*(4), 429–435.

2

Digital Channels Catalysing Businesses in Fast-Expanding African Markets

Esi A. Elliot, Robert E. Hinson, Anthony Annan, and Martin J. Eppler

2.1 Introduction

In recent times, advances in social media and related business models have created dynamic platforms for social interactions and the formation of commercial social networks (Bharadwaj et al., 2013; Hoffman et al., 2012). The digital channels could benefit billions of people by spurring inclusive growth that adds \$3.7 trillion to the GDP of fast-expanding markets within a decade (Hoontrakul, 2017). Hoffman and

E. A. Elliot (✉)
University of Texas Rio Grande Valley, Edinburg, TX, USA

R. E. Hinson
University of Ghana Business School, Accra, Ghana

A. Annan
Caldwell University, Caldwell, NJ, USA

M. J. Eppler
University of St. Gallen, St. Gallen, Switzerland

O. Adeola et al. (eds.), *Digital Service Delivery in Africa*, Palgrave Studies of Marketing in Emerging Economies,
https://doi.org/10.1007/978-3-030-83909-3_2

Novak (2012) stated that digital is evolving into a unique social medium for communication, information, and commerce. Therefore, our research question is how digital advances the dual goals of profitability and social impact in fast-expanding markets? Fast-expanding markets are defined as new markets that emerge at industry, business, or even individual levels with vibrant, robust, and fast-growing economies (Tse et al., 2016). Such markets are highly significant to marketers for upscaling digital payments. The key questions are how this upscaling emerges and the role social networks play within this domain. We, therefore, also investigate the lessons offered regarding the rapid scaling of social media activities by social network structures.

Digital financial services take on many forms, including long-distance remittances, micropayments, and other applications that go by various names, such as digital banking, digital transfers, and digital payments (Donner & Tellez, 2008). Social networks in this context are webs of social ties that bind individuals together based on factors such as friendships, common interests, and shared professional activities. Social networks become even more dynamic when they evolve into social ecosystems, which are complex forms of social ties whereby individuals are part of multiple overlapping commercial contexts and interact with others in other social networks at the same or different times. Ecosystems, in this sense, are open, flexible, dynamic, and interactive market spaces that are highly demand-driven (Boley & Chang, 2007). Social ecosystems typically overlap more freely in various ways, such as social networks formed around the family, profession, or social interests.

Our research context is the fast-expanding markets of Kenya and Ghana, Digitisation in African markets such as the five KINGS countries, namely Kenya, Ivory Coast, Nigeria, Ghana, and South Africa, has opened up several marketing opportunities (Frynas & Mellahi, 2003). In such markets as chosen for our study, social ecosystems occur in multiple tech hubs, working spaces, and accelerators that provide innovation, creativity, and entrepreneurship. Some studies (Elliot et al., 2018) have discussed how mobile phone technology is customized to mitigate marketing channel inefficiencies. Other researchers have also explored non-traditional channels and innovative access to consumers Sheth, 2011), reverse innovation (Govindarajan & Ramamurti, 2011) to demonstrate how innovations can be scaled in African markets. While recent studies have discussed how digitisation and other opportunities are advancing marketing in fast-expanding markets (Mayer, 2019), there has been limited discussion on the role of *social ecosystems* in digitisation in such markets. According to Boley and Chang (2007), individuals in a social ecosystem are proactive and responsive in their interactions regarding their own benefits while supporting collaboration and communication in order to ensure sustainability.

To answer our research question, we first conducted rigorous and systematic secondary research to expose key constructs related to the goals of profitability and digital of FSPs. We followed up with a qualitative study in the form of phenomenological interviews conducted in Ghana, West Africa, with 15 dyads of financial services providers (FSPs) and their microenterprise customers (CMEs). The contribution of this paper is, therefore, an expansion on Hoffman and Novak's (2012) exposition on how digital evolves into a unique social medium for communication, information, and commerce by the provision of an upscaling framework of social media to meet the dual goals of profitability and social sustainability.

The contents of this paper are organised as follows: following the discussion on related research in the next section, the methodology section describes the qualitative approach of this study in the form of ethnographic interviews informed by the phenomenological school of thought. In the fourth section, we present and analyze our findings on digital ecosystems in African markets and their role in scaling up business activities. We compare digital ecosystems with other non-social media that emerge from the data. Finally, we conclude with a discussion on the policy implications of social media and discuss future research opportunities and needs.

2.2 Conceptual Foundations

2.2.1 Digitisation in Fast-Expanding Markets

Digitisation capability refers to advanced ability to use smart and connected digital products and data analytics to facilitate the development and delivery of service offerings (Cenamor et al., 2017). Visconti and Quirici (2014) assert that access to the Internet, social networks, and cashless electronic payments softens the conflicts of interest among stakeholders, reinforces the FSPs business model, with positive externalities on both sustainability and outreach.

McKay and Pickens (2010) found that branchless banking, including mobile banking, was 19% cheaper on average than alternative services. At low transaction amounts or for informal money transfer options, this difference reached almost 40%. Successful mobile phone technologies[1] such as Kenya's M-Pesa and the Philippines' BanKO have been lauded as offering customers a simple, efficient, and cost-effective method of savings, transfer money and make payments.

Digitisation assists firms to adjust service and delivery process designs according to customer needs quickly without a substantial trade-off in cost, delivery, and quality of services (Wright, 2002). According to Hinson et al. (2007), e-business facilitates the execution of export-related functions like financial management, marketing management, strategy leverage, production management, information systems, logistic management, customer relationship management, and human resources management. We, therefore, argue in this study that digital ecosystems have opened up opportunities to leverage unique socio-cultural factors in fast-expanding markets. According to Boley and Chang (2007), 'digital ecosystems transcend the traditional, rigorously defined, collaborative environments from centralised, distributed or hybrid models into an open, flexible, domain cluster, demand-driven, interactive environment'

[1] Mobile technology refer collectively to a set of applications that enable financial institutions' clients to use their mobile telephones to manipulate their bank accounts, store value in an account linked to their handsets, transfer funds or even access credit or insurance products. Services include M-banking, M-payments, M-transfer and M-finance.

(p. 1). A digital ecosystem is a networked architecture and collaborative environment (Boley & Chang, 2007). Socially, microenterprises have been accustomed to traditional modes of communication such as face-to-face interactions in marketplaces, churches, and other open spaces from which they receive immediate feedback and trust (Trigkas et al., 2020). These communication channels have now been mostly replaced by digital versions to provide convenience, save time and enhance business performance. While these studies expose how digital enhances business performance for firms. Our study builds on these studies to discover how social media in the emerging market contexts upscales business performance for both the microenterprise customer and financial services firms as they engage in digital interactions.

2.2.2 Social Media and Social Networks in Emerging Markets

Social media is digital, computer-based technology that facilitates the sharing of ideas, knowledge and networks in communities (Dollarhide, 2019). Social media has been indicated to have seven building blocks—identity, conversations, sharing, presence, relationships, reputation, and groups (Kietzmann et al., 2011). This study focuses on the relationship block, which represents the extent to which users can be related to other users having some form of association that leads them to converse, share objects of sociality, meet up, or list each other as a friend. There are three dimensions of social structure, each rooted in different types of relations: (a) *market relations*, in which products and services are exchanged for money or bartered, (b) *hierarchical relations*, in which obedience to authority is exchanged for material and spiritual security, (c) *social relations*, in which favours and gifts are exchanged (Adler & Kwon, 2002).

Social networks are the relationships through which individuals receive opportunities to use financial and human capital (Burt, 2000). Social networks in emerging markets exist in at least three separate forms: *kinship ties* that link together components of extended family enterprises; *social ties* that form through shared social histories, for example, attendance at the same school or membership in the same clubs; and *professional ties* based on connections formed in the course of repeated business transactions (Bräutigam, 2003). Authors such as Sussan and Acs (2017) have provided insights on the role of digitisation for economic development in entrepreneurial ecosystems.

Social media is likely to be more prevalent in emerging markets where consumers tend to have a collectivist approach to life and form social networks, which are a key conduit for survival in their environment (Sridharan & Viswanathan, 2008). Collectivism stands for a society in which people from birth onwards are integrated into strong, cohesive in-groups, who throughout continue to protect the individual throughout the lifetime in exchange for unquestioning loyalty (Hofstede, 2007). Additionally, in collectivist cultures, group interests prevail, and there is a reciprocation of favour, a sense of belonging, and respect for tradition (Hofstede, 2003). Social obligations also create interdependence woven together with strands of information, shared contacts, finance (credit or investment), and a degree of trust (Talib & Rahman, 2010). This socio-cultural environment comprises risk-takers, information brokers, and resource providers who foster the emergence of new ideas leading to a cycle of wealth creation (Venkataraman, 2004). Our study explores the significance of these digital payments in the context of the interactions between two key players in fast-expanding markets—microenterprises and financial services firms.

2.2.3 Interactions Between Microenterprises (CMEs) and Financial Services Firms (FSPs)

Microenterprises form over 92% of businesses in fast-expanding markets such as Africa. These businesses have fewer than 10 employees, with an average of five workers (O'Dwyer & Ryan, 2000). Mobile phone owners have surpassed the number of people who own bank accounts in the region, and mobile payments hold great potential for the unbanked (Etim et al., 2013). Most of these microenterprises operate in geographically dispersed locations, mostly in informal sectors and have a high dependence on family. The potential of microenterprises as powerful agents of economic growth in emerging markets lies in their capacity to apply ingenuity and resourcefulness in their societies (McDade & Spring, 2005). These microenterprises need access to the full range of financial services to generate income, build assets, smooth consumption, and manage risks. Financial services providers (FSPs) are characterised by four essential features, which are essential to their provision of value to customers.

FSPs are a unique set of financial institutions because they have a *double bottom line*—that is, they pursue a combination of financial and social impact goals. FSPs thus follow good banking principles to sustain profitability while also pursuing their social impact objective of alleviating poverty. The financial performance goal of profitability entails reducing dependence on subsidies and reducing risk exposure. The social performance goals vary and include achieving a stated social mission and commitments to corporate social responsibility. Examples include reducing financial exclusion and poverty, empowering women, and following ethical standards for consumer protection.

Opportunities have been created by digital interactions between microenterprises and financial services firms for enterprise networks, professional communities, e-business platforms, research networks, education networks, and virtual communities such as LinkedIn, Facebook, Twitter, or YouTube (Hervas-Oliver et al., 2011; Etim et al., 2013).

2.3 Research Methodology

An initial search was conducted with advanced search options of peer-reviewed scholarly journals with the specification of 'Microfinance' and 'Profitability', resulting in the peruse of 232 papers. A google scholar search of 'mobile communication technology and microfinance profitability improvement', yielded 12,300 results, sorted by relevance as shown in the search results diagram below.

Search Results Diagram

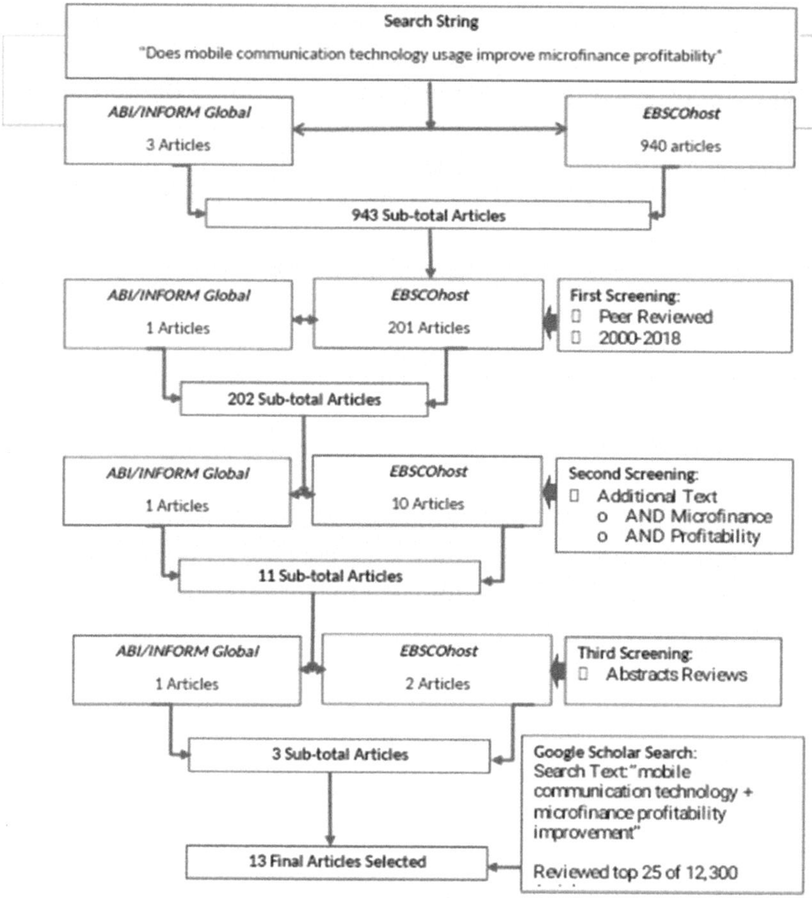

As a follow-up to investigating constructs exposed from the secondary research, we incorporate interviews and observations into an interpretative study. Interpretative studies also provide respondents with room to articulate responses through open-ended questions (Denzin, 1997) (see Tables 2.1 and 2.2). The qualitative method was considered ideal for this study because, in contrast to quantitative research, the qualitative approach enables the researcher to unveil what people say and do so as a result of how they interpret the world. Through an empathetic understanding and process of interpretation, it is possible to reproduce the thoughts, feelings, and motives behind the actions of others (Bodgan &

Table 2.1 Demographic profile of participants—microenterprise customers in Ghana and Kenya

Participant (pseudonym)	Business type	Age	Gender	Education	Length of relationship
CME1	Concrete products manufacturer	33	Male	Certificate	6
CME2	Interior decorating	31	Male	High School	4
CME3	Hydraulic equipment wholesaler	50	Male	Undergraduate	15
CME4	Beauty products retailer	48	Female	Elementary	7
CME5	Health equipment retailer	45	Male	Undergraduate	5
CME6	Clothing retailer	42	Female	Elementary	4
CME7	Contractor	43	Male	Elementary	5
CME8	Confectionery and cosmetics retailer	38	Female	Elementary	5
CME9	Citrus farmer	49	Male	Graduate	15
CME10	Contractor	49	Male	High School	5
CME11	Lingerie and general goods hawker	33	Female	Elementary	8
CME12	Commodities wholesaler	45	Female	Elementary	15
CME13	Wigs wholesaler	31	Female	High School	4
CME14	Cosmetics/ perfumery retailer	50	Female	Elementary	4
CME15	Caterer	44	Female	High School	6
CME16	Entrepreneur	46	Male	College	6
CME17	Sales woman	52	Female	High School	6

Table 2.2 Demographic profile of participants—financial services firms in Ghana

Participant (by Pseudonym)	Bank	Age	Gender	Education (degree)
FSP1	Imex Bank	36	Male	Graduate
FSP2	Imex Bank	44	Male	Graduate
FSP3	Imex Bank	41	Female	Graduate
FSP4	Imex Bank	42	Female	Graduate
FSP5	Plabo Microcredit Company	49	Male	Undergraduate
FSP6	Imex Bank	27	Male	Graduate
FSP7	Imex Bank	39	Female	Graduate
FSP8	Sunny International Bank	42	Male	Graduate
FSP9	Sumir Microcredit Company	37	Male	Graduate
FSP10	Imex Bank	39	Male	Graduate
FSP11	Plabo Microcredit Company	31	Male	Graduate
FSP12	Sunny International Bank	29	Male	Undergraduate
FSP13	Sunny International Bank	33	Female	Graduate
FSP14	Sumir Microcredit Company	47	Male	Graduate
FSP15	Sumir Microcredit Company	49	Male	Graduate

Taylor, 1975). This is achieved through observations and immersion in the cultural context, in order to gain insights into the inner world of the participants in digital ecosystems. The features of the qualitative method, therefore, facilitate: (1) understanding the processes by which events and actions take place (such as the scaling-up process); (2) developing contextual understanding (such as regarding cultural aspects) (3) facilitating interactivity between researcher and participants (4) adopting an interpretive stance and (5) maintaining design flexibility.

2.3.1 Data Collection

Informants were identified by both snowball and purposive sampling. Snowball sampling was used based on the informants' relevance to the research question. Purposive sampling was used based on the informants' willingness to impart their knowledge and experiences with researchers. The FSPs and CMEs dyads in this study worked together for a minimum of four years and have jointly developed at least one new service design which involves digital ecosystems. Prior to interviews and during follow-up interviews, we built rapport and trust with participants via email exchanges and/or in-person meetings. Interviews were conversational to allow themes to emerge that participants were comfortable sharing. We conducted 72 in-depth interviews with both FSP and CME participants in Ghana. Specifically, we conducted depth interviews plus follow-up interviews with 15 FSP-CME dyads (30 participants in total). This selection of an FSP and CME dyad was to maintain the qualitative integrity of the study by choosing related dyads and ensure richness of data when saturation is reached. The general recommendation for in-depth interviews is a sample size of 30 (Dworkin, 2012), and since the study was a dyadic one, the total number of participants was 72. Data was collected over an eight-month period, with one month of intensive face-to-face interviewing and observations preceded by four months of telephone interviews and followed by two months more of telephone interviews. Interviews were conducted with FSPs and CMEs individually, with each dyad, and on multiple occasions. Complementing data from secondary research and ethnographic interviews are data derived from observational data and photographs. Collectively, this data helps to enhance methodological rigour and to facilitate a more comprehensive understanding and theorising. In addition to gathering the interview data, we observed and took notes during eight in-situ meetings between the CME and FSP, which were later followed up with digital conversations. Observational notes provide a greater contextual understanding of the recordings and transcripts (Lévi-Strauss, 2008). When permitted, photographs were taken, and interviews were audio-recorded.

2.3.2 Data Analysis

The recorded interviews were transcribed and analysed. Analysis was a multilayered process using the Atlas Ti software for open and axial coding. The goal of open coding is to reduce large amounts of data to smaller, more manageable amounts and involves a process where concepts and categories are identified. Codes were assigned to each participant's response based on the value co-creation activities of collaboration, dialogical interactions, learning, and creativity. Axial coding is the process of relating categories to their subcategories and linking categories at the level of properties and dimensions. Axial coding involved the categorisation of data into themes and subthemes, a process commonly used in study designs that aim to describe a phenomenon, especially when research literature on the phenomenon is limited (Kondracki et al., 2002).

Three types of scategorisation were used for data analysis—thematic, affective, and strategic—to assess how value is co-created between microenterprises and financial services firms in subsistence markets. Thematic analysis identifies, analyses, and reports patterns (themes) within the data (Hayes & Krippendorff, 2007). Affective analysis tracks the expressions of emotion (both positive and negative) and provides insight into the subjective and idiosyncratic perception of the value co-created and contextual factors. Strategic analysis evaluates the types of rhetorical strategies used by a particular group of stakeholders (in this case, microenterprises and relationship managers). We present the themes emerging from our findings in the next section.

2.4 Findings and Discussions

Our findings demonstrate how digital interactions with customers leverage the social networks of the collectivist African markets for socially creative outcomes. Three themes emerge from our study: (1) Social Network *Construction*, (2) Social Network *Animation*, and (3) Social Network *Reinvention*. These themes highlight the dynamic marketing possibilities that digital channels offer in Ghana and Kenya, where social networks are highly dynamic.

2.4.1 Social Network Construction

Social network construction occurs when the actors deepen their relationships and therefore create a space that supports collaborations. The actors further strengthen their connections through their collaborations, which results in social media. Social media is a form of creativity that is expressed when one or several individuals choose new strategies to solve social problems or enhance social activities in larger groups (Mouchiroud & Lubart, 2002), CMEs build a group of peers and experts who want to help them and stay updated on the entire process of their marketing plan. Peers may be dynamic networkers or businessmen with trade works and show up opportunities in unusual places. These networks consist of ties that provide resources such as information, providing an inclusive support structure (Putnam, 2000). The following quote from FSP5 illustrates how digital channels can be used to construct new social networks in his narration:

> The social inclusion and the fact that our culture allows us to connect easily, it makes it easier to connect with the market. We have apps as a payment platform app which anyone can download and use this for their transactions. So, a digital platform is making life comfortable and easy for the ordinary Ghanaian, so we intend to push it to the school going children to understand it and grow up with it to understand it. People are finding it difficult to understand how this financial inclusion would help their life since they are not earning much.

FSP5 points out the fact that the digital payment platform provided by FSPs makes life easier for customers. The advantage of such social networks in African markets is that the *collectivist values lead to extremely fast patronage of products. The word-of-mouth effects are extremely dynamic in collectivist social networks.* Social networks are where social interactions occur, which improves the individual's knowledge and ability to generate feasible ideas. Having loose ties to many other individuals in different social circles enables access to a greater variety of information and diverse perspectives (Perry-Smith, 2006). These weak ties, therefore, contribute to a greater ability to grasp subtle differences suggested by alternative solutions to problems and overall boosts innovativeness but also the rapid scaling of innovative solutions. Social relationships, therefore, stimulate a more expansive view and raise the potential for making unique connections between ideas such as narrated by FSP5. Similarly, CME12 indicates:

> Communication is vital to every facets of life, you can get more ideas and solve problems *so anyone who interacts more with customers get more.* Now the banks are really using the online applications. Money transfers has become easy and settlement of funds has become easy. I am an internet merchant. Without Internet my business wouldn't exist. I buy and sell products without moving an inch. Mobile technology makes it even better because it allows me to conduct business while on the go or during a vacation. Mobile payment can help expand my business because it would make payments for my goods and services less cumbersome. Mobile Payment technology helps move cash and goods seamlessly. The faster and easier you get paid, the quicker your business expands. With mobile apps we can have more financial literacy training for customers to expand the customer networks and also interact with customers to exchange ideas.

CME12 points out two essential advantages that social ecosystems provide to digitisation. The first is that digitisation would lead to market share expansion and competitiveness and would create more efficiency. The second is that while face-to-face contact is important, the leverage of social networks with digitisation will put a human face to the FSP-CME interaction and thus construct a more efficient social networking platform with the customer. The infusion of technology to service encounters is dramatically changing their 'high-touch, low-tech' nature since the competitive marketplace is driving all firms to incorporate services within their key offerings to customers (Bitner et al., 2000). With digital payments, CMEs and FSPs have less costs and are thus more efficient. CME5 illustrates this fact in his quotation

> Mobile transfers would help to give more and get more from more customers. As a businessman you need to bring the supply and demand together and then make your profit. Mobile transfers help me to do this because I save money and I can connect with more people. I cast my net wider and obtain more customers who pay directly into my account. I therefore spend less time creating a large customer base, so my business is growing.

CME 5 exposes how the leverage of social networks with digitisation would help him to create as well as capture more value. As exposed by CME5, digital channels link the firm and employees and enables marketers to deliver services and observe instant responses and effects of their marketing activities. This aspect validates the assertion that the link between employees and customers is represented by interactive marketing where promises made to customers become instant reality and moments of truth in which customers and employees interact, and the service is jointly produced (Bitner, 1995; Bitner et al., 2000). In African markets, more value is created for more customers simultaneously, as highlighted by CME5, creating new, socially constructed networks. Adler and Kwon (2000) distinguish among three dimensions of social structure, each rooted in different types of relations: (a) market relations, in which products and services are exchanged for money or bartered, (b) hierarchical relations, in which obedience to authority is exchanged for material and spiritual security, (c) social relations, in which favours and gifts are exchanged. The exchanges by the actor in these social networks create beneficial market and social relations.

A CME from Kenya (CME16) explains how social media has resulted in social network construction and the frugal upscaling of digital and the enhancement of businesses in the fast-expanding markets of Kenya. CME16 delares:

> Social media has expanded businesses to no end in Kenya. Entrepreneurs just need to put up the picture of their businesses on Instagram, Facebook... and their business is set up. All they need is a motor bike to deliver packages to their workplace to get the business running. Look at how businesses have progressed and now you hear about the African

> Continental Free Trade Area. Social media can be used to advertise products, interact with customers and this increases profits and cut down costs. We save time and maintain our stocks since we communicate easily with customers and suppliers.

CME13 highlights how the use of social media for business, reduces the costs of entrepreneurs in Kenya. It also enhances their brand and makes the running of business seamless. She perceives great opportunities with social media for businesses even at the macro level to the extent of regional and global trade and she mentions the African Continental Free Trade Area.

2.4.1.1 Social Network Animation

Social network animation occurs when communication among social networks progresses dynamically over time. Social capital characterises the interpersonal relationships that an individual has with other members in a surrounding community, and it provides the basis for analysing the sense of community and the degree to which the individual is connected with others in the community (Fischer et al., 2002). Weak social ties in the networks strengthen over time with consistent communication on issues of common interest. Social ecosystems are spurred on by empowerment through social network animation on a face-to-face level by FSPs, which augments the imagination and hope of CME communities. Tacit knowledge, knowledge based on the experience of individuals, is largely acquired and transmitted through informal face-to-face interactions. It is expressed in the form of attitudes, points of view, evaluations, motivations, commitments, etc. (Polanyi, 1966). Beyond this knowledge interchange and enhancement, the co-creation occasioned by social network animation results in social media. A form of social media is *co-creation*, which is the process leading to the emergence and sharing of creative activities and meanings in a socio-technical environment (Fischer et al., 2004). FSP11 narrates:

> We have transformation officers who are charged to perform *financial literacy training*, so they have laptops and weekly training is provided

to them through WhatsApp. They show videos to the women in the communities. They talk to them on how to manage their business … so in a maximum of six weeks, you can qualify for a loan… (FSP11)

In this social ecosystem context, customer interaction involves varying degrees of digital activities—financial literacy training through videos and WhatsApp messaging. After six weeks of exposure to these activities, customers can then qualify for a loan. These activities in social media *provide structural social capital*. Structural social capital facilitates mutually beneficial collective action through established roles and social networks supplemented by rules, procedures, and precedents (Hitt et al., 2002). To qualify for a loan means the CME is ready to follow the rules and procedures to ensure the loan is paid back with interest.

Financial inclusion is enhanced with this social network animation. This financial inclusion occurs as social network animation provides increased knowledge, resources, exchange of ideas, and referral opportunities. FSP11 speaks of *transformation officers who animate the community social networks*. The transformation refers to transformational programs advocated by FSPs to promote policies that empower Social Networks. Social ecosystems are formed from these loosely linked groups. These social ecosystems thrive in communities with relatively cohesive social structures with leaders that can be held *accountable*. As each group in the network receives information and training, it is synthesised and new ideas spring forth. This offers greater scope to expand the social ecosystem to benefit from transformational financial services. Second, it enables the FSPs as well as the communities to *extend their skill base*. Additionally, the training, services, facilities, and assistance provided to the community members empower them to emerge linkages within the social ecosystem to ensure the successful implementation of transformative projects initiated by the FSPs. Whereas creativity is still a product of the individual actor, the action of working together is a generative stimulus. FSP15 details some aspects of the social ecosystems inspired by social network animation:

Our church is a place where everybody knows everybody, and we interact a lot at social functions where we share ideas, information and other resources, so the mobile app makes it easy for us to donate when we have to. We use the mobile app to donate and pay our tithes. We use the MTN and Vodaphone app. The church has an account like any other individual. It is convenient, and we don't need to have any physical cash to pay tithe. You can put money into your mobile account before transferring, and some people can use this as savings. Based on necessity, this can be used. Any amount can be used to pay anyone else who has that account. This payment platform helps churches create liquidity for the church and saves them from counting after church with no need for counting. It helps the church administration and prevents fraud in the church since everything is digital.

This process of digitalisation validates recommendations when building and managing customer interaction channels, as highlighted by FSP15. These are: (1) Provide multiple interaction channels to the customers to allow them to choose which channels are more convenient for them; (2) Design each experience gateway considering the building blocks of value co-creation processes; (3) Manage experience quality management across all interaction channels; (4) Ensure best practices to standardise the quality of customer service across all interaction channels and cocreator agents (Prahalad & Ramaswamy, 2004). The digital realm allows firms to choose the right approach and method for responding to a customer's requirement based on a common view of his/her experience context (Romero & Molina, 2011). As illustrated by FSP 15 and in line with insights on the value co-creation by Prahalad and Ramaswamy (2004), digital facilitates multiple customers' choices from a simple financial transaction process to an overall co-creation experience. FSP8 throws further light on this social network animation occasioned by digital:

Mobile applications like WhatsApp allow 250 people in a group to interact at a go and I have a couple of groups like that where people contribute on a monthly basis. So, loans can be rotated and provided to each customer as group loans. Sometime WhatsApp works like magic.

The intensely relational nature of African markets is shown in the above narration of FSP10. This collectivist relationship expands the knowledge set of the FSP or CMEs in the social ecosystems and can be animated for dynamic benefits through social media. Social relationships stimulate a more expansive view and raise the potential for making unique connections between ideas (Steiner, 2000). FSP10 also highlights how digital can afford her some connections she may otherwise not be privy to:

> We can drop customer emails. The one difference between that and face-to-face contacts is that it can be sent through your iPhone. Can connect with my relationship manager anywhere and discuss an urgent business deal with him, even when I am far away from my business location and communities.

Face-to-face contacts are in such situations facilitated through digital, and both channels become useful for customer interactions, which eventually result in innovations (Purser & Montuori, 1999). Our findings also suggest that digital channels facilitate interaction with the customer by bridging relational distances. Sook Kwon et al. (2014) found out that individuals respond positively to the merging of the boundary between online and offline participation in communities.

CME 17, who is an IT personnel in a bank and entrepreneur also notes the current animation of social networks with digital. He details:

> You know with the youth in Kenya, they interact a lot in their social networks on Facebook, twitter and other social media. They uses this to advertise their business, get recommendations etc. These recommendations go a long way to enhance their businesses. Now, we have this trend of flowing the influencer. Youtube is used a lot and many influencers emerge. Youtube is used for education, for the family, for the business and many aspects of satisfying the business needs.

From the narration of CME 17, we see that social media has resulted in a lot of animation in social networks for entrepreneurs in Kenya. The fact that they can obtain recommendations from Facebook to expand market share and educate themselves and their families from Youtube saves them time and provides convenience. These benefits result from the social network animation that digital occasions.

2.4.1.2 Social Networks Reinvention

Social Networks reinvention occurs when the social network platforms are transformed into a new state with new service delivery innovations that engender new behaviours. Social media happens when a society reinvents itself (Domingues, 2000). Social media entails taking a new perspective on how we design the supporting technological, social, and organisational environments (Fischer et al., 2002). FSP-11 exposes this role of digital approaches in rural areas:

> In Ghana, because of the rural-urban migration, it also makes transferring money to the rural areas very simple. It is only the susu that we depend on for capital injection in such communities, but problems can arise, and this person says I have travelled and am not available, but with mobile payments, these problems can be eliminated. Sometimes in church communities, we help ourselves, and they keep the records and know you make regular payments so that you cannot be cheated. When you are travelling to purchase stock, for example, you can get some help. We have formed various groups and given each group a name – names from the bible.

Susu savings is a procedure that credit operators use to help people within the lowest income brackets to save small amounts on a daily or weekly basis (Osei-Assibey, 2009). With mobile payments, FSPs can expand their physical reach of Susu into poor and rural areas and reduce their financial exclusion for savings and loans. As illustrated above by FSP11, mobile payments reduce the risks involved in the operation of such as breach of trusts or being prone to robbery attacks (Aryeetey, 1994). CME 9 sheds light on social networks reinvention that digitisation makes possible:

> Mobile money is used by the savings and loans is linked to savings. 'Mazumma' or 'Zpay' is used to transfer money across networks, to buy airtime and pay bills and to send money to other people. This has been very convenient for me, and in the comfort of my house, I can conduct business on the go, and I do not have to travel long distances. Now almost all the businesses have businesses you can pay through, so it makes our

> consumer experience simple – it is cashless. Crowdfunding is also easy because of the communal system, so generating funds for business associations make donations easier and simpler. I see more start-ups and more online businesses. A new sector of online services and businesses have emerged.

CME9 illustrates three different modes of social networks reinvention that is made possible as a result of digitisation—digital transfer of money across networks, crowdfunding, and the emergence of new online businesses. These new processes of digitisation bring the FSP and CME together in new ways. Social media is spiralled where CMEs can choose new strategies to solve social problems or enhance social activities, within dyads or in larger groups (Mouchiroud & Lubart, 2002) (Table 2.3).

Our study, therefore, expands on Hoffman and Novak's (2012) exposition on how digital evolves into a unique social medium for communication, information, and commerce by the provision of an upscaling framework of social media. Table 2.4 exposes the upscaling of social media that emerge from social media through the exchange of knowledge, ideas, and networks between the CME and FSP in fast-expanding markets. Digitisation here becomes more than using digital technologies as a unique social medium for communication, information, and commerce but also as a means to develop social ecosystems and meet dual goals of profitability and social impact. The FSPs participation in CME social ecosystems opens new ideas and knowledge for the social networks to reinvent themselves economically. Social relationships stimulate a more expansive view and raise the potential for making unique connections between ideas (Perry-Smith, 2006). Having loose ties to many other CMEs in social networks provides access to a greater variety of information and diverse perspectives and contributes to a greater ability to grasp alternative solutions to problems.

2.5 Conclusions and Implications

Our study shows how social ecosystems meet the dual goals of profitability and social impact through digital platforms. Our findings show

Table 2.3 Social media and outcomes of digital social networks

Themes	Outcomes
Social network construction	*Business performance enhancement* • Development of a shared identity in the performance of business and financial transactions • Modeling the use of digital tools for business performance enhancement • Interaction with experts beyond the business arena • Participate in constructive dialogue for creating shared voice and vision • Reflect CMEs opinions and points of view • Iterative feedback on business ideas • Scaffolding and assessing CME understanding • Enhancement of scholarship in business • Practice of self-promotion
Social network animation	*Service delivery innovations* • Stimulate learning, ideas and new innovations • Sharing and developing observations and opinions of peers and forming enduring attitudes • Develop trust and facilitating participation in the community through provision of a safe arena for exploring identity and personal relationships • Transfer of explicit and tacit knowledge • Practice collaborative skills of negotiating • Catalyst for participation and reification of knowledge • Contribution to the economy of knowledge production and dissemination • Engaging with and responding to the work of peers • Engagement in the broader education community

(continued)

that digitisation provides more value in the interaction between the CME and FSP by being more than a unique social medium for communication, information, and commerce. Most importantly, social media in social media facilitate the meeting of the dual goals of the FSP and CME. Social media facilitate the outreach to the poor as well as women's

Table 2.3 (continued)

Themes	Outcomes
Social network reinvention	*Market share expansion* • Design of new resources • Design of new business models • Stimulate discussion, problem solving and innovation • Induced to objectives and strategies and accounting for the opinions of others • Development of shared scholarly practices through critical engagement with peers' contributions • A diversity of perspectives strengthens social media • New representations for imparting business knowledge • Reporting on thoughts in the public domain encourages deep reflection • Develop shared language and practices in the scholarly discipline • Develop and refine professional informed opinions • Learning is anywhere, on the go

Source Adapted from Duncan and Chandler (2011)

empowerment in fast-expanding markets. Two groups of metrics that have been used extensively in the microfinance literature are outreach to the poor (Cull, 2009; De Bruyne & Sarma, 2008; Lensink et al., 2011; Mersland & Strøm, 2010; van den Berg et al., 2015), and women's empowerment.

2.5.1 Theoretical Implications

Our study expands on Hoffman and Novak's (2012) exposition on the evolution of digital into a unique social medium for communication, information, and commerce through knowledge, ideas, and networks shared by CMEs and FSPs. We highlight how the various aspects of social media that interplay with digital are drivers of knowledge creation and sharing and innovation through social networks construction, social networks animation, and social networks reinvention. Most significant

Table 2.4 Upscaling of social media ecosystems

Digital cocreation activities	Social network construction	Social network animation	Social network reinvention
Knowledge	The FSP is exposed to the cognitive abilities, memory, motivations, prior knowledge and emotions of the CME networks. Also bridges the psychological distance between the CME and FSP by reducing their cognitive tasks when learning	FSP opens a plethora of opportunities to share knowledge with CMEs that can be used for other projects in communities and that could not take place at a distance	Social networks can be reinvented as the CMEs enter into dialogues and problem-solving activities with the FSP
Ideas	There is also learning that stimulates CMEs and FSPs to 'filter, choose and recognise' relevant information in various situations (Koole, 2009)	The 'media spaces' and new media technologies such as videos spirals the collaboration and ideation in the socio-cultural setting (Preece, 2002)	New. Immediate and ongoing access to ideas, knowledge and networks of CME and FSP peers provides additional motivation and empowerment for reinvention of networks
Networks	Bridge between CMEs horizontal networks and FSPs by maintaining high physical and psychological comfort levels	In the collaborative networks, meaning is negotiated from different perspectives (Ragan & Smith, 1999) and the network interaction takes into consideration all the needs of the distant CME and FSP learners	Upscaling of network activities spirals business growth at the supranational, national, regional, industrial, cluster, sector, corporate and product levels with new business models

are the indirect network effects that compound the social media of the FSP and CME to meet their dual goals of profitability and social impact. Indirect network effects occur through such social learning (Stremersch et al., 2007) (Tables 2.5 and 2.6).

2.5.2 Managerial Implications

Social network construction, animation, and reinvention have implications for the dual goals of CMEs and the FSPs - profitability goals as well as social impact and for upscaling social media through its indirect effects on business performance (Stremersch et al., 2007). These social media activities. Clear indicators and strategies to support such goals are often lacking, however. Some critics have cautioned that FSPs that become too focused on financial performance at the expense of outreach to poorer customers drift from their objectives of serving the poor (Cull, 2009; Murdoch, 2000). Digital systems facilitate the realisation of both profitability and social goals by improving customer relationship management (Raddats et al., 2014) and relationships with suppliers (Saccani et al., 2014) and the design, integration, and delivery of product service systems (Vendrell-Herrero et al., 2017).

Yet, some of the challenges of social media must be recognised. The financial benefits to firms are often hard to quantify, making the original investment difficult to justify. Some CME participants mentioned their disapproval of increased charges imposed by FSPs as a result of digitisation. Additionally, some CMEs may prefer the social aspects of interacting on a face-to-face level with FSPs during service encounters. Some FSPs in our study also mentioned that CMEs were very slow in adopting the use of digital platforms for financial service delivery and interactions, thus limiting the emergence of social media. Issues of customer privacy and the confidentiality of information may be salient as a result of digital infusion (Milne, 2000). Firms that consider the implementation of social media should closely involve customers in the design process. Satisfying specific customer needs and creating an open dialogue to address concerns are important ways of overcoming some of the negative repercussions of social media. To address these barriers to

Table 2.5 Table of participant narrations

Theme	Definition	Narration
Social network construction	New collaborative business networks are created	Society dwells on relationships and helping each other and this is the core of business advancement as others can support the business anytime and this saves time Social networks through digital above all boost relationships and business in terms of remittances People can get capital no matter how small and this provides capital to plan business, time and actives. Once someone remits money to you, you can meet your obligations and plan how to spend

Theme	Definition	Narration
Social network animation	Relationships in social networks become more dynamic with more knowledge and idea sharing	With financial services all they want is that you meet your obligations, and they are there for you for the long haul You build up rapport so that the client and you understand the business very well, and the relationship becomes more keener, and obligations are met As the relationship develops, more knowledge is shared, and the bank is able to give out more loans because we can pay back on time

(continued)

Table 2.5 (continued)

Theme	Definition	Narration
Social network reinvention	New social network channels are created from the old ones or old channels are significantly improved leading to greater profitability	Because microenterprises can meet their obligations on a regular basis, the relationship is becoming better and better and more innovations are coming up Social networks on various social media channels like Facebook are creating connections between financial services, operators and their customers to transfer money, and this is developing businesses even faster Now customers can scan bar codes and use this for payments, so with this, business for certain services that accept these bar codes is expanding fast. These businesses also have online channels, so mobile networks of businesses are growing very fast with these innovations and the banks are cashing in

Table 2.6 Social ecosystems illustrations with indirect network effects

Indirect network effects	How it occurs
Horizontal reach: CME to CME networks facilitated by FSP—**Social network construction**	Case 1: The CME builds a relationship with other CMEs in business associations. The FSP facilitates the exchange of money, products, knowledge, ideas, networks and other resources through supporting a mobile wallet. This social network is constructed at a horizontal level of CME to CME support to meet dual goals of profitability and social impact
A vertical reach: FSP to CME facilitated by FSP—**Social network animation**	Case 2: The CME builds a relationship with the FSP through social networks. The FSP facilitates the dual goals of profitability and social impact for both CME and FSP through supporting CME mobile wallet as well as training CME using digital. Social network is animated at a vertical through the joint creativity and learning
A diagonal reach: CME and FSP create new value chain networks facilitated by FSP— **Social network reinvention**	Case 3: Both CME and FSP develop relationships with other CMEs in new digital networks that include other regional and global networks. The FSP facilitates the dual goals of profitability and social impact through the support of expanding a mobile wallet across regions and nations on a digital social platform. This social network is reinvented at a diagonal level with new business models and innovations

effective implementation, the firm must provide convincing evidence of the benefits of the digital ecosystems to all stakeholders.

2.5.3 Policy Implications

The post-COVID 19 era has brought to policymakers in fast-expanding markets additional opportunities through digitisation. Social ecosystems in these fast-expanding markets can be leveraged to enhance strategies for conserving, protecting, and enhancing natural resources to provide an enabling environment that meets the duals goals of profitability and social impact. It has been found that digitisation in the form of mobile money has been responsible for improving the economic lives of about 2% of the Kenyan population—out of poverty (Muthiora, 2015). There is also growing evidence of digitisation in fast-expanding markets mobilising domestic resources, and assisting to boost government revenue. Policymakers can leverage this influence for financing models to support banks, microfinance institutions, money transfer companies, and mobile network operators and cooperatives and to extend the reach of financial markets.

2.5.4 Future Research Directions

To provide further insight into the increased use of and enhancement of digital service ecosystems by FSPs in service encounters with CMEs, several questions need to be explored in further research. Assessments of satisfaction and loyalty, as well as attributions or complaining, are all factors that may have unique characteristics in social media. Social media allow for many more service encounters. Several other research questions that need to be addressed include: how should FSPs plan, implement, and measure the impact of social media on service encounters with the CME? What can be done to ensure that social media is beneficial to both FSP and CMEs? Answers to these questions will not only represent scholarly contributions; they will also benefit marketing in African markets, where many growth opportunities exist.

References

Adler, P. S., & Kwon, S.-W. (2000). Social capital: The good, the bad, and the ugly. *Knowledge and Social Capital, 89*.

Adler, P. S., & Kwon, S. W. (2002). Social capital: Prospects for a new concept. *Academy of Management Review, 27*(1), 17–40.

Aryeetey, E. (1994). *Supply and demand for finance of small enterprises in Ghana.* No. 251. World Bank Publications.

Bharadwaj, A., El Sawy, O. A., Pavlou, P. A., & Venkatraman, N. (2013). Digital business strategy: Toward a next generation of insights. *MIS Quarterly, 37*, 471–482.

Bitner, M. J. (1995). Building service relationships: It's all about promises. *Journal of the Academy of Marketing Science, 23*(4), 246–251.

Bitner, M. J., Brown, S. W., & Meuter, M. L. (2000). Technology infusion in service encounters. *Journal of the Academy of Marketing Science, 28*(1), 138–149.

Bodgan, R., & Taylor, S. J. (1975). *Introduction to qualitative research methods: A phenomenological approach to the social sciences.* John Willey & Sons.

Boley, H., & Chang, E. (2007). Digital ecosystems: Principles and semantics. In *2007 Inaugural IEEE-IES Digital EcoSystems and Technologies Conference,* 21(2), 398–403.

Bräutigam, D. (2003). Close encounters: Chinese business networks as industrial catalysts in Sub-Saharan Africa. *African Affairs, 102*(408), 447–467.

Burt, R. S. (2000). The network structure of social capital. *Research in Organisational Behavior, 22*(1), 345–423.

Cenamor, J., Rönnberg Sjödin, D., & Parida, V. (2017). Adopting a platform approach in servitisation: Leveraging the value of digitalisation. *International Journal of Production Economics, 192*, 54–65.

Cull, N. J. (2009). *Public diplomacy: Lessons from the past. No. s 12.* A Figueroa Press.

Denzin, N. K. (1997). *Interpretive ethnography: Ethnographic practices for the 21st century.* Sage.

De Bruyne, B., & Sarma, J. (2008). Fractional flow reserve: A review. *Heart, 94*(7), 949–959.

Dollarhide, M. (2019). Social media definition. *Investopedia.*

Domingues, J. M. (2000). Creativity and master trends in contemporary sociological theory. *European Journal of Social Theory, 3*(4), 467–484.

Donner, J., & Tellez, C. A. (2008). Mobile banking and economic development: Linking adoption, impact, and use. *Asian Journal of Communication, 18*(4), 318–332.

Duncan, J. C., & Chandler, P. D. (2011). A community of practice for early career biology teachers: Social networking and digital Technologies. *Proceedings of contemporary approaches to research in mathematics, science, health and environmental education.*

Dworkin, S. L. (2012). Sample size policy for qualitative studies using in-depth interviews. *Archives of Sexual Behavior, 41*, 1319–1320.

Elliot, E. A., Ngugi, B., & Malgwi, C. A. (2018). Mitigating microfinance marketing channels inefficiencies with customerisation of mobile technology. *International Marketing Review, 35*, 619–636.

Etim, N. A. A., Thompson, D., & Onyenweaku, C. E. (2013). Measuring efficiency of yam (Dioscorea spp) production among resource poor farmers in rural Nigeria. *Discourse Journal of Agriculture and Food Sciences, 1*(3), 42–47.

Fischer, R. A., Santiveri, F., & Vidal, I. R. (2002). Crop rotation, tillage and crop residue management for wheat and maize in the sub-humid tropical highlands: I. Wheat and legume performance. *Field Crops Research, 79*(2–3), 107–122.

Fischer, G., Giaccardi, E., Ye, Y., Sutcliffe, A. G., & Mehandjiev, N. (2004). Meta-design: A manifesto for end-user development. *Communications of the ACM, 47*(9), 33–37.

Frynas, J. G., & Mellahi, K. (2003). Political risks as firm-specific (dis)advantages: Evidence on transnational oil firms in Nigeria. *Thunderbird International Business Review, 45*(5), 541–565.

Govindarajan, V., & Ramamurti, R. (2011). Reverse innovation, emerging markets, and global strategy. *Global Strategy Journal, 1*(3–4), 191–205.

Hayes, A. F., & Krippendorff, K. (2007). Answering the call for a standard reliability measure for coding data. *Communication Methods and Measures, 1*(1), 77–89.

Hervas-Oliver, J. L., Garrigos, J. A., & Gil-Pechuan, I. (2011). Making sense of innovation by R&D and non-R&D innovators in low technology contexts: A forgotten lesson for policymakers. *Technovation, 31*(9), 427–446.

Hinson, R., Sorensen, O., & Buatsi, S. (2007). Internet use patterns amongst internationalizing Ghanaian exporters. *The Electronic Journal of Information Systems in Developing Countries, 29*(1), 1–14.

Hitt, M. A., Lee, H.-U., & Yucel, E. (2002). The importance of social capital to the management of multinational enterprises: Relational networks among Asian and Western firms. *Asia Pacific Journal of Management, 19*(2–3), 353–372.

Hoffman, D. L., & Novak, T. P. (2012). 12 Social media strategy. In *Handbook of marketing strategy* (p. 198). Edward Elgar.

Hoffman, D. L., Novak, T. P., & Stein, R. (2012). Flourishing independents or languishing interdependents: Two paths from self-construal to identification with social media. *SSRN Electronic Journal*. https://doi.org/10.2139/ssrn.1990584

Hofstede, G. (2003). *Culture's consequences: Comparing values, behaviors*. Sage.

Hofstede, G. (2007). Asian management in the 21st century. *Asia Pacific Journal of Management, 24*(4), 411–420.

Hoontrakul, P. (2017). *Economic transformation and business opportunities in Asia*. Springer.

Kietzmann, J. H., Hermkens, K., McCarthy, I. P., & Silvestre, B. S. (2011). Social media? Get serious! Understanding the functional building blocks of social media. *Business Horizons, 54*(3), 241–242.

Kondracki, N. L., Wellman, N. S., & Amundson, D. R. (2002). Content analysis: Review of methods and their applications in nutrition education. *Journal of Nutrition Education and Behavior, 34*(4), 224–230.

Koole, S. L. (2009). The psychology of emotion regulation: An integrative review. *Cognition and Emotion, 23*(1), 4–41.

Lévi-Strauss, C. (2008). *Structural anthropology*. Basic books.

Mayer, J. (2019). *Digitalization and industrialization: Friends or foes?* UN.

Mersland, R., & Øystein Strøm, R. (2010). Microfinance mission drift? *World Development, 38*(1), 28–36.

McDade, B. E., & Spring, A. (2005). The 'new generation of African entrepreneurs': Networking to change the climate for business and private sector-led development. *Entrepreneurship & Regional Development, 17*(1), 17–42.

McKay, C., & Pickens, M. (2010). *Branchless banking 2010: Who's served? At what price? What's next?* (Vol. 66). CGAP Focus Note.

Milne, G. R. (2000). Privacy and ethical issues in database/interactive marketing and public policy: A research framework and overview of the special issue. *Journal of Public Policy & Marketing, 19*(1), 2000.

Montuori, A., & Purser, R. (1999). *Social media* (Vol. 1). Hampton Press.

Moro Visconti, R., & Quirici, M. (2014). The impact of innovation and technology on microfinance sustainable governance. *Corporate Ownership & Control, 11*, 420–428.

Mouchiroud, C., & Lubart, T. (2002). Social media: A cross-sectional study of 6- to 11-year-old children. *International Journal of Behavioral Development', 26*(1), 60–69.

Murdoch, J. (2000). Networks—a new paradigm of rural development? *Journal of Rural Studies, 16*(4), 407–419.

Muthiora, B. (2015). *Enabling mobile money policies in Kenya: Fostering a digital financial revolution.* GSMA Mobile Money for the Unbanked.

O'Dwyer, M., & Ryan, E. (2000). Management development issues for owners/managers of micro-enterprises. *Journal of European Industrial Training, 24*(6), 345–353.

Osei-Assibey, E. (2009). Financial exclusion: What drives supply and demand for basic financial services in Ghana? *Savings and Development*, 207–238.

Perry-Smith, J. E. (2006). Social yet creative: The role of social relationships in facilitating individual creativity. *Academy of Management Journal, 49*(1), 85–101.

Putnam, R. D. (2000). Bowling alone: America's declining social capital. In *Culture and politics* (pp. 223–234), Palgrave Macmillan.

Polanyi, M. (1966). The logic of tacit inference. *Philosophy, 41*(155), 1–18.

Purser, R., & Montuori, A. (1999). *Social creativity* (vol. 2). Hampton Press.

Raddats, C., Burton, J., Zolkiewski, J., Story, V. M., Baines, T., & Lightfoot, H. (2014). Servitisation capabilities for advanced services: A multi-actor perspective. *Industrial Marketing Management, 60*, 54–68.

Romero, D., & Molina, A. (2011). Collaborative networked organisations and customer communities: Value co-creation and co-innovation in the networking era. *Production Planning and Control, 22*(5–6), 447–472.

Preece, J. (2002). Building. *Communications of the ACM, 45*(4), 37.

Prahalad, C. K., & Ramaswamy, V. (2004). Co-creation experiences: The next practice in value creation. *Journal of Interactive Marketing, 18*(3), 5–14.

Ragan, T. J., & Smith, P. L. (1999). *Instructional design.* Macmillan.

Saccani, N., Visintin, F., & Rapaccini, M. (2014). Investigating the linkages between service types and supplier relationships in servitized environments. *International Journal of Production Economics, 149*, 226–238.

Sheth, J. N. (2011). Impact of emerging markets on marketing: Rethinking existing perspectives and practices. *Journal of Marketing, 75*(4), 166–182.

Sook Kwon, E., Kim, E., Sung, Y., & Yun Yoo, C. (2014). Brand followers: Consumer motivation and attitude towards brand communications on Twitter. *International Journal of Advertising, 33*(4), 657–680.

Sridharan, S., & Viswanathan, M. (2008). Marketing in subsistence marketplaces: Consumption and entrepreneurship in a South Indian context. *Journal of Consumer Marketing*.

Stremersch, S., Tellis, G. J., Franses, P. H., & Binken, L. G. (2007). Indirect network effects in new product growth. *Journal of Marketing, 71*(3), 52–74.

Steiner, J. (2000). Containment, enactment and communication. *International Journal of Psycho-Analysis, 81*(2), 245–255.

Sussan, F., & Acs, Z. J. (2017). The digital entrepreneurial ecosystem. *Small Business Economics, 49*(1), 55–73.

Talib, F., & Rahman, Z. (2010). Critical success factors of TQM in service organizations: A proposed model. *Services Marketing Quarterly, 31*(3), 363–380.

Trigkas, M., Partalidou, M., & Lazaridou, D. (2020). Trust and other historical proxies of social capital: Do they matter in promoting social entrepreneurship in Greek rural areas? *Journal of Social Entrepreneurship, 12*, 338–357.

Tse, T., Esposito, M., & Soufani, K. (2016). Fast-expanding markets: The revolution of the microeconomy. *Thunderbird International Business Review, 58*(1), 5–11.

Van den Berg, M., Wendel-Vos, W., Van Poppel, M., Kemper, H., van Mechelen, W., & Maas, J. (2015). Health benefits of green spaces in the living environment: A systematic review of epidemiological studies. *Urban Forestry & Urban Greening, 14*(4), 806–816.

Vendrell-Herrero, F., Bustinza, O. F., Parry, G., & Georgantzis, N. (2017). Servitisation, digitisation and supply chain interdependency. *Industrial Marketing Management, 60*, 69–81.

Venkataraman, S. (2004). Regional transformation through technological entrepreneurship. *Journal of Business Venturing, 19*(1), 153–167.

Wright, A. (2002). Technology as an enabler of the global branding of retail financial services. *Journal of International Marketing, 10*(2), 83–98.

3

The Role of African Founded Firms in the Growth of the Digital Economy

Ebimo Amungo

3.1 Introduction

The COVID-19 pandemic created unprecedented socio-economic challenges with widespread lockdowns that led to the closure of schools, businesses, and even entertainment venues. Digital technology has been critical in responding to these disruptions especially in the developed countries. The World Bank noted that the COVID-19 pandemic showed the crucial role in the digital technologies now play in mitigating unforeseen shock. To a large extent, the digital technologies has allowed businesses to continue operating despite the lockdown caused by the pandemic (World Bank, 2021).

The impact of the pandemic on Africa has been particularly devastating, as the majority of the countries of the region lack the technological infrastructure to swiftly respond to the challenges of Covid 19. The

E. Amungo (✉)
Amungo Consulting Limited, Abuja, Nigeria

O. Adeola et al. (eds.), *Digital Service Delivery in Africa*, Palgrave Studies of Marketing in Emerging Economies,
https://doi.org/10.1007/978-3-030-83909-3_3

pandemic ushered in a new reality of tele-working, tele-conferencing, and an increased reliance on tele-medicine, distance learning, and e-commerce became part of a "new normal" that is still changing every day. At the centre of the shift in the digital economy are firms like Amazon, Netflix, Zoom, Alibaba, and Google.[1]

In Africa, the effect of Covid 19 has been particularly excruciating as the continent lags behind every region of the world in the development of digital technology and the digital economy it supports (Broadband Commission, 2016). The response to the challenge and opportunities presented by the pandemic has nevertheless been robust. Propelled by policy initiatives of African governments, African entrepreneurs have been at the heart of creating new solutions to address the challenges of Covid 19. According to the World Bank, there have been 191 digital policy responses to COVID 19 recorded for 31 countries in the period March–July 2020 (World Bank, 2021).

When addressing digital economy in Africa, it is important to consider the barriers and obstacles prevalent on the continent such as access to electricity, internet connectivity, infrastructure, policies and regulations, and the ability of people to use the digital solutions (Eziakonwa, 2020). Despite these challenges, the digital economy has grown significantly in Africa, with incubators, start-ups, and IT activities spreading across the continent. Using technology and experience, Africans have created many digital solutions to provide immediate help for the pandemic (Eziakonwa, 2020).

African Founded Firms are also taking the lead in the provision of digital services. African Founded platforms make up 85% of digital platforms on the continent (Johnson et al., 2020). They also lead in the provision of services like e-commerce and ride hailing (The International Trade Centre and Amsterdam University of Applied Sciences, 2020). African Founded Firms have also played a pivotal role in the growth of mobile money services in Africa (GSMA, 2020). Meanwhile, Fintechs and payment solution providers like Interswitch and Flutterwave, have

[1] Tech giants are getting creative to manage the COVID-19 crisis. https://www.theverge.com/interface/2020/3/17/21181691/google-verily-trump-website-trials-amazon-hiring-covid-19-response.

facilitated the growth of e-commerce, mobile banking, and mobile insurance (GSMA, 2019), while healthtech start-ups have provided innovative solutions as Covid 19 has focussed attention on healthcare systems around the world (World Bank, 2021).

This chapter aims to chart a course of the involvement of African Founded Firms in expanding digital economy on the continent. This chapter points out the contributions of African firms to the growth of the digital economy in Africa. The emphasis is to show that African economic and business entities have been at the heart of the growth of the digital economy. The chapter does not seek to understate the role of foreign investors in the digital economy space, nevertheless, the role of African firms is not often given the same prominence it deserves by scholars and policy makers. This may be due to paucity of research and case studies on the contributions of African Founded Firms in the economic development of the continent.

The need for studies that highlight the contributions of African Founded Firms is made more imperative by a recent report by Google and IFC highlighting the future of the digital economy in Africa (Google & IFC, 2020). In a travesty of facts, the highly cited and circulated report focussed on proposed submarine cables by Facebook and Google in Africa while ignoring the huge investments by several African Founded Firms that has given the continent a robust submarine cable network.[2] Misrepresentations like these are being addressed by some authors who chronicle the contributions of African Founded Firms and multinationals to the economic development of African (Ibeh et al., 2018).

This chapter is an expository analysis of the role that African Founded Firms, some of which are today multinationals, played in putting the investments that have spurned a vibrant digital economy on the continent (Verhoef, 2017). Even then, a proposition asserting a significant role by African Founded Firms in the digital economy needs to stand on some facts that give an indication of their role. Measures of the relative size of African Founded Firms in Africa's digital economy are

[2] These contributions are recorded annually by Steven Song in the African Infrastructure Report. https://manypossibilities.net/2020/01/africa-telecoms-infrastructure-in-2019/.

inferred from the size of their investments across the digital economy value chain, which includes investments in infrastructure that enable the digital economy, like mobile networks, fibre optic networks broadband, submarine cables, data centres. These investments have propelled the growth internet penetration to 40% in Africa today. African Founded Firms like MTN, Econet, GLO, Telcom and Sonatel, Maroc Telecom have been significant investors across Africa (Amungo, 2020).

This chapter is an industry and firm-level look at most of the actors whose investments, innovation, and other ancillary know-how, helped engender the birth, growth, and expansion of the digital economy in Africa. The first part of the chapter discusses the definition, size, and components of the digital economy. The second section addresses the digital economy in Africa by highlighting the investments in digital infrastructure that enabled the birth, growth, and expansion of the digital economy. The third section examines the impact of the digital economy in Africa. Finally, the fourth part discusses issues affecting the digital economy in Africa.

3.2 What Is the Digital Economy?

The internet is now a significant part of the socio-economic fabric of many countries transforming the very nature of human societies. Across the world, economies are being driven by this digital transformation across several sectors and digital technology is playing a greater role in people's daily lives. The critical role of these changes towards digitalisation is amplified by target 9.c of the United Nations Sustainable Development Goals (SDGs) which seeks universal access to information and communication technologies (ICTs) as an enabler of several services needed to achieve universal identification, more efficient delivery of government services, financial inclusion, and job creation (Broadband Commission, 2016). Digital technology has transformed the economic landscape across the world. It impacts key sectors of the economy such as health, agriculture, education, and trade, among others.

The term digital economy describes all economic transactions that take place on the internet. It is also known as the internet economy or the web economy (Bukht & Heeks, 2017). The internet has enabled access to information and technology, a key component of accelerating the pace of the digital economy and connecting markets. Today the digital economy is global, propulsive, foundational, and characterised by very large, global firms (Atkinson, 2021).

Firms like Amazon, Facebook, Netflix, Alibaba, PayPal, are integral parts of present-day economic realities. These firms offer services that range from e-commerce, ride hailing, media content delivery to payment solutions (UNCTAD, 2019). In China, Xinhua News agency reported the influence of digital firms when it said "WeChat (owned by Tencent) has more than one billion active users and, together with Alipay, an Alibaba company, its payment solution has captured virtually the entire Chinese market for mobile payments. Meanwhile, Alibaba has been estimated to have close to 60% of the Chinese e-commerce market."[3]

Empirical studies on the digital economy have focussed largely on technology infrastructure, IT and communications sector investment, e-Commerce, and broadband penetration rates to determine the size of the digital economy. However, new thinking has expanded the size of the digital economy to include spillovers from the use of digital technology (Huawei & Oxford Economics, 2017).

In a report published by Accenture Strategy, Knickrehm et al. (2016) believe that the digital economy has three levers which consist of a number of broad and specific indicators. These include digital skills, which measures factors such as the information, communications, and technology expertise in the workforce. The second lever is digital technologies, which includes access to the broadband connectivity and the economy's ability to utilise the Internet. The third lever relates to digital accelerators which include the environmental, cultural, and behavioural aspects of the digital economy that support digital entrepreneurship or activities (Knickrehm et al., 2016).

[3] Xinhua News agency China's digital economy sees robust growth amid pandemic. http://www.xinhuanet.com/english/2021-04/26/c_139907279.htm.

3.2.1 The Size of the Digital Economy

The contribution of digital economy to total economic output has been increasing in several countries. A study by Oxford Economics and Huawei found that it has grown 2.5 times faster than global GDP over the past 15 years (Huawei & Oxford Economics, 2017). UNCTAD in a report noted that China and the United States of America are the two dominant players in the global digital economy as they both account for 75% of all patents that relate to blockchain technologies, 50% of global spending on Internet of Things, and more than 75% of the world market in public cloud computing. The two countries also account for 90% of the market capitalisation value of the world's 70 largest digital platforms. Europe's share is just 4% while Africa and Latin America together account for only 1% (UNCTAD, 2019).

Hauwei and Oxford Economics believe the digital economy worldwide was worth US$11.5 trillion in 2016, or 15.5% of global GDP when spillovers from the digital economy are considered (Huawei & Oxford Economics, 2017). China's digital economy enjoyed a robust 9.7% growth rate in 2020 despite the pandemic and global economic downturn. China's digital economy was estimated to be worth 6 trillion U.S. dollars, accounting for 38.6% of the GDP.[4]

Besides the developed countries, the level of digitalisation of the economy taking place in some developing economies is also increasing. While the digital economy ranges in size from 10 to 35% of GDP in advanced economies it represents 2–19% of GDP in developing economies. Malaysia, Chile, and China match advanced economies in their use of digital assets (Herbert & Loudon, 2020).

3.3 The Digital Economy in Africa

Africa's digital economy has been growing rapidly over the past two decades. The growth is spurred by a number of factors that include

[4] Xinhua News agency China's digital economy sees robust growth amid pandemic. http://www.xinhuanet.com/english/2021-04/26/c_139907279.htm.

increased investment in digital infrastructure that has led to increased access to the internet, an expanding urban population, increase in digital skills, and a booming start-up ecosystem (Google & IFC, 2020).

In a bid to increase the role of the digital economy in Africa, 48 African governments have enacted 48 ICT policy documents (Friederici et al., 2017). The aim of policy makers is to use ICTs and the Internet to speed up the economic development of countries, level the playing field, bridge previous structural and infrastructural deficiencies, increase productivity and employment (Solomona & van Klytonb, 2020). Propelled by enabling policies from governments, several African Founded Firms have played important roles in the birth and growth of Africa's digital economy through their investments in digital infrastructure and by kickstarting the start-up ecosystem on the continent. Huge investments in mobile networks, submarine cables, data centres, fibre optic networks by African Founded Firms have increased access to the internet for a lot of Africans while some African Founded Firms provide digital services through establishment of internet platforms, fintech, healthtech, media and entertainment, e-commerce, e-mobility, e-logistics, and other ancillary digital services (Amungo, 2020).

Africa now has a plethora of digital start-ups that are driving innovation and providing solutions across several sectors (Jacques et al., 2013). These start-ups are increasingly contributing to the GDP of several African countries (Google & IFC, 2020). International Finance Corporation, IFC, noted that young talented digital entrepreneurs are driving African Internet opportunity by establishing start-ups that are solving some of Africa's most challenging issues, such as access to healthcare for remote populations, employment opportunities for women, and the ability to securely send and receive money. The report added that "Advanced technologies—tailored to data-driven, scalable, and pan-African approaches—are providing new ways for Africans to conduct business and earn income" (Google & IFC, 2020).

Indication of the innovativeness of African Founded Firms was their response to the Covid 19 and subsequent constraints caused by the pandemic. In one example, Flutterwave, a Nigerian digital payment solutions provider, was able to rapidly set up digital storefronts for 20,000 customers, when pandemic lockdowns hit brick-and-mortar businesses in Africa, throwing them a lifeline at a time when most countries where in lockdown.[5] Companies like Flutterwave, MTN, Globacom, and Econet have been the drivers of digital economy through their investments in digital technology and infrastructure as well as providing the digital services.

The involvement of these African Founded Firms in Africa's digital economy is a function of exigency and opportunity. Exigencies because a lack of interest in investments on the continent from foreign investors have created gaps in the market. And opportunity because many African firms have been founded with the aim of providing goods and services to fill these gaps (Amungo, 2020).

A regional comparison of the flow of foreign investments shows Africa lagging in all measures of investment from most of the countries driving the digital economy or even the companies that offers services in this economic space. Repeatedly, World Investment Report from UNTAD has over the past decade revealed Africa's poor showing as an investment destination for both developed and emerging economies multinationals (UNCTAD, 2020). An analysis of the investments spending of the largest firms driving the global digital economy shows Africa's stark position as an investment blackhole. For this reason, African Founded Firms were created to fill gaps in the market. With their presence across the whole gamut of the digital economy value chain, African Founded Firms played significant roles in kickstarting the digital economy on the continent through their investments in digital technology and infrastructure.[6]

3.3.1 Investments in Digital Technology in Africa

The transformation into the digital age in Africa has been slow, hampered by myriad issues including the low investment in the enabling infrastructure (Broadband Commission, 2016). Even then, Africa's breakthrough

[5] Time Magazine: Flutterwave Powering retailers. https://time.com/collection/time100-companies/5949986/flutterwave/.

[6] African Infrastructure Review 2021: Steven Song runs a website that publishes a review on African Telecommunications infrastructure since 2014. There are details on investments on mobile network operations, submarine cables and data bases and fibre optics. https://manypossibilities.net/2020/01/africa-telecoms-infrastructure-in-2019/.

into the digital age can be said to have been kickstarted between 1990 and 2000 as African governments enacted policies to deregulate, liberalise, and privatise the telecommunications sectors (Gutman et al., 2015). Governments then called for bids from the foreign and domestic investors for mobile network licences (Sepulveda, 2016). As has been the case in other sectors. A few countries like Egypt, Morocco, South Africa, and Kenya were able to attract investments from foreign firms like Vodafone and Orange. But a large swathe of Africa could only attract investments from African founded mobile network operators. African multinational telecoms operators like Orascom Telcom, Sonatel Mobile, Econet Wireless, Maroc Telecom, and MTN were often duelling against each other or against telecom multinationals like Vodafone, Orange, and Millicent Telecoms at various licencing rounds across the continent.

Nigeria, Africa's largest and most profitable market was only able to attract these two African Founded Firms, MTN and Econet and a local competitor, GLOBACOM for its mobile licence bid rounds in 2000.[7] Today, Africa's largest network operators include MTN, Maroc Telecoms, Globacom, Econet Wireless, and Vodacom. Between them, they have more than 250 million subscribers on the continent (Amungo, 2020) (Fig. 3.1).

Amungo (2020) noted that African multinational telecoms operators have also been the main investors in smaller African countries like Rwanda, Benin, Lesotho, Zambia, Ghana, Côte d'Ivoire, and Cameroon effectively redistributing capital that they had been able to raise in their bigger more profitable markets as they expand their networks across the continent.[8]

Investments in submarine cable networks have improved connectivity between Africa, Europe, Asia and also increased access to the internet on the continent. There are now 16 submarine cable systems between Africa and Europe, Asia, America, and South America and most of them are owned by consortia of African Founded Firms. These include GlobaCom, MainOne, SEACOM, ESSY, and WAC. Other African

[7] ASOKO INSIGHTS Africa's Top Mobile Telco Operators. https://www.asokoinsight.com/content/market-insights/africa-top-mobile-telco-operators.

[8] The term African Lions is used by Amungo (2020) to describe African founded Multinational Enterprises.

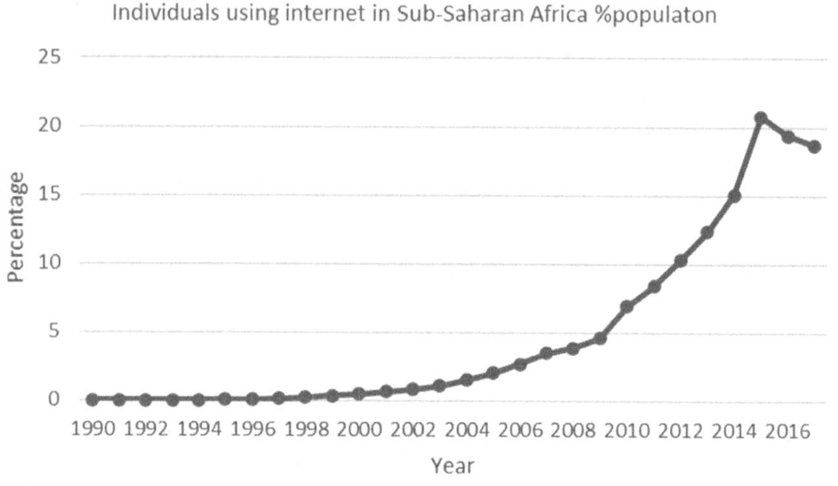

Fig. 3.1 Individuals using internets in Sub-Saharan Africa (*Source* World Bank Development Indicators)

Founded Firms are the main providers of other value added downstream and midstream services like data centres, and internet service gateways as well as other broadband services. Notable among these is South African firm, Telkom, which has 38 subsidiaries across Africa. Liquid Telecom, a subsidiary of Econet Wireless, which provides value added services across East, Central and Southern Africa including laying an extensive fibre optic network across Africa. The quest for efficiency in the telecom sector spurned the formation of companies that manage base stations and towers. The most prominent being IHS Towers and Helios Towers (Amungo, 2020).

As the digital economy expands, there is increased demand for data centres. The African Founded Firms leading investments in data centres include Vodacom/Safaricom, MTN, MainOne, Rack Centre Nigeria, Africa Data Centres and Teraco. It is estimated that African Founded Firms own more than 95% of data centre capacity in the region (Fig. 3.2).[9]

[9] Why Hasn't Africa Gone Digital?. https://www.scientificamerican.com/article/why-hasnt-africa-gone-digital/.

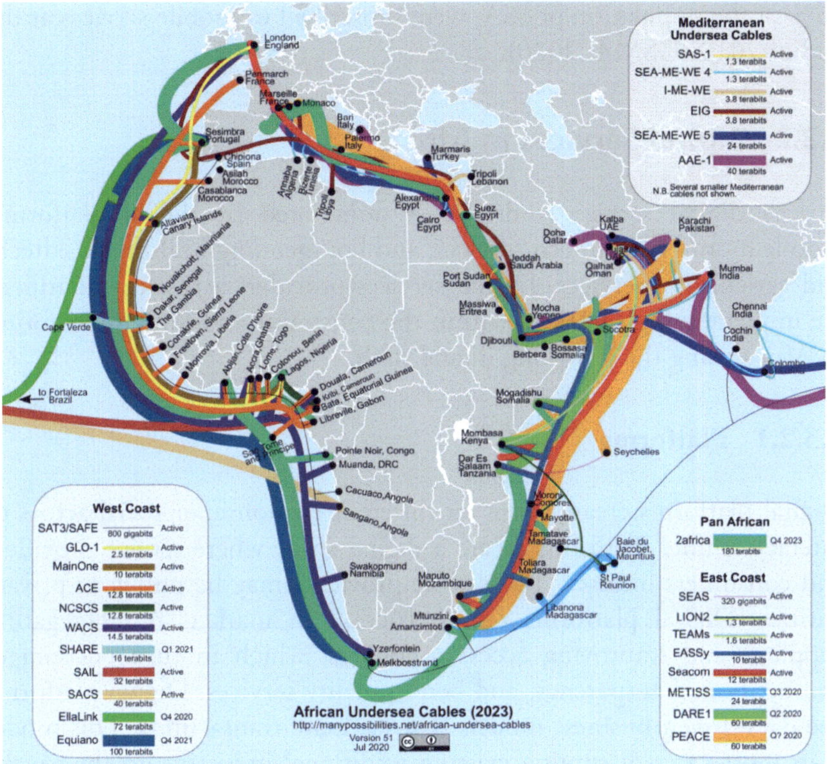

Fig. 3.2 Map showing the various submarine cables in Africa (*Source* Steven Song: Many possibilities)

Today, most Africans access the internet through their mobile phones. Mobile network operators like MTN, Globacom, EthiopTelecom, Safaricom, and Vodacom are leading the dynamic pace of growth of the digital economy through their investment in broadband and mobile internet. GSMA in its 2020 report on mobile economy in Africa noted that mobile phone subscriptions across the continent have grown from 87 million in 2005 to 760 million in 2017, growing 20% per annum. Mobile network coverage ranges from 10 to 99% in Africa - an average of 70%. Meanwhile, it is estimated that 477 million people, which is

45% of the population of SSA, were subscribed to mobile services at the end of 2019 (GSMA, 2020).

3.3.2 Digital Services in Africa

Africa's digital service landscape is dominated by digital platforms, mobile money and fintech services, and bourgeoning healthtech, edtech, and agricultural services. Digital services providers across the continent are implementing solutions within the constraint and limitations found in Africa using the following digital tools.

3.3.2.1 Platforms

Digital platforms create space for different economic or social actors to interact online. Platforms create a digital space where service providers and consumers interact. The service providers may be public or private entities. Digital platforms reduce friction in markets by aggregating suppliers and improving access to buyers, which in turn encourages competition, transparency, and better-quality services. Digital platforms use data-driven business models that facilitate transactions. This model is in most cases disrupting existing traditional industries in their wake (David-West & Evans, 2016). After a detailed study published by Cenfri, it was found that there has been robust growth in digital platforms in Africa. A total of 365 unique operating platforms were identified in 2019. African digital platforms that match online shopping, freelance, and e-hailing activities represent the majority of platforms (Johnson et al., 2020).

Another study by Makuvaza et al. (2018) found that more than 80% of the digital platforms operating in Africa were founded by home grown firms. The remainder of the platforms primarily originates from North America (7.8%), Europe (6.8%) and Asia (1.4%). The study also found that 37 platforms operate in more than one African market.

3.3.2.2 Retail and e-Commerce

Ecommerce is growing in Africa even though it still is the continent with the smallest transactions globally (Google & IFC, 2020). A study by The International Trade Centre and Amsterdam University of Applied Sciences in 2019, found that there were 631 online marketplaces in Africa managing 1,900 websites in 58 countries and territories (The International Trade Centre and Amsterdam University of Applied Sciences, 2020).

Five African countries accounted for most marketplace web traffic in 2019. South Africa led marketplace web traffic in Africa, with a 30% share. Four major Arabic-speaking countries in North Africa—Algeria, Egypt, Morocco, and Tunisia—together accounted for 41%. Other countries with relatively high shares were Nigeria (12%) and Kenya (5%). The study noted that most of these platforms were founded in Africa by African entrepreneurs. The listed top 10 African marketplaces in 2019 were Jumia, Ouedkniss, Gumtree, Souq, OLX, Takelot.com, JiJi, Avito, Cars.co.za, and Autrader.co.za. which collectively generated about 64% of all online traffic in Africa.[10]

The largest e-commerce marketplace in Africa is Jumia. Jumia operates in 12 African countries with Egypt and Nigeria its largest markets. Jumia was responsible for almost 24% of web traffic in 2019. The platform had 6.7 million customers as of the third quarter of 2020.

3.3.2.3 Healthcare and Healthtech

There has been a spirited response to the healthcare challenges engendered by COVID-19 pandemic in Africa. An analysis by the World Health Organisation[11] found that the pandemic catalysed the development of more than 120 health technology innovations that were piloted or adopted in Africa. The study found that Africa accounted for 12.8% of the innovations following the analysis of 1000 new or modifications of existing technologies that were developed worldwide to target

[10] The International Trade Centre and Amsterdam University of Applied Sciences, 2020.

[11] https://www.afro.who.int/news/covid-19-spurs-health-innovation-africa.

different areas of the COVID-19 response. These response areas included surveillance, contact tracing, community engagement, treatment, laboratory systems, and infection, prevention and control. However, even before the pandemic, African Healthtech innovators and health focussed platforms have sought to tap into all aspects of healthcare delivery in Africa as the pharmaceutical market worth $14 billion faces challenges such as sprawling supply chains, low order volumes, and exorbitant prices (Conway et al., 2019). Some healthcare providers are using digital solutions to address this challenge.

The prominent platforms include Lifestores Healthcare, a Lagos-based three-year-old start-up, is focussing its efforts on primary healthcare delivery by targeting thousands of local pharmacies and small-scale chemist shops by improving efficiencies in their supply chain. South Africa Udok runs a Connected Care Platform using an innovative software they developed in-house. mPharma, a Ghanaian health tech start-up that manages prescription drug inventory for pharmacies. It specialises in vendor-managed inventory, retail pharmacy operations, and market intelligence serving hospitals, pharmacies, and patients.

Ilara Health, a Kenya-based healthtech firm uses a platform to distribute medical devices to clinics across Kenya. Some firms find solutions to the perennial problem of fake drugs in Africa. MPedigree uses text messages, among other simplified solutions, to root out fake goods in the market. Other notable health tech firms include Medsaf which buys pharmaceuticals directly from the manufacturers at fair prices, and distributes them to hospitals, clinics, and pharmacies. Helium Health 82, a Nigerian start-up that gives healthcare providers a comprehensive suite of technology solutions to improve their healthcare delivery. 54gene83, a start-up building the first pan-African commercial Genetics BioBank.

3.3.2.4 Logistics

Africa's logistics start-up space is getting very competitive and has been attracting multi-million-dollar investments with global backing. African Founded Firms like Kenyan company Sendy has an on-demand platform that connects clients to drivers and vehicles for goods delivery.

Nigerian trucking logistic start-up Kobo360 provides a digital platform connecting drivers to cargo that needs distribution.

Lori Systems—a Nairobi-based logistics start-up started by a South African, Kenyan, and Togolese is also another African Founded Firms that is attracting capital and increasing digital access to logistics. Lori System's tech-enabled and operations-driven marketplace connects transport to cargo.

3.3.2.5 Mobile Money

Mobile money has been described as "a digital payment platform that allows for the transfer of money between cellphone devices."[12] It is driven by technology that is installed in the SIM card of mobile devices. The main feature of mobile money is that users can receive, withdraw, and send money without being connected to the formal banking system. No bank account is required to facilitate the transaction.

The adoption of mobile money has made Africa the enduring epicentre of the service. In the 2020 edition of its annual report on the mobile economy, GSMA noted that two-thirds of total global mobile money transactions were driven by users in sub-Saharan Africa (SSA). In all, there were 548 million registered accounts in the region, over 150 million of which were active on a monthly basis (GSMA, 2020). The massive adoption of mobile money services in Africa has helped financial inclusion across the region.

The key to the success of mobile money adoption in the continent is the adaptation of technology firms to the African reality. According to an article in The Africa Report,[13] the technology driving mobile money growth is the Unstructured Supplementary Service Data (USSD) and Short Messaging Service (SMS). These two technologies are the backbone of feature phone communications. Feature phones are still prevalent in sub-Saharan Africa so companies have adopted the use of

---

[12] Africa's Mobile Money Boom. https://www.forbes.com/sites/ilonalimonta-volkova/2020/12/07/mobile-money-in-africa/.

[13] The Africa Report Three reasons why African mobile connectivity is misleading. https://www.theafricareport.com/14567/three-reasons-why-african-mobile-connectivity-is-misleading/.

USSD/SMS to reach end-users. USSD channels allow digital platforms to reach mobile subscribers who do not have internet access in rural areas where mobile internet adoption is lower.

Kenya is a leader in mobile payment technology. Kenyan mobile network operator, Safaricom pioneered a mobile money service called Mpesa which facilitates mobile to mobile payments via SMS. It is estimated that there are 16m Mpesa transactions a day. MTN Group is another big firm expanding its mobile money offering. The company opened its Mobile Money API programme in 2019 across seven countries to foster innovation and enhance financial inclusion. So far, 3,700 developers have already registered to the programme that is now driving millions of digital transactions (GSMA, 2020).

A report published by McKinsey noted the diversified nature of mobile money operations in Africa. In the report, the authors noted that Fintechs are increasing their influence in the market and share of mobile banking customers. However, mobile network operators have been the dominant providers of mobile money services in Africa for the past decade (Chironga et al., 2017). The report categorised mobile money service providers to include;

1. *MNO-dominant* model where the MNO is responsible for most steps of the value chain. A bank usually acts as the deposit holder. Examples are M-Pesa with 26 million registered users in Kenya, and MTN Mobile Money, with 41 million registered customers across 15 countries.
2. *MNO-led partnerships* where a banking partner supports the MNO in providing products beyond payments such as small consumer loans and deposits. An example is M-Shwari in Kenya, a partnership between Safaricom and CBA, a mid-sized bank in Kenya.
3. *Bank-led partnerships with MNOs.* This service allows customers to conduct banking transactions from their accounts. An example of this model is Equitel, a partnership between Equity Bank and Airtel in Kenya.
4. *Bank models that include banking apps for smartphones and text-based money transfer services using basic handsets.* For these services, the sender needs to be a customer of the bank providing the service. It is,

however, not required for the recipient to be a bank customer. This is the predominant model in Nigeria with banks like GTBank, Access Bank, and First Bank offering various code-based banking services through leading Telcos including MTN, Glo, and Airtel.

5. *Fintech solutions.* These include services provided by firms like Chipper Cash, Flutterwave, and is Paga. These firms provide payments solutions that allow customers to send money via their phones and pay for online purchases on merchant websites.[14]

3.3.2.6 FinTechs

As the digital economy is growing in Africa, payment solutions have become imperative and burgeoning start-up industry of financial technology companies are flourishing in Africa today. These fintechs are finding solutions to Africa's poor integrations into global financial markets. The demand for these payment solutions has spawned innovation among Africa's technology-skilled youths who are developing a plethora of apps and platforms. Overall, there has been significant growth in mobile payments and money transfer platforms which indicates strong demand for and adoption rates of these services. Through their investments and innovation African Founded Firms like Interswitch, Flutterwave, Chipper, and Paga are facilitating payments between African merchants and consumers.

Chironga et al. (2017) observed that "FinTechs in Africa have launched a number of mobile-first solutions that are building momentum." These solutions cut across several financial services sectors like insurance, credit and loans, and remittance. One significant fintech is Interswitch which has helped transform the payment infrastructure for the banking system in Nigeria, and has operations across 23 other countries.

[14] Chironga, M., De Grandis, H., & Zouaoui, Y. (2017). *Mobile financial services in Africa: Winning the battle for the customer*. McKinsey & Company.

Other major players include JumiaPay as well as Savings and lending fintechs like M-Shwari, Fuliza, and KCB M-PESA. BIMA offers mobile-based insurance services in four African countries while Jumo uses telco data to underwrite credit for clients across Africa (Table 3.1).

African founded Fintechs are also providing solutions for remittance payments by Africa's growing diaspora. International remittances processed via mobile money increased by 65% in 2020 (GSMA, 2020). According to the World Bank migrants from SSA remitted US$48 billion in 2018. Fintechs like Sasai Remittance service and Afriex provides instant, zero-fee transfers to Africans at home and in the diaspora.

3.3.2.7 EdTech and e-Learning?

Education was one of the sectors most impacted by Covid 19. Schools were closed and some countries migrated to online learning using education technology. Thus, digital technology and the internet has thus enabled education at all levels to continue. Education technology used innovative learning techniques to facilitate teacher and student interaction. In several African countries the migration to online learning has been facilitated by technologies developed mainly by local start-ups. This has involved building the right infrastructure and providing the right hardware and software to facilitate the teaching and learning process.

Some of the notable providers of edtech services include Eneza Education which operates in Kenya, Ghana, and Ivory Coast. Eneza delivers tailored educational content either online, via applications, or basic feature phones. Co-founded by Kenyan technologist Kago Kagichiri and educator Toni Maraviglia, Eneza Education has over 800,000 users.[15] Method-based mainly on SMS, users pay for the service by airtime and the payment is integrated within all major mobile network operators.

Chalkboard Education is a Ghanaian platform that offers low tech software and services for institutions to create and track training programmes on mobile phones, without the internet. O'Genius Priority, Rwanda: O'Genius Panda is an educational platform where students

---

[15] EdTech: how technology is changing education in Africa. https://www.worldremit.com/en/stories/story/2019/11/14/edtech-africa.

Table 3.1 Some of the largest Fintechs in Africa

Name	Founders	City and country founded in	Year founded	Amount raised from investors by April 2021	Services
Flutterwave	Iyinoluwa Aboyeji, Olugbenga Agboola	Lagos, Nigeria	2016	$234.7M	Business-to Business payment gateway systems
Chipper Cash	Ham Serunjogi, Maijid Moujaled	San Fransisco, USA[a]	2018	$152.2M	Peer-to-peer mobile payments services using text message
Jumo	Andrew Watkins-Ball	Cape Town, South Africa	2015	$156.7M	Banking services through the Jumo digital app
Paymob	Alain El Hajj, Islam Shawky, Mostafa Menessy	Cairo, Egypt	2015	$18.5M	Payment and banking gateway for merchants and consumers
Fawry	Ashraf Sabry, Mohamed Okasha	Cairo, Egypt	2007	$122M	Electronic payment network
Interswitch	Charles Ifedi, Mitchell Elegbe	Lagos, Nigeria	2002	$210.5M	Digital payments
PalmPay	Transsion	Lagos, Nigeria	2019	$106M	P2P transactions, mobile payments
DPO group	Eran Feinstein, Offer Gat	Nairobi, Kenya	2006	$15M	Online payments processing

(continued)

Table 3.1 (continued)

Name	Founders	City and country founded in	Year founded	Amount raised from investors by April 2021	Services
Cellulant	Bolaji Akinboro, Ken Njoroge	Nairobi, Kenya	2004	$54.5M	Multinational digital payments
Yoco	Bradley Wattrus, Carl Wazen, Katlego Maphai, Lungisa Matshoba	Cape Town, South Africa	2013	$23M	Point-of-sale payments provider for small businesses in Africa
Paga	Jay Alabraba, Tayo Oviosu	Lagos, Nigeria	2009	$36.7M	Mobile payment
OPay	Opera	Lagos, Nigeria	2018	$170M	Mobile payment service

Note [a]Chipper Cash was founded by two African immigrants Ham Serunjogi and Maijid Moujaled in San Fransisco
Source Compiled by the author with information from the websites of the companies and multiple online sources including Crunchbase (https://www.crunchbase.com)

use computers to perform laboratory experiments equipping them with experiential and practical scientific knowledge.

3.4 The Impact of the Digital Economy in Africa

There is a well-documented contention that digitalisation creates economic growth and several studies have sought to measure the impact of the digital economy in Africa.[16] Some scholars have argued that a measure of the digital economy should reflect the economic returns being made to digital investments. However, other scholars contend that the full economic returns of investment in technology are greater than that. Some scholars posit those digital investments lead to knock-on effects throughout the economy, which amplify their final impact (GSMA, 2020).

Studies have suggested that the impact of ICT policy and investment in Africa has not been as promised and projected (Solomona & van Klytonb, 2020). Despite investment efforts, African countries have faltered in reaping the expected economic prosperity associated with digitalisation because of a persistent digital divide, including digital skills shortages, deficits in ICT infrastructure, and high-cost structures (Banga & Willem te Velde, 2018). Some scholars believe that despite the grand promise of economic growth of ICT and the internet, the vision has not been realised in Africa. Some studies on the other hand have reported positive impact on the growth of digital economy in Africa (Friederici et al., 2017).

Nevertheless, Abendin et al. (2021) concluded that digitalisation has had a positive impact on international trade and has thus spurred economic growth in Africa. In a study of the impact of the digitalisation on the Kenyan economy, Banga and Willem te Velde (2018) found that Kenyan firms with internet are more productive and have a higher share

[16] Bukht R., & Heeks R. (2017). Defining, conceptualising and measuring the digital economy. http://www.informatics.manchester.ac.uk/news/latest-stories-updates/defining-conceptualising-and-measuring-the-digital-economy/ [Google Scholar] [Ref list].

of skilled workers than firms without access to the internet (Banga & Willem te Velde, 2018).

These empirical studies have, however, failed to acknowledge the nominal growth in the digital economy in Africa and the impact this has had on a broad spectrum of economic activities. In their report, Google and IFC strike a positive note on the growth and impact of the digital economy in Africa. The report believes that "Africa's internet economy is transforming development on the continent by fostering economic opportunities, creating jobs, and providing innovative solutions to complex challenges, including access to health care, education and finance." Google and the IFC estimate that the Gross Value Add of Africa's "internet economy was $100 billion in 2019, or 3.9 per cent of GDP" (Google & IFC, 2020).

The World Bank also believes that mobile broadband and the internet has had a positive impact on welfare and poverty reduction in Africa. Using data from Nigeria, the World Bank asserted that mobile broadband usage when sustained for a year increases consumption by 6%. The effect on consumption rises to 8% after two years of coverage. The World Bank noted that "The proportion of households below the extreme poverty line drops by about 4 per cent after one year of gaining mobile broadband, and by about 7 per cent after 2 or more years of mobile broadband coverage" (World Bank, 2021).

GSMA estimates that mobile technologies and services generated 9% of GDP in Sub-Saharan Africa in 2019. This amounted to $155 billion of economic value added. The mobile ecosystem also sustained 3.8 million jobs (directly and indirectly). There was also substantial benefit to governments as the mobile ecosystem contributed to public sector funding, with $17 billion raised through taxation (GSMA, 2020).

The IFC believes investments like the ESSY submarine cable have improved access to the internet for more than 250 million people across Africa. It is also their belief that greater access to affordable and faster Internet has spawned the growth of new industries. This has invariably led to the creation of new jobs, increasing employment in some areas by as much as 10%. The report believes that improved internet access is responsible for a 14% increase in East Africa's gross domestic product since 2009.[17]

3.5 Key Issues Affecting Digital Economy in Africa

There are a number of factors impeding the development of the digital economy in Africa and these include (1) weak digital infrastructure; and (2) a lack of digital skills among workers and consumers. Despite the remarkable growth, the internet is still not available to three-quarters of people of the continent's population. Moreover, it is comparatively costlier to access the internet in Africa than in advanced economies and the reliability and speed of internet connections are generally much worse (Solomona & van Klytonb, 2020). Notwithstanding, the advances in digital access to the internet are still beyond the reach of most Africans, with only 22% reporting access in 2017 (World Bank, 2021). Digital start-ups still have the problem of access to funding. Even then, adoption of digital technologies and platforms to boost productivity and sales by businesses is still slow. Policy initiatives by governments to develop digital infrastructure, services, skills, and entrepreneurship are not in tandem with the physical and institutional realities challenging African youths and entrepreneurs.

3.5.1 Digital Infrastructure

Despite the investments in telecommunication, Africa still lags behind in the availability of essential Digital infrastructure. As the world transitions to 5G, the adoption of this technology is the lowest in Africa. Statistical evidence has determined that improved telecommunications infrastructure is important for economic growth. Digital infrastructure and access to the internet are also important to the success of entrepreneurs.

---

[17] IFC. https://www.ifc.org/wps/wcm/connect/news_ext_content/ifc_external_corporate_site/news+and+events/news/cm-stories/cm-connecting-africa#page3.

Africa still needs vast investment in digital infrastructure to improve internet access. A report by The Broadband Commission estimates that Africa needs $100 billion investments that would include the construction of 250,000 new 4G base stations and at least 250,000 kilometres of new fibre across the region to achieve universal access to broadband connectivity by 2030 (Broadband Commission, 2016).

3.5.2 Lack of Digital Skills

There is an increased need for skilled personnel to power the growing digital transformation across Africa but the continent lags behind in the availability of Tech talents. It is estimated that most countries across the continent have workforces that are severely lacking in digital skills and are only half that of the global average.

While appraising the availability of digitally skilled youths in Africa Google & IFC (2020) estimated that there 700,000 professional developers on the continent. Fifty per cent of them are concentrated in five countries, Egypt, Kenya, Morocco, Nigeria, and South Africa. Nevertheless, the proportion of people lacking basic digital skills is much higher in Africa than in the advanced economies. High-level digital skills, such as coding, are rare in Africa. Google and IFC found that the digital skills with the highest penetration among youths are social media and graphic design, digital literacy, and web development. It was observed that advanced topics such as artificial intelligence, scientific computing, and human–computer interaction remain relatively unpenetrated (Google & IFC, 2020).

Initiatives to improve basic digital skills and to build a cadre of highly skilled workers is being undertaken through several policy initiatives by governments and multilateral development partners (Herbert & Loudon, 2020). Additionally, African Founded Firms and edtech start-up have also been involved in the push for digital proficiency among Africa's youth. Moringa School, Andela, Gebeya, Decagon, Semicolon, and Umuzi are promoters of this new wave of education and training.

3.5.3 Regulatory Hurdles

Traditional financial services providers are pushing back in some countries against the growing incursion of FinTechs and money market providers into their market. Banks and insurance companies have long enjoyed the privilege of being the main purveyors of financial services but, MNOs and FinTechs are disrupting traditional models of finance and banking in Africa and indeed across the world. This has led to increased regulatory scrutiny and intervention in some African countries including Nigeria, Ethiopia, and Morocco.

In Nigeria different regulatory moves from some of the country's financial bodies have been targeted towards payments, crypto, and wealth tech start-ups.[18] While these regulators claim to foster the interests of the Nigerian public and protect consumers, their moves reek of innovation stifling and jurisdictional play.

3.6 Conclusion

The Covid 19 pandemic has shown the vibrancy resilience and relevance of digital technology. Digital economy is now a significant contributor to GDP. For Africa, the birth and growth of the digital economy has been driven mainly by African Founded Firms. Their investment in the digital technology and digital infrastructure was the foundation on which entrepreneurs have built on to set up digital service firms.

The contribution of the digital economy to GDP is still relatively small in Africa. This is due to poor internet penetration and lack of digital skills. But the rate of growth of the digital economy is one of the fastest in the world and this has triggered optimism. Investments in digital infrastructure are increasing as African Founded Firms are expanding their digital infrastructure. Additionally, Google, Facebook, and other foreign multinational firms are involved in different submarine cable projects to

[18] Nigeria's Biggest Bank Targets 30% Profit Outside Home Market. https://www.bloomberg.com/news/articles/2021-02-19/nigeria-s-biggest-bank-targets-30-profit-outside-home-market.

enhance broadband connectivity on the continent. Mobile telecom operators are also increasing internet access by rolling out 5G and fibre optics networks. The adoption of smartphones continues to rise in Africa and has reached 50% of total connections.

Indeed, the optimism regarding the prospects of the digital economy can be inferred from the increasing ability of African start-ups to raise capital. Increasingly, Africa's flourishing start-up ecosystem is attracting venture capital investment from American, Chinese, and European investors. This increase in investor confidence is fuelled by ongoing changes on the continent that include improved macroeconomic indicators, rapid urbanisation, improved business environments, and a large youth population. Meanwhile African governments are promoting better cooperation between regions through instruments like the African Continental Free Trade Agreement.

According to figures released by Partech Ventures Africa, African tech start-ups attracted $2.02 billion in investments in 2019. This represents 74% year on year growth. These investments were in deals that took place across 18 countries, with Nigeria, Kenya, Egypt, and South Africa as the major investment destinations.

Meanwhile the digital economy is shifting the investing landscape in Africa by creating new economic linkages. With a combined size of 70% of the digital economy between them, investments and technology from America and China are driving the growth of Africa's digital boom. Ironically, investors from European countries, including those that have had a long-established historical, trading and financial relationships with Africa, have contributed less to Africa's growing digital economy.

Investments in digital technology, and the internet economy that it enables, is growing in Africa and African Founded Firms and start-ups are playing a leading role in that growth. The obvious implication of these findings for policy makers is that African governments should develop strategies and enact policies that support the ability of African Founded Firms to continue to invest and expand their operations across the continent.

References

Abendin, S., Pingfang, D., & Nsiah, C. (2021). International trade and economic growth in Africa: The role of the digital economy. *Cogent Economics & Finance, 9*(1). https://doi.org/10.1080/23322039.2021.1911767

Amungo, E. (2020). *The rise of the African Multinational Enterprise (AMNE): The lions accelerating the development of Africa.* Springer Nature.

Atkinson, R. D. (2021). *A U.S. grand strategy for the global digital economy.* Information Technology & Innovation Foundation.

Banga, K., & Willem te Velde, D. (2018). *Digitalisation and the future of manufacturing in Africa.* ODI. Retrieved May 14, 2021, from https://set.odi.org/wp-content/uploads/2018/03/SET_Digitalisation-and-future-of-African-manufacturing_Final.pdf

Broadband Commission. (2016). *Connecting Africa through broadband: A strategy for doubling connectivity by 2021and reaching universal access by 2030.* ITU and UNESCO.

Bukht, R., & Heeks, R. (2017). *Defining, conceptualising and measuring the digital economy.* Development Informatics (Working Paper no. 68). https://ssrn.com/abstract=3431732 or https://doi.org/10.2139/ssrn.3431732

Chironga, M., De Grandis, H., & Zouaoui, Y. (2017). *Mobile financial services in Africa: Winning the battle for the customer.* McKinsey & Company.

Conway, M., Holt, T., Sabow, A., & Sun, I. Y. (2020). *Should sub-Saharan Africa make its own drugs?* McKinsey & Co. Downloaded from https://www.mckinsey.com/~/media/mckinsey/industries/public%20and%20social%20sector/our%20insights/should%20sub%20saharan%20africa%20make%20its%20own%20drugs/should-sub-saharan-africa-make-its-own-drugs.pdf?shouldIndex=false

David-West, O., & Evans, P. C. (2016). *The rise of African platforms: A regional survey.* The Center for Global Enterprise.

Eziakonwa, A. (2020). *Africa's digital solutions to tackle COVID-19.* European Investment Bank.

Friederici, N., Ojanperä, S., & Graham, M. (2017). The impact of connectivity in Africa: grand visions and the mirage of inclusive digital development. *The Electronic Journal of Information Systems in Developing Countries, 7*, 1–20.

Google & IFC. (2020). *e-Conomy Africa 2020.* Google and IFC, a member of the World Bank Group.

GSMA. (2019). *State of the industry report on mobile money.* GSMA.

GSMA. (2020). *The mobile economy in Sub-Saharan Africa 2020.* GSMA.
Gutman, J., Amadou, S., & Soumya, C. (2015). *Financing African infrastructure: Can the world deliver?* Brookings Institution.
Herbert, G., & Loudon, L. (2020, December 01). *The size and growth potential of the digital economy in ODA-eleigible countries*. Helpdesk Reports.
Huawei & Oxford Economics. (2017). *Digital spillover. Measuring the true impact of the digital economy.* Huawei Technologies.
Ibeh, K., Ifedapo, A., & Olawale, A. (2018). The rise of African multinationals: Are IB scholars paying sufficient attention? *AIB Insights, 18*(4), 10–14.
Jacques, B., Chui, M., & Manyika, J. (2013). *Ten IT-enabled business trends for the decade ahead.* McKinsey Quarterly.
Johnson, C., Bester, H., Janse van Vuuren, P., & Dunn, M. (2020). *Africa's digital platforms: An overview of emerging trends.* insight2impact.
Knickrehm, M., Berthon, B., & Daugherty, P. (2016). *Digital disruption: The growth multiplier.* Accenture Strategy.
Makuvaza, L., Johnson, C., & Smit, H. (2018). *The rise of African digital platforms*. Impact.
Sepulveda, E. (2016). *Creating mobile telecom markets in Africa*. International Finance Corporation.
Solomona, E. M., & van Klytonb, A. (2020). The impact of digital technology usage on economic growth in Africa. *Utilities Policy, 67*. https://doi.org/10.1016/j.jup.2020.101104
The International Trade Centre and Amsterdam University of Applied Sciences. (2020c). *Business and policy insights: Mapping e-Marketplaces in Africa.* ITC. Retrieved May 19, 2021, from https://www.intracen.org/uploadedFiles/intracenorg/Content/Publications/B2C-marketplaces-20201221_final_Low-res.pdf
UNCTAD. (2019). *Digital economy report.* United Nations Conference on Trade and Development.
UNCTAD. (2020). *World investment report.* United Nations Conference on Trade and Development.
Verhoef, G. (2017). *The history of business in Africa.* Springer.
World Bank. (2021, Spring). Digital economy for Africa. *Digital Economy for Africa.* Retrieved May 15th, 2021, from https://thedocs.worldbank.org/en/doc/b618f9ef700dde6e605c994f2170b704-0360022021/original/DE4A-newsletter-Spring-2021-spread-Final.pdf

4

Customer Relationship Management and Business Performance: Do Digital Platform Capabilities Matter?

Jude N. Edeh

4.1 Introduction

Research on how firms benefit from their customer relationships is very important for both scholars and practitioners (Christopher et al., 1991; Meena & Sahu, 2021; Ngai, 2005; Reimann et al., 2010). With the rapid change in customer beliefs and behaviour, companies need to build sustainable relationships with their customers and leverage deep insights to deliver superior customer value (Al-Weshah et al., 2019). It is widely agreed that retaining or managing existing customers is more cost-effective than finding new ones (Kotler & Keller, 2009). Customer relationship management (hereafter, CRM) is a critical source of competitive advantage and superior performance of firms (Jackson, 1994; Migdadi, 2021; Mithas et al., 2005; Wang & Feng, 2012). CRM

J. N. Edeh (✉)
Kedge Business School, Marseille, France
e-mail: jude.edeh@kedgebs.com

O. Adeola et al. (eds.), *Digital Service Delivery in Africa*, Palgrave Studies of Marketing in Emerging Economies,
https://doi.org/10.1007/978-3-030-83909-3_4

is a "strategic approach that is concerned with creating improved shareholder value through the development of appropriate relationships with key customers and customer segments" (Payne & Frow, 2005: 168).

The concept of CRM developed in the early 1970s as a sales force automation tool, which enabled companies to track and manage sales interactions between their sales teams and customers (Buttle, 2004). Over time, CRM has evolved to become a "business strategy [that] leverages marketing, operations, sales, customer service, human resources, R&D and finance, as well as information technology and the Internet to maximise the profitability of customer interactions" (Chen & Popovich, 2003: 673). As customer tastes and preferences are speedily changing, companies implementing CRM processes have the potential of developing and bringing innovative goods and services to the marketplace (Reinartz et al., 2004; Valmohammadi, 2017). Prior studies support a positive relationship between CRM capability and firm performance (Battor & Battor, 2010; Coltman et al., 2011; Foltean et al., 2019).

Furthermore, digital transformation has become a strategic imperative in customer relationship management. In the business context, digital transformation is the use of new digital technologies such as social media, mobile analytics, artificial intelligence, cloud, blockchain, to create new business models and enhance customer experience (Fitzgerald et al., 2014; Warner & Wäger, 2019). In recent years, small and medium-sized enterprises (SMEs) have been important drivers of economic development. However, they face survival and competitive pressures in today's highly dynamic and globalised marketplace. In response to these challenges, they are increasingly integrating digital technologies, such as digital platforms, into their strategy to attract new customers as well as manage existing customer relationships (Kamalaldin et al., 2020). Research reveals that digital platforms are transforming the way companies conduct operations (Cenamor et al., 2019), build competitive advantages (Parker et al., 2016) and create customers values (Bresciani et al., 2018).

This trend highlights the close linkage between customer relationships and digital technologies in satisfying customer needs and sustaining performance. However, the mere possession of CRM tools as well as digital technology resources may be insufficient to thrive in today's highly competitive marketplace. On the one hand, customer attitudes are continuously evolving, as such, only companies with the capability of building sustainable relationships with new customers as well as existing customers can create long-lasting customer loyalty. On the other hand, digital technologies create rapid changes and advancements (Vithayathil, 2018), hence, companies need to reconfigure their digital technology resources to match the customer needs. In this context, the dynamic capability view (DCV) proposes that adaptive companies are more likely to survive and achieve superior performance (Teece, 2007). Scholars contend that dynamic capabilities allow companies to integrate, reconfigure, acquire and release resources to match the changes and opportunities in the marketplace (Eisenhardt & Martin, 2000).

Thus, this chapter draws on DCV to investigate how two forms of dynamic capabilities, namely, CRM capability and digital platform capability interact to influence the performance of SMEs in the lower-middle-income country of Nigeria. The research focus is very important for the following reasons: First, as values have become more global, small companies in emerging markets, especially in Sub-Saharan Africa, are struggling to win, retain and manage their customers effectively. Second, unlike their peers in developed economies, these companies face more severe resource challenges that are more likely to influence their operations, strategies, and performance. Accordingly, this chapter contributes to the literature by shedding light on how these companies use CRM capability and digital platform capability to enhance their performance. Specifically, it explores the mediating role of digital platform capability in the relationship between CRM capability and performance.

The chapter proceeds as follows. The theoretical background and hypothesis development are presented in the next section. Then the research methodology is presented. This will be followed by the presentation of the results. Finally, a discussion of the findings will be presented alongside the study's limitations and suggested future research directions.

4.2 Theoretical Background

The resource-based view (RBV) of firms is one of the main perspectives in the strategy literature (Acedo et al., 2006; Newbert, 2007). At its core, it seeks to explain why companies in the same industry perform differently (Zott, 2003). In this regard, it posits that valuable, rare, inimitable, and non-substitutable resources are the basis of competitive advantages (Barney, 1991; Grant, 1991; Wernerfelft, 1984). In other words, survival as well as superior performance depends on a company's ability to create new resources and make them difficult for competitors to duplicate (Barney, 2001; Peteraf, 1993; Uhlenbruck et al., 2006). On this view, capabilities broadly refer to the "complex bundles of skills and accumulated knowledge that enable firms to coordinate activities and make use of their assets" (Day, 1990). Prior studies following the RBV suggest that superior customer-relational capability is one of the most important capabilities of companies as it confers sustainable competitive advantages (Coltman et al., 2011; Day, 1994, 2000). For example, Wang and Feng (2012) find that CRM capabilities were positively related to the performance of firms (Wang & Feng, 2012). Similarly, in a study of internet service providers, Keramati et al. (2009) find that the implementation of CRM resources leads to better firm performance. However, other studies found insignificant relationships (Ramaswami et al., 2009).

While still useful, RBV has been criticised for its static consideration of resources (Kraaijenbrink et al., 2010; Priem & Bulter, 2001). In today's changing business environment, mere possession of resources does not necessarily result in sustainable competitive advantage and performance (Battisti & Deakins, 2017; Eisenhardt & Martin, 2000; Vithessonthi & Racela, 2016). As a result, the dynamic capability view (DCV) scholars extended the RBV to explain how companies survive and grow in dynamic markets (Helfat & Peteraf, 2003; Rindova & Kotha, 2001). According to Teece et al. (1997: 516), a dynamic capability is a firm's "*ability to integrate, build, and reconfigure internal and external competencies to address rapidly changing environments*". The DCV reminds us that companies must reconfigure their resource bases, structures, and processes to grow and create sustainable value < in volatile environments (Eisenhardt & Martin, 2000; Peteraf et al., 2013). Moreover, Zollo and Winter (2002: 340) maintain that *"dynamic capability is a learned and stable pattern of collective activity, through which organizations systematically generate and modify their operating routines to enhance their effectiveness"*. Even though there is a substantial body of studies exploring the relationship between dynamic capabilities and performance outcomes (Karna et al., 2016; Rashidirad & Salimian, 2020; Teece et al., 2016; Wilhelm et al., 2015), SMEs in Africa are yet to receive sufficient attention.

On this basis, this chapter draws on DCV to explore how these SMEs use customer relationship management and digital platform capabilities to enhance their performance. This research focus has overarching implications because these companies, unlike their peers from developed economies, face severe resource constraints, lack of required skills and experience. In addition, they originate from weak institutional environments (LiPuma et al., 2011). Research shows that institution plays a critical role in the structure and performance of firms (Allred & Steensma, 2005). Overcoming these difficulties will require these companies to build various capabilities and continually renew them to effectively respond to the contingency of the marketplace. In this regard, Teece (2007) suggests that companies should adapt their resources to the evolving market demands through the sensing, seizing, and reconfiguration of resources.

First, African SMEs need to develop *sensing capabilities*. That is, they need to identify trends, challenges, and opportunities linked to their internal and external environments. For example, information and communication technology (ICT) is creating new opportunities in Africa (Hjort & Poulsen, 2019; Ndubuisi et al., 2021). SMEs incorporating these tools into their scanning strategy can acquire and filter information from the environments. Consequently, by evaluating and interpreting these ideas and insights, African SMEs can discover new opportunities and better understand customer needs.

Once opportunities have been identified, these companies must understand the resource needs and, accordingly, deploy the adequate resources to capture value from those opportunities and respond to threats (*seizing capabilities*. Again, new technologies can help African

SMEs to integrate digital processes and structures into their decision-making and business model development. For example, research shows that companies deploying digital technological resources as well as introducing innovative products and services can address customer needs (Cenamor et al., 2019).

Third, African SMEs need to develop *reconfiguration capabilities*. That is, the ability to integrate, and continually renew resources and organisational structures in line with the changes in markets conditions. For example, these companies can revamp their routines, redesign their business models and constantly refreshing their digital resources to better establish and nurture long-term relationships with customers. Taken together, by sensing, seizing, and reconfiguring their resources, African SMEs can gain deep insight into market needs, customer expectations and in turn, create superior customer values (Goerzig & Bauernhansl, 2018).

4.2.1 Customer Relationship Management Capabilities and Performance

Scholars have distinguished between resources and capabilities. According to Amit and Schoemaker (1993: 35), resources are stocks of factors that are available, owned or controlled by a firm. They are closely tied to the focal companies, thereby representing the static nature of resources (Katz & Kahn, 1966; Wernerfelt, 1984). Capabilities, on the other hand, are the ability of a company to effectively utilise its resources. Accordingly, to develop capabilities, a company needs to possess the skills and competencies of creating, leveraging, recombining, and releasing its resources (Eisenhardt & Martin, 2000). Customers are important stakeholders, thus, it is not surprising that CRM capability is critical to firm performance. CRM capability is the ability of a company to integrate adequate resources into its process of identifying and maintaining customer relationships and consequently, leveraging these relationships to create customer value (Morgan et al., 2009). Day (1994) refers to CRM capability as a valuable and hard-to-imitate source of competitive advantage.

Prior research reveals that companies with superior CRM capabilities have greater performance (Krasnikov & Jayachandran, 2008; Wang & Feng, 2012). For example, in a seminal study, Reichheld and Sasser (1990) find that CRM capabilities lead to higher customer retention rates and profitability. Similarly, Ryals (2005) reveals that business units implementing CRM activities achieved a 270% increase in profits. Battor and Batter (2010) find that CRM has a direct positive effect on firm performance. In a recent study, Al-Weshah et al. (2019) find that the four dimensions of CRM, namely system quality, information quality, system usage, and user satisfaction, have a significant impact on the performance of Jordanian telecommunication companies. To this end, this chapter argues that CRM capabilities form the basis on which African SMEs can understand the changing customer needs and find efficient ways of meeting their expectations (Day, 1994). In other words, this capability will allow them to retain their existing customers, build long-term customer relationships and consequently, achieve superior performance. Thus, the first hypothesis is proposed as follows:

Hypothesis 1: There is a positive relationship between CRM capability and business performance.

4.2.2 Digital Platform Capability and Performance

Unlike in the traditional contexts, digital transformation is accelerating the pace of change, thereby causing more volatility and uncertainty in the global marketplace (Dehnert, 2020; Loonam et al., 2018). As a result, many companies are exploring and exploiting digital technologies to survive and achieve superior performance (Warner & Wäger, 2019). Hess et al. (2016) highlight that digital technologies shape business models, organisational structures, and processes of companies. In other words, these technologies offer companies a variety of tools, systems, and structures that enable them to interact, collaborate, and create customer values (Nambisan, 2017). In this regard, digital platforms such as social media, chatbots, video conference tools, online communities are powerful sources of competitive advantages (Parker et al., 2016; Wang,

2020). Accordingly, digital platform capability is the ability of a company to gather and integrate available digital technological resources, skills and competence into its activities and processes to produce desired outcomes (Stoel & Muhanna, 2009). For example, companies possessing digital platform capability can utilise enormous opportunities in the digital space, enhance their operational efficiency and performance (Salleh et al., 2017; Yunis et al., 2018).

As evidence is still scarce in emerging markets such as Africa, there is a need for more studies to advance the understanding of the impact of digital platforms on the performance of SMEs (Alavi, 2016). Even though digital platforms are useful, the lack of resources faced by the majority of African SMEs is likely to affect their outcomes (Hamdan et al., 2016). In this context, this chapter contends that companies with the relevant skills and competencies can use digital platforms to improve their performance. This is in line with studies suggesting that mere possession of digital platform resources is not sufficient for achieving competitive advantages and performance (Salleh et al., 2017). In other words, digital platform capability enables these companies to leverage and align digital structures and systems for competitive and performance objectives. Therefore, the following hypothesis is proposed:

Hypothesis 2: There is a positive relationship between digital platform capability and business performance.

4.2.3 Digital Platform Capability and CRM Capability

Digital platforms are changing the ways companies interact and engage with their customers. The digital platform can promote ecosystems, where companies can interact, and exchange ideas with customers (Helfat & Raubitschek, 2018; Nambisan et al., 2019). In other words, digital platforms can play an important role in shaping the CRM capabilities of companies (Kamalaldin et al., 2020). Specifically, digital platforms can help African SMEs to create channels that promote a free flow of information and constant sharing of ideas between them and customers (Ritter & Pedersen, 2020). Specifically, it can improve the customer interactions, collection, and filtering of market-related information critical to understanding customer needs (Melville et al., 2004). Thus, African SMEs possessing appropriate skills and competence can incorporate these insights to better track, evaluate and understand customers evolving demands. Furthermore, digital platforms can enable these companies to capture customer needs and expectations in real-time. Accordingly, African SMEs integrating digital platform capability into their CRM capability can create and deliver superior customer value, maintain a large base of loyal customers, and consequently, sustain superior performance (Eisenmann et al., 2011). Therefore, the last hypothesis is proposed:

Hypothesis 3: The positive relationship between CRM capability and business performance is mediated by digital platform capability.

4.3 Research Design

4.3.1 Sample and Data Collection

To test the proposed hypotheses, a survey targeting SMEs in the manufacturing and service sectors in Nigeria was conducted. The focus on SMEs is due to their important contributions to developing economies. Thus, examining the role of CRM and digital platform capabilities will further uncover the antecedents of their productivity. The survey instrument was pre-tested on three (3) scholars and two (2) practitioners to ensure the validity and clarity of the questionnaire items. Based on their feedback, adjustments were made to the survey questionnaire. The final version of the questionnaire was emailed to 400 companies in 2020. In line with other studies, the survey was directed to the owner-managers as they have more reliable information about their companies' activities and overall performance (Zahra & Covin, 1995). A total of 113 responses was received, yielding a response rate of 28.24%. However, due to missing data, 10 were omitted, leaving a total of 103 completed questionnaires, yielding a response rate of 25.75%.

4.3.2 Measures

The focal variables in this study are CRM capability, digital platform capability, and business performance, which are measured by multiple-item scales. These items were all operationalised based on a five-point Likert-type scale.

4.3.2.1 Business Performance

Business performance was operationalised as two-dimensional constructs, namely, financial performance and market performance (Spanos & Lioukas, 2001). Subjective measures were adopted in this study because of the difficulty in obtaining absolute values of actual performance. Specifically, in an emerging market context such as Nigeria, small companies are often reluctant to disclose their financial information (Haugland et al., 2007). Research shows that subjective assessment of firm performance is fitting because it reflects a company's true position relative to others (Slotegraaf & Dickson, 2004). Accordingly, following previous studies, first, financial performance was measured with two items, profitability and sales growth. Second, market performance was measured with three items: customer satisfaction, customer retention, and market share. The respondents were asked to indicate their companies' performance relative to their competitors. The items ranged from *much worse than competitors* (1) to *much better than competitors* (5).

4.3.2.2 Customer Relationship Management Capability

The CRM capability is conceptualised as a second-order construct following Battor and Battor (2010). Accordingly, it consists of three first-order components, namely customer information, relationship orientation, and configuration (Reinartz et al., 2004).

4.3.2.3 Digital Platform Capability

To measure digital platform capability, this study conceptualised it as a second-order construct that contains three first-order components, namely, ICT adoption, digital orientation, and digital skills (Li & Chan, 2019; Zhou & Wu, 2010).

4.4 Analysis and Results

4.4.1 Analytical Method

To test the research model and hypotheses, this study adopted a Partial Least Squares Path Modelling approach (Hair et al., 2019). In PLS-SEM, the ten (10) times rule is recommended for the determination of the right sample size (Barclay et al., 1995). The structural model of this study has three constructs, that is, two independent variables (CRM capability and digital platform capability) and a dependent variable (Business performance). The sample size used in this study is above the minimum requirement; and thus, appropriate for the analysis (Hair et al., 2017). Accordingly, the two standard procedures to structural equation modelling analysis were applied, first, the measurement model was assessed to determine the reliability and validity of the constructs; and second, the structural model was used in the hypothesis testing.

4.4.2 Assessing Measurement Models

4.4.2.1 Validity and Reliability

The convergent validity involves the verification of three indices, namely, the factor loadings, average variance extracted (AVE), and composite reliability (CR). After removing two items with poor outer loading value (BF2, BF 5), the measurement model of Business Performance was reduced to three items. The results of convergent validity presented in Table 4.1 show that the outer loading for all the items is above the 0.7

Table 4.1 Convergent validity results

Construct	Item	Outer loading (>0.7)	Cronbach's alpha (α > 0.7)	Rho-A (>0.7)	Composite reliability (>0.7)	AVE (>0.5)
Business performance			0.823	0.835	0.894	0.739
	BF3	0.854				
	BF4	0.905				
	BF6	0.817				
CRM capability			0.811	0.861	0.888	0.727
	CRM1	0.915				
	CRM2	0.909				
	CRM3	0.720				
Digit Platform capability			0.748	0.765	0.854	0.661
	DPC1	0.795				
	DPC2	0.815				
	DPC3	0.828				

thresholds. More so, Cronbach's alpha is a common test for internal reliability of latent constructs (Bryman & Bell, 2011) with a recommended value of 0.70 or higher. Likewise, the composite reliability (CR) verifies the internal consistency and reliability of the constructs; and it is recommended to be 0.70 or higher. The Cronbach' alpha: >0.748 and CR: >0.854 are above the recommended values. Finally, the convergent validity is achieved by AVE values higher than 0.50; and as shown in Table 4.1, all the constructs have sufficient convergent validity: AVE is >0.661 (Hair et al., 2011).

4.4.2.2 Discriminant Validity

The discriminant validity guarantees the uniqueness of a measurement construct. The values in Table 4.2 show that each of the constructs shares more variance with its associated items than with any other constructs (Hair et al., 2014: 105). More precisely, as shown in the first section of Table 4.2, the square root of each construct's AVE (see the diagonal

Table 4.2 Discriminant validity (Fornell-Larcker criterion) (Heterotrait-Monotrait Ratio)

Latent constructs	BP	CRMC	DPC	BP	CRMC	DPC
Business performance (BP)	0.860					
CRM capability (CRMC)	0.603	0.853		0.725		
Digital platform capability (DPC)	0.679	0.486	0.813	0.849	0.575	

entries) is greater than its highest correlation with any other construct (see the non-diagonal entries). The results show that the measurement model satisfies the discriminant validity criteria recommended by Fornell and Larcker (1981). Likewise, the measurement model satisfies the Heterotrait–Monotrait (HTMT) ratio criterion of discriminant validity. As shown in the second section of Table 4.2, the values are lower than 0.90 (Henseler et al., 2016).

Lastly, the variance inflation factor (VIF) took values under the 2.6 limit (inner VIF between 1.0 to 1.3; outer VIF between 1.4 to 2.6). These values indicate the absence of collinearity (Diamantopoulos & Siguaw, 2006). In sum, the fulfilment of the reliability, convergent validity, and discriminant validity criteria confirm that the proposed model meets all measurement requirements recommended by the literature (Hair et al., 2014).

4.4.3 Structural Model Evaluation and Results

Since the adequacy of the measurement model was confirmed, structural equation modelling was used to test the hypotheses. First, the results show that the model explains 55.9% of the variance in the endogenous latent variable—business performance (Chin, 1998). Second, the values of the effect size (f2) are adequate for the two exogenous latent variables—CRM capability (0.222) and digital platform capability (0.442). Finally, the value of the Goodness of Fit of the Model of this study is (SRMR = 0.074), which is below the 0.08 threshold (Hu & Bentler, 1999); and the predictive power (Q2 = 0.392), which confirms the relevance of the model.

Table 4.3 Results of the structural equation model test

Hypotheses	β	*t*-value	*p*-value
H1: CRM capability (CRMC) → Business performance (BP)	0.315	2.193	0.029
H2: Digital platform capability (DPFC) → BP	0.662	4.922	0.000
H3: CRMC → DPFC → BP	0. 396	3. 261	0.001

The results of the relationship between the constructs operationalised in this study are presented in Table 4.3. The first hypothesis posits that there is a direct positive relationship between CRM capability and business performance. The results support this hypothesis ($\beta = 0.315$; t-value $= 2.193$; $p = 0.029$). The second hypothesis states that there is a direct positive relationship between digital platform capability and business performance. Likewise, the results support this hypothesis ($\beta = 0.662$; t-value $= 4.922$; $p = 0.000$). Finally, a mediation test is performed to see if the digital platform capability mediates the positive relationship between CRM capability and business performance. In support of hypothesis 3, the specific indirect effects test results show that digital platform capability fully mediates the relationship between CRM capability on business performance is positive and significant ($\beta = 0.$ 396; t-value $= 3.$ 261; $p = 0.001$).

4.5 Discussions

In today's globalised and rapidly changing business environment, digitalisation is regarded as a source of competitive advantage and superior performance due to its potential for new value creation. Despite the burgeoning literature in this area, there is a paucity of evidence on how emerging market firms, African SMEs, in particular, utilise digital technologies in managing their customer relationship. Consequently, the primary objective of this chapter was to examine the simultaneous effects of CRM capability and digital platform capability on the performance of SMEs in Nigeria. This chapter has some important implications for the small companies in Africa.

First, the study reveals that CRM capability contributes to business performance. In the current dynamic marketplace, the customer-centric strategy is the key to the business survival and success of companies (Coltman et al., 2011; Ho et al., 2020). This finding is very important for SMEs in Africa as it reemphasises the importance of CRM practices as means of customer engagement and understanding of customer needs. However, the dynamic capability literature reminds us that the mere existence of resources may be inappropriate or insufficient to sustain competitive advantages, especially when the market conditions change (Battisti & Deakins, 2017). Thus, this finding is consistent with prior studies highlighting the need for developing adequate capabilities when adopting and implementing CRM practices (AlQershi et al., 2020). As customer demands and preferences are rapidly evolving across Africa, CRM capability help SMEs in the region better understand those needs and develop appropriate responses. The knowledge acquired from customer relationships, customer involvement, and joint problem sharing can help African SMEs introduce products and services that match changes in customer expectations (Valmohammadi, 2017). In so doing, they can build customer loyalty and consequently achieve superior performance (Rapp et al., 2010).

Second, in line with burgeoning evidence, this study provides support for a positive relationship between digital platform capability and business performance. In this digital era, there is a wide range of new technologies that create value for SMEs (Bharadwaj et al., 2013; Bouwman et al., 2019). However, these new technologies are rapidly increasing the pace of change in the marketplace, thereby placing additional constraints on the life cycles of products. In other words, moving with technological advancement is no longer an option, but an imperative if a company wants to survive and grow sustainably. However, given the vast amount of digital resources and data, companies, especially SMEs, need to have the appropriate capabilities in place. In this regard, this study reveals that digital platform capability is essential to achieving superior performance. The need for developing digital platform capability is higher for African SMEs due to their severe resource constraints. Without appropriate capability, mere investment in digital technological resources can lead to spreading their companies' resource too thin. Thus, this finding suggests that SME managers in Africa should take capability development seriously when adopting digital platforms to achieve their desired outcomes.

Third, in addition to the direct effects discussed above, an interesting finding in this study is that the digital platform capability fully mediates the positive relationship between CRM capability and business performance. The rise of new technologies is enabling companies to integrate digital platforms into their CRM practices. For example, the use of social media networks has become one of the widely used platforms by companies to interact with customers and deliver services (Ayodeji & Kumar, 2019). Research suggests that information sharing, customer engagement, joint problem-solving, and long-lasting relationship are greater when a company can integrate available digital technological resources, skills, and competence into its CRM activities and processes (Kamboj et al., 2018). The mediating effect found in the current study supports that prior studies highlight the importance of incorporating digital technologies in their existing CRM system to sustain superior performance (Foltean et al., 2019; Wang & Kim, 2017). Thus, these findings suggest that SME managers in Africa should integrate and utilise digital capabilities in their CRM practices to win and retain customers.

4.5.1 Limitations and Future Research Directions

This study is not without limitations. First, the firms in our sample are from a single country, Nigeria. The results obtained in this study cannot be fully generalised to companies in other emerging economies. Therefore, this study calls for future studies to validate the impact of CRM capability and digital capability on business performance, especially in Sub-Saharan Africa.

Second, digital platform capability is a complex construct and, as such, capturing all its dimensions in a single study is very challenging. Likewise, there are other variables not included in the study (e.g. market orientation, brand management capability) that may influence the relationship between CRM capability and business performance. Thus, this study calls for future studies to explore other measures to further uncover the factors influencing the relationships examined in this study.

Finally, relative to their peers in developed economies, SMEs in Africa are more exposed to resource constraints and weak institutional background. This study acknowledges that these liabilities are likely to affect their level of digital technology adoption and implementation. Thus, future research needs to explore the mechanisms underpinning their resource allocation and capability development.

4.6 Conclusion

Digital technologies are changing markets, business environments, and customer interactions. With the rise of digital technology, the adoption and implementation of CRM has drastically changed. As a result, SMEs are now incorporating digital platforms into their existing CRM systems. While CRM practices have the potential of increasing performance, this chapter has shown that SMEs in Africa need to develop adequate CRM and digital platform capabilities to enhance their success. Specifically, this chapter shows that digital platform capability is critical to explaining the impact of CRM capability on business performance. Despite the limitations of this study, it has the potential of opening up more productive fields for future research.

References

Acedo, F. J., Barroso, C., & Galan, J. L. (2006). The resource-based theory: Dissemination and main trends. *Strategic Management Journal, 27*, 621–636.

Alavi, S. (2016). New paradigm of digital marketing in emerging markets: From social media to social customer relationship management. *International Journal of Management Practice, 9*(1), 56–73.

AlQershi, N. A., Mokhtar, S. S. M., & Abas, Z. B. (2020). CRM dimensions and performance of SMEs in Yemen: The moderating role of human capital. *Journal of Intellectual Capital*. https://doi.org/10.1108/JIC-05-2020-0175

Al-Weshah, G. A., Al-Manasrah, E., & Al-Qatawneh, M. (2019). Customer relationship management systems and organizational performance: Quantitative evidence from the Jordanian telecommunication industry. *Journal of Marketing Communications, 25*(8), 799–819.

Allred, B., & Steensma, H. (2005). The influence of industry and home country characteristics on firms' pursuit of innovation. *MIR: Management International Review, 45*(4), 383–412.

Amit, R., & Schoemaker, P. J. H. (1993). Strategic assets and organizational rent. *Strategic Management Journal, 14*, 33–46.

Ayodeji, O. G., & Kumar, V. (2019). Social media analytics: A tool for the success of online retail industry. *International Journal of Services Operations and Informatics, 10*(1), 79–95.

Barclay, D., Higgins, C., & Thompson, R. (1995). The partial least squares (PLS) approach to causal modelling: Personal computer adoption and use as an illustration. *Technology Studies, Special Issue on Research Methodology, 2*(2), 285–309.

Barney, J. B. (1991). Firm resources and sustained competitive advantage. *Journal of Management, 17*(1), 19–120.

Barney, J. B. (2001). Resource-based theories of competitive advantage: A ten-year retrospective on the resource-based view. *Journal of Management, 27*(6), 643–650.

Battisti, M., & Deakins, D. (2017). The relationship between dynamic capabilities, the firm's resource base and performance in a post-disaster environment. *International Small Business Journal, 35*(1), 78–98.

Battor, M., & Battor, M. (2010). The impact of customer relationship management capability on innovation and performance advantages: Testing a mediated model. *Journal of Management Management, 26*(9–10), 842–857.

Bharadwaj, A., El Sawy, O., Pavlou, P., & Venkatraman, N. (2013). Digital business strategy: Toward a next generation of insights. *MIS Quarterly, 37*(2), 471–482.

Bouwman, H., Nikou, S., & de Reuver, M. (2019). Digitalization, business models, and SMEs: How do business model innovation practices improve performance of digitalizing SMEs? *Telecommunications Policy, 43*(9). https://doi.org/10.1016/j.telpol.2019.101828

Bresciani, S., Ferraris, A., & Del Giudice, M. (2018). The management of organizational ambidexterity through alliances in a new context of analysis: Internet of Things (IoT) smart city projects. *Technological Forecasting and Social Change, 136*, 331–338.

Bryman, A., & Bell, E. (2011). *Business research methods* (3rd ed.). Oxford University Press.

Buttle, F. (2004). *Customer relationship management: Concepts and tools*. Elsevier Buttlerworth-Heinemann.

Cenamor, J., Parida, V., & Wincent, J. (2019). How entrepreneurial SMEs compete through digital platforms: The roles of digital platform capability, network capability and ambidexterity. *Journal of Business Research, 100*, 196–206.

Chen, I. J., & Popovich, K. (2003). Understanding customer relationship management (CRM): People processes and technology. *Business Process Management Journal, 9*(5), 672–688.

Chin, W. W. (1998). The partial least squares approach to structural equation modelling. *Modern Methods for Business Research, 295*(2), 295–336.

Christopher, M., Payne, A., & Ballantyne, D. (1991). *Relationship marketing*. Butterworth-Heinemann.

Coltman, T., Devinney, T. M., & Midgley, D. F. (2011). Customer relationship management and firm performance. *Journal of Information Technology, 26*(3), 205–219.

Day, G. S. (1990). *Market driven strategy: Processes for creating value*. Free Press.

Day, G. S. (1994). The capabilities of market-driven organizations. *Journal of Marketing, 58*(4), 37–52.

Day, G. S. (2000). Managing marketing relationships. *Journal of the Academy of Marketing Science, 28*(1), 24–30.

Dehnert, M. (2020). Sustaining the current or pursuing the new: Incumbent digital transformation strategies in the financial service industry. *Business Research, 13*, 1071–1113.

Diamantopoulos, A., & Siguaw, J. A. (2006). Formative vs reflective indicators in organizational measure development: A comparison and empirical illustration. *British Journal of Management, 17*(4), 263–282.

Eisenhardt, K. M., & Martin, J. A. (2000). Dynamic capabilities: What are they? *Strategic Management Journal, 21*(1), 1105–1121.

Eisenmann, T. R., Parker, G., & Van Alstyne, M. (2011). Platform envelopment. *Strategic Management Journal, 32*(12), 1270–1285.

Fitzgerald, M., Kruschwitz, N., Bonnet, D., & Welch, M. (2014). Embracing digital technology—A new strategic imperative. *MIT Sloan Management Review, 55*(2), 1–12.

Foltean, F. S., Trif, S. M., & Daniela Liliana Tuleu, D. L. (2019). Customer relationship management capabilities and social media technology use:

Consequences on firm performance. *Journal of Business Research, 104*, 563–575.
Fornell, C., & Larcker, D. F. (1981). Evaluating structural equation models with unobservable variables and measurement error. *Journal of Marketing Research, 18*(1), 39–50.
Goerzig, D., & Bauernhansl, T. (2018). Enterprise architectures for the digital transformation in small and medium-sized enterprises. *Procedia CIRP, 67*, 540–545.
Grant, R. M. (1991). The resource-based theory of competitive advantage: Implications for strategy formulation. *California Management Review, 33*, 114–135.
Hair, J. F., Hult, G. T. M., Ringle, C. M., & Sarstedt, M. (2017). *A primer on partial least squares structural equation modeling (PLS-SEM)* (2nd ed.). Sage.
Hair, J. F., Ringle, C. M., & Sarstedt, M. (2011). PLS-SEM: Indeed a silver bullet. *Journal of Marketing Theory and Practice, 19*(2), 139–152.
Hair, J. F., Risher, J. J., Sarstedt, M., & Ringle, C. M. (2019). When to use and how to report the results of PLS-SEM. *European Business Review, 31*(1), 2–24.
Hair, J. F., Sarstedt, M., Hopkins, L., & Kuppelwieser, V. G. (2014). Partial least squares structural equation modeling (PLS-SEM): An emerging tool in business research. *European Business Review, 26*(2), 106–121.
Hamdan, A. R., Yahaya, J. H., Deraman, A., & Jusoh, Y. Y. (2016). The success factors and barriers of information technology implementation in small and medium enterprises: An empirical study in Malaysia. *International Journal of Business Information Systems, 21*(4), 477–494.
Haugland, S. A., Myrtveit, I., & Nygaard, A. (2007). Market orientation and performance in the service industry: A data envelopment analysis. *Journal of Business Research, 60*(11), 1191–1197.
Helfat, C. E., & Peteraf, M. A. (2003). The dynamic resource-based view: Capability lifecycles. *Strategic Management Journal, 24*, 997–1010.
Helfat, C. E., & Raubitschek, R. S. (2018). Dynamic and integrative capabilities for profiting from innovation in digital platform-based ecosystems. *Research Policy, 47*(8), 1391–1399.
Henseler, J., Hubona, G., & Ray, P. A. (2016). Using PLS path modeling in new technology research: Updated guidelines. *Industrial Management & Data Systems, 116*(1), 2–20.
Hess, T., Matt, C., Benlian, A., & Wiesböck, F. (2016). Options for formulating a digital transformation strategy. *MIS Quarterly Executive, 15*(2), 123–139.

Hjort, J., & Poulsen, J. (2019). The arrival of fast Internet and employment in Africa. *The American Economic Review, 109*(3), 1032–1079.

Ho, M. H.-W., Chung, H. F. L., Kingshott, R., & Chiu, C.-C. (2020). Customer engagement, consumption and firm performance in a multi-actor service eco-system: The moderating role of resource integration. *Journal of Business Research, 121*, 557–566.

Hu, L., & Bentler, P. M. (1999). Cutoff criteria for fit indexes in covariance structure analysis: Conventional criteria vs new alternatives. *Structural Equation Modeling: A Multidisciplinary Journal, 6*(1), 1–55.

Jackson, D. Jr. (1994). Relationship selling: The personalization of relationship marketing. *Asia-Australia Marketing Journal*, 45–54.

Kamalaldin, A., Linde, L., Sjödin, D., & Parida, V. (2020). Transforming provider-customer relationships in digital servitization: A relational view on digitalization. *Industrial Marketing Management, 89*, 306–325.

Kamboj, S., Yadav, M., & Rahman, Z. (2018). Impact of social media and customer-centric technology on performance outcomes: The mediating role of social CRM capabilities. *International Journal of Electronic Marketing and Retailing, 9*(2), 109–125.

Karna, A., Richter, A., & Riesenkampff, E. (2016). Revisiting the role of the environment in the capabilities–financial performance relationship: A meta-analysis. *Strategic Management Journal, 37*(6), 1154–1173.

Katz, D., & Kahn, R. L. (1966). *The social psychology of organizations.* John Wiley and Sons.

Keramati, A., Mehrabi, H., Mojir, N., & Mousakhani, M. (2009). Customer relationship management and performance, a resource-based view of Iranian internet service industry. *International Journal of Electronic Customer Relationship Management, 3*(2), 103–120.

Kotler, P., & Keller, K. (2009). *Marketing management* (10th ed.). Pearson Education.

Kraaijenbrink, J., Spender, J.-C., & Groen, A. J. (2010). The resource-based view: A review and assessment of its critiques. *Journal of Management, 36*(1), 349–372.

Krasnikov, A., & Jayachandran, S. (2008). The relative impact of marketing, research-and-development, and operations capabilities on firm performance. *Journal of Marketing, 72*(4), 1–11.

Li, T., & Chan, Y. E. (2019). Dynamic information technology capability: Concept definition and framework development. *The Journal of Strategic Information Systems, 28*(4). https://doi.org/10.1016/j.jsis.2019.101575

LiPuma, J., Newbert, S., & Doh, J. (2011). The effect of institutional quality on firm export performance in emerging economies: A contingency model of firm age and size. *Small Business Economics, 40*, 817–841.

Loonam, J., Eaves, S., Kumar, V., & Parry, G. (2018). Towards digital transformation: Lessons learned from traditional organizations. *Strategic Change, 27*(2), 101–109.

Meena, P., & Sahu, P. (2021). Customer relationship management research from 2000 to 2020: An academic literature review and classification. *Vision.* https://doi.org/10.1177/0972262920984550

Melville, N., Kraemer, K., & Gurbaxani, V. (2004). Review: Information technology and organizational performance: An integrative model of IT business value. *MIS Quarterly, 28*(2), 283–322.

Migdadi, M. M. (2021). Knowledge management, customer relationship management and innovation capabilities. *Journal of Business & Industrial Marketing, 36*(1), 111–124.

Mithas, S., Krishnan, M. S., & Fornell, C. (2005). Why do customer relationship management applications affect customer satisfaction? *Journal of Marketing, 69*(4), 201–209.

Morgan, N. A., Vorhies, D. W., & Mason, C. H. (2009). Market orientation, marketing capabilities, and firm performance. *Strategic Management Journal, 30*, 909–920.

Nambisan, S. (2017). Digital entrepreneurship: Toward a digital technology perspective of Entrepreneurship. *Entrepreneurship Theory and Practice, 41*(6), 1029–1055.

Nambisan, S., Wright, M., & Feldman, M. (2019). The digital transformation of innovation and entrepreneurship: Progress, challenges and key themes. *Research Policy, 48*(8), 1–9.

Ndubuisi, G., Otioma, C., & Tetteh, G. K. (2021). Digital infrastructure and employment in services: Evidence from Sub-Saharan African countries. *Telecommunications Policy*. https://doi.org/10.1016/j.telpol.2021.102153

Newbert, S. L. (2007). Empirical research on the resource-based view of the firm: An assessment and suggestions for future research. *Strategic Management Journal, 28*, 121–146.

Ngai, E. W. T. (2005). Customer relationship management research (1992–2002): An academic literature review and classification. *Marketing Intelligence & Planning, 23*(6), 582–605.

Parker, G., Van Alstyne, M., & Choudary, S. (2016). *Platform revolution.* W. W. Norton.

Payne, A., & Frow, P. (2005). A strategic framework for customer relationship management. *Journal of Marketing, 69*(4), 167–176.

Peteraf, M. A. (1993). The cornerstones of competitive advantage: A resource-based view. *Strategic Management Journal, 14*(3), 179–191.

Peteraf, M., Stefano, G. D., & Verona, G. (2013). The elephant in the room of dynamic capabilities: Bringing two diverging conversations together. *Strategic Management Journal, 34*(12), 1389–1410.

Priem, R. L., & Butler, J. E. (2001). Is the resource-based 'view' a useful perspective for strategic management research? *Academy of Management Review, 26*(1), 22–40.

Ramaswami, S., Srivastava, R., & Bhargava, M. (2009). Market-based capabilities and financial performance of firms: Insights into marketing's contribution to firm value. *Journal of the Academy of Marketing Science, 37*(2), 97–116.

Rapp, A., Trainor, K. J., & Agnihotri, R. (2010). Performance implications of customer-linking capabilities: Examining the complementary role of customer orientation and CRM technology. *Journal of Business Research, 63*(11), 1229–1236.

Rashidirad, M., & Salimian, H. (2020). SMEs' dynamic capabilities and value creation: The mediating role of competitive strategy. *European Business Review, 32*(4), 591–613.

Reichheld, F. F., & Sasser, W. E. Jr. (1990). Zero defections: Quality comes to services. *Harvard Business Review, 68*(5), 105–111.

Reimann, M., Schilke, O., & Thomas, J. S. (2010). Customer relationship management and firm performance: The mediating role of business strategy. *Journal of the Academy of Marketing Science, 38*, 326–346.

Reinartz, W., Krafft, M., & Hoyer, W. D. (2004). The CRM process: Its measurement and impact on performance. *Journal of Marketing Research, 41*, 293–305.

Rindova, V. P., & Kotha, S. (2001). Continuous morphing: Competing through dynamic capabilities, form and function. *Academy of Management Journal, 44*(6), 1263–1280.

Ritter, T., & Pedersen, C. L. (2020). Digitization capability and the digitalization of business models in business-to-business firms: Past, present, and future. *Industrial Marketing Management, 86*, 180–190.

Ryals, L. (2005). Making customer relationship management work: The measurement and profitable management of customer relationships. *Journal of Marketing, 69*(4), 252–261.

Salleh, N. A. M., Rohde, F., & Green, P. (2017). Information systems enacted capabilities and their effects on SMEs' information systems adoption behaviour. *Journal of Small Business Management, 55*(3), 332–364.

Slotegraaf, R. J., & Dickson, P. R. (2004). The paradox of a marketing planning capability. *Journal of the Academy of Marketing Science, 32*(4), 371–385.

Spanos, Y. E., & Lioukas, S. (2001). An examination into the causal logic of rent generation: Contrasting Porter's competitive strategy framework and the resource-based perspective. *Strategic Management Journal, 22*, 907–934.

Stoel, M. D., & Muhanna, W. A. (2009). IT capabilities and firm performance: A contingency analysis of the role of industry and IT capability type. *Information & Management, 46*(3), 181–189.

Teece, D. J. (2007). Explicating dynamic capabilities: The nature and microfoundations of (sustainable) enterprise performance. *Strategic Management Journal, 28*(13), 1319–1350.

Teece, D. J., Pisano, G., & Shuen, A. (1997). Dynamic capabilities and strategic management. *Strategic Management Journal, 18*, 509–533. https://doi.org/10.1002/(SICI)1097-0266(199708)18:7<509::AID-SMJ882>3.0.CO;2-Z

Teece, D., Peteraf, M., & Leih, S. (2016). Dynamic capabilities and organizational agility: Risk, uncertainty, and strategy in the innovation economy. *California Management Review, 58*(4), 13–35.

Uhlenbruck, K., Hitt, M. A., & Semadeni, M. (2006). Market value effects of acquisitions involving internet firms: A resource-based analysis. *Strategic Management Journal, 27*, 899–913.

Valmohammadi, C. (2017). Customer relationship management: Innovation and performance. *International Journal of Innovation Science, 9*(4), 374–395.

Vithayathil, J. (2018). Will cloud computing make the Information Technology (IT) department obsolete? *Infomation Systems Journal, 28*, 634–649.

Vithessonthi, C., & Racela, O. C. (2016). Short- and long-run effects of internationalization and R&D intensity on firm performance. *Journal of Multinational Financial Management, 34*, 28–45.

Wang, F. (2020). Digital marketing capabilities in international firms: A relational perspective. *International Marketing Review, 37*(3), 559–577.

Wang, Y., & Feng, H. (2012). Customer relationship management capabilities: Measurement, antecedents and consequences. *Management Decision, 50*(1), 115–129.

Wang, Z., & Kim, H. G. (2017). Can social media marketing improve customer relationship capabilities and firm performance? Dynamic capability perspective. *Journal of Interactive Marketing, 39*, 15–26.

Warner, K. S., & Wäger, M. (2019). Building dynamic capabilities for digital transformation: An ongoing process of strategic renewal. *Long Range Planning, 52*(3), 326–349.

Wernerfelt, B. (1984). A resource-based view of the firm. *Strategic Management Journal, 5*, 171–180.

Wilhelm, H., Schlömer, M., & Maurer, I. (2015). How dynamic capabilities affect the effectiveness and efficiency of operating routines under high and low levels of environmental dynamism. *British Journal of Management, 26*(2), 327–345.

Yunis, M., Tarhini, A., & Kassar, A. (2018). The role of ICT and innovation in enhancing organizational performance: The catalysing effect of corporate entrepreneurship. *Journal of Business Research, 88*, 344–356.

Zahra, S. A., & Covin, J. G. (1995). Contextual influences on the corporate entrepreneurship-performance relationship: A longitudinal analysis. *Journal of Business Venturing, 10*(1), 43–58.

Zhou, K. Z., & Wu, F. (2010). Technology capability, strategic flexibility and product innovation. *Strategic Management Journal, 31*(5–6), 547–561.

Zollo, M., & Winter, S. (2002). Deliberate learning and the evolution of dynamic capabilities. *Organization Science, 13*(3), 339–351.

Zott, C. (2003). Dynamic capabilities and the emergence of intraindustry differential firm performance: Insights from a simulation study. *Strategic Management Journal, 24*, 97–125.

5

Digital Supply Chain in Sub-Saharan Africa: A Multi-Country Study

Marvel Ogah and Raymond Onuoha

5.1 Introduction

Innovative digital technologies have the potential to improve supply chain performance. While the nexus between digital technologies and supply chain management has received considerable academic attention in the last decade (Ageron et al., 2020; Arenkov et al., 2019; Boone & Ganeshan, 2007; Büyüközkan & Göçer, 2018; Jabbour et al., 2020; Kache & Seuring, 2017; Lancioni et al., 2003; Núñez-Merino et al., 2020; Sanders et al., 2019; Wang et al., 2016), not much is known concerning sustainable digital supply chains, especially in the context

M. Ogah (✉) · R. Onuoha
Lagos Business School, Lekki, Nigeria
e-mail: mogah@lbs.edu.ng

R. Onuoha
e-mail: ronuoha@lbs.edu.ng

O. Adeola et al. (eds.), *Digital Service Delivery in Africa*, Palgrave Studies of Marketing in Emerging Economies,
https://doi.org/10.1007/978-3-030-83909-3_5

of Africa. Addressing this knowledge gap is fundamental to understanding the longer-term imperative of the fourth industrial revolution in reshaping supply chain operations and management within the continent for greater socio-economic development of the countries within it, as it relates directly to their competitiveness (Miethlich et al., 2020). While most prior studies have focused on either business sectors or individual enterprises, the discourse in this chapter will examine some countries within the continent of Africa largely understudied unit of analysis within the domain of supply chain management.

From a sustainability standpoint, a digital supply chain leverages a wide range of emerging 'industry 4.0' technologies (e.g. big data, blockchain and augmented reality) to advance the effectiveness and efficiency of the supply chain (SC) to meeting customer demand, in a manner that is economically plausible, environmentally favourable and socially responsible, as determined by SC stakeholders (Seuring & Müller, 2008; Song et al., 2017). Within this purview, therefore, this chapter is motivated to answer the questions:

- What do we know about digital supply chains in Africa?
- What are the key factors for assessing the sustainability of digital supply chains in sub-Saharan Africa?

These research questions are answered based on a conceptual framework developed by the authors that draw out a comparative assessment of the case studies concerning the select countries in Africa–Nigeria, South Africa, Kenya and Tanzania. The countries have been selected based on the respective peculiarities of these countries in sub-Saharan Africa. Building on the country-based study, the chapter elucidates some of the barriers and policy pathways to sustainable digital supply chains in Africa.

5.2 Literature Review

The competitiveness of any supply chain value stream management is hinged on responsiveness, innovativeness and cost-effectiveness. In this regard, the increasing levels of connectivity driven by higher computing powers and ubiquitous internet technology are creating new possibilities in supply chain functionalities since the turn of the decade, engendering a strong imperative to assessing their transformational effects with regards to digital strategies (Bharadwaj et al., 2013; Sambamurthy et al., 2003). Dominant themes in recent literature focus on the creation and capture of value (Bechtsis et al., 2018; Brinch, 2018; Mittal et al., 2018; New, 1997; Pagani, 2013; Pal & Sandberg, 2017; Skilton, 2014), optimising cost-revenue efficiencies (Masoud & Mason, 2017; Nooraie, 2017), and risks (Barry, 2004; Hofmann et al., 2018; Kache & Seuring, 2017; Kwak et al., 2018; Sheffi, 2018) within a digitally enabled supply chain. In this domain, the extant literature posits divergent supply chain management approaches in varying digital business environments for industry conformance, chiefly attributable to information asymmetry effects of digitally enabled business systems (Mithas et al., 2013).

Globally, the shift from hierarchical to fragmented supply chain networks concerning integration and strategic partnerships by contemporary firms have been catalysed by the forces of technology globalisation and its requirements on firm agility as a competitive advantage (Lavikka et al., 2017; Mol & Birkinshaw, 2009; Pagani, 2013; Sambamurthy et al., 2003; Straub et al., 2004). The digitisation of a supply chain has the potential to dramatically elicit lower costs, increase product availability and even create new markets unknown or unavailable before the availability of key technologies (Swanson, 2017). Recent developments concerning digitalisation are expected to play an increasingly significant role in the management and design of global supply chains. The shift of value from physical artefacts to 'smart' product offerings and the data that the digitalisation processes re-creating pose particular problems, especially to companies actively involved in manufacturing and logistics systems or, more general, in value-adding activities.

However, the rather disruptive process concerning the transformation of companies into their digitalised counterparts constitutes an element of uncertainty and difficulty for many decision-makers (Porter & Heppelmann, 2014). Consequently, companies still have idle inventory and other resources that are not 'working' for them. To remain competitive, therefore, supply chain managers must constantly improve their processes and react to ever-growing and evolving customer preferences in a changing business environment. With increasing information capabilities, firms now can better understand how and where their supply chain is working efficiently, and importantly, where it is not. Supply chain visibility is therefore increased, allowing firms to achieve a greater level of performance and competitive advantage (Swanson, 2017).

Recent research by the New York-based Center for Global Enterprises (CGE)'s Digital Supply Chain Institute (DSCI)[1] identified digital transformation as the most critical competitive factor in global supply chains over the next three years, with an improvement value of 20% and 10% to both cost and revenues, respectively, by optimising the staging and flow of materials and firm resources (Rai et al., 2006). Despite this competitive imperative, it remains a daunting challenge for firms in the digital transformation of their supply value chains, with many going into extinction being unable to cope with the pressure of evolution (Loonam et al., 2018). Within this purview, there has been limited application of appropriate theoretical underpinnings in interrogating the digital transitioning of supply chain systems and processes (Seyedghorban et al., 2020; Straub et al., 2004). Consideration of these phenomena within the supply chain management perspective has critical implications for theory and practice that necessitate further research (Holmström & Partanen, 2014).

This empirical research within the domain of supply chain management has been limited especially in developing economy contexts and in conceptual validating of practical country cases (Arlbjørn & Paulraj, 2013; Arlbjørn et al., 2011; Banker et al., 2006; Baramichai et al., 2007; Büyüközkan & Göçer, 2018; Frohlich, 2002; Mithas et al., 2013; Loonam et al., 2018; Rai et al., 2006; Sabri et al., 2018). The chapter bridges this knowledge gap by applying the conceptual framework that follows to analysing the select country cases in Africa; but first, we make a definition about the scope of the paper.

[1] CGE: going digital can reduce supply chain costs by 50%. https://supplychaindigital.com/supply-chain-2/cge-going-digital-can-reduce-supply-chain-costs-50.

5.3 Digital Supply Chain Transformation

A digital supply chain can be defined as one that leverages 'digital resources to create differential value' by optimising performance and minimising risks (Bharadwaj et al., 2013: 472). It is mainly characterised by efficiently coordinated communication linkages and collaboration between stakeholders in the supply chain ecosystem (Korpela et al., 2017). This invariably leads to higher efficiencies in cost optimisation and lower cycle times for firms operating in the supply value chain (Bharadwaj et al., 2013). Despite these positive externalities, there persist the critical issues of technology risks and cost of deployment especially in instances where intended outcomes are not fully justified (Hazen & Byrd, 2012).

5.4 Sustainable Digital Supply Chains (DSC): A Conceptual Framework

A conceptual foundation for the cross-country comparative on sustainable digital supply chains is based on a deductive theoretical framework consisting of dynamic capability, stakeholder and institutional theories. The comparative case analysis explores country orientations in sustainably digitalising their supply chains.

First, drawing on dynamic capability theory (DCT), the authors develop an assessment instrument for sustainable digital supply chains in select African countries. DCT underscores the need for countries to develop dynamic capabilities to overcoming supply chain challenges and gain competitive advantage via digital (Chowdhury & Quaddus, 2017). The dynamic capabilities paradigm in supply chain management research provides a theoretical lens for interrogating the nuanced adaptation differences in the digital transformation of supply chains within countries. The concept relates the systematic, change-inducing capabilities of countries for their supply chains and the contextual operational and institutional environment (Barreto, 2010; Schilke et al., 2018; Winter, 2003).

In their definition, Teece et al. (1997: 516) explicated the dynamic capability construct as a 'firm's ability to integrate, build, and reconfigure internal and external competencies to address rapidly changing environments'. This perspective is built on the assumption that the firm's dynamic capabilities are created based on a specific path-dependent evolution of their organisational processes, which lays credence to heterogeneity across different firms even to competitive outcomes (Karimi & Walter, 2015; Lavie, 2006). In the context of supply chain management, Beske (2012) delineates the dynamic capability framework into supply chain partnerships, co-evolvement, reconstruction, flexibility and knowledge assessment, all combined to generate sustainable and competitive supply chains. Within the structural contingency paradigm, the contextual institutional and business environment play a significant moderating role in the explication and adaptation of firm dynamic capabilities to changes in technology (Brandon-Jones & Knoppen, 2018; Donaldson, 2001; Gruchmann & Seuring, 2018).

Second, and tying from the DCT concept is the framework of institutional theory. Institutional theory assesses beyond firms, the broader influence of the contextual socio-political structure in the evolution of digital supply chains (Scott, 2005). It elucidates the processes via which rules, policies, regulations and agencies impact firm behaviours in the digital transformation of their supply chains, albeit in a sustainable manner over time. We position the institutional pressure to construct within this chapter by asking in the cases what the primary institutional drivers of transformation are, and how these drivers influence the response of firms within the countries in digitally transforming their supply chains sustainably.

Third, and in line with our introductory position, as the sustainability of the digital supply chain (SC) is determined by SC stakeholders, we infuse stakeholder theory to explain how firms within the different countries are socially responsive to the obligations of the stakeholders within the supply chain ecosystems in their digital transformation evolution (Gupta et al., 2020). From the analytical perspective of stakeholder theory, we assess how the different supply chain digital transformation fits within the broader supply chain ecosystem in country, regarding sustainability requirements in creating value for sustainable competitive advantage (Freeman et al., 2010; Hörisch et al., 2020).

The above theoretical frame is integratively deduced to undertake the comparative case analysis for sustainable digital supply chains in the select African countries.

1. Country-based Studies of Sustainable Digital Supply Chains – Nigeria, Kenya, SA and Tanzania

- Nigerian Digital Supply Chain

The digital supply chain in Nigeria is evolving and adapting to the needs of most value chains. The supply chain ecosystem is currently harnessing the power of digital transformation towards shaping its relevance for an efficient and interconnected operation. Currently, with the advent of COVID-19 and other related incidents of disruptions occasioned by the peculiarities of the Nigerian environment, most industrial players want to remain relevant to the changing needs to embrace the advantages of digitalisation and interactive supply chain. While most Nigerian organisations in the supply chain environment are working towards incorporating new technologies that would drive efficiency, speed and connectivity, and to allow greater utilisation of its available workforce to drive greater supply chain success, there abound some challenges. However, according to a diagnostic report by the World Bank Group (2019), access acceleration to digital technologies will spur innovation, efficiency and production in the Nigerian drive towards digital supply chain value streams, but most players are excluded from the digital ecosystem as a result of limited access to enabling digital infrastructure.

According to research anchored by Digital Economy for Africa, there is an expedient drive towards digital technologies in a bid to elicit innovation, efficiency and productivity in the Nigerian digital ecosystem; however, this development has been hampered by limited access to broadband and lack of adequate devices amidst enabling progress in digital infrastructure, finance, digital skills and entrepreneurship (Fisher et al., 2014; Herold & Mikl, 2021; Hohenstein et al., 2014; Wood et al., 2016). Recent research has also revealed that the digital supply chain ecosystem in Nigeria is still evolving largely characterised by its fragmented nature, how the Nigerian supply chain networks cum collaborations are struggling to flourish in a volatile, and unpredictable nature of the Nigerian business environment (Oyedijo et al., 2021). Albeit, the emerging digital supply chain in Nigeria is characterised by barriers and drivers, which can be segmented into three distinct levels interplaying among external, internal and local supply value chain vagaries.

- South African Digital Supply Chain

Aside from the issues of the rising cost of material inputs, increasing supply chain costs, deteriorating infrastructure, and lack of digital capability among the South African workforce as a requirement for the changing consumer demands which also affecting the consumer value chain in South Africa (Accenture Strategy, 2019; World Economic Forum & Accenture, 2017).

However, with a projection into the future, the adoption of digital technologies would attract immense value-add for the South African consumer value chain by 2026 (Accenture Strategy, 2019; WEF & Accenture, 2017). Albeit, with an ever-increasing consumer expectation hinged on the adoption of digital technologies towards driving the South African digital supply chain, there abound critical challenges occasioned by penetration in new markets and the operational exigency for efficient and competitive value chain networks. This trend has necessitated the plank for both local supply chain organisations and other stakeholders to explore and create policy reforms geared towards enabling digital supply chain transformation in South Africa. Comparatively, like other developing African countries, aside from digital supply chain impact, other aspects of digital supply chain flow such as AI, rapid and technological advances hold massive benefits for the future regarding the generation of the appropriate environment for digital advancement in South Africa (Aly, 2020; Park & Choi, 2019).

- Kenyan Digital Supply Chain

Kenya is one of the African countries that was affected by a reduction in agricultural exports due largely to production and supply chain disruption posed by risks hinged on the labour-intensive segment, which was dependent on efficient logistics due to the high perishability rate of production, and gridlock in national supply occasioned by the COVID-19 bottlenecks (Oxford Business Group, 2020). Inter alia, post-COVID-19 has necessitated a robust shift towards digital supply chain process architecture that has enabled producers and consumers in Kenya to grow accustomed to the DSC ecosystem characterised by strong mobile money and cashless technological platforms. The emergence of a digital supply architecture in Kenya has helped to strengthen the agricultural value chain and it has also augmented the steady supply of fresh agricultural products especially for basic consumption (Oxford Business Group, 2020). This situation has significantly impacted on the relevance of the digital supply chain ecosystem in Kenya during the post-Covid era.

The digital supply chain ecosystem in Kenya has evolved due to the modularisation and interface standardisation which hitherto has made it more accessible to businesses and users alike irrespective of inherent digital challenges (Bramann, 2017; Drouillard et al., 2014). This trend has not only re-inforced emergent entrepreneurial architecture in tandem with other governmental, non-governmental agencies, and potential investors (Kelly & Firestone, 2016; Park et al., 2017).

Like other emergent digital imperatives, the drive and adoption of the digital supply chain have been slow and characterised by a design-reality gap in developing nations inclusive of Kenya, Nigeria and Tanzania (Ahmad et al., 2013; Al-Hujran et al., 2015; Carter et al., 2016; Elkadi, 2013; Heeks, 2003; Kumar & Best, 2006; Lee et al., 2011). Within the African digital framework, Kenya is a leader in digitalisation in terms of both access to and use of digital technologies, including robotics, artificial intelligence and cloud computing; however, there is a significant digital divide within the country in both access to and use of this technology, and compared with manufacturing firms in more developed and sub-Saharan Africa (Cooke, 2018). With an incremental focus on the Kenyan manufacturing sector, the government policies have sought to improve this aspect of the digital supply chain by improving digital capabilities, fostering competitiveness and managing digital change in an inclusive way; this drive is inclusive of the Kenyan service sector.

- Tanzanian Digital Supply Chain

The supply chain management architecture in Tanzania has been largely responsive to emergent customers' demand. Albeit, the Tanzanian government, has undertaken several measures to support the evolution of the digital supply chain despite incidents of constraint inherent in the supply chain ecosystem (Ekblom, 2016; Mollel, 2015; Nkwabi, 2019). These constraints include low supply chain management, poor inventory management, lack of proper pricing strategies, technology-related issues, lack of capital investment, lack of information flow, managerial incapability and poor governance infrastructures. However, despite these challenges, the digital supply chain in Tanzania has had recourse to resilience-enhancing strategies towards improving the quality of targeted infrastructure, developing alternative corridors, building capacity to accelerate post-disaster recovery solution in tandem with policies to support coping mechanisms with the emergent supply chain geared towards e-sourcing and inventory capabilities (Colon et al., 2019).

Although, Tanzania is well-positioned to integrate into the global digital supply chain due to its growing economy and a rapidly developing innovation ecosystem; this goal is hampered by the high cost of internet access, poor quality of internet service and low last-mile connectivity challenges (Colon et al., 2019; UNCTAD, 2020) Sustainably, this development would not only situate the digital supply chain in Tanzania to the test of time but also to vagaries of the global supply chain ecosystem.

5.5 Barriers to Sustainable Digital Supply Chains in Africa

A sustainable digital supply chain exploits digital technology that facilitates supply chain collaboration and leads to new levels of operational excellence (Lammers et al., 2019). Digital capabilities from blockchain to artificial intelligence (AI), to the internet of things to machine learning and intelligent automation protect supply chains against future disruptions (KPMG, 2020). Moreover, for organisations operating in the African market building, a sustainable digital supply chain will be an essential differentiator. There is huge economic potential in Africa's consumer markets such as Nigeria, South Africa, Kenya, Tanzania, but many organisations struggle to successfully do business in these markets (Inclusive Business, 2013), and this has been ascribed to their inability to adopt a sustainable digital supply chain strategy (KPMG, 2020). Lammers et al. (2019) posited that there are two main reasons responsible for the slow adoption of digitalisation across the supply chain; barriers preventing companies from implementing digitalisation strategies throughout the whole supply chain and the absence of facilitating element or drivers that might help speed-up adoption of the digital supply chain. They developed a framework that describes these barriers and drivers of the digital supply chain (Lammers et al., 2019). The discourse will leverage this framework to understand the barriers to a sustainable digital supply chain in Africa.

1. **Financial Barrier**: This barrier refers to the high cost of system improvements (Lammers et al., 2019); which is often associated with the cost of implementing new digital technologies into an organisation and comprise of cost of innovation (Hjalmarsson et al., 2014), investment costs, cost of setting up digital tools/equipment and implementation cost (Peansupap & Walker, 2005). Digital technologies are very capital intensive and will require huge funding to acquire in terms of, team training, research and development and technology artefacts, etc. Especially in an emerging market context where resources are scarce, this is a huge barrier. Another very important aspect of the financial barrier that discourages managers from investing in digital innovations in organisations (especially in the Africa supply chain) is as it relates to the return on investment. It is often difficult to demonstrate how the addition of new digital technology to existing operation will positively impact the bottom-line in terms of cost–benefit analyses (Hjalmarsson et al., 2014), and these

uncertainties according to Molinillo and Japutra (2017), are due to the lack of demonstrated business cases that justify the investment in the first place. So, investment in digital technology should not be because it is a new technology, but each organisation should demonstrate clearly how it intends to capture value from its investment in a particular technology.

2. **Knowledge and Skills Barrier**: This is a critical barrier impacting not just Africa but the global digital supply chain. It is a situation whereby organisations are not able to find competent personnel with the right skills either within the company (intra-level) or on the market (meta-level) to drive solution in the digital supply chain (Hjalmarsson et al., 2014; Lammers et al., 2019). New technologies in the market today are complex and will require entirely new skills or a combination of critical skills to drive them (Pflaum & Gölzer, 2018). Critical digital skills such as Programming, Web and App Development, data science and data analytics, decision making for leaders, digital marketing, etc. are quite rare in the continent. Technology competence according to Ramilo and Embi (2014), comprising the organisation's internal technology resources, technology infrastructure and IT skills, which are considered drivers of digital transformation. The digital divide present in Africa is still a setback in deploying a sustainable digital supply chain.
3. **Regulatory Barrier**: Regulation is very important as they help safeguard and protect people, information and infrastructure; they can also serve as a great equaliser in the market so that all market players benefit from a level playing field (International Telecommunication Union, 2019). Digital Technology is among the fastest-moving sectors which necessitate fast-moving regulatory responses (International Telecommunication Union, 2019). It is becoming less visible, more prevalent and embedded in many sectors and systems. As we can now find complex applications of new digital technologies such as artificial intelligence (AI), big data, the app economy, cloud computing, Internet of Things, social media and mobile technology in the supply chain putting regulatory paradigms to the test. Regulatory response in Africa is plodding and has become a barrier to the

swift adoption of a digital supply chain in the continent. It represents an important external obstacle at the market level in some cases (Lammers et al., 2019). The actions of the government can in many ways drive digital transformation or be a limiting factor to the digital revolution.

4. **Infrastructural Barrier**: One of the most common technological barriers at the meta-level is represented by privacy and security concerns around digital technologies and lack of infrastructure. Security issues include concerns on confidentiality, fear of fraud, security and privacy. Similarly, the lack of IT or needed infrastructure to effectively drive the digital supply chain or the lack of the technology/maturity level needed is a very common barrier. In Africa, this poses a great challenge because of the high level of infrastructural deficit (i.e. power, poor internet broadband services, poor transportation facility; poor road network, etc.), making it impossible to achieve a sustainable digital supply chain (Hjalmarsson et al., 2014; Lammers et al., 2019; Peansupap & Walker, 2005; Pflaum & Gölzer, 2018).
5. **Environmental Barrier**: From the businesses' external environment, the most important barrier for the supply chain perspective (intra-level) is the lack of collaboration and cooperation between players. Digital supply chains can enable players to achieve higher levels of collaboration and communication with the associated benefits (Asiegbu, 2021). However, a lack of collaboration and cooperation between the supply chain players can foster a barrier to the implementation of digital transformation (Asiegbu, 2021; Karim et al., 2017). Thus, effective Integration with stakeholders (i.e., vendors' and suppliers') throughout the supply chain is essential to unlocking the full potential provided by the digitalisation of the whole chain. This can be a critical barrier to sustainable digital supply chain implementation in Africa.
6. **Organisational Barrier**: Organisational barriers arise when decisions are to be made involving the transformation of business processes within the organisation, the first perception of relative advantage is fundamental. Does it ask the question what do we stand to gain by acquiring this new technology? The degree to which an innovation can bring benefits to an organisation by reducing costs and

increasing sales defines the basis of its acceptance into the organisation (Ramilo & Embi, 2014). Most organisations in Africa have not imbibed a digital first strategy, and execute weak digital innovation strategies, which are often considered a barrier to the efficient development of a sustainable digital supply chain. Their systems, process, practice and value system are not digitally savvy or compatible with new digital technology. Implementing a digital supply chain will entail a holistic digital transformation, which is a difficult decision to make due to cost and time constraints.

7. **Cultural Barrier:** Cultural barrier is closely linked to the organisational barrier. This barrier addresses behaviours and attitudes and represents one of the major barriers to digital transformation in Africa. Most of our cultural beliefs and stereotypes about technology influence the desire to invest in acquiring them. To address the changes needed to implement a digital transformation, the culture of innovation and building the right environment that encourages collaboration, communication and open discussion among key players within and without the organisation is significant (Asiegbu, 2021; Hjalmarsson et al., 2014). An unsupportive organisational culture such as organisational inertia (referred to as fear of or resistance to innovative change) and lack of interest (in the knowledge of digital technologies), poor organisational attitude towards innovation, insufficient team commitment, the adversarial relationship among the staff and lack of support of managerial staff can represent a barrier when introducing digital innovation (Lammers et al., 2019; Peansupap & Walker, 2005)

5.6 Pathways to Sustainable Digital Supply Chains in Africa

We propose the following pathways to developing sustainable digital supply chains in Africa, based on the country cases that have been elucidated and the consequent barriers that have been identified in Sections 4 and 5 above:

1. *Sustainable digital supply chain strategy integration*: For businesses in African countries to ensure global competitiveness, the imperative to innovate their supply chain ecosystems leveraging digital transformation is fundamental. This will entail integrating a sustainable digital supply chain strategy into their overall corporate strategy (Patterson et al., 2003). The integration will have a significant impact on accelerating their pace of technology adoption, considering the sizeable levels of investments that would be required to executing the strategy. Furthermore, a strategic integration will help broaden the traditional narrow focus of supply chain managers beyond suppliers, logistic providers and customers to longer-term strategic alliances and partnerships. This readjustment will help maximise their competitiveness within the global supply chain network.
2. *Access to digital (broadband) infrastructure*: Internet (broadband) connectivity significantly impacts the rate of adoption of digital supply chains in African countries, especially considering the export-oriented nature of production operations within global value chains (Gereffi et al., 2005; Stephenson et al., 2021). While the last decade has witnessed significant growth in broadband infrastructure investments across African countries, including the landing of eight fibre-optic cables estimated to cost almost $4 billion (Song, 2014), African countries must ensure that ongoing broadband infrastructure projects are aligned to maximising their impact for the digital supply chain ecosystem.
3. *Funding/Investment*: Supply chain digitalisation necessitates increased investments and financial requirements in both upgrading supply chain capital equipment as well as working capital impacts. Analysis by the Oxford Economics and Global Infrastructure Hub (2018) estimates that by 2040, there will be a financing shortfall (exacerbated by economic downturns as a consequence of the COVID-19 pandemic) of almost $1 trillion for digital infrastructure investments, more so as required for the digital transformation of supply chains across African countries. This funding gap will imply accessing appropriate finance for the execution of a digital supply chain strategy. African countries will need to synergise with Development Finance Institutions, such as the Industrial Development Corporation (IDC), whose

primary focus is on providing appropriate low-cost financing for these kinds of processes, especially in developing countries and economies. Attracting such financing for the digital transformation of the supply chains in African countries is a critical medium for enhancing their competitiveness in a globally digitalising world (Ciuriak, 2020).

4. *Enabling policy and regulatory environment*: As a region with a largely weak digital supply chain ecosystem, the development policies of African countries must begin to incorporate the promotion of technology adoption within the supply chains of countries. Supply chain integration as a consequence of digitalisation has significant development imperatives for the region, especially for small and medium-sized businesses (SMEs)—which constitute a significant component of its industrial sector. An enabling policy and regulatory environment are therefore fundamental for promoting these businesses in accessing affordable digital solutions for their supply chain operations, to ensure the markets remain competitive in the face of market dominance risks posed by digital first-movers, who are mostly larger companies. More so, digitalisation comes with increasing data flows—both human and machine-generated; therefore, the regulatory frameworks for ensuring data protection and the security of digital systems also needs to be put in place within countries in Africa.
5. *Create Partnerships and Industry-based Coalitions*: Ultimately, creating partnerships and industry-based coalitions will be an important pathway for scaling sustainable digital supply chains across Africa (Stephenson et al., 2021). Such a multistakeholder framework would bring together businesses (large and small), policymakers, industry experts and practitioners in driving the digitalisation agenda for the supply chains in African countries from a broad-based perspective. This broad-based framework will allow for enhanced synergies in facilitating both financings for digital infrastructure investments, as well as for stakeholder-agreeable policy-making for supply chain digitalisation within African countries.

5.7 Conclusion

The digital transformation of the traditional supply chain architecture in response to emerging consumer needs globally has its inherent opportunities and challenges, both for developed economies and emerging countries. While this paradigm shift is enabled by the adoption of innovative technologies towards supply chain agility and customer service improvement (Ageron et al., 2020), it would also be a source of competitive advantage for businesses and governments, especially for some countries in Africa (Ageron et al., 2020; CapGemini, 2016; EY, 2016). Inter alia, the evolution of the digital economy has helped some countries in the sub-Saharan Africa to be responsive to the COVID-19 pandemic regarding emerging opportunities in sectors such as digital deliverable services, e-commerce, online work and digital-driven platforms (Banga, 2020). These digital imperatives have also occasioned a major paradigm shift in terms of value delivery, but in vagaries of value offerings. These attributes of DSC and evolutional trends have not only impacted the developed business community but also the developing or emerging continents like Africa, especially concerning sub-Saharan Africa countries—Nigeria, Kenya, South Africa and Tanzania. In varying dimensions, the digital supply chain has not only induced massive developments in these countries but has been characterised by challenges and opportunities for the future in the continent of Africa.

References

Accenture Strategy. (2019). *Unlocking digital value for South Africa's consumer industry*.

Ageron, B., Bentahar, O., & Gunasekaran, A. (2020). Digital supply chain: Challenges and future directions. *Supply Chain Forum: An International Journal, 21*(3), 133–138. https://doi.org/10.1080/16258312.2020.1816361

Ahmad, M. O., Markkula, J., & Oivo, M. (2013). Factors affecting e-government adoption in Pakistan: A citizen's perspective. *Transforming Government: People, Process and Policy, 7*(2), 225–239.

Al-Hujran, O., Al-Debei, M. M., Chatfield, A., & Migdadi, M. (2015). The imperative of influencing citizen attitude toward e-government adoption and use. *Computers in Human Behavior, 53*, 189–203.

Aly, H. (2020). Digital transformation, development and productivity in developing countries: Is artificial intelligence a curse or a blessing? *Review of Economics and Political Science.* Emerald Publishing Limited e-ISSN: 2631–3561 p-ISSN: 2356–9980. https://doi.org/10.1108/REPS-11-2019-0145

Arenkov, I., Tsenzharik, M., & Vetrova, M. (2019, September). Digital technologies in supply chain management. In *International Conference on Digital Technologies in Logistics and Infrastructure (ICDTLI 2019)* (pp. 448–453). Atlantis Press. https://download.atlantis-press.com/article/125918549.pdf. Accessed April 13, 2021.

Arlbjørn, J. S., de Haas, H., & Munksgaard, K. B. (2011). Exploring supply chain innovation. *Logistics Research, 3*(1), 3–18.

Arlbjørn, J. S., & Paulraj, A. (2013). CCon innovation in business networks from a supply chain perspective: Current status and opportunities for future research. *Journal of Supply Chain Management, 49*(4), 3–11.

Asiegbu, G. U. (2021). Business intelligence-driven supply chain optimization in emerging markets: Pathways for African businesses. In *Africa's platforms and the evolving sharing economy* (pp. 121–140). IGI Global.

Banga, K. (2020) Can the digital economy help mitigate the economic losses from COVID-19 in Kenya? *Supporting Economic Transformation.* Retrieved June 4, 2021: https://set.odi.org/wp-content/uploads/2020/04/Can-the-digital-economy-help-mitigate-the-economic-losses-from-COVID-19-in-Kenya.pdf

Banker, R. D., Bardhan, I. R., Chang, H., & Lin, S. (2006). Plant information systems, manufacturing capabilities, and plant performance. *MIS Quarterly*, 315–337.

Baramichai, M., Zimmers, E. W., Jr., & Marangos, C. A. (2007). Agile supply chain transformation matrix: An integrated tool for creating an agile enterprise. *Supply Chain Management: An International Journal, 12*(5), 334–348.

Barreto, I. (2010). Dynamic capabilities: A review of past research and an agenda for the future. *Journal of Management, 36*(1), 256–280.

Barry, J. (2004). Supply chain risk in an uncertain global supply chain environment. *International Journal of Physical Distribution & Logistics Management, 34*(9), 695–697.

Bechtsis, D., Tsolakis, N., Vlachos, D., & Srai, J. S. (2018). Intelligent autonomous vehicles in digital supply chains: A framework for integrating innovations towards sustainable value networks. *Journal of Cleaner Production, 181*, 60–71.

Beske, P. (2012). Dynamic capabilities and sustainable supply chain management. *International Journal of Physical Distribution & Logistics Management, 42*(4), 372–387.

Bharadwaj, A., El Sawy, O., Pavlou, P., & Venkatraman, N. (2013). *Digital business strategy: Toward the next generation of insights*. https://papers.ssrn.com/sol3/papers.cfm?abstract_id=2742300. Accessed July 17, 2018.

Boone, T., & Ganeshan, R. (2007). The frontiers of eBusiness technology and supply chains. *Journal of Operations Management, 25*(6), 1195–1198.

Bramann, J. U. (2017). Building ICT entrepreneurship ecosystems in resource-scarce contexts: Learnings from Kenya's 'Silicon Savannah'. In B. Ndemo, & T. Weiss (Eds.), *Digital Kenya*. Palgrave Studies of Entrepreneurship in Africa. Palgrave Macmillan.

Brandon-Jones, A., & Knoppen, D. (2018). The role of strategic purchasing in dynamic capability development and deployment: A contingency perspective. *International Journal of Operations & Production Management, 38*(2), 446–473.

Brinch, M. (2018). Understanding the value of big data in supply chain management and its business processes: Towards a conceptual framework. *International Journal of Operations & Production Management*.

Büyüközkan, G., & Göçer, F. (2018). Digital supply chain: Literature review and a proposed framework for future research. *Computers in Industry, 97*, 157–177.

CapGemini, I. (2016). GTNexus. *The current and future state of digital supply chain transformation, GT Nexus*, 1–12.

Carter, L., Weerakkody, V., Phillips, B., & Dwivedi, Y. K. (2016). Citizen adoption of e-government services: Exploring citizen perceptions of online services in the United States and United Kingdom. *Journal of Information Systems Management, 33*(2), 124–140.

Ciuriak, D. (2020, June). Economic rents and the contours of conflict in the data-driven economy. *Policy Brief, Centre for International Governance Innovation*. https://papers.ssrn.com/sol3/papers.cfm?abstract_id=3496025

Colon, C., Hallegatte, S., & Rozenberg, J. (2019). Transportation and supply chain resilience in the United Republic of Tanzania. In *Background study to LIFELINES: The resilient infrastructure opportunity*. World Bank.

Chowdhury, M. M. H., & Quaddus, M. (2017). Supply chain resilience: Conceptualization and scale development using dynamic capability theory. *International Journal of Production Economics, 188*, 185–204.

Cooke, G. (2018). *Digital transformation in Kenyan manufacturing and job creation*. Event Report.

Donaldson, L. (2001). *The contingency theory of organizations*. Sage.

Drouillard, M., Taverner, D., Williamson, C., & Harris, M. (2014). *Digital entrepreneurship in Kenya*. GSMA.

Ekblom, M. (2016). *Challenges facing food processing MSEs in Tanzania: A qualitative case study of the sunflower oil industry in Babati, Manyara*. http://www.divaportal.org/smash/record.jsf?pid=diva2:935700

Economic Forum and Accenture, Unlocking Digital Value to Society: A new framework for growth, White Paper 2017.

Elkadi, H. (2013). Success and failure factors for e-government projects: A case from Egypt. *Egyptian Informatics Journal, 14*, 165 –173. https://doi.org/10.1016/j.eij.2013.06.002

Ernst & Young. (2016). Digital supply chain: It is all about data, Report, 1–15.

Fisher, R., McPhail, R., You, E., & Ash, M. (2014). Using social media to recruit global supply chain managers. *International Journal of Physical Distribution & Logistics Management, 44*, 635–645. https://doi.org/10.1108/IJPDLM-07-2013-0179

Freeman, R. E., Harrison, J. S., Wicks, A. C., Parmar, B. L., & de Colle, S. (2010). *Stakeholder theory: The state of the art*. Cambridge University Press, Cambridge.

Frohlich, M. T. (2002). E-integration in the supply chain: Barriers and performance. *Decision Sciences, 33*(4), 537–556.

Gereffi, G., Humphrey, J., & Sturgeon, T. (2005). The governance of global value chains. *Review of International Political Economy, 12*(1), 78–104.

Gruchmann, T., & Seuring, S. (2018). Explaining logistics social responsibility from a dynamic capabilities perspective. *The International Journal of Logistics Management*.

Gupta, S., Modgil, S., Gunasekaran, A., & Bag, S. (2020, July). Dynamic capabilities and institutional theories for Industry 4.0 and digital supply chain. In *Supply chain forum: An International Journal* (Vol. 21, No. 3, pp. 139–157). Taylor & Francis.

Hazen, B. T., & Byrd, T. A. (2012). Toward creating competitive advantage with logistics information technology. *International Journal of Physical Distribution & Logistics Management*.

Heeks, R. (2003). *Most eGovernment-for-development projects fail: How can risks be reduce Institute for Development Policy and Management* Manchester, M13 9GH, UK: University of Manchester, Harold Hankins Building, Precinct Centre.

Herold, D. M., & Mikl, J. (2021). The emergence and adoption of digitalization in the logistics and supply chain industry: An institutional perspective. *Journal of Enterprise Information Management Emerald Publishing Limited*, 1741–0398. https://doi.org/10.1108/JEIM-09-2020-0382

Hjalmarsson, A., Johannesson, P., Jüll-Skielse, G., & Rudmark, D. (2014). Beyond innovation contests: A framework of barriers to open innovation of digital services.

Hofmann, E., Strewe, U. M., & Bosia, N. (2018). Discussion—How does the full potential of blockchain technology in supply chain finance look like? In *Supply Chain Finance and Blockchain Technology* (pp. 77–87). Springer, Cham.

Holcomb, M. C., Krul, A., & Thomas, D. (2015). Supply chain talent squeeze: How business & universities are collaborating to fill the gap. *Supply Chain Management Review.*

Hohenstein, N. O., Feisel, E., & Hartmann, E. (2014). Human resource management issues in supply chain management research: A systematic literature review from 1998 to 2014. *International Journal of Physical Distribution & Logistics Management, 44*, 434–463. https://doi.org/10.1108/IJPDLM-06-2013-0175

Holmström, J., & Partanen, J. (2014). Digital manufacturing-driven transformations of service supply chains for complex products. *Supply Chain Management: An International Journal, 19*(4), 421–430.

Hörisch, J., Schaltegger, S., & Freeman, R. E. (2020). Integrating stakeholder theory and sustainability accounting: A conceptual synthesis. *Journal of Cleaner Production, 275*, 124097.

Inclusive Business. (2013). *Supply chain impact—Some key challenges in Africa.* Retrieved from web address on 26 April 2021: https://www.inclusivebusiness.net/ib-voices/supply-chain-impact-some-key-challenges-africa

International Telecommunication Union. (2019). *Policy and regulatory environments for digital transformation.* Retrieved from web address on 26 April 2021: https://www.itu.int/en/mediacentre/backgrounders/Pages/Policy-and-regulatory-environments-for-digital-transformation.aspx

Jabbour, C. J. C., Fiorini, P. D. C., Ndubisi, N. O., Queiroz, M. M., & Piato, É. L. (2020). Digitally-enabled sustainable supply chains in the 21st century: A review and a research agenda. *Science of the Total Environment, 725*, 138177.

Kache, F., & Seuring, S. (2017). Challenges and opportunities of digital information at the intersection of Big Data Analytics and supply chain management. *International Journal of Operations & Production Management*.

Karimi, J., & Walter, Z. (2015). The role of dynamic capabilities in responding to digital disruption: A factor-based study of the newspaper industry. *Journal of Management Information Systems, 32*(1), 39–81.

Karim, S., Al-Tawara, A., Gide, E., & Sandu, R. (2017, May). Is big data too big for SMEs in Jordan? In *2017 8th International Conference on Information Technology (ICIT)* (pp. 914–922). IEEE.

Kelly, T., & Firestone, R. (2016). *How tech hubs are helping to drive economic growth in Africa* (Background Paper for the World Development Report 2016: Digital Dividends). Washington, DC: The World Bank. Retrieved from https://openknowledge.worldbank.org/bitstream/handle/10986/23645/WDR16-BPHow-Tech-Hubs-are-helpingto-Drive-Economic-Growth-in-Africa-Kelly-Firestone.pdf

Korpela, K., Hallikas, J., & Dahlberg, T. (2017, January). Digital supply chain transformation toward blockchain integration. In *Proceedings of the 50th Hawaii International Conference on System Sciences*. http://128.171.57.22/bitstream/10125/41666/1/paper0517.pdf

KPMG. (2020). *Building supply chain resilience through digital transformation.* Retrieved from web address on 26 April 2021: https://assets.kpmg/content/dam/kpmg/xx/pdf/2020/06/building-supply-chain-resilience-through-digital-transformation.pdf

Kumar, R., & Best, M. (2006). Impact and sustainability of e-government service, s in developing countries: Lessons learned from Tamil Nadu, India. *The Information Society, 22*, 1–12. https://doi.org/10.1080/01972240500388149

Kwak, D. W., Seo, Y. J., & Mason, R. (2018). Investigating the relationship between supply chain innovation, risk management capabilities and competitive advantage in global supply chains. *International Journal of Operations & Production Management, 38*(1), 2–21.

Lammers, T., Tomidei, L., & Trianni, A. (2019, August). Towards a novel framework of barriers and drivers for digital transformation in industrial supply chains. In *2019 Portland International Conference on Management of Engineering and Technology (PICMET).*

Lancioni, R. A., Smith, M. F., & Schau, H. J. (2003). Strategic internet application trends in supply chain management. *Industrial Marketing Management, 32*(3), 211–217.

Lavie, D. (2006). Capability reconfiguration: An analysis of incumbent responses to technological change. *Academy of Management Review, 31*(1), 153–174.

Lavikka, R., Hirvensalo, A., Smeds, R., & Jaatinen, M. (2017, September). Transforming a supply chain towards a digital business ecosystem. In *IFIP International Conference on Advances in Production Management Systems* (pp. 295–301). Springer, Cham.

Loonam, J., Eaves, S., Kumar, V., & Parry, G. (2018). Towards digital transformation: Lessons learned from traditional organizations. *Strategic Change, 27*(2), 101–109.

Masoud, S. A., & Mason, S. J. (2017, September). Assessing the cost impact of multiple transportation modes to enhance sustainability in an integrated, two stage, automotive supply chain. In *Informatics* (Vol. 4, No. 4, p. 34). Multidisciplinary Digital Publishing Institute.

Miethlich, B., Belotserkovich, D., Abasova, S., Zatsarinnaya, E., & Veselitsky, O. (2020). Digital supply chain management-new competitiveness imperative for economic development. *International Journal of Supply Chain Management, 9*(5), 495.

Mithas, S., Tafti, A., & Mitchell, W. (2013). How a firm's competitive environment and digital strategic posture influence digital business strategy. *MIS Quarterly, 37*(2), 511–536.

Mittal, N., Agarwal, R., & Selen, W. (2018). Value creation and the impact of policy interventions: Indian LPG supply chain case study. *The International Journal of Logistics Management, 29*(1), 64–89.

Molinillo, S., & Japutra, A. (2017). Organizational adoption of digital information and technology: A theoretical review. *The Bottom Line.*

Mol, M. J., & Birkinshaw, J. (2009). The sources of management innovation: When firms introduce new management practices. *Journal of Business Research, 62*(12), 1269–1280.

Mollel, A. (2015). *Impact of supply chain management practices on Organizational performance in food processing Firms of Dar es salaam, Tanzania.* Masters. Mzumbe University. http://hdl.handle.net/11192/1171

New, S. J. (1997). The scope of supply chain management research. *Supply Chain Management: An International Journal, 2*(1), 15–22.

Nkwabi, J. M. (2019). Supply chain management constraints in Tanzanian small and medium enterprises. *African Journal of Business Management, 13*(16), 564–570. https://doi.org/10.5897/AJBM2019.8876

Nooraie, S. V. R. (2017). *Mitigating supply and demand risk of disruptions through tradeoff among risk, cost and supply chain capabilities* (Doctoral dissertation, North Carolina Agricultural and Technical State University).

Núñez-Merino, M., Maqueira-Marín, J. M., Moyano-Fuentes, J., & Martínez-Jurado, P. J. (2020). Information and digital technologies of Industry 4.0 and Lean supply chain management: A systematic literature review. *International Journal of Production Research, 58*(16), 5034–5061.

Oxford Business Group. (2020). Digital solutions enhance resilience of Kenya's agriculture sector amid COVID-19 pressures. *Economics News*. Retrieved May 10, 2021: https://oxfordbusinessgroup.com/news/digital-solutions-enhance-resilience-kenya-s-agriculture-sector-amid-covid-19-pressures?utm_source=feed&utm_medium=rss&utm_campaign=eus_all_all

Oyedijo, A., Adams, K., & Koukpaki, S. A. F. (2021). Supply chain systems in Africa: insights from Nigeria. In *Business in Africa in the Era of Digital Technology*. Springer Publisher.

Oxford Economics and Global Infrastructure Hub. (2018). *Global infrastructure outlook: Investment need in the compact with Africa countries*. https://www.gihub.org/sectors/communications/

Pagani, M. (2013). Digital business strategy and value creation: Framing the dynamic cycle of control points. *MIS Quarterly, 37*(2), 617–632.

Pal, R., & Sandberg, E. (2017, October). Sustainable value creation through new industrial supply chains in apparel and fashion. In *IOP Conference Series: Materials Science and Engineering* (Vol. 254, No. 20, p. 202007). IOP Publishing.

Park, H., & Choi, S. O. (2019). Digital innovation adoption and its economic impact focused on path analysis at national level. *Journal of Open Innovation: Technology, Market, and Complexity, 5*(3), 56.

Park, E., Hain, D. S., & Jurowetzki, R. (2017). *Entrepreneurial ecosystem for technology start-ups in Nairobi: Empirical analysis of Twitter networks of start-ups*.

Patterson, K. A., Grimm, C. M., & Corsi, T. M. (2003). Adopting new technologies for supply chain management. *Transportation Research Part E: Logistics and Transportation Review, 39*(2), 95–121.

Peansupap, V., & Walker, D. (2005). Factors affecting ICT diffusion. *Engineering, Construction and Architectural Management*.

Pflaum, A. A., & Gölzer, P. (2018). The IoT and digital transformation: Toward the data-driven enterprise. *IEEE Pervasive Computing, 17*(1), 87–91.

Porter, M. E., & Heppelmann, J. E. (2014). How smart connected products are transforming competition. *Harvard Business Review, 92*(11), 64–88.

Rai, A., Patnayakuni, R., & Seth, N. (2006). Firm performance impacts of digitally enabled supply chain integration capabilities. *MIS Quarterly*, 225–246.

Ramilo, R., & Embi, M. R. B. (2014). Critical analysis of key determinants and barriers to digital innovation adoption among architectural organizations. *Frontiers of Architectural Research, 3*(4), 431–451.

Sabri, Y., Micheli, G. J., & Nuur, C. (2018). Exploring the impact of innovation implementation on supply chain configuration. *Journal of Engineering and Technology Management*. https://www.sciencedirect.com/science/article/pii/S0923474816302260. Accessed July 19, 2018.

Sambamurthy, V., Bharadwaj, A., & Grover, V. (2003). Shaping agility through digital options: Reconceptualizing the role of information technology in contemporary firms. *MIS Quarterly*, 237–263

Sanders, N. R., Boone, T., Ganeshan, R., & Wood, J. D. (2019). Sustainable supply chains in the age of AI and digitization: Research challenges and opportunities. *Journal of Business Logistics, 40*(3), 229–240.

Schilke, O., Hu, S., & Helfat, C. E. (2018). Quo vadis, dynamic capabilities? A content-analytic review of the current state of knowledge and recommendations for future research. *Academy of Management Annals, 12*(1), 390–439.

Scott, W. R. (2005). Institutional theory: Contributing to a theoretical research program. *Great Minds in Management: The Process of Theory Development, 37*(2), 460–484.

Seuring, S., & Müller, M. (2008). From a literature review to a conceptual framework for sustainable supply chain management. *Journal of Cleaner Production, 16*(15), 1699–1710.

Seyedghorban, Z., Tahernejad, H., Meriton, R., & Graham, G. (2020). Supply chain digitalization: Past, present and future. *Production Planning & Control, 31*(2–3), 96–114.

Sheffi, Y. (2018). What lurks beneath: Deep supply chain risks. In *The Routledge Companion to Risk, Crisis and Security in Business* (pp. 116–135). Routledge.

Skilton, P. F. (2014). Value creation, value capture, and supply chain structure: Understanding resource-based advantage in a project-based industry. *Journal of Supply Chain Management, 50*(3), 74–93.

Song, S. (2014). Hilary: Note that all of a sudden they put a period after the doi number. African undersea cables. https://manypossibilities.net/african-undersea-cables/

Song, M., Cen, L., Zheng, Z., Fisher, R., Liang, X., Wang, Y., & Huisingh, D. (2017). How would big data support societal development and environmental sustainability? Insights and practices. *Journal of Cleaner Production, 142*, 489–500.

Stephenson, M., Hamid, M. F. S., Peter, A., Sauvant, K. P., Seric, A., & Tajoli, L. (2021). More and better investment now! How unlocking sustainable and digital investment flows can help achieve the SDGs. *Journal of International Business Policy, 4*(1), 152–165.

Straub, D., Rai, A., & Klein, R. (2004). Measuring firm performance at the network level: A nomology of the business impact of digital supply networks. *Journal of Management Information Systems, 21*(1), 83–114.

Swanson. (2017). The impact of digitization on product offerings: Using direct digital manufacturing in the supply chain. In *Proceedings of the 50th Hawaii International Conference on System Sciences* (pp. 4202–4209). URI: http://hdl.handle.net/10125/41668

Teece, D. J., Pisano, G., & Shuen, A. (1997). Dynamic capabilities and strategic management. *Strategic Management Journal, 18*(7), 509–533.

United Nations Conference on Trade and Development. (2020). *Tanzania, Malawi prepare to reap benefits of digital economy*. https://unctad.org/news/tanzania-malawi-prepare-reap-benefits-digital-economy

Wang, G., Gunasekaran, A., Ngai, E. W., & Papadopoulos, T. (2016). Big data analytics in logistics and supply chain management: Certain investigations for research and applications. *International Journal of Production Economics, 176*, 98–110.

Winter, S. G. (2003). Understanding dynamic capabilities. *Strategic Management Journal, 24*(10), 991–995.

Wood, G., Dibben, P., & Meira, J. (2016). Knowledge transfer within strategic partnerships: The case of HRM in the Brazilian motor industry supply chain. *International Journal of Human Resource Management, 27*, 2398–2414. https://doi.org/10.1080/09585192.2016.1221841

World Bank Group. (2019). Nigeria Digital Economy Diagnostic Report. World Bank. License: Creative Commons Attribution CC BY 3.0 IGO.

World Economic Forum and Accenture. (2017). *Unlocking digital value to society: A new framework for growth*. White Paper.

Part II

Country- Based Themes and Practices

6

Digital Entrepreneurship in Africa: Case Studies of Nigeria and South Sudan

Itoro Emembolu, Charles Emembolu, Olumide Aderinwale, and Emmanuel Lobijo

6.1 Introduction

In the literature, the internet has been referred to as a global leveller of opportunity, particularly for entrepreneurs, due to the way digital technologies have transformed the way we live, work and interact (Friederici et al., 2020; Nambisan, 2017; Ngoasong, 2018; Roundy & Fayard, 2019). Digital technologies have allowed entrepreneurs to go

I. Emembolu (✉)
Northumbria University, Newcastle upon Tyne, UK
e-mail: itoro@tqstem.org

C. Emembolu
Crestsage Limited, Lagos, Nigeria

I. Emembolu · O. Aderinwale
TechQuest STEM Academy, Lagos, Nigeria

E. Lobijo
Junub Open Space, Juba, South Sudan

O. Adeola et al. (eds.), *Digital Service Delivery in Africa*, Palgrave Studies of Marketing in Emerging Economies,
https://doi.org/10.1007/978-3-030-83909-3_6

beyond traditional constraints of engagements previously encountered. They have provided access to larger reach, irrespective of location, utilising the combinatory effects of globalisation and digitalisation, thereby enabling entrepreneurs to operate on a more global scale, creating equal opportunities (Taura et al., 2019).

The concept of digital entrepreneurship revolves around the pursuit of market opportunities by making use of or leveraging digital technologies or information and communication technologies (Friederici et al., 2020; Roundy & Fayard, 2019). It has been defined in the literature as the interaction between digital technologies and entrepreneurial processes and how they impact each other in terms of design, use and commercialisation of digital technologies, in pursuit of market opportunities, and creation and adaptation of economic activities (Friederici et al., 2020; Nambisan, 2017; Recker & Briel, 2019; Roundy & Fayard, 2019). Attributes of digital technologies such as being editable, combinable and the ease of distribution have aided their adoption into entrepreneurial activities, informed how businesses are being re-imagined and created for more robust and sustainable ventures (Dal Zotto & Omidi, 2020; Elia et al., 2020; Nambisan, 2017).

Some fundamental dimensions of digital entrepreneurship have been identified in the literature (Davidson et al., 2018; Recker & Biel, 2019; Wagner & Wäger, 2019) with regards to digital technologies. One of these dimensions is digital technologies '***as a digital enabler***' of entrepreneurial activities or processes (Davidson et al., 2018; Nambisan, 2017; von Briel et al., 2018; Wagner & Wäger, 2019). Leveraging digital technologies by entrepreneurs play a critical role in promoting and supporting innovation (Leong et al., 2020). The second dimension is ***'as a digital outcome'*** of entrepreneurial activities, in terms of business architecture, products or market offerings. The third dimension is ***'as a digital context'***, where the entrepreneurial activities occur in terms of environment, sector, industry and even ecosystems (Davidson et al., 2018; Von Briel et al., 2018). The success of entrepreneurs relies not only on their business venture and capabilities but also largely depends on the entrepreneurship ecosystem they operate in (Elia et al., 2020). Digital entrepreneurship highlights how practice, theory and education are changed by digital technologies.

While there is an increasing body of research on digital entrepreneurship, many of these studies focus mainly on developed economies. Thus, there are relatively few studies in the contexts of developing countries, particularly in Africa (Leong et al., 2020; McAdams et al., 2019; Nambisan, 2017). To this end, this chapter presents the emergence of digital entrepreneurship in Africa, highlighting the role of innovation and organisational skills as critical to successful entrepreneurial activities. Then it also reviews the challenges and opportunities of digital entrepreneurship from a female entrepreneur's perspective.

6.2 The Emergence of Digital Entrepreneurship in Africa

The interdisciplinary field of digital entrepreneurship has been rapidly gaining prominence in the global economy and research community (Recker & Briel, 2019). Although there has been much spotlight on the possibilities of a digital boom in Africa, as evidenced by the interests of many Tech Giant organisations in Africa (Friederici et al., 2020; Taura et al., 2019) and the gradual increase in the number of technology hubs across Africa, the business models and approaches adopted in developed economies do not necessarily have the same effects in developing countries in Africa. Also, due to the scarcity of reliable data in many developing countries, there are not many studies on the actual landscape of digital entrepreneurship in Africa.

Current research (Friederici et al., 2020) suggests that many startups and entrepreneurial journeys in countries in Africa do not necessarily follow tested international models in terms of attracting funds and scaling beyond the indigenous economy. Many of the entrepreneurial activities adopt and adapt digital technologies—**digital technologies *as enablers*** (Nambisan, 2017; Wagner & Wäger, 2019), rather than causing massive industry disruptions—***digital outcomes.***

The population of Africans online (using the internet) has steadily increased from 81 million in 2010 to about 294 million in 2019 (UN Broadband Commission, 2020). While this is significant traction, these figures represent 7.79% and 22.48%, respectively, of the African population (worldometers.info) for those years. This indicates that about 77% of individuals on the continent are still not online (are disconnected). These statistics provide a glimpse of the digital gaps that persist in Africa.

For even the areas that have online access, studies suggest that while digital entrepreneurship has started gaining prominence in some African countries, its distribution across the continent is uneven (Friederici et al., 2020). Of the 54 African countries, 15 accounts for about 85% of the digital entrepreneurship activities on the continent, of which 60% comes from only four countries, namely South Africa, Nigeria, Kenya and Egypt, while the remaining 25% come from eight other African Countries (Friederici et al., 2020). The adoption of digital entrepreneurship is clustered in specific African countries. Even though African entrepreneurs experience many challenges, they can largely overcome them by leveraging available digital technologies.

6.3 Challenges and Opportunities of Digital Entrepreneurship in Africa

Many of the challenges faced by digital entrepreneurs in Africa are similar to those of other emerging economies. In what follows, we shall outline some of the challenges identified in the literature.

- **Lack or inadequate Internet and digital technology access** (Counted & Arawole, 2015; Solomon & van Klyton, 2020; Steel, 2021): Access to the internet has been identified as an essential enabler for digital entrepreneurs, although as mentioned in the previous sections, a large percentage of Africans do not have access to the internet. For those connected, there are still high data and access costs. Some developing economies in East Africa have started exploring collaborations under the One Network Area (ONA) roaming initiative to reduce the high costs of mobile roaming. Some of the beneficiaries of this initiative include South Sudan, Kenya, Burundi and Tanzania.
- **Poor or lack of adequate infrastructure:** lack of basic infrastructure makes attempts to bridge the digital divide more challenging. In

Nigeria, for example, there is epileptic or no power supply in some areas, poor roads and other infrastructure deficiencies (Solomon & van Klyton, 2020; Steel, 2021; UN Broadband Commission, 2018).

- **Insufficient access to finance /funding** (Groza et al., 2020; Solomon & van Klyton, 2020; UN Broadband Commission, 2018): Availability or access to capital is necessary to keep an organisation operational. The high transactional costs of running businesses underscore the need for capital for many entrepreneurs and small businesses in developing countries. While access to funding is a concern for all entrepreneurs, the amount of funding received by female entrepreneurs, in particular, is disproportionately little in comparison with their male colleagues (Groza et al., 2020). It has been argued in the literature that this occurs because there is usually not enough female representation in the decision-making process of funding sources (for example, venture capital).
- **Insufficient collaborations between organisations:** Different organisations have knowledge resident within their respective organisations and competencies. Without enough collaborations, relevant knowledge would continue to exist in silos and cause inefficiencies through replication of efforts across organisations. Collaborations between industry, government and academia would foster innovation (UN Broadband Commission, 2018) and reduce inefficiencies. More impact will be achieved if there are collaborations, co-creation and repositories where knowledge banks can be accessed and utilised across organisations.
- **Restrictions and unavailability of global e-payment systems** (Samara & Terzian, 2021; Solomon & van Klyton, 2020): There are currently many restrictions around suitable payment gateways across many countries that cannot accommodate international transactions. There are also restrictions on some payment links if originating from specific African countries. This is a significant issue for many entrepreneurs as it limits participation on a global scale. Even within Africa, financial transactions between African countries face difficult hurdles, which constitute barriers to trade and access to markets.

- **Institutional voids** (Chakrabarty, 2009; McAdam et al., 2019): Institutional voids develop as a result of the underdevelopment of institutional frameworks in terms of policies, infrastructure, norms and national culture that could support entrepreneurs. For example, it takes an average of 25 business days to set up a business in Sub-Saharan Africa compared to 4 days it takes to set up a similar business in Europe (UN Broadband Commission, 2018). Digital entrepreneurship provides a pathway to overcoming the limitations and barriers caused by institutional voids (McAdams, 2019). Governments in developing countries can provide an enabling environment and supporting policies that bring together relevant stakeholders to tackle the challenges and explore the opportunities within the respective economies.
- **Human capital with under-developed skillsets and structural unemployment** (Coward & Fellows, 2018; Madichie et al., 2019; Solomon & van Klyton, 2020; UN Broadband Commission, 2018): Although access to the internet and digital infrastructure have been identified as necessary conditions for the success of digital entrepreneurship in Africa, they are not sufficient independently (Briel et al., 2018; Friederici et al., 2020), but have to be reviewed with consideration of available resources, skills, capabilities and other complex environmental factors. Improving digital literacy and competencies should help reduce inequalities and improve future job or business opportunities for citizens of African economies. There has to be an alignment with workforce competencies to suit the demands of the current digital landscape (Solomon & van Klyton).
- **Poor Technology Adoption:** Concerns have been raised in some studies that while individuals might have access to the internet, they might not make use of some of the tools and technologies available (Friederici et al., 2020). For instance, people might use their phones for calls, texts and to chat on social media platforms (Facebook, WhatsApp, etc.), nothing more. The level of literacy and digital literacy could impact the degree and value derivable from the adoption and use of the internet.

Technology adoption is also as important and requires some digital competencies and skills. Since there have been rapid changes in technological advancements across many frontsy, the world of work has been changing too, and so are the skills required to keep up and adapt to these changes. The World Economic Forum (WEF, 2020) has predicted that by the year 2030, one billion people will need to be reskilled for future jobs (many of which are not in existence yet). Therefore, entrepreneurs will need to balance their current collection of existing capabilities while also developing new digital competencies and capabilities (Warner & Wäger, 2019). Despite investment efforts to leverage digitalisation, many African countries are still yet to benefit fully from outcomes of the digitalisation process because of persistent digital gaps in terms of skills and competencies.

Irrespective of these challenges, there are also opportunities that are available to digital entrepreneurs in Africa.

- **Opportunities to improve digital skills** to learn, improve digital literacy levels, increase the number and quality of technology users that can, in turn, support innovation.
- **Barriers to entry for digital entrepreneurship are low,** and there are also opportunities to create solutions that address some of the challenges mentioned. For example, an opportunity to innovate around a payment system that is global and tailored to African needs.

Availability and access to digital infrastructure is an external enabler for digital entrepreneurs (Friederici et al., 2020) that could be harnessed. Also, digital entrepreneurship can help female entrepreneurs bridge the digital divide and remove some barriers and local restrictions they might have been directly or indirectly subjected to (Roundy & Fayard, 2019). **Digital entrepreneurship as an enabler for marginalised group**s such as females that experience additional constraints as a result of cultural, social and environmental factors (Roundy & Fayard, 2019). Therefore, this paper reviews challenges to digital entrepreneurship from a female perspective and across two African countries (Nigeria and South Sudan).

6.4 Organisational Skills in Digital Entrepreneurship

While the proliferation of new technologies has brought about many opportunities, one of the main challenges is the skills gap that has emerged, particularly around digital skills and technology adoption (Coward & Fellows, 2018).

Digital skills can be categorised along a continuum. The more popular categories in the literature are

- *Basic digital skills* (minimum level of digital literacy, foundational skills that enable one to function in the digital world),
- *Intermediate digital skills* (skills that enable one to perform work or job-related functions and create content using technology. They consist of a wide array of skill sets) and
- *Advanced digital skills* (these are skills needed by specialists in their different fields or subject areas).

The DigComp framework by the European Commission provides a valuable reference for planning digital competencies (Khan & Vuopala, 2019; UNESCO, 2019). DigComp 2.0 outlines eight proficiency levels across five areas of competencies, namely: (1) Information and data literacy, (2) communication and collaboration, (3) digital content creation, (4) safety and (5) problem-solving. Each of these competencies has knowledge, skill sets and proficiencies associated with the competency. The DigComp framework could support the harnessing of digital technologies to innovate, deal with the rise of digital skills and competencies needed for personal development, social inclusion and business development. Improving the digital literacy rates and digital skill competencies in Sub-Saharan Africa should help reduce inequalities and improve future job opportunities for her citizens. One way to explore competencies is using the dynamic capabilities framework to provide a lens on how entrepreneurs can respond to the technological changes and digital economy through their capabilities and competencies.

6.5 Dynamic Capabilities

Calls in the literature have suggested exploring the concepts of digital entrepreneurship through a dynamic capabilities' theoretical lens (Dal Zotto & Omidi, 2020; Dong, 2019; Warner & Wäger, 2019). The Dynamic Capabilities (DC) Theory provides an innovation-based framework that explicates the capabilities of firms to integrate, build and modify from their existing resource base. It helps organisations respond rapidly to market, environmental or technological changes for competitive advantage (Dillon et al., 2020; Dong, 2019; Helfat & Peteraf, 2015; Roundy & Fayard, 2019; Teece, 2007, 2018; Warner & Wäger, 2019).

Proponents of this theory broadly categorise dynamic capabilities into three groups. 1. Digital sensing, which is concerned with making sense of the emerging technological and market landscapes. This capability could be subdivided into scouting, scenario planning and mindset crafting. 2. Digital seizing, which is concerned with experimenting with methods and collaborating to be able to respond to changes. It could be subdivided into strategic agility, prototyping and organisation of digital portfolios. 3. Transforming capabilities, which refers to the managing and stabilising of internal and external structures of the organisation and attaining digital maturity, through the digital upskilling of its workforce. Subcategories for this capability are navigating ecosystems, reorganising internal structures and digital maturity.

Organisations have to constantly balance the use and adaptation of their existing capabilities while at the same time reviewing new organisational capabilities and evaluating where they could fit within the existing capabilities and alignments to dynamic market trends. As such, organisations need to build strong dynamic capabilities (Helfat & Peteraf, 2015; Teece, 2007, 2018; Warner & Wäger, 2019).

Some of the new technologies have helped change the nature, and the way organisations react to uncertainties (Nambisan, 2017). Organisations have learnt to create stronger dynamic capabilities through technologies such as the Internet of Things (IoT), BlockChain, Cloud Computing and Artificial Intelligence (to mention a few). The use of social media has also helped organisations to expand their dynamic capabilities.

The attributes of digital technologies (editable, combinable and ease of distribution) help organisations re-configure and re-combine organisational resources and capabilities to form distinct dynamic competencies that are adaptable to the rapidly changing digital environment. They provide modular architecture that is combinable.

Studies (Warner & Wäger, 2019) have suggested improving the digital maturity of organisational workforce (ability to add value through digital means and processes), as an essential dynamic capability. One of the ways organisations have been able to leverage technology is through the use of platforms. Digital platforms are online platforms comprised of different tools and processes that individuals develop or build on to operate and deliver digital services; they help organisations to innovate.

6.6 Role of Innovation in Digital Entrepreneurship

Entrepreneurs and digital organisations do not thrive in isolation; they require supportive, innovative ecosystems that enable them to develop networks, build capabilities and collaborate (Global Entrepreneurship Monitor, 2020). Digital innovation is derived from applying digitising techniques to everyday products, services, or human experiences (Yoo, 2010), such as understanding how to use collaborative tools, adding web and mobile applications to products or services, or improving user experiences. In order to perform some of these functions, organisations need to build organisational knowledge of relevant digital technologies.

Organisational knowledge has been identified as a main driver of innovation (Pinchot & Soltanifar, 2021), which can be improved by increasing the number of organisation's workforce that understands and knows how to use the acquired knowledge. Apart from the intersections between the collective workforce organisational knowledge, and leveraging digital technologies, there are innovation potentials embedded within the heterogeneity and idiosyncrasies of entrepreneurial human capital and their individual competencies (Elia et al., 2020).

A major constraint to developing and leveraging an organisation's knowledge is when the organisation's management lack the adequate understanding, skills and confidence required to adopt and use new digital technologies. In essence, it is critical that an organisation's management or lead entrepreneur acquires some digital skills and technological understanding and also buy-in to required technology adoption for business success. Upskilling and reskilling through programmes, seminars and networking engagements could help bridge this gap. Leveraging digital technologies by entrepreneurs play a critical role in promoting and supporting innovation (Leong et al., 2020).

6.7 Methodology

This study adopts a mixed-method multi-case study approach (Ngoasong, 2018; Yin, 2003) with perspectives from female entrepreneurs as individual cases within African contexts, in order to gain insights into individual and collective lived experiences of female entrepreneurs. Two African countries were chosen from different African regions to explore differences and similarities in context. The countries used for this study are Nigeria and South Sudan. The use of multiple case studies allowed for comparisons between the female entrepreneurs in each country and across entrepreneurs from Nigeria and South Sudan (Stubbs & Myers, 2015; Yin, 2003).

The dimension of digital technology utilised for this study is digital technologies as 'digital enablers' (Nambisan, 2017; Wagner & Wäger, 2019). The competency explored in this research in line with the Digital Competency Framework is on 'communication and collaborations'—that explores how the entrepreneurs are interacting with digital technologies through sharing, engaging, collaborating and managing their digital identity or brands (European Commission, 2014; Vuorikari et al., 2016). It also aligns with the collaborative sub-capabilities of the strategic agility from the seizing capability (dynamic capabilities framework).

Nigeria is situated in West Africa with a population of over 206 million, while South Sudan is situated in East Africa with a population of 11.3 million. Both countries have a young population with over 50% of the population between the ages of 15 to 64, with Nigeria at 53.57%

and South Sudan at 55.06% (Statista.com). The two countries are classified as low-income countries (Global Entrepreneurship Monitor, 2021), with a high unemployment rate. The rate of unemployment in Nigeria is at an all-time high of 33% (Bloomberg, 2021), according to the Nigerian National Bureau of Statistics (2020), with the rate of unemployment higher for women (35.2%) compared to Men (31.8%). While the rate of unemployment in South Sudan is not as high as in Nigeria, it stands at 12.7% (Knoema, 2020). The economic situation of both countries has exacerbated poverty and unemployment, with unequal effects on young people and women (African Development Bank, 2020a, 2020b).

Data was collected from 422 female entrepreneurs from the two countries (Nigeria [N] = 392; South Sudan [N] = 30). Surveys were used to capture entrepreneurs' business demographics, their confidence in using technology or collaborative tools, and their perceived challenges and opportunities as entrepreneurs in Nigeria and South Sudan.

Qualitative aspects of the data were analysed using thematic analysis and descriptive statistics. Responses were coded into themes which are tabulated in Table 6.2, with examples of entrepreneur's direct references included.

6.8 Results

The entrepreneurs that participated in this research had their business interests spread across different sectors, as shown in Table 6.1. Based on this dataset, the top three sectors for Nigerian female entrepreneurs are Food and Beverage (16.9%), Fashion and Beauty (15.5%) and textile (14.7%). On the other hand, the entrepreneurs from South Sudan have businesses mainly around commerce (53.3%), food and beverages (similar in spread like Nigeria at 16.7%) and then fashion, beauty and tourism (both at 6.7%). Some other sectors that stood out for both Nigerian and south Sudanese entrepreneurs were textile, agriculture, education and training, arts and culture and media and communication.

6.8.1 Distribution of Survey Responses from Participating Female Entrepreneurs

When participating female entrepreneurs were asked to rate their ability in the use of online business development resources, 35.8% of the participants indicated that they could not or did not know how to use the online business development resources (as shown in Fig. 6.1). This constituted 36.7% of the Nigerian participants and 23.3% of the South Sudanese participants. On the other hand, 21.3% of the participants indicated confidence in their ability to use online resources (that they were good at it or very good at it), which constitute 19.7% of the Nigerian participating entrepreneurs and 43.3% of the entrepreneurs from South Sudan.

When asked to rate their ability in the use of online collaborative tools, 23.2% of the participating entrepreneurs indicated that they could not, or did not know how to use collaborative tools, which constituted 24% of the Nigerian participants and 13.3% of the South Sudanese participants (See Fig. 6.2). Also, 29.2% of the participants indicated confidence in their ability to use online resources (that they were good at it or very good at it), which constitute 27.6% of the Nigerian participating entrepreneurs and 50% of the entrepreneurs from South Sudan.

When participating female entrepreneurs were asked to rate their ability in leveraging technology for their businesses (see Fig. 6.3), 32.5% of the participants indicated that they could not or did not know how to

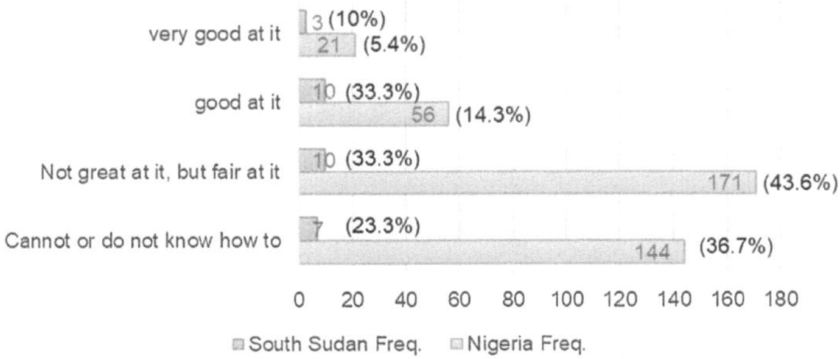

Fig. 6.1 Ability to use of business development resources

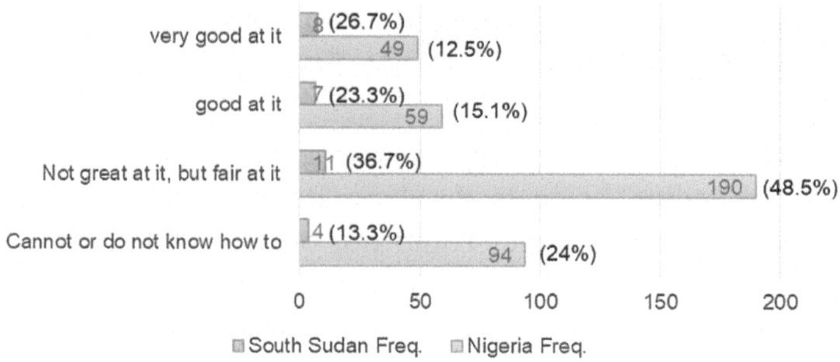

Fig. 6.2 Ability to use of collaborative tools

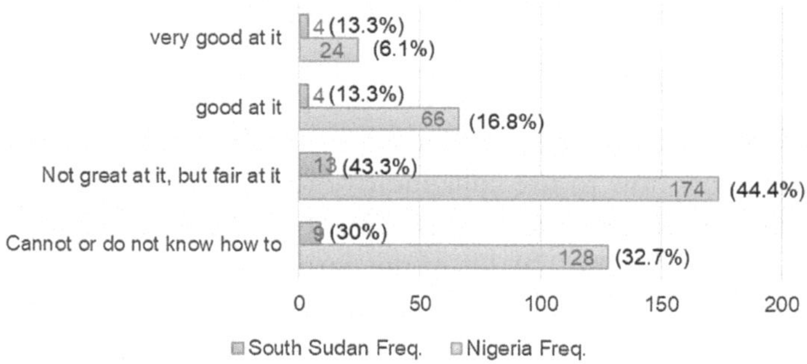

Fig. 6.3 Ability to leverage technology for business

leverage technology for their businesses, which constituted 32.7% of the Nigerian participants and 30% of the South Sudanese participants. On the other hand, 23.2% of the participants indicated confidence in their ability to use online resources (that they were good at it or very good at it), which constitute 22.9% of the participating Nigerian entrepreneurs and 26.6% of the entrepreneurs from South Sudan.

6.8.2 Challenges of Digital Entrepreneurship in Africa

African female entrepreneurs were asked to indicate challenges they faced, particularly with respect to the respective digital economies. Across country comparisons were carried out, based on the number of mentions for each theme that emerged. Distribution of emerged factors can be seen in Table 6.1.

Majority of the participating female entrepreneurs across both countries identified the lack of capital as the largest major challenge, the lack of or insufficient access to funds, grants and even loans necessary to keep their businesses running and also to enable them to innovate. From Nigeria, 48% of the entrepreneurs mentioned capital as a major concern, while 35% of South Sudanese entrepreneurs did same.

The second top challenge identified by Nigerian entrepreneurs is the environment (11%) due to insurgency, political instability, high taxes, corruption and gender inequality. This is followed by high costs and access to utilities (7%). Lack of access or insufficient supplies of utilities such as electricity, water, access to the internet and high data costs were identified to cause an increase in the transactional costs of running a business.

On the other hand, environment ranked second largest challenge (at 19%) for female entrepreneurs from South Sudan, closely followed by insufficient knowledge of business management processes, technologies, tools and requisite skills.

6.8.3 Opportunities for Digital Entrepreneurship in Africa

Furthermore, entrepreneurs were asked to indicate what they saw as opportunities for the African female entrepreneurs. Table 6.2 shows the distribution of emerged outcome.

The main opportunity identified by Nigerian entrepreneurs is the potential to harness the manpower and skillsets from the large population in Africa (21% of mentions by the entrepreneurs). As of 2021, Africa had a population of over 1.3 billion (worldometers.info), with Nigeria and South Sudan at 210.7 million and 11.3 million, respectively. Other opportunities identified can be derived from the growing economies (18%) and market opportunities in Africa. In joint third are the education/training and Investment opportunities (both at 15%).

Table 6.1 Identified challenges of digital entrepreneurship in Africa

Challenge(s)	Entrepreneurs' description of challenge(s)	Nigeria (Freq.)	%	South Sudan (Freq.)	%
Capital	Lack of capital/funds, finances, access to grants and poor access to loan facilities	234	48	15	35
Tech/digital skills	Technology to improve business, insufficient Tech and digital skills, inability to reach out to customers through digital marketing	10	2	0	0
Resources	Lack of resources or access to resources, difficulty in getting resources at affordable prices/high costs of goods, lack of infrastructure, transportation/logistics issues, lack of facilities and logistics for expansion, lack of collateral to access available funds	16	3.3	3	7
Visibility	How to gain more visibility for their businesses	15	3.1	0	0
Human resources	People	2	0.4	0	0

Challenge(s)	Entrepreneurs' description of challenge(s)	Nigeria (Freq.)	%	South Sudan (Freq.)	%
Environment	High taxes by government, multiple taxation, government policies and incentives to support businesses, insecurity, insurgency and political instability, most things in-country are imported making it hard to set prices, COVID 19 pandemic, less value on local currency, gender inequality, corruption	51	11	8	19
Competition	Price fluctuations, unequal playing ground for local talent, too much competition	11	2.3	0	0
Support	Lack of business development support	14	2.9	4	9.3
Marketing/sales	Insufficient knowledge of marketing, branding	28	5.7	1	2.3
Business management	Insufficient knowledge of business management and financial management, financial literacy, lack of requisite skills for business development	24	4.9	5	12

(continued)

Table 6.1 (continued)

Challenge(s)	Entrepreneurs' description of challenge(s)	Nigeria (Freq.)	%	South Sudan (Freq.)	%
Customers	Ignorance of the public/customers, low patronage, customers patronising imported products or solutions	9	1.8	1	2.3
Mentors	Lack of mentorship or access to mentors	13	2.7	0	0
Network	Insufficient knowledge about useful networks, poor or insufficient network access, difficulty in engaging networks, struggles with partnerships	16	3.3	1	2.3
Utilities	High cost of data, lack of electricity to perform online task, lack of access to basic amenities (power supply, water, etc.), disabilities support	34	7	1	2.3
Capabilities	Lack of requisite skills	8	1.6	2	4.7
Sustainability	Facilities and logistics for expansion and scaling	3	0.6	0	0

Source Authors

Education and training programmes provide avenues to improve digital literacy, offers capacity building programmes and opportunities to reskill and upskill.

For South Sudanese entrepreneurs, the main opportunity identified is the ability to leverage technology and make use of the digital market opportunities (17%). This is followed by education and training opportunities (14%), similar to their Nigerian counterparts. In the joint third, innovation and resilience (10%) stood out with regards to smart logistics and innovative solutions as a means to reduce poverty and manage scarce resources. On the other side, the possibility of harnessing the workforce/human capital (10%) from the population was identified.

6.9 Discussion

This chapter explores digital entrepreneurship, its current state and adoption in Africa. Digital entrepreneurship removes many of the constraints that previously limited the traditional entrepreneur, such as the boundlessness of entrepreneurial activities. Organisations are no longer limited to providing services and products to markets within their vicinity. The boundary of distance is transcended, and opportunities to scale very quickly are provided through digital infrastructure. Digital platforms help entrepreneurs scale, get their goods, products or services to a wider market base and remove previous constraints that made them only sell to their local markets.

The dynamic capabilities theory provided a useful framework to view and react to the dynamic digital skills and capabilities needed for the work of the future in the very disruptive and rapidly changing technological world we are in.

Findings from the study suggest that over a third of the participating female entrepreneurs from both countries indicated their inability to use online business development resources, with another third of the participants indicating basic perceived knowledge of online business development tools. Findings are consistent with other studies (Friederici et al., 2020) on limited technology adoption as a result of a lack of technical know-how. An implication of this finding is the need to provide

Table 6.2 Identified opportunities for digital entrepreneurship in Africa

Opportunities	Entrepreneurs' description of opportunities	Nigeria (Freq.)	%	South Sudan (Freq.)	%
Innovation and resilience	Creativity, smart logistics, conducive environment to create new ideas, ability to manage and utilise resources under harsh conditions, using acquired business ideas to reduce poverty rates	27	14	3	10
Technology	Digital market, leveraging technology, IT development, ecommerce, internet in rural areas and for marketing, investments in science and technology, developing the social power of the internet, using technology to accelerate the African market	23	12	5	17
Agriculture	Agribusiness and market opportunities, resources to feed countries, food processing and packaging, agricultural imports and exports	13	6.9	1	3.4

Opportunities	Entrepreneurs' description of opportunities	Nigeria (Freq.)	%	South Sudan (Freq.)	%
Nascent market/growing economy	Good economy, support being given, market opportunities, free market, markets not oversaturated, untapped and not ventured areas, agribusiness, ecommerce, African businesses led by Africans, investments, opportunities to establish industries, availability of target market, good environment for startups	34	18	8	28
Education and training opportunities	Capacity building programmes and initiatives, skill acquisition, youth training, training on entrepreneurship, mentorship, empowerment, government approach towards readiness of individuals, sponsorships, seminars, Nation-building	29	15	4	14
Investment opportunities	Support from big organisations, financial support, sponsorship, investors, grants/funding by foreign bodies/agencies, soft loans	28	15	2	6.9

(continued)

Table 6.2 (continued)

Opportunities	Entrepreneurs' description of opportunities	Nigeria (Freq.)	%	South Sudan (Freq.)	%
Collaboration opportunities/coalitions	Networking, global businesses, support systems, connections	18	9.5	2	6.9
Large population/cheap labour	Availability of eligible and skilled workforce large markets, labour force, enough population to serve different products, creating job opportunities to the unemployed market, manpower and resources	39	21	3	10
Unfulfilled needs	improve the way of life, meeting populations unfulfilled needs	6	3.2	2	6.9
Reducing unemployment	creating jobs to tackle unemployment, establish industries	9	4.8	3	10
Access to raw materials	availability of resources, enough raw materials	18	9.5	2	6.9

Source Authors

more support, digital skills training and information sessions to female entrepreneurs in Africa, to enable them to gain the required knowledge or information to adopt and leverage digital technologies. It will also help provide a top-down management buy-in for useful digital technologies.

While 72.5% of female entrepreneurs from Nigeria indicated inability or limited ability in using collaborative tools, the percentages were lower for the South Sudanese entrepreneurs at about 50%. These results reinforce the need for upskilling to be able to keep up the skills for the future and enable the entrepreneurs to function effectively.

Over 70% of female entrepreneurs across both countries indicated their inability or limited ability to leverage technology for their businesses. Leveraging technology has been argued as critical for innovation (Leong et al., 2020). Inability to leverage technology would constrain entrepreneurs' ability to build dynamic capabilities that offer competitive advantages and help organisations innovate (Dillon et al., 2020; Teece, 2018).

The challenges and opportunities of digital entrepreneurship were also reviewed in this chapter, in general, and in the context of two African countries (Nigeria and South Sudan) and from a female entrepreneurship perspective.

The need for access to capital seemed to resonate for entrepreneurs from both countries and consistent with current literature (Groza et al., 2020). Recently, active players and organisations within the tech space identified the need to support female entrepreneurs and create interventions that provide access and opportunities to access fund. Other recent avenues include online crowdfunding and grants.

It was also interesting how the need for digital skills did not seem to have many mentions from the Nigerian Entrepreneurs and no mention at all from the South Sudanese entrepreneurs. This is despite the high percentage of entrepreneurs on both sides indicating inability or limited ability in using collaborative tools and leveraging technology. It may indicate the focus of the management team on raising capital for the business. This would still require the teams to develop their organisational knowledge and capabilities to be able to innovate.

This study is not without some limitations. In this chapter, we have reviewed digital entrepreneurship within the context of female entrepreneurs in Nigeria and South Sudan. While the findings provide insights that could be applicable in other African contexts, further research can include other African countries at different levels of economic developments to explore similarities and differences. Other studies can also explore the pre-effects as well as and post-effects of interventions that improve digital entrepreneurial skills and capabilities.

The study also used only one dimension of digital technologies 'as digital enablers. Future studies could explore digital technologies as digital outcomes of entrepreneurial activities from African digital entrepreneurs. The study provides insights into barriers and opportunities experienced by entrepreneurs in Nigeria and South Sudan, if not built upon by further research (reviewing other contextual nuance or comparisons with other countries); they become just another silo of knowledge. While silos of innovative solutions and products exist, they may work better, scale faster and have more impact if they are part of a larger ecosystem where individual parts, processes, services and solutions complement each other, and collectively improve the digital economies across Africa.

6.10 Conclusion

This chapter contributes to the conversations on contextual evidence of digital entrepreneurship and the literature on digital entrepreneurship from a female perspective. This is relevant because many extant studies focus on more developed economies and a large male representation, with less focus on emerging economies in Africa and under-represented groups.

The chapter highlights the large and uneven digital gaps in Africa, the need for upskilling and reskilling, particularly for female entrepreneurs. Improving digital literacy, building competencies and providing support for digital entrepreneurship, should enable innovation, help reduce inequalities, improve future job or business opportunities for the citizens of African economies and further develop their digital economies.

Acknowledgements The authors thank the editors for their review and patience. Special thanks to AfriLabs for their support of the FESP initiative from the AfriLabs Capacity Building Programme (ACBP) awards, funded by Agence Francaise De Development (AFD), through the Digital Africa seed fund. Many thanks also to all the entrepreneurs in Nigeria and South Sudan and mentors across the world that participated and supported the FESP.

References

African Development Bank. (2020a). *Nigeria economic outlook*. https://www.afdb.org/en/countries/west-africa/nigeria. Accessed May 14, 2021.

Africa Development Bank. (2020b). *South Sudan economic outlook*. https://www.afdb.org/en/countries/east-africa/south-sudan. Accessed May 14, 2021.

Bloomberg. (2021). *Nigeria's unemployment rate rises to second highest on global list*. https://www.bloomberg.com/news/articles/2021-03-15/nigeria-unemployment-rate-rises-to-second-highest-on-global-list. Accessed May 14, 2021.

Chakrabarty, S. (2009). The influence of national culture and institutional voids on family ownership of large firms: A country level empirical study. *Journal of International Management, 15*(1), 32–45.

Counted, A. V., & Arawole, J. O. (2015). 'We are connected, but constrained': Internet inequality and the challenges of millennials in Africa as actors in innovation. *Journal of Innovation and Entrepreneurship, 5*(1), 1–21.

Coward, C., & Fellows, M. (2018). *Digital skills toolkit*. International Telecommunication Union.

Dal Zotto, C., & Omidi, A. (2020). Platformization of media entrepreneurship: A conceptual development. *Nordic Journal of Media Management, 1*(2), 209–233. https://doi.org/10.5278/njmm.2597-0445.5234

Davidsson, P., Recker, J., and von Briel, F. (2018). External enablement of new venture creation: A framework. *Academy of Management Perspectives*.

Dillon, S. M., Glavas, C., & Mathews, S. (2020). Digitally immersive, international entrepreneurial experiences. *International Business Review, 29*(6), 101739.

Dong, J. Q. (2019). Moving a mountain with a teaspoon: Toward a theory of digital entrepreneurship in the regulatory environment. *Technological Forecasting and Social Change, 146*, 923–930.

Elia, G., Margherita, A., & Passiante, G. (2020). Digital entrepreneurship ecosystem: How digital technologies and collective intelligence are reshaping the entrepreneurial process. *Technological Forecasting and Social Change, 150*, 119791.

European Commission. (2014). *Measuring digital skills across the EU: EU wide indicators of digital competence—digital single market—European Commission*. Retrieved 11 September 2019, from https://ec.europa.eu/digital-single-market/en/news/measuring-digital-skills-across-eu-eu-wide-indicators-digital-competence

Friederici, N., Wahome, M., & Graham, M. (2020). *Digital entrepreneurship in Africa: How a continent is escaping Silicon Valley's long shadow*. The MIT Press.

Global Entrepreneurship Monitor—GEM. (2020). *Covid impact report—Executive summary*. https://www.gemconsortium.org/news/executive-summary. Accessed October 5, 2021.

Global Entrepreneurship Monitor. (2021). *2020/2021 global report*. Retrieved November 16, 2021 from https://www.gemconsortium.org/report/gem-20202021-global-report

Groza, M. P., Groza, M. D., & Barral, L. M. (2020). Women backing women: The role of crowdfunding in empowering female consumer-investors and entrepreneurs. *Journal of Business Research, 117*, 432–442.

Helfat, C. E., & Peteraf, M. A. (2015). Managerial cognitive capabilities and the microfoundations of dynamic capabilities. *Strategic Management Journal, 36*(6), 831–850.

Knoema. (2020). *South Sudan unemployment rate*. https://knoema.com/atlas/South-Sudan/Unemployment-rate. Accessed May 14, 2021.

Khan, F., & Vuopala, E. (2019). Digital competence assessment across generations: A finnish sample using the digcomp framework. *International Journal of Digital Literacy and Digital Competence (IJDLDC), 10*(2), 15–28.

Leong, C., Tan, F. T. C., Tan, B., & Faisal, F. (2020). The emancipatory potential of digital entrepreneurship: A study of financial technology-driven inclusive growth. *Information & Management*, 103384.

Madichie, N. O., Taura, N. D., & Bolat, E. (2019). What next for digital etrepreneurship in Sub-Saharan Africa? In *Digital entrepreneurship in Sub-Saharan Africa* (pp. 221–240). Palgrave Macmillan, Cham.

McAdam, M., Crowley, C., & Harrison, R. T. (2019). "To boldly go where no [man] has gone before"—Institutional voids and the development of women's digital entrepreneurship. *Technological Forecasting and Social Change, 146*, 912–922.

Nambisan, S. (2017). Digital entrepreneurship: Toward a digital technology perspective of entrepreneurship. *Entrepreneurship Theory and Practice, 41*(6), 1029–1055.

Ngoasong, M. Z. (2018). Digital entrepreneurship in a resource-scarce context: A focus on entrepreneurial digital competencies. *Journal of Small Business and Enterprise Development*.

Nigerian National Bureau of Statistics. (2020). *Labor force statistics: Unemployment and underemployment report (Q4 2020)*. Retrieved November 16, 2021 from https://nigerianstat.gov.ng/elibrary

Pinchot, G., & Soltanifar, M. (2021). Digital intrapreneurship: The corporate solution to a rapid digitalisation. In *Digital entrepreneurship* (pp. 233–262). Springer, Cham.

Recker, J., & von Briel, F. (2019, November). The future of digital entrepreneurship research: Existing and emerging opportunities. In *ICIS*.

Roundy, P. T., & Fayard, D. (2019). Dynamic capabilities and entrepreneurial ecosystems: The micro-foundations of regional entrepreneurship. *The Journal of Entrepreneurship, 28*(1), 94–120.

Samara, G., & Terzian, J. (2021). Challenges and opportunities for digital entrepreneurship in developing countries. *Digital Entrepreneurship, 283*.

Solomon, E. M., & van Klyton, A. (2020). The impact of digital technology usage on economic growth in Africa. *Utilities Policy, 67*, 101104.

Steel, G. (2021). Going global–going digital. Diaspora networks and female online entrepreneurship in Khartoum, Sudan. *Geoforum, 120*, 22–29.

Stubbs, E. A., & Myers, B. E. (2015). Multiple case study of STEM in school-based agricultural education. *Journal of Agricultural Education, 56*(2), 188–203.

Taura, N. D., Bolat, E., & Madichie, N. O. (2019). Introduction to African digital entrepreneurship. In *Digital entrepreneurship in Sub-Saharan Africa* (pp. 3–7). Palgrave Macmillan, Cham.

Teece, D. J. (2007). Explicating dynamic capabilities: The nature and microfoundations of (sustainable) enterprise performance. *Strategic Management Journal, 28*(13), 1319–1350.

Teece, D. J. (2018). Business models and dynamic capabilities. *Long Range Planning, 51*(1), 40–49.

UN Broadband Commission. (2018). *Digital entrepreneurship.*

UN Broadband Commission for Sustainable Development. (2020). The State of Broadband 2020: Tackling digital inequalities. A decade for Action.

UNESCO. (2019). *Recommendations on assessment tools for monitoring digital literacy within UNESCO's digital literacy global framework*. Retrieved

September 11, 2019 from http://uis.unesco.org/sites/default/files/documents/ip56-recommendations-assessment-tools-digital-literacy-2019-en.pdf

von Briel, F., Davidsson, P., & Recker, J. (2018). Digital technologies as external enablers of new venture creation in the IT hardware sector. *Entrepreneurship Theory and Practice, 42*(1), 47–69.

Vuorikari, R., Punie, Y., Gomez, S. C., & Van Den Brande, G. (2016). *DigComp 2.0: The digital competence framework for citizens.* Update phase 1: The conceptual reference model (No. JRC101254). Joint Research Centre (Seville site).

Warner, K. S., & Wäger, M. (2019). Building dynamic capabilities for digital transformation: An ongoing process of strategic renewal. *Long Range Planning, 52*(3), 326–349.

WEF. (2020). *Reskilling revolution.* Retrieved May 16, 2021 from https://www.reskillingrevolution2030.org/

Yin, R. K. (2003). Designing case studies. *Qualitative Research Methods*, 359–386.

Yoo, Y. (2010). Computing in everyday life: A call for research on experiential computing. *MIS Quarterly, 34*(2), 213–231.

7

Digital Informal Credit System for Student Entrepreneurship Promotion in Higher Learning - The Case of South Africa

Ishmael Obaeko Iwara

7.1 Introduction

Informal credit systems have no universally accepted constructs and/or definitions; hence, they are coined and defined along cultural lines. The initiative can be referred to as Rotating Savings and Credit Associations (ROSCAs) or Accumulating Savings and Credit Associations (ACSAs) (Hossein, 2017; Koenane, 2019; Luthuli, 2017; Matuku & Kaseke, 2014; Mulaudzi, 2017; Smets, 2000). It is also commonly known as esusu in Nigeria (Moses et al., 2015) and chama in Kenya (Sile & Bett, 2015). In the context of South Africa, where this study was conducted, Stokvel (*tshitokofela* as it is known in vhaVenda) is the indigenous version of the initiative (Mulaudzi, 2017; Kok & Lebusa, 2018). Regardless of the diverse terminologies, the underlying idea is homogenous. It is an arrangement, where a network of community members, with a

I. O. Iwara (✉)
University of Venda, Thohoyandou, South Africa
e-mail: 16023142@mvula.univen.ac.za

O. Adeola et al. (eds.), *Digital Service Delivery in Africa*, Palgrave Studies of Marketing in Emerging Economies,
https://doi.org/10.1007/978-3-030-83909-3_7

common vision, pool their resources to actualise their goal (Bäckman Kartal, 2019; Iwara, 2020; Lebusa, 2018). This is an informal system with no intermediation and subsidy, or any form of government regulations (Rodima-Taylor, 2020). There are many forms of stokvels in South Africa, one of which is the digital stokvel, however, the primary and central aim of each is premised on capital mobilisation for small businesses operation, informal saving/banking for future endeavours, lending and borrowing money.

This chapter discusses how digital stokvel is harnessed to mobilise resources for student-related entrepreneurial activities, its formation and function, benefits and associated challenges in the context of the University of Venda, in South Africa. As a historically disadvantaged institution of higher learning, in 2018/2019, the University started to encourage entrepreneurial activities among students, as part of its mission to become an entrepreneurial university. This chapter was part of an investigation into what entrepreneurial activities already exist, and what needs to be done to promote these activities on campus. The details in the following chapter includes: an overview of a stokvel, detailing its role in Africa; the background of digital entrepreneurship, explaining its inception, operations and relevance, followed by the methodology, result and discussion of findings.

7.2 The Role of Stokvel in Africa

Generally, stokvels hold a promise for economic and social development, especially among marginalised individuals (Gugerty, 2007; Ramagoshi, 2016; NASASA, 2018; Menze & Tsibolane, 2019). Kok and Lebusa (2018) and Menze and Tsibolane (2019) emphasise that informal credit initiatives such as Stokvel have become one of the most popular means for income generation, as well as a measure of maintaining financial independence in Africa. Many entrepreneurs in the continent rely on such initiative for business start-up capital, resource mobilisation for business expansion and saving. Essentially, it provides alternative and traditional financial arrangements where access to formal financial institutions is limited (Iwara et al., 2021). Stokvels also play a central role in interconnecting individuals towards the development of a cohesive society, given that it entails bringing together community members onto platforms to interact financially (UNESCO, 2012; Sile & Bett, 2015). Ideally, the concept is resourceful in building a community advantage and social capital. As a result of these standpoints, it has occupied a strong position in Africa's culture and has gained momentum, promoted in many societies and practised by many people on the continent regardless of gender, age and social status.

In a systematic review of the stokvel model, Iwara and Netshandama (2021) highlighted two significant standpoints through which traditional African entrepreneurs, especially those in rural areas, can promote entrepreneurship using the initiative. Firstly, enterprise capital mobilisation through the different types of stokvel system—saving, rotating systems and loan initiatives. In this context, trust is the main criteria for credit accessibility (Dare & Okeya, 2017); hence, this makes funds available to businesses without any form of security. Mungiru and Njeru (2015), Dare and Okeya (2017), similarly, suggest that, unlike formal financial institutions, which require evidence of business registration, stock of sales and collateral during loan transaction, access to credit in an informal structures such as stokvel is often based on trust and recommendation from a member. As a result of these conditions, it is acknowledged that capital mobilisation for small businesses through stokvel is relatively flexible and convenient when compared to formal credit systems (Moloi, 2011; Backman Kartal, 2019). In addition to capital mobilisation, traditional stokvel is a community of practice where members meet and network. Accordingly, it presents opportunities for building strong social capital for business operation such as product marketing and customer mobilisation (Iwara & Netshandama, 2021). It can then be inferred that stokvels offer businesses in Africa an essential resource for entrepreneurship promotion.

7.3 Digital Stokvel for Entrepreneurship Promotion

In the recent decade, globalisation has brought about a digital-driven stokvel wherein interactions rely on smart technological resources. Computers (smartphones, laptops and desktops) and electronic communication platforms like internet banking applications, WhatsApp, Facebook, e-mail, Skype and Zoom have become usual avenues through which e-stokvel functions. E-stokvels make it possible to periodically assemble a group of individuals through online platforms, to pool stipulated premiums into a lump-sum, which then becomes available for an identified purpose (Kariuki & Ofusori, 2017; Menze & Tsibolane, 2019). Aside from capital mobilisation, e-stokvel also provides business opportunities as it enables entrepreneurs to network digitally and accumulate customers, market their product, transact and deliver different types of services and goods (Biyela et al., 2018; du Pisanie, 2018; Menze & Tsibolane, 2019). Currently, e-stokvel has become a pivotal business operation tool amid the Covid-19 pandemic, given that there have been lock-down regulations, movement restrictions and a shutdown of many businesses operating physically. In this context, digital platforms, such as e-stokvel, present alternative avenues for business operation and sustainability.

The efficacy of e-stokvels in entrepreneurship promotion, in serving as an emerging business niche has been well-established in certain societies. However, it is only at present time that they have become areas of research in South Africa. For instance, Kariuki and Ofusori (2017) explore the role of WhatsApp-operated informal credit systems in promoting youth entrepreneurship in Durban, detailing how online credit platforms provide exciting and innovative ways to raise business start-up capital. Biyela et al. (2018) highlight the domestication of ICTs in informal banking, explaining the significant role the concept plays in influencing easy access to finance and social cohesion in Cape Town. Du Pisanie (2018) elucidates the contribution of the digital system towards empowering young farming entrepreneurs; Menze and Tsibolane (2019) contributed to a better conception of a system to help in shaping the daily application of technology and unearthing the use of online informal credit in enhancing the social inclusion of the marginalised in South Africa. Overall, these studies make significant contribution to this body of knowledge, particularly the place of e-stokvel in the provision of capital for entrepreneurial activity, networking and job creation. However, its formation and functions, advantages and underlining challenges remain unexplained. Lack of essential knowledge about e-stokvel may allow its overwhelming benefits to obscure its equally significant challenges. This is knowledge of interest in different contexts, for example, in historically disadvantaged location, University of Venda, where a vast number of the students come from a low-income background and tend to become involved in the initiative to operate small businesses for sustainability.

7.4 Methodology

This study was conducted at the University of Venda in South Africa. The choice for the University as a study area was informed by the fact that it is among the Historically Disadvantaged Institutions (HDI) of higher learning in the country and is characterised by vast middle and low-income class students. Some of the students participate in various forms of stokvel to manage a micro or small enterprise for financial independence while pursuing their degrees. The research participants, which consisted of students who are actively involved in e-stokvels and online/physical forms of businesses, provided essential knowledge.

The qualitative Appreciative Inquiry (AI) research methodology was followed in this study. An appreciative inquiry is a strength-based subjective approach to organisational change, wherein individuals engage in discourse to explore measures that give a better understanding, meaning and new shape to their organisation (Armstrong, 2017; Dent, 2019). AI is based on a 5-D cycle (defining, discovering, dreaming, designing and destiny implementing stages) that involves asking open-ended questions to a group of stakeholders (in this case, students who are actively involved in stokvels) to craft and implement action plans towards entrepreneurial activities on campus. The aim was to give student participants time during the interviews to relate their views, options and feelings in their responses to the questions. This process was to encourage them to reshape (design) what they had by making them understand that they could bring a positive change in the entrepreneurial activities on campus. The participants felt free to narrate their views, and the interviews assisted them to give in-depth information based on their context.

Before embarking on this study, the researcher had to conceptualise the whole project, hence, in accordance with the 5-D cycle. During the 'defining' stage, the researcher clarified the topic of the study which was to explore and describe digital student stokvel system for student entrepreneurship promotion in higher learning. The background and problem statement were clearly articulated to explain the extent of the challenges being addressed. At this stage, the AI-approach interview was developed to guide questions. The discovery stage involved an assessment of the formation, functions, motivation, merits and demerits of digital stokvels. AI-approach questions were designed to allow students to analyse both the positive and negative aspects of digital stokvel. The 'discovery' stage assisted the participants to continue with the next stage which entailed 'dreaming about what could be'. The 'dream' stage was to enable the participants to envisage'what could be done', based on the negative experiences of the discovery stage. The AI-approach questions were to obtain information, such as what the participants' experience with stokvels was and what progress and growth students would like to prevail on campus to facilitate stokvels and entrepreneurial activities. The 'design' stage, thus, involved reshaping the future through dialogue. The main reason for this stage was to create a supportive environment for responsive policy formulation, conversation and interaction on the topic. In the 'destiny' stage, the results of the dream stage and what had been planned in the design stage were implemented. The feasibility of implementing the 'dream' and the design stages in the operational plan (or the work plan) was evaluated. This involved transforming the design stage into more specific sets of tasks or activities to be put into action. Implementation and monitoring are essential parts of this process.

7.4.1 Data Collection Procedures

Semi-structured interviews were conducted with participants sampled through the purposive and snowball sampling techniques as these were deemed convenient for the selection of student entrepreneurs operating enterprises intertwined with digital stokvels. The sampling process continued until the point of data saturation was met. Respondents were made aware of their voluntary participation and the right to withdraw from the study at any time. Only participants who consented to the University of Venda's ethical conditions were sampled and interviewed accordingly. In all, 31 students were drawn from the University for this study, out of which 16 were South Africans (SA), eight from Zimbabwe (Zim), three from Nigeria (Nig), three from the Democratic Republic of Congo (DRC) and one from Cameron (CR). Undergraduate students (Ug) constituted approximately 84% (26) of the participants, while the remaining were postgraduate students (Pg); the females accounted for 68% and 32% were their male counterparts. As presented in Table 7.1, using x to indicate the nature of businesses operated, online enterprises are predominant, however, some students combined online and physical approaches. Both undergraduate and postgraduates, as well as South African and International (Intl) students involved in businesses.

7.4.2 Data Analysis

The semi-structured interviews were audio-taped and transcribed verbatim in typed format for the data analysis. The transcribed data were subjected to an analysis modelled on Atlas-ti v8 software—open coding system for thematic analysis. Coding ensured that a number of themes or categories were generated. Interrogating participants' experiences about e-stokvel from this approach provided a comprehensive understanding of the context from an individual's perspective and gave a precise narrative about the initiative for policy formulation and practice.

Table 7.1 Nature of student enterprises at the university

	Business Method		Qualification		Designation	
Nature of enterprise	Online	Physical	Undergrad	Postgrad	SA	Intl
Event management design and decoration	x	x	x		x	x
Printing/photocopying	x	x	x	x	x	
Stationary		x	x		x	
Home delivery laundry service	x	x	x		x	x
Snacks		x	x	x	x	
Coaching, data analyst, editing	x	x		x		x
Bolt transportation	x		x	x	x	
Supplement and body fit items	x			x	x	x
Web and graphic designer	x		x	x	x	x
Photographer	x	x	x		x	
YouTube videos—traditional	x		x	x	x	x
Re-selling products	x		x	x	x	x
Loan shark	x	x		x	x	
Manicure and natural products	x	x	x	x	x	x

7.5 Result and Discussions

The findings in this study are organised into four segments. First, e-stokvel formation/functions which highlighted its nature, operation and functionality; second, the motivation for involvement in e-stokvel; third, its merits and last, its demerits.

7.6 E-Stokvel: Formation and Functions

E-stokvel presents similar savings, investment and income-generation opportunities for entrepreneurial activities and/or other forms of projects as traditional stokvels do. The main disparity existing between the two lies in the use of e-platforms, which is not peculiar to traditional stokvels.

While the primary purpose of e-stokvel platforms is credit mobilisation, entrepreneurial-minded students also use them to run efficient businesses.

> *... online platforms are the main sources for the enrolments of members, meetings and transactions. A group is formed by creating a communication link (normally Facebook or WhatsApp) and subsequently, the administrator adds other members who might share the same business interest ....* (Male; Pg, DRC)
>
> *... there are also instances where an individual creates a group and share the link to social media platforms for interested parties to join. ... I once joined this type of stokvel group to invest ... The link is customised to reach the desired maximum number (30) of individuals and then deactivated so that members may commence with meeting and contribution arrangements....* (Female; Pg, CR)

Often, the initiator of the idea serves as the group administrator, although this mostly applies in platforms with a high volume of participants as smaller groups may not require such a hierarchy to operate. Other positions, like finance administrator and secretary, may be appointed in the first online meeting, after the enrolment processes have been completed. All activities in this context are limited to online platforms; thus, members must have basic knowledge of using smart devices and online communication platforms.

> *... we don't convene in a physical meeting, the moment it is time for us to discuss, all of us will log in and talk business. We have one account where all the money for our business goes to and the finance officer takes charge ... ... in the event where we need to contribute, the agreed sum of money can be paid to the account to make a pool, which is then handed to one member as a lump-sum ....* (Female; Ug, Zim)
>
> *... e-wallet (an electronic money transfer made to someone's phone number) is another resource payment option, however, proof of each transaction is made accessible to other members of the group ... Sending evidence of transaction to the group is to ensure transparency and accountability ... ... the administrator will consolidate all payments and report accordingly ....* (Male; Ug, SA)

Through e-stokvels, a group of students who share the same vision can contribute money to a pool that is given to one of the members. This lump sum payment to beneficiaries is based on the principle of 'first to join, first served' in the form of a pyramid until everyone in the group has received the benefits. In rare instances, exceptions would be made in reaction to members' special personal circumstances. Members have the option to continue or exit the group after a successful round transaction.

> *... So I was introduced to a link for stokvel where we invest and have about 50% interest after 6 months, however, one has to pay consistently every month for the entire duration. What happens is that the initial capital paid is invested in a financial market to generate profit. Besides the investments, group members can do other businesses there. I usually advertise my herbal-life products on the group and supply to any member who places an order ....* (Male; Ug, SA)

Essentially, students save or invest their little daily/ monthly income, through e-stokvels which then makes a lump sum for projects such as starting or expanding a business. The activity is based on principles, one of which is, the use of online platforms. The platform is coordinated by one of the members, often the initiator of the idea. An agreed fixed amount is contributed regularly to a pool which is given to members on a rotational basis; all members convene through an online platform to contribute to a pool which, in the end, is used for an agreed purpose. The collection is once-off in a circle and this makes it affordable for students from middle and low-economic background as predominantly found at the University.

7.7 Motivation for Involvement in E-Stokvel

One of the strengths of e-stokvel lie in the similar mindset and mission of the participants. Like every other form of a stokvel, participants were motivated to involve in e-stokvel for several reasons. As depicted in Fig. 7.1, these include their desires to become entrepreneurs of influence in the future; to connect with people, discuss ideas, learn and

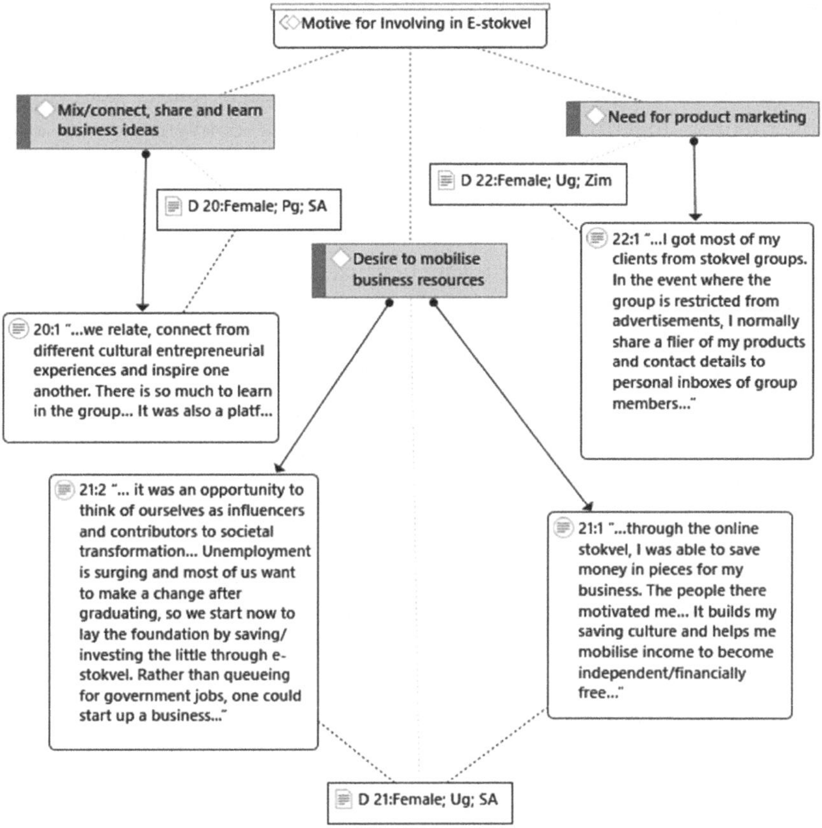

Fig. 7.1 Motivation for involvement in E-Stokvel consolidated by the author

operate a business; harness platforms for product marketing, and the need to mobilise resources for business start-up/expansion for income generation, while to some, it was out of necessity and a survival strategy. Joining the initiative, hence, is based on the students' need for alternative income-generation platforms for sustainable livelihood. This result is consistent with Bäckman Kartal (2019) in whose study, cultural, economic and normative factors appear as important motivators for joining stokvel in selected areas of KwaZulu-Natal Province in South Africa; however, the economic factors stand out as the strongest indicator among others.

7.8 Merits of E-Stokvel Systems

In terms of the merits of e-stokvel activities, participants believe it is convenient as meetings can be held at members' convenience; in addition, it attracts diverse groups and individuals, given that participation is not limited to any cultural lines or certain locations. Efficiency is another factor as the use of online platforms for meetings and transactions make them fast, smart, and lastly, it is safe because it avoids one-on-one contact that could expose an individual to physical threats which are very possible in financial interactions.

7.8.1 Convenience

E-stokvel participation is easy and comfortable as it enabled participants to engage with other activities and responsibilities while attending to stokvel matters at the same time. Aside from the fact that it gives students the leverage to multitask, it enabled them to continue stokvel activities despite lockdown regulations amidst the Covid-19 pandemic.

> *... it makes life easy and simple. I attend our meetings while cooking, watching TV or working on my assignments at the same time. All I need to do is to have my smartphone close to me; Wi-Fi is free on campus ....* (Female; Ug, Zim)
>
> *It does not matter where I find myself, all I have to worry about is the internet and my phone battery. I was doing stokvel and at the same time selling my products in there throughout the lockdown periods for Covid-19.* (Male; Ug, SA)

In e-stokvel, members can conveniently play their roles without having to worry about regular physical meetings in a designated location which is a central tenet of a traditional stokvel (Kariuki & Ofusori, 2017; du Pisanie, 2018). Meetings are flexible and can be held at any time. This enables group members to reduce the number of times they have to meet in person (Biyela et al., 2018), cutting down on the logistics of a physical meeting, unlike a traditional stokvel setting wherein hosting of physical meetings are rotated among members.

... we don't need to meet each other, everything is done on WhatsApp. It saves me the cost of hosting people in my place ... ... usually, one has to host their group members. When it gets to my turn, I have to rent chairs, cook food and buy drinks to entertain them. Since we migrated to digital, I no longer spend time on such .... (Other; Pg, SA)

7.8.2 Diverse

Typically, traditional stokvel draws members from a known environment, such as family members, peers, trusted colleagues, community members and sometimes those residing in the same area (Matuku & Kaseke, 2014; van Wyk, 2017). This is essential for quality assurance required to build trust. On the contrary, e-stokvel draws participants from a wider spectrum of societies. In most cases, members do not share the same cultural background and/or work in the same sphere, thus, multicultural drawing on people from varied contexts.

... I saw the hyperlink on Facebook. The moment I clicked to join, I was sent a WhatsApp link to the group ..., ... It was easy .... We are over 100 individuals in the group which cut across areas, not only from my University. I am sure almost every tribe in the country is represented because we use all South African official indigenous languages to interact in the group, and it does not affect our operation ... we only meet once a week to talk and do business.... (Male; Ug, SA)

... online stokvel is good because it offers people the opportunity to play [participate] stokvel regardless of where they are. Currently, I belong to three groups, two of which operate online ...; one is a traditional stokvel in my village. This group is predominantly made up of grannies [aged people], specifically women. So, I send money monthly from my NSFAS bursary to my mum to play [contribute] ..., ... another one is at my former University; it has people from different areas... except for an emergency, we only meet on WhatsApp once in two weeks to contribute ... ... the last one is here in UNIVEN which comprises of students; some are not even South Africans .... (Female; Ug, SA)

As narrated, distance is the least barrier to e-stokvel activities. Members may reside in different areas and still participate actively (du

Pisanie, 2018; Menze & Tsibolane, 2019). The desire and ability to comply with agreed terms and existing principles of the group, regardless of the geographical area, is what matters. This narrative is substantiated by a participant:

> *... it is far better because we don't necessarily have to be in one place. One of the groups I have at the moment is a committee of five friends; two are in different places in Mpumalanga Province, one is in Gauteng Province, then mina [myself] and one other are here in Limpopo Province; we still play and get in touch with each other ....* (Female; Ug, SA)

7.8.3 Efficiency

Transactions are instantaneous, and at the comfort of members due to the fact that e-stokvels are limited to online banking, unlike the traditional stokvel where procedures occur only during physical meetings with all or majority of the members in attendance.

> *... we make contributions directly into my account during meetings. It takes a few seconds to transfer the lump-sum to the qualified member as soon as the meeting ends, without having to move an inch ....* (Male; Pg, Zim)
>
> *In a pressing financial need, a member can easily send a message to the group for assistance. It is easier for other members to vote immediately in support or against without having to gather for decisive decisions ... e-stokvel promises money at the time you need it ....* (Female; Ug, SA)

Easy and quick access to capital is among the key advantages of e-stokvels (Kariuki & Ofusori, 2017; Biyela et al., 2018). The expected amount of money is made available almost immediately after the meeting and upon request. With the traditional format, urgent issues are deliberated upon the next available meeting day when all members would have gathered. To get a lump sum for an emergency, it sometimes requires the appointed person to make house-to-house visits for collection of the agreed-upon amount that is contributed to the pool. Apart from being time-consuming and stressful, chances of robbery/theft and physical attacks are some of the risks involved in the traditional approach to stokvel.

7.8.4 Safety

Amid the COVID-19 pandemic, digital stokvel is an ideal system. It provides members with an opportunity to be involved in informal financial activities as well as operate businesses without any adherence to lockdown regulations that have implications on physical gatherings.

> *... while the country was in complete lockdown, and students sent home, e-platform was the only option to continue with stokvel contribution we had started before Covid-19 pandemic disorganised our plans. It enabled me to save up to R300 each month from the government social relieve grant given to me. By the time we resume, I would have gathered enough money to expand my hairpiece and cosmatic business on campus ....* (Female; Pg, SA)

Online transactions curtail organised attacks and theft arrangements that often occur in the case of traditional stokvels when a member receives a lump sum (Thomas, 2015; Wyk, 2017). E-stokvels also limit face-to-face interactions necessary among members in a traditional stokvel. This helps to control rifts like quarrel and/or fight that may arise when members disagree during a meeting.

> *... years ago, our house in the village was ransacked, and a huge amount of money taken from it. This happened the night after my mother had received a lump-sum from her stokvel group, a contribution she made with the little benefits that accrue from our tuck-shop. We don't know how the thief got the information but my father had suspected that it must be an arrangement from one of the group members ....* (Female; Ug, SA)
> *... it gives peace of mind and controls enmity that comes with traditional stokvel. Sometimes people exchange blows for a minor issue... Regardless of the penalty to defaulters, the damage would have been done. I could recall, during a traditional stokvel meeting, a colleague fought me publicly for pointing out my concerns about lateness ... I was embarrassed ....* (Female; Pg, SA)

In a well-constituted e-stokvel, the administration is made open to every member. Proof of each transaction—be it a contribution, investment, penalty fine or a lump sum to a bona fide contact—is displayed on the group; hence, the information is made accessible to every member. This reduces irregularities that occur when one member uses paper-based ledgers for book-keeping, in the context of a traditional stokvel (Kariuki & Ofusori, 2017; Menze & Tsibolane, 2019). Even though, in the latter, reports are given in each meeting, it is often difficult to investigate inaccuracies in cases where group members fail to document each transaction made in previous events in traditional stokvel system.

> *… our WhatsApp group is where all records on the stokvel are. Because we put everything there (a snapshot of each transaction), one can see clearly where things have gone wrong and raise a concern immediately … … we don't need to document our transactions in a book and give an account at the end where people sit at home to manipulate figures. Each transaction is sent to our group so that everyone can make a personal record and refer to it in future. It is open to everybody ….* (Male; Ug, Zim)

7.9 Demerits of E-Stokvel Systems

Some of the demerits of an e-stokvel lie in its non-promotion of social bonding which is one of the key essences of stokvel initiative; it is discriminatory given that many who would have joined may not have the capacity; expensive in the sense that internet services are required to meet and some transactions attract bank charges and lastly, it is vulnerable to fraudulent practices.

7.9.1 Lack of Social Cohesion

Social cohesion is inherent to African cultural values and is held in high esteem even in stokvel. However, income generation is the principal objective of e-stokvels. People are interested in the money they make from being a member of the group and not relationships, which is an integral part of a traditional stokvel system (Iwara, 2020; Ledeneva,

2018; Sile & Bett, 2015; Storchi, 2018). The online approach limits one-on-one interactions among members, thus, the opportunity to meet each other, familiarise and bond are limited, deterring kinship ties, towards a cohesive society.

> *... the only difference I have noticed about online stokvel, which is not very pleasant to me, is lack of cordial relationship ... all people do there is business. People should have stokvels not only to generate income but meet, gist, eat and play together. It gives a sense of belonging and relief from anxiety ..., it is not the case here [in e-stokvel] ... If one is in a critical situation, other members should visit to support morally and materially ..., this aspect is entirely missing in e-stokvel ....* (Female; Pg, SA)

A traditional stokvel is embedded in societal clusters where a group of individuals with a common interest meet physically to share and also do business (Matuku & Kaseke, 2014; Sile & Bett, 2015). Trust in this context is paramount and is built through familiarisation. Communication between members in such settings happens freely, regularly and face-to-face, in close physical proximity during meetings (Menze & Tsibolane, 2019); this is fundamental to community engagements, kinship, cohesive society, and attracting customers for businesses. Social media-based communication has considerably less direct interaction between members, defeating peer-to-peer interaction and *koinonia* (relationship) that usually come with the initiative.

7.9.2 Discriminatory

E-stokvel is diverse, however, limited to a certain category of individuals. It is youth-friendly and mostly participated by people with digital knowledge in areas where basic services, such as electricity and internet coverage, are provided. This leaves other classes of individuals behind even though the generally understood mandate of a stokvel is assisting the marginalised with income security, cohesive society and business promotion (Dare & Okeya, 2017). In reality, this purpose is not met decisively, leaving concerns on how such a problem can be solved.

... in as much as I like the online stokvel, it has a lot of limitations. There was a time I lost my phone in the village during a semester break. As a result, I lost contact with the group. It made me skipped three meetings and contributions, and this got me disqualified and removed from the group. I could not fight because it was part of the terms and conditions. Eventually, I lost the money I had contributed to the group too .... (Male; Ug, Zim)

... I have been fined twice for failing to attend a general meeting ..., it was not my fault. Each time I travel home, the internet signal is poor because my village is very remote. I have to catch up with a signal somewhere close to town. I had to quit the group at some point because I feel they are not considerate of others .... (Female; Ug, SA)

E-stokvel opens to criticism on the basis that it lacks physical interaction and social bonding through which people talk and promote their businesses in person; it is discriminatory since entrepreneurs without digital knowledge and resources cannot get involved.

7.9.3 Expensive

In as much as e-stokvel is efficient and convenient, it has cost implications as meetings and transactions require internet coverage. In circumstances where internet resources are not subscribed for students, it may be a challenge for some to afford sufficient data for online conversations. Similarly, bank charges apply for some of the transaction made, hence, one may end up 'spending more to save a less'.

Chatting on WhatsApp group is easy and cheap, ... sometimes it could be difficult to buy enough data for group video calls during Zoom or Skype meetings ... It is expensive here in the village. My group members do not understand that ... they want everyone to meet on a conference video call every week. (Female; Ug, SA)

... entry fee to the group is R200 non-refundable, and one is registered after the money has been paid. We must add 5% of each money we transfer for administration purpose such as bank charges. If I check, my bank also charges for each transfer I make ..., I think it is rather expensive to join e-stokvel .... (Male; Ug, SA)

7.9.4 Fraudulent

While e-stokvel presents important opportunities for networking, smart businesses and income mobilisation, it is also gradually setting a stage for cybercrimes where fraudsters exploit people.

> *... I have been a victim of stokvel fraud. Someone who claimed to be a student, created an account and shared the link, most of us joined and contributed a pool using e-wallet with the hope of getting a lump-sum when it reaches out turn. To my greatest surprise, the group was dissolved after a while. I tried to call the contact used on the WhatsApp group but it never did connect after that ....* (Female; Ug, Zim)
>
> *The group I joined had over 100 members, it was only when I had deposited R200 enrolment non-refundable fee I was given a date for my lump-sum showing that I was the last in the circle. It was not a big deal since I needed the cash in December to start a business for my mother in the village. Unfortunately, the group ended after contributing R150 each Sunday for 6 weeks. No refunds were made, and the group administrator is nowhere to be found ....* (Male; Ug, SA)

Fraudulent practices include the initiator of a stokvel collecting money from those being recruited without paying back as agreed; in this situation, typically, the members lose their investments. These narratives are consistent with this point:

> *... my experience with one online group was horrific ..., to qualify for enrolment, one must recruit at least two people to the group; this I did and my two friends contributed the same as me ... I paid R200 [a compulsory enrolment fee] and also paid an additional R500 (monthly premium) as an instant contribution to a pool to get R6000 in 12 months ... I was contributing from my NSFAS money to have bulk money to change my snack business to printing on campus ... After three months of continued contribution, the group manager exited, and that was the end of it ....* (Female; Ug, SA)

E-stokvel-related frauds have not attracted scientific attention, however, there have been concerns in the public media space. De Villiers in Business Insider SA (2019), for instance, stresses that people in 'WhatsApp stokvel' should be cognisant of the fact that they are exposed to scam. Most of them are managed by unknown individuals who facilitate the exchange of money and who may take the opportunity to illegally access the money (Lindeque—Eye Witness News, 2019). The platform enables individuals with ulterior motives to easily fraud vulnerable people, especially, the unemployed and the marginally educated in e-matters. Some WhatsApp stokvels operate like a pyramid wherein the overlords persuade people to act as mediators who then lure the poor masses to contribute a premium that will never be accounted for. This is an important security issue for intervention as this may impact negatively on students' businesses, economic and academic survival, should it occur.

7.10 Conclusion and Recommendations

The strength of the students who participated in this study lies in their resilience and their dream to harness e-stokvel for business, start-up/expansion resource mobilisation which gives alternative means of income generation, share and exchange business ideas with people of different cultures, market product and mobilise clients through the online platforms. Through this study, it can be confirmed that stokvels can strengthen both online and physical entrepreneurial activities of students on campus, training them on different savings' orientations, injecting an imagination of the digital future as well as how they might influence a similar culture in their home communities. Using digital platforms for stokvel practices and businesses is a novelty. The University students have shown that African traditional informal initiatives can exist and operate successfully in the digital future, and this offers a window of opportunity for entrepreneurs on the continent to emulate learning points. The main merits are that e-stokvel is convenient to students given that its activities are held through online platforms and also flexible as it attracts people with diverse cultural contexts to convene, digitally, and share ideas. The swiftness of transactions and the safety in terms of limiting physical attacks while the collected cash of the stokvel is in transit constitutes part of the merit. On the other hand, e-stokvel limits physical bonding for entrepreneurial promotion among members. In reality, customer mobilisation and relationship are strengthened through physical interactions in African traditional business environments. More so, it can only accommodate people with digital knowledge and smart devices, making it discriminatory. The cost of banking/transaction, as well as the administration fee which applies to some groups, is expensive and unaffordable to some students, and lastly, it has the potential to produce fraudulent practices or e-scams. Based on the key findings, it is recommended that:

- The University should explore policies and structural arrangements that would formalise support for students engaged in stokvels. Campus e-stokvel group could be registered and regulated, such that it will minimise some of the challenges student entrepreneurs grapple with when participating in this initiative.
- Future studies should explore ideal format and tools for the re-orientation of the University to become more nurturing and supportive towards students' entrepreneurial activities, such as stokvels and others.

Acknowledgements This study emanated from the South Africa—Sweden Research Forum (SASUF) project: '"Who runs the world?" Women and Informal Finance: Now and Then'.

Professor Elise Dermineur, Umeå University, Sweden, and Professor Vhonani Olive Netshandama, University of Venda, South Africa, play a supervisory role in this book chapter. I would like to appreciate the students at the University of Venda who accepted to share their digital stokvel experiences.

References

Armstrong, A. C. (2017). Considering metaphors and appreciative enquiry as approaches to qualitative research. In *Proceedings of the school of education research and capacity building workshop 2016 (p. NA)*. School of Education, USP.

Bäckman Kartal, H. (2019). *How to empower a country using informal financial systems: Stokvels, the South African economical saviour*. Honours Thesis, Umeå University.

Biyela, N., Tsibolane, P., & Van Belle, J. P. (2018). Domestication of ICTs in community savings and credit associations (Stokvels) in the Western Cape, South Africa. In *International development informatics association conference* (pp. 35–47). Springer.

Creswell, J. W., & Creswell, J. D. (2017). *Research design: Qualitative, quantitative, and mixed methods approaches*. Sage.

Dare, F. D., & Okeya, O. E. (2017). The impact of informal capital market on the economic development and health of rural areas. *Journal of Humanities and Social Science, 22*(8), 23–33.

de Villiers, J. (2019). *If you joined a 'WhatsApp stokvel' you've probably been scammed*. Business Insider SA. https://www.businessinsider.co.za/whatsapp-stokvel-scam-national-stokvel-association-of-sa-nasasa-pyramid-scheme-2019-10.

Dent, N. (2019). Appreciating collaborative service improvement—A case study on using appreciative inquiry methodology in co-production in mental health. *Mental Health and Social Inclusion, 23*(3), 105–111.

du Pisanie, K. (2018). Stokvel Empowers Young Farmers. *Stockfarm, 8*(10), 18–19.

Gugerty, M. K. (2007). You can't save alone: Commitment in rotating savings and credit associations in Kenya. *Economic Development and Cultural Change, 55*(2), 251–282.

Hossein, C. S. (2017). Fringe banking in Canada: A study of Rotating Savings and Credit Association (ROSCAsAs) in Toronto's inner suburbs. *Canadian Journal of Nonprofit and Social Economy Research, 8*(1), 29–43.

Iwara, I. O. (2020). *Towards a model for successful enterprises centred on entrepreneurs' exogenous and endogenous attributes: Case of Vhembe District, South Africa*. Doctoral dissertation, University of Venda.

Iwara, I. O., & Netshandama, V. O. (2021). Small-enterprise capital mobilization and marketing in rural areas: A review synthesis of Stokvel model. *Academy of Entrepreneurship Journal, 27*(2), 1–12.

Iwara, I. O., Adeola, O., & Netshandama, V. O. (2021). Traditional savings association for entrepreneurial success in Africa: A case study of Rotative Stokvel enterprise. *Academy of Entrepreneurship Journal, 27*(2), 1–15.

Kariuki, P., & Ofusori, L. O. (2017, March). WhatsApp-operated stokvels promoting youth entrepreneurship in Durban, South Africa: Experiences of young entrepreneurs. In *Proceedings of the 10th International Conference on Theory and Practice of Electronic Governance* (pp. 253–259).

Koenane, M. L. (2019). Economic development in Africa through the Stokvel system: 'our' indigenous way or 'theirs'. Filosofia Theoretica. *Journal of African Philosophy, Culture and Religions, 8*(1), 109–124.

Kok, L., & Lebusa, M. (2018). *The savings schemes clubs (Stokvels) in South Africa: The Stokvels as an informal way to finance black entrepreneurship in South Africa.* LAP Lambert Academic Publishing.

Ledeneva, A. (Ed.). (2018). *Esusu—Global encyclopaedia of informality, volume 2: Towards understanding of social and cultural complexity*. UCL Press.

Lindeque, M. (2019). *WhatsApp Stokvels: How fraudsters use group chats to steal money*. Eye Witness News. https://ewn.co.za/2019/10/09/whatsapp-stokvels-how-fraudsters-use-group-chats-to-steal-money.

Luthuli, S. N. (2017). *Stokvel groups as a poverty reduction strategy in rural communities: A case of uMlalazi Municipality, KwaZulu-Natal*, Doctoral dissertation.

Matuku, S., & Kaseke, E. (2014). The role of Stokvels in improving people's lives: The case in orange farm, Johannesburg, South Africa. *Social Work, 50*(4), 504–515.

Menze, A., & Tsibolane, P. (2019). Online stokvels: The use of social media by the marginalized. In *CONF-IRM* (p. 26).

Moloi, T. P. (2011). *An exploration of group dynamics in "stokvels" and its implications on the members' mental health and psychological well-being* (Doctoral dissertation, University of Zululand).

Moses, C., Akinbode, M., & Obigbemi, I. F. (2015). Indigeneous financing; an effective strategy for achieving the entrepreneurial objectives of SSEs. *Journal of Entrepreneurship: Research & Practice*, 1–12.

Mulaudzi, R. (2017). *From consumers to investors: an investigation into the character and nature of Stokvels in South Africa's urban, peri-urban and rural centres using a phenomenological approach*, Doctoral dissertation, University of Cape Town.

Mungiru, J. W., & Njeru, A. (2015). Effects of informal finance on the performance of small and medium enterprises in Kiambu County. *International Journal of Scientific and Research Publications, 5*(11), 338–362.

NASASA. (2018). *The national Stokvels association of South Africa*. http://nasasa.co.za/site/#intro.

Ramagoshi, R. (2016). Stokvels in the African communities: This is how we do it. *Plus 50, 11*(4), 51.

Rodima-Taylor, D. (2020, January 21–23). *African informal 'sharing economies' and the advent of the digital age.* In International symposium Informal financial markets: Now and then. From pre-banking to bitcoins, Umeå University.

Sile, I., & Bett, J. (2015). Determinants of informal finance use in Kenya. *Research Journal of Finance and Accounting,* 6–19.

Smets, P. (2000). ROSCAs as a source of housing finance for the urban poor: An analysis of self-help practices from Hyderabad, India. *Community Development Journal, 35*(1), 16–30.

Storchi, S (2018). *Impact evaluation of savings groups and Stokvels in South Africa.* http://saveact.org.za/wp-content/uploads/2018/11/FMT_Stokvels-and-SGs-Report_10-October-2018_final.pdf.

Thomas, A. (2015). Revolving loan scheme (Esusu): A subtitute to the Nigerian commercial banking? *Journal of Business and Management, 17*(6), 62–67.

UNESCO. (2012). *Intangible cultural heritage: Decision of the intergovernmental committee: 7.COM 8.6.* https://ich.unesco.org/en/Decisions/7.COM/8.6.

Van Wyk, M. M. (2017). Stokvels as a community-based saving club aimed at eradicating poverty: A case of South African rural women. *The International Journal of Community Diversity, 17*(2), 13–26.

8

Banking the Cocoa Farmer in Ghana: The Role of Mobile Technology

Robert E. Hinson and Louis Numelio Tettey

8.1 Introduction

In sub-Saharan Africa, cell phone coverage and acceptance have surged remarkably over the last decade (PWC, 2016). Till 1999, below one per cent of the population had access to a cell phone, and this has risen to above 55 per cent (GSMA, 2009). Mobile phone acceptance and usage in Ghana, in particular, have surged from 150,000 mobile phone subscribers in 2000 to around eleven million subscribers in 2009 (Narteh et al., 2017; Wireless Intelligence, 2012). This figure keeps increasing owing to the services of telecommunications operators spreading across the continent. Mobile banking technology is one such novel service

R. E. Hinson · L. N. Tettey (✉)
University of Ghana Business School, Accra, Ghana
e-mail: lntettey@ug.edu.gh

R. E. Hinson
e-mail: rhinson@ug.edu.gh

O. Adeola et al. (eds.), *Digital Service Delivery in Africa*, Palgrave Studies of Marketing in Emerging Economies,
https://doi.org/10.1007/978-3-030-83909-3_8

offered through the mobile phone. Mobile technology is a technology that is portable and lets users perform several tasks (Hur, 2019). In inference, it is a mobile technological device that enables its users to carry out different tasks.

In recent years, the formal banking sector in Ghana has seen some positive marginal growth (from 14.9 per cent in February 2018 to 15.2 per cent in February 2019) (Bank of Ghana, 2019). Yet, there is a low rate of penetration of banking activities. There is an increase in account ownership from 29 per cent in 2011 to 58 per cent in 2017 (Demirgüç-Kunt et al., 2018). Nonetheless, financial inclusion, especially among rural cocoa farmers in Ghana, remained low. This is primarily due to the financial institutions' location drawback, low educational levels of rural farmers, absence of collateral required for loans, inability to save owing to rural farmers' insecure incomes, and other explanatory as well as personal risks (Okello et al., 2010).

A study in the Philippines reveals that without access to proper financial services or products, farmers in the rural areas can resort to money lenders or loan sharks, as well as friends and families who could lend to them on some conditions (see Owens, 2007). An example of good financial services or products lacking by rural cocoa farmers in Ghana is mobile banking technology. Some studies have revealed that mobile technology adoption influences agricultural activities (see Lomotey et al., 2018; Peprah et al., 2020; Issahaku et al., 2018). For example, it enhances the welfare, wealth, and farm output of smallholder cocoa farmers (Peprah et al., 2020). It helps boost some of the economic outcomes of smallholder farmers that are important to poverty reduction and rural development (Peprah et al., 2020). It also enhances the productivity of rural farmers and helps cocoa farmers to maximise the quantity and quality of agricultural yield (Issahaku et al., 2018; Lomotey et al., 2018). Consequently, policymakers and stakeholders are now interested in the development of mobile technology to address infrastructural voids that impede an all-inclusive financial system, especially in underdeveloped and low-income nations (Peprah et al., 2020).

Contemporary technology and telecommunications have now made it possible to bank the unbanked and make available financial services to the deprived rural farmers. For example, mobile technology such as cell phones and other digital media permit smallholder agrarian farmers to use financial services without going to a bank (Kirui et al., 2012). Interestingly, mobile technology (m-money) plays a vital role in the cocoa value chain. It enhances proficiency and accountability and offers cocoa farmers access to structured savings accounts, micro-credit, and insurance (WCF, 2015). However, regardless of the moderately progressive state of mobile technology and the high level of knowledge of it among farmers in Ghana, the use of the service is presently restricted to personal money transfers and does not apply to farming activities or to the broader use of financial services that can boost their financial lives (WCF, 2015).

There are several studies on mobile technology: mobile technology and smart agriculture, mobile money and agriculture productivity, mobile money and welfare of smallholder farmers, mobile phone technology and agriculture, among others (see Peprah et al., 2020; Issahaku et al., 2018; Narteh et al., 2017). Authors such as Lomotey et al. (2018) believe that there is an enormous lacuna between agriculture production and the adoption of appropriate aiding mobile technology among farmers in Ghana. This chapter responds to such a claim by emphasising the benefits of mobile technology adoption by rural cocoa farmers in the context of an emerging economy.

8.2 Literature Review

8.2.1 Ghana's Cocoa Sector

The general saying that "Cocoa is Ghana, Ghana is Cocoa" reveals the magnitude of cocoa production in Ghana (Lundstedt & Pärssinen, 2009). In the world cocoa market, Ghana is considered as one of the largest suppliers of cocoa and employs millions of people in its cocoa sector (ibid.). Not only are small-scale farmers reliant on cocoa proceeds, but so is the Ghanaian economy since cocoa became Ghana's primary source of export revenue in 2004 (Lundstedt & Pärssinen, 2009). Cocoa trees, indigenous to South America, first arrived in Ghana in 1876. Since then, the cocoa sector has grown rapidly, and today it forms a core part of the Ghanaian economy (Waldron et al., 2020). Cocoa production is the main export of agro-based products in Ghana and accounts for over USD 2.2 billion in 2011 (Lomotey et al., 2018; McKinley et al., 2016). In 2015, the nation was the second-largest cocoa producer in the world and production is expected to increase to 850,000–900,000 tonnes in the coming years (Oludare, 2016). In 2018, Ghana exported USD 2.4 billion worth of raw cocoa beans, constituting 26 per cent of world production and second only to Côte d'Ivoire in value (UN Comtrade, 2020). With such demand, in Ghana, cocoa is not only seen as a state economic sustenance but the sole source of income for millions of people in the cocoa farming value chain (Lomotey et al., 2018; McKinley et al., 2016).

It is thus anticipated that cocoa producers in Ghana will make use of new technological tools to increase yield as well as mobile technology for their business transactions. Amazingly, there is a vast lacuna between stakeholders in cocoa production and the adoption of current technology in Ghana. Peprah (2015) and Nana, Asuming-Brempong and Nantui (2013) posit that the educational status of farmers in Ghana compromises their adoption and use of new technology and knowledge expansion. In complementing the above, a more recent study by Peprah et al. (2020) pinpoints a higher than the basic level of education as an important factor influencing the acceptance of mobile technology among Ghanaian smallholder farmers. An observation by Lomotey et al. (2018) shows that although most countries, including the UK, are greatly adopting technologies such as mobile technology for agriculture yield maximisation and other benefits, the same could not be said of Ghana. From the above, it is evident that there is little work on mobile banking technology and cocoa farmers in Ghana. This paper then contributes to the literature on mobile banking technology usage by Ghanaian cocoa farmers by considering how it can be leveraged to improve digital financial services delivery to the cocoa farmers in the cocoa value chain.

8.2.2 Mobile Technology Adoption and Cocoa Farmers in Ghana

The dawn of "CocoaLink" exposed the enthusiasm of farmers in Ghana to the usage of cell phones, suggesting the likely adoption of mobile technology (Peprah et al., 2020). For farmers in Ghana, the use of cell phones is not recent. The Ghana Cocoa Board initiated the "CocoaLink (an outreach program)" in 2010 to deliver cell phone services to farmers (Peprah et al., 2020). For two-way interaction, the service makes use of voice as well as text messages via a particular short-code on the cell phone. It enables cocoa farmers to "send text or photo inquiries" directly to experts for diagnosis and obtain accurate and appropriate agricultural as well as other relevant information (Peprah et al., 2020). "CocoaLink's" messaging platform is supplemented by weekly training sessions aimed at equipping farmers with knowledge on cell phone usage, social issues such as child labour and agronomy, among others.

Since rural cocoa farmers have no access to the conventional banking system, we believe that mobile technology could provide them with alternative banking services. Bankole et al. (2011) contend that in determining the adoption behaviour of mobile banking users, culture plays a vital role. By inference, we envisaged that certain cultural factors or variables would affect cocoa farmers' adoption of mobile technology through the acceptance model process (refer to Fig. 8.1). Among these external cultural issues is cocoa farmers' perception that banks are for "the rich" and, as such, banks are not for them (Lonie et al., 2018). The level of education of cocoa farmers could compromise their adoption of mobile technology (Peprah, 2015; Peprah et al., 2020) since they need some level of knowledge to aid them in operating the technology. Self-efficacy, such as the ability of a cocoa farmer to own and use a mobile phone (Issahaku et al., 2018), is essential. Non-availability of banks branches in their rural locations will necessitate them to travel to the nearest city to transact business which most often comes at a cost (Peprah et al., 2020) and causes a delay in receiving payment from licensed buying companies (LBCs) for the sales of their yield among others. In short, all these factors may, one way or the other, affect the adoption of mobile banking technology by cocoa farmers. Aside from this, we also propose that other

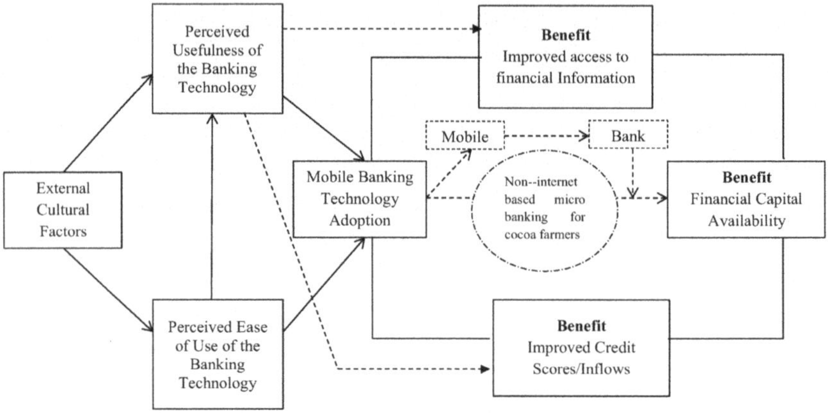

Fig. 8.1 Cocoa farmer access to mobile banking technology benefit (CFAMBTB) model (*Source* Authors)

factors, such as perceived usefulness and ease of use of mobile banking technology could also affect the adoption of mobile technology by cocoa farmers.

Smallholders typically own small-scale land plots and depend mainly on household labour for the growing of subsistence crops along with some other cash crops. Smallholder farmers' production systems are characterised by the usage of essential, outdated technologies, high seasonal labour fluctuations, low returns, and women playing a significant part in the production process (Peprah et al., 2016). Also, smallholder farmers differ in characteristics, farm size, livestock, and off-farm activities, allocation of resources between food and cash crops, the use of external inputs and hired labour, patterns of household spending, and share of sold food crops (Peprah et al., 2016).

According to Asuming-Brempong et al. (2004), smallholder farming is described in Ghana as "based on the method of preserving soil fertility and the level of technology". They describe such features of agricultural systems as land-use patterns, yield, capital inputs, the permanence, and impermanence of cultivation rights and strength of cultivation.

8.2.3 Mobile Money in the Cocoa Value Chain

Dissimilar to the "CocoaLink messaging platform", conventional mobile money services offer the means for sending and receiving money and also making payments. In this study, the researcher's definition of mobile money is in line with Gosavi (2018), who described mobile money as a "mobile phone-based financial tool that can transfer money safely and quickly across a wide geographical area". In Ghana, three major telecommunications companies (MTN Ghana, Tigo/Airtel, and Vodafone Ghana) are currently offering mobile money services. MTN is the market leader with the widest coverage across the country. Since the passage of the "Electronic-Money Issuers and Agents Guidelines" in July 2015 to take over from the 2008 "Branchless Banking Guidelines", mobile money in Ghana has experienced a bolster.

A study conducted by the World Cocoa Foundation discloses that cell phone ownership is high among cocoa farmers in Ghana. Cell phone ownership far exceeds the populace's level of involvement in the formal banking system. The high presence of cell phone ownership among these cocoa farmers and the low levels of financial inclusion presents a great market opportunity for mobile money in Ghana (WCF, 2015). Furthermore, per the World Cocoa Foundation report in 2015, there is a high level of cognisance of mobile money services by cocoa growers in Ghana (out of 520 cocoa farmers surveyed in Ghana and Côte d'Ivoire, 80 per cent or 416 were aware of mobile money). This finding is consistent with other researchers who posit that there is enormous market growth in mobile money in Ghana. The mobile money products brands in Ghana are so apparent to the extent that some farmers appeared to perplex the Mobile Network Operators (MNOs) universal telecommunications product with the unique offering of mobile money (WCF, 2015).

Notwithstanding the high level of cognisance of the mobile money services, the study revealed that mobile money adoption by cocoa farmers in Ghana is low. In another 2018 report of WCF, less than 50 per cent of cocoa farmers surveyed carried out a mobile money transaction. The primary use by those using mobile money was to send and receive money connected to non-farming activities (WCF, 2018). In essence, the low-level acceptance of mobile money services by the cocoa farmers is not because of the unavailability of access to the service, but rather due to the farmers' restricted perspective of the service offerings as only a money transfer service.

Undeniably, mobile money plays a significant role in the cocoa value chain. In other words, in the cocoa payment chain, mobile money payment services provide the likelihood of enhanced proficiency and transparency (WCF, 2015). Also, mobile money services can offer cocoa farmers access to structured savings accounts, micro-credit, and insurance; thus, mobile money banking can be a gateway to financial services that can enhance the livelihoods and communities (WCF, 2015). This is the right time to assess the potential and mechanism for integrating mobile money technology into the cocoa value chain due to the maturing mobile money market and growing levels of customer awareness. Cocoa purchasers have started to explore the usage of mobile money as a mode of paying Côte d'Ivoire's cocoa-producing farmers. In Ghana, there is a high interest among mobile money service providers to reach farmers in the cocoa-producing area with their mobile money services packages (WCF, 2015). For instance, In Côte d'Ivoire, Orange has partnered with at least two cocoa buyers as a means to motivate the usage of mobile money by farmers for their produce transactions (Lonie et al., 2018).

In Ghana, Mobile Network Operators (MNOs) have shown a high interest in cocoa farmers' mobile money uptake, and numerous pilots are said to be ongoing. Still, the product reach for this segment has yet to be expanded. Also, Ghana COCOBOD has realised the difficulty of providing cocoa farmers with financial services and has expressed its support for the Cocoa Sika digital payment platform proposed by MTN. MTN aims to work with COCOBOD through the digital payment concept of Cocoa Sika to cooperate on bulk mobile payments and bulk SMS messaging to incorporate information at all phases in the cocoa chain payment procedure, including approvals and payment updates (WCF, 2015).

8.3 Cocoa Farmer Access to Mobile Banking Technology Benefit (CFAMBTB) Model

8.3.1 Perceived Usefulness of Mobile Banking Technology

Perceived usefulness is described by Venkatesh and Davis (1996), as "the extent to which a person perceives that adopting a system or technology will enhance their job performance/productivity". Per the view of Tobbin and Kowornu (2011), the desire to use mobile technology, specifically mobile money, will rise if the trust in its usefulness also rises. From the conceptual model in (Fig. 8.1), we assume that when a person perceives banking technology as easy to use, the person will appreciate its usefulness more. Nonetheless, literature indicates that the adoption of mobile payment is positively correlated with perceived usefulness (Kim et al., 2010; Narteh et al., 2017; Padashetty & Kishore, 2013). In the CFAMBTB model (Fig. 8.1), we suggest that mobile technology, compared to the traditional banking system, will be much more beneficial to the cocoa farmers by helping them receive quick payment for the sales of their yield from licensed buying companies (LBCs). This, in turn, will allow them to quickly buy their inputs and start the cycle of growing and selling.

Additionally, they no longer need to use their productive hours in a queue in banks to transact their business, thus saving them time. Also, there are other services embedded in mobile technology that will be of much benefit to them. For example, they can use mobile money platforms to pay their personal expenses such as school fees for their children or receive remittance money from family and supporters worldwide.

8.3.2 Perceived Ease of Use of Mobile Banking Technology

Perceived ease of use is the magnitude to which a person trusts that a system would be simple to use and that to facilitate its acceptance or adoption, the system should not be complicated (Carter & Belanger,

2004; Rogers, 1995). This implies that little effort should be required to use a specific type of technology by the user (Liu & Li, 2010; Narteh et al., 2017). In the view of scholars such as Taylor and Todd (1995) and Davis (1993), this effort may be mental and physical. By implication, from the proposed framework (Fig. 8.1), we suggest that for cocoa farmers to adopt and use mobile technology; the person should see the mobile technology to be easy to use with minimal technical knowledge or effort. Therefore, in the (CFAMBTB) model, perceived ease of use includes accessibility of mobile technology in rural areas, a simple registration process for mobile banking platforms, a streamlined payment process, and banking platforms that can be operated on low-tech phones. In short, we believe that perceived ease of use of the banking technology will impact cocoa farmers' behavioural intention of adoption.

8.3.3 Mobile Banking Technology Explained

According to Redmond and Henson (2018), "mobile technology is any information and communication technology that is battery operated and can be used without power in a range of locations. Mobile Technologies can range from laptops to mobile phones, to Apple watches". In this article, mobile technology in the CFAMBTB model (Fig. 8.1) is conceptualised as portable technology (to be more specific, any cell phone that either supports the internet or not) that helps users (cocoa farmers) to perform any financial transactions digitally everywhere they are. In the CFAMBTB model, mobile banking technology is proposed as an alternative to the traditional banking services for the rural cocoa farmers in Ghana, to close their financial inclusion gap. With this technology, cocoa farmers can always transact business on their phones everywhere they are at any time.

8.4 Benefits of Mobile Technology to Stakeholders Involved in the Cocoa Value Chain in Emerging Market

8.4.1 Benefit for COCOBOD

In Ghana, COCOBOD is the sole purchaser of all Ghanaian cocoa from licensed buying companies (LBCs) which it then sells to domestic and foreign processors. The adoption of mobile banking technology by cocoa farmers will eventually improve the efficiency of COCOBOD by ensuring greater security and transparency, better fraud detection, higher personal security, and transparent and traceable transactions within the cocoa value chain. This will eventually lead to an increase in revenue to the government as a consequence of the growth of suppliers through financial capital availability or easy access to capital.

8.4.2 Benefit for Banks

Mobile banking technology will help the bank determine the creditworthiness of cocoa farmers, allowing banks to assess farmers' affordability and repayment timelines for loans. Banks no longer have to set up their physical branches in all rural communities where these cocoa farmers live. They could instead partner with telecommunication networks such as MTN, Vodafone, and AirtelTigo to strengthen their resources and widen the coverage area of the services.

8.4.3 Benefits for Licensed Buying Companies (LBCs) and Local Purchasing Companies (LPCs)

It is prudent to mention that other actors in the cocoa value chain will also benefit from the CFAMBTB model. The model is also intended to encourage licensed buying companies (LBCs) to move from the conventional cash-based method of payment to the use of digital means (mobile technology, banks, or both). According to the World Cocoa Foundation, in the status quo scheme, the LBC, which buys cocoa on behalf of upstream processors, receives its payments digitally from those processors, mainly via bank transfers (WCF, 2015). However, purchases further down the supply chain appear to be in cash from that point onwards (Buruku et al., 2020). In the current scenario, the vast volumes of cash that pass through this supply chain expose district offices (DOs), purchasing clerks (PCs) and even, to some extent, farmers to major risks of fraud and insecurity. Due to this, at each point in the supply chain, LBCs lose because of the inability to track funds. The status quo is still focused on paper receipts, which are unreliable and make audits more difficult. In all, adopting mobile technology will prevent LBCs and PCs from physical cash theft and insecurity for all the actors in the cocoa value supply chain.

8.4.4 Benefits for Cocoa Farmers

Some scholars have documented the evidence of the benefits of mobile technology (such as m-money, among others) adoption by consumers (see Adaba et al., 2019; Kikulwe et al., 2014; Narteh et al., 2017). A more recent one by Peprah et al. (2020) found that the adoption of mobile technology such as mobile money has an enhancing effect on cocoa farmers' wealth, welfare, and farm output in Ghana. This study further adds to the benefits of mobile technology adoption by cocoa farmers in Ghana. From the CFAMBTB model (Fig. 8.1), we suggest that the adoption and usage of mobile technology as an alternative banking service will aid the cocoa farmers to get improved access to financial information and, thus, bridge the information asymmetry gap. This is so because after a cocoa farmer adopts the mobile technology if he/she needs any information related to their accounts and the services available, all that he/she needs is to dial a code on their phone. Within a few seconds, he/she gets the information. This is far superior to the traditional banking system, where the customer will have to walk to the bank and speaks to a representative who sometimes may give incomplete or incorrect information, creating an information gap. Also, it will amount to improved credit scores/inflow to the cocoa farmer since all their transaction records are kept and can be traced. The usefulness of the enhanced scores/inflows is that it can be used to determine the creditworthiness of a cocoa farmer, which can allow them to quickly access loans from banks for the expansion of their business.

8.5 Implications for the African Continent

Generally, in the African cocoa supply chain, payment is mostly dominated by physical cash. In the status quo mode of the payment system, it is only licensed buying companies (LBCs) that receive payment through digital means, to be more specific, through a bank transfer (Buruku et al., 2020). The rest of the actors (purchasing clerks, district officers, and farmers) in the supply chain tend to transact business in cash. The huge amount of physical cash that district officers, purchasing clerks, and farmers will have to deal with exposes them to a significant risk of robbery and other forms of danger (Buruku et al., 2020). The risk situation outlined above demonstrates the dire need for the actors in the cocoa supply chain on the African continent to embrace mobile banking technology to be safe and to promote transparency. This study requests the use of a digital mode of payment (mobile banking technology) for cocoa farmers, instead of the current traditional cash-based method.

Also, policy decisions in the leading cocoa-producing countries in Africa should consider expanding mobile banking technology services to smallholder cocoa farmers in rural areas. This can be achieved by enhancing education and advertisement on the benefits of the use of mobile banking technology to cocoa farmers through community-based organisations as well as community radio.

8.6 Conclusion

Ghana's cocoa sector, despite its many challenges, has a fantastic opportunity to adopt digital financial services across the supply chain, thereby strengthening businesses, boosting income and financial inclusion, and driving economic opportunities and development. This article proposes mobile banking technology to the deprived cocoa farmers in the rural areas of Ghana as an alternative to traditional banking services. This, as laid out in the study, will promote improved access to financial information, hence, bridge the information asymmetry gap, and improve farmers' credit scores/inflow, which will eventually get them access to loans (easy access to capital) to expand their farming activities. Overall, the adoption of Mobile banking technology by cocoa farmers will lead to the avoidance of the high risk associated with the traditional cash payment method and remote access to financial services. This article provides a significant contribution to theory as well as policy articulation. The conceptualisation of a model (Cocoa Farmers Access to Mobile Banking Technology Benefit) of mobile banking technology services for the disadvantaged cocoa farmers in the rural areas of emerging economy countries is the theoretical contribution. The chapter suggests that this model may help develop pathways to improve financial access to the locationally disadvantaged rural cocoa farmers. Future studies should aim at empirically testing the Cocoa Farmers Access to Mobile Banking Technology Benefit (CFAMBTB) model proposed in this article to evaluate its usefulness in the provision of digital financial services to deprived cocoa farmers.

Acknowledgements This work was supported by NWO-WOTRO project "Information transparency system as a low-cost scalable solution to farmers' access to credit and services in Ghana", Application number W08.250.203.

References

Adaba, G. B., Ayoung, D. A., & Abbott, P. (2019). Exploring the contribution of mobile money to well-being from a capability perspective. *The Electronic Journal of Information Systems in Developing Countries*, *85*(4), e12079.

Asuming-Brempong, S., Al-Hassan, R., Sarpong, D. B., Kwadzo, G. T. M., Akoena, S. K. K., Sakyi-Dawson, O., ... & Ashley, S. (2004). Poverty and Social Impact Analysis (PSIA) studies for Ghana: Economic transformation of the agricultural sector. In *Final report submitted to National Planning Development Commission, Ministry of Food and Agriculture and DFID*, Accra, Ghana.

Bank of Ghana. (2019). *Banking sector report*. Bank of Ghana.

Bankole, F. O., Bankole, O. O., & Brown, I. (2011). Mobile banking adoption in Nigeria. *The Electronic Journal of Information Systems in Developing Countries, 47*(1), 1–23.

Buruku, B., Chaintreau, M., & Kahonde, O (2020). *Digitizing payments in Ghana's cocoa supply chain-four building blocks for responsible and scalable digitization*. Better Than Cash Alliance.

Carter, L., & Belanger, F. (2004). The influence of perceived characteristics of innovating on e-government adoption. *Electronic Journal of E-Government, 2*(1), 11–20.

Davis, F. D. (1993). User acceptance of information technology: System characteristics, user perceptions and behavioral impacts. *International Journal of Man-Machine Studies, 38*(3), 475–487.

Demirguc-Kunt, A., Klapper, L., Singer, D., Ansar, S., & Hess, J. (2018). *The global findex database 2017: Measuring financial inclusion and the fintech revolution*. The World Bank.

Gosavi, A. (2018). Can mobile money help firms mitigate the problem of access to finance in Eastern sub-Saharan Africa? *Journal of African Business, 19*(3), 343–360. https://doi.org/10.1080/15228916.2017.1396791.

GSMA. (2009). *GSMA announces that global mobile connections surpass 5 billion*. www.gsmworld.com/newsroom/press-releases/2010/5265.htm on 1 November, 2020.

Hur, J. W. (2019). Mobile technology integration and English language learners: A case study. In *Early childhood development: Concepts, methodologies, tools, and applications* (pp. 1049–1065). IGI Global.

Issahaku, H., Abu, B. M., & Nkegbe, P. K. (2018). Does the use of mobile phones by smallholder maize farmers affect productivity in Ghana? *Journal of African Business, 19*(3), 302–322.

Kikulwe, E. M., Fischer, E., & Qaim, M. (2014). Mobile money, smallholder farmers, and household welfare in Kenya. *PloS one, 9*(10), e109804.

Kim, C., Mirusmonov, M., & Lee, I. (2010). An empirical examination of factors influencing the intention to use mobile payment. *Computers in Human Behavior, 26*(3), 310–322.

Kirui, O. K., Okello, J. J., & Nyikal, R. A. (2012). Awareness of mobile phone-based money transfer services in agriculture by smallholder farmers in Kenya. *International Journal of ICT Research and Development in Africa (IJICTRDA), 3*(1), 1–13.

Liu, Y., & Li, H. (2010). Mobile internet diffusion in China: An empirical study. *Industrial Management & Data Systems, 110*(3), 309–324.

Lomotey, R. K., Mammay, A., & Orji, R. (2018). Mobile technology for smart agriculture: Deployment case for cocoa production. *International Journal of Sustainable Agricultural Management and Informatics, 4*(2), 83–97.

Lonie, S., Martinez, M., Oulai, R., & Tullis, C. (2018). *Opportunities for digital financial services in the cocoa value chain in Côte d'Ivoire: Insights from new data.* World Bank.

Lundstedt, H., & Pärssinen, S. (2009). Cocoa is Ghana, Ghana is cocoa-evaluating reforms of the Ghanaian cocoa sector. *Lund University Publications Student Papers.* http://lup.lub.lu.se/student-papers/record/1511300.

McKinley, J., Nalley, L. L., Asare, R. A., Dixon, B. L., Popp, J. S., & D'Haese, M. (2016). Managing risk in cocoa production: Assessing the potential of climate-smart crop insurance in Ghana. *J. Int. Agric. Trade Dev, 10*, 53–79.

Nana, Y. C. F., Asuming-Brempong, S., & Nantui, M. F. (2013). Analysis of cocoa-based agricultural knowledge and information systems in the eastern region of Ghana. *Russian Journal of Agricultural and Socio-Economic Sciences, 14*(2).

Narteh, B., Mahmoud, M. A., & Amoh, S. (2017). Customer behavioural intentions towards mobile money services adoption in Ghana. *The Service Industries Journal, 37*(7–8), 426–447.

Okello, J. J., Ofwona-Adera, E., Mbatia, O. L., & Okello, R. M. (2010). Using ICT to integrate smallholder farmers into agricultural value Chain: The case of DrumNet project in Kenya. *International Journal of ICT Research and Development in Africa (IJICTRDA), 1*(1), 23–37.

Oludare, M. (2016). *Ghana to expand cocoa production coverage—Industry regulator, global financial digest* [online]. http://www.globalfinancialdigest.com/2016/02/ghana-to-expandcocoa-production.html.

Owens, J. (2007, September 17–19). *Leapfrogging access to finance with mobile phone technology: Philippine rural banks offering M-banking & M-commerce services.* Presentation at IFC/CGAP Conference (pp. 17–19), Washington, DC.

Padashetty, S., & Kishore, K. S. (2013). An empirical study on consumer adoption of mobile payments in Bangalore city-A case study. *Researchers World, 4*(1), 83.

Peprah, J. A., Afoakwah, C., & Koomson, I. (2016). Crop yield volatility among smallholder farmers in Ghana. *United Nations University Institute for Natural Resources in Africa*. ISBN: 9789988633110.

Peprah, J. A., Oteng, C., & Sebu, J. (2020). Mobile money, output and welfare among smallholder farmers in Ghana. *SAGE Open, 10*(2), 2158244020931114.

Peprah, K. (2015). Sustainability of cocoa farmers' livelihoods: A case study of Asunafo district, Ghana. *Sustainable Production and Consumption, 4*, 2–15.

PWC. (2016). *Ghana banking survey: How to win in era of mobile money*. https://www.pwc.com/gh/en/assets/pdf/2016-banking-survey-report.pdf on 1 November, 2020.

Redmond, T. A., & Henson, J. (2018). Innovations in mobile photography for digital-age teachers and learners. In J. Keengwe (Ed.), *Handbook of research on mobile technology, constructivism, and meaningful learning* (pp. 90–105). IGI Global.

Rogers, E. M. (1995). *Diffusion of innovations* (4th ed.). Free Press.

Taylor, S., & Todd, P. (1995). Assessing IT usage: The role of prior experience. *MIS quarterly*, 561–570.

Tobbin, P., & Kuwornu, J. K. (2011). Adoption of mobile money transfer technology: Structural equation modeling approach. *European Journal of Business and Management, 3*(7), 59–77.

UN Comtrade. (2020). *International trade statistics database*. https://comtrade.un.org/data.

Venkatesh, V., & Davis, F. D. (1996). A model of the antecedents of perceived ease of use: Development and test. *Decision Sciences, 27*(3), 451–481.

Waldron, D., Chaintreau, M., & Kahonde, O. (2020). *The hidden costs of cash to Ghana's cocoa sector*. Better Than Cash Alliance.

Wireless Intelligence. (2012). *Dashboard, Africa*. https://wirelessintelligence.com/analysis/2012/04/dashboard-africa-2012 on November 1, 2020.

World Cocoa Foundation (2015*). Mobile money market for the world cocoa foundation final report*. Strategic Impact Advisors.

World Cocoa Foundation. (2018). *Future of mobile money for cocoa farmers in Côte d'Ivoire, Ghana*. https://www.cgap.org/blog/future-mobile-money-cocoa-farmers-cote-d'Ivoire-ghana.

9

Strategy in Digital Business—The East African Perspective

Paul Katuse

9.1 Introduction

Digital business entails the integration of digital technology in business practices to generate new value in business models. This integration enhances internal capabilities and business operations and in turn customer experiences. Chaffey et al. (2019) differentiated the term digital business from e-business by arguing that digital business has a broader scope than e-business. Digital business as a terminology was first coined by IBM in 1997. There is a very minimal difference between digital business and traditional information technology (IT). Digital business entails the integration of the buy-side e-commerce, intranet, and sell-side e-commerce. The buy-side entails the supplier value management,

P. Katuse (✉)
United States International University-Africa, Nairobi, Kenya

Chandaria School of Business, United States International University-Africa, Nairobi, Kenya

O. Adeola et al. (eds.), *Digital Service Delivery in Africa*, Palgrave Studies of Marketing in Emerging Economies,
https://doi.org/10.1007/978-3-030-83909-3_9

the intranet entails the organisational processes and functioning units, and the sell-side e-commerce entails the management of the interaction of the customer value chain activities. Therefore, digital business is about applying digital technology and media geared towards improving the competitiveness of the organisation through the optimisation of internal processes with online and traditional channels to market and supply. Converting analogue systems and information from physical to digital systems is called digitisation, whereas the utilisation of digitised data and technologies to influence workflow, transform customers and organisation interaction and engagement, and build better streams of revenue is called digitalisation.

The emergence of digitisation in eastern Africa can be traced to the mid-1980s. It was preceded by the IMF/World Bank initiated changes through structural adjustment programmes (SAPs) and enhanced structural adjustment facilities (ESAF) in the mid-1990s. In its early days, digitisation came to the east African business sphere enveloped as ICT. However, it was not until the mid-2000s when mobile phone affordability and governments' policy frameworks coupled with the growth of telecommunication companies that the need for digitisation was felt in a significant manner. Kenya got connected to the World Wide Web in October 1995, by means of a leased connection line providing internet for the first time at 32 Kbps (Mureithi, 2017). *Celtel* was the first firm to offer mobile telephone services in May 1995 (International Telecommunications Union, 2001). Tanzania was connected in 1995 (Sheriff, 2008) and Rwanda in 1996 (Mlay et al., 2013). The bandwidth of these systems was very low compared to today.

Digitalisation in East Africa by African-owned businesses still lags behind their peers. According to Banga and Velde (2018), there still is a window of opportunity to develop the less automated sectors in Africa. This window, however, may have a short duration. A comparative example in furniture manufacturing is the difference between Kenya and the US. In the US, the use of robots is likely to become cheaper than US labour by the year 2023; the Kenyan inflection point only comes a decade later, that is, in 2034, clearly indicating a window of opportunity, which is approximately ten years later. Robots financing and operating costs in the US are likely to become cheaper than wages in Kenya in manufacturing by around 2033. Accordingly, the inflection point for Ethiopia would be between 2038 and 2042, indicating a variance in digitalisation adoption and diffusion in different African countries. The African Digital Maturity report (Siemens, 2017), stipulates that African countries are at different levels of digital maturity comparatively. In the report, countries were categorised as emerging, developing, established, and advanced in their level of digitalisation. The difference is a clear indication of specific designs and patterns; and also, levels of digital preparedness or literacy in each country. The enhancement of access for customers to products and services, and suppliers to manufacturers have been quickened by increased broadband and fourth-generation (4G) networks and systems. The comparison of broadband penetration and 4G coverage in Rwanda and Kenya showed that without affordability, access alone does not have any impact. For instance, the rollout of 4G technology in Rwanda is almost 100 per cent compared to that of Kenya at 53 per cent, whereas broadband penetration in Rwanda (11.3 per cent) is less than half of Kenya's (47.8 per cent) (Mkalama & Ndemo, 2020).

It is under digitalisation that the elements of McKinsey 7S model can be appropriated. Abidin et al. (2015) argued that the McKinsey model is divided into seven areas of regions "soft" and "hard" element within the organisation. Strategy, structure, and system are the hard elements whereas staff, skills, shared values, and style are the soft elements. The hard elements are more infrastructural in outlook whereas the soft elements deal more with the human element and may be determined by the kind of people in the organisation. The emergence of business strategies oriented to technology such as business-to-business (B2B), business-to-customer (B2C), business-to-government (B2G), and business-to-employee (B2E) makes it possible to digitalise some aspects of the 7S model. Smartphone applications, e-commerce specialised websites, electronic marketplaces, and online auctions are practically the most exploited kinds of online platforms (Bresciani et al., 2016), which can be anchored on the proposed platformisation model (Adeola et al., 2021).

This chapter discusses the context of digitalisation processes in the East African marketing sector. It addresses the issues of digital value creation in marketing activities; the roles and challenges of digital business framework; and the importance of understanding a business's competitive landscape. The chapter uses Mckinsey 7S model as its basis and draws a parallel with the traditional strategy processes whose activities are focused on a firm's mission and vision. Finally, it provides recommendations on how organisations can use digitalisation to sustain their market positioning through platformisation and, consequently, deliver optimal services to their stakeholders.

9.2 The Influence of Digital Business on the Existing Marketing Sector

Digital business has had a multifaceted impact not only on the East African marketing front but also on the entire business sector. Shah (2018) argued that digital marketing guarantees a direct interconnection between firms and their consumers. Platforms thereof give appropriate opportunities for organisations' to connect with customers and get instantaneous feedback on the consumer's feelings. These help these organisations improve their overall performance.

The impact of digitalisation on players, resources and activities may be felt by an entire organisations' value chain. Pagani and Pardo (2017) proposed three main types of impacts of digitalisation. These are:

1. *Activity-links-centred digitalisation* when the digital resource optimises existing activities—for instance, the digital transformation centre of Rwanda (The Digital Transformation centre of Rwanda, 2020).
2. *Resource-ties-centred digitalisation* when the digital resource supports the creation of new activities—for instance, the mpesa academy in Kenya (Mpesa Foundation Academy, 2020)
3. *Actor-bonds-centred digitalisation* when the digital resource supports new bonds between actors—for instance, Uganda digital acceleration programme by the World Bank (The World Bank, 2020).

Grishikasvili, Dibbs and Meadows (2014) suggested that organisations require big data to make important business decisions for the exploitation of new commercial opportunities; To date, the coverage of 4G technology in East Africa is up 70 per cent of the population (OECD-Development Centre, 2021). The impact of digital technology has always varied from one industry to another. Businesses from various sectors and industries have continuously challenged the traditional marketing approaches and models and at the same time disrupting the digital landscape—brands such as Amazon, Airbnb, Netflix, Uber, and Deliveroo—by providing seamless crossover of offline and online activities (Briddle, 2017). East African examples are as *mpesa*, and *masoko* in Kenya, *abanista* and *kaymu* in Uganda, *zudua* in Tanzania, *iduka* in Rwanda, and *kukasoko* in Burundi. Digitalisation has spread its influence on many areas and activities of the business, a few of those areas, such as, costs, training, digital value creation, pricing, and pricing models.

9.3 Influence on Cost

The cost structure of businesses has been impacted by digitalisation and especially through the hard S's of the McKinsey model, i.e., strategy, structure, and system in a firm. Goldfarb and Tucker (2019) believe that digital technology, or the act of presenting information in binary digits or simply bits, has structurally lowered costs in five different cost centres in the marketplace. Felix (2018) corroborated this information when he established that, due to low levels of digitisation in Tanzania, businesses in Tanzania, compared to others in the East African region, had higher costs.

He proposed that both the Tanzania Communication and Regulatory Authority, alongside the private sector and other related stakeholders, could find out ways of promoting digitalisation in the Tanzanian economy. Sridhar and Fang (2019) corroborated this in their seminal paper on marketing strategies and digital environments. In 2020, the United Nations Capital Development Fund in 2016 published a case in Tanzania, which shows that increased digitalisation coupled with widespread adoption of Person-to-Government (P2G) and Business-to-Government (B2G) payments in Tanzania, focusing on the period from 2012 to 2016 helped reduce costs (United Nations Capital Development Fund, 2020). The five cost centres are:

1. **Information search costs.** The adoption of digital technology has created ease for individual business agents and firms in gathering information faster. For instance, customers can obtain and receive information on products and services at zero to minimal costs. Firms on the other side of the spectrum can also gather information on rivals' prices, at almost zero to no cost, on third-party websites and rivals' websites.
2. **Replication costs or the cost of producing goods.** With the advancement of digital technology, digital goods that have a marginal cost of almost zero have been created, as opposed to all physical goods, that have non-zero cost. For instance, software developers can recreate codes they own with zero direct cost by the use of open-source platforms. Their competitors can also obtain this same code at no cost also from open-source platforms.
3. **Transportation costs or the cost of information transportation and goods/product from one place to another.** As it is clearly evident, there is no physical distance deterrent for obtaining information on digital technology, goods, and products (e.g., physical products), services (e.g., in the hospitality industry), and expertise (e.g., skills of the workforce).
4. **Tracking costs or the costs incurred on obtaining stage/phase-by-stage/phase information on the production, stage of delivery, or readiness for utilisation of goods or services.** With reduced costs on tracking, it has become even easier for firms and industries to carry out activities such as customisation (e.g., of products like computing equipment, etc.), personalisation (e.g., for products like apparels and fashion, etc.), and also continuous customer engagement in the process of customer expectation of service (e.g., vacations, pizza delivery, updates of the stage of delivery, etc.).
5. **Verification costs or the costs incurred when validating the identity, authenticity, and reputation of an agent.** The advancement

of digital technology has significantly reduced the verifying costs of product quality through online reviews and brought down the friction and asymmetry to the paucity of verifiable information in the customer experience process.

9.4 Influence on Training

Through digitalisation, the approach by firms to the application of McKinsey's soft S's: skills, staff style, and shared values is changing. This dynamism has brought in new challenges which many firms struggle with. Some of these challenges are emerging as new customer segments, socio-cultural diversity in the global marketplace, heightened market volatility, unprecedented customer expectations about price, quality, delivery speed, employee turnover and skill maintenance, and the effect of the internet on an organisation's core business (Sousa & Rocha, 2018).

Components of digital business such as artificial intelligence are changing the rate at which dynamism in the industry is happening, particularly in areas that require close interaction and collaboration between computers and people. Big Data is re-orienting how we access, organise, visualise, select, and utilise the information for training purposes. Machine learning and the internet of things have caused significant changes, specifically in the manufacturing industry, aeronautics, as well as the service sector, for example, in the hospitality and health industries. Thanks to nanotechnology, the skill requirements in the computer industry, energy health sectors, and complementary sectors are changing at tremendous speed. Several scholars have argued that these technological effects have led to new business opportunities along with new risks in organisation's value chains and customer expectations (Fan & Zhou, 2011; Hui, 2014; Sun et al., 2012). Porter and Heppelman (2014) believe that the process of integrating digitalisation to training is inextricably transforming work processes through the interactions between machines and people. When combined with other factors, digitised training has seen an increment in the number of youths who are attaining more skills and entering into business in East Africa, particularly Kenya (Andeweg et al., 2020) and Uganda (Wafudu & Kamin, 2021).

9.5 On Digital Value Creation

Shared values, a key component of McKinsey's model, addresses culture, core values, and firm's cohesion. This is likely to lead organisations to embrace digital innovation, resulting in new processes, service, and products offerings. Regardless of whether they are interacting with their stakeholders physically or through web-based technology, many firms use digital technologies to create, sustain, and add value, hence providing great significance and benefits to the entire value chain (Yoo et al., 2010). Studies suggest that the adoption of digital business through innovation may alter not only specific business operations and the business models but also the entire innovation ecosystems (Adner & Kapoor, 2009; Loebbecke & Picot, 2015). On the dimension of digital innovation, firms create value from their activities and interactions with stakeholders; this is referred to as co-creation of value. This interplay happens within the context of digital innovation ecosystems of the specific regulatory, market, and other external environmental contexts such as industry technology absorption and levels of competition under which the firms operate as established by Jelassi and Martínez-López (2020) in the Kenyan market.

In their seminal paper, Ahmad and Osama (2015) argued that digital application marketplaces are continuously becoming significant to digital platform owners working towards gaining the benefits of distribution, brokerage, and applications by third-party developers. Two critical goals drive the owners of those marketplaces: to address the needs and requirements of heterogeneity of end-users and captivate the attention of third-party developers. Accommodating organisational goals is vital for value creation.

In Rwanda, Kirabo et al. (2020) established that businesses respond to the change brought about by digitalisation of business by focusing on the creation and development of digital service capacities and capabilities, which makes firms maintain better relationships and connections with their customers, therefore contributing to value creation. Research suggests that digital service capacities and capabilities are harnessed from the critical interaction between similar to value creation processes and service components: technology, people, information, and business resources (Chuang & Lin, 2015; Maglio et al., 2009; Spohrer et al., 2007). In their framework of value creation and the multi-dimensionality of value-creating practices in the digital innovation ecosystem, Susenoa et al. (2018) proposed that the creation of value from digital innovation can be elaborated through new ways distinguish different categories of value.

As indicated by Sweeny and Souter (2001), value can be looked at from the dimension of it being functional, emotional, and social. The functional value essentially deals with the quality perceptions or performance of the product and/or service delivery or how the product or service satisfies the needs of the firm's customers. Furthermore, functional value is specifically the utility derived from the use of such product and/or service offering, that is, whether the product and /or service is value for consumers' or customers' money. On the other hand, social value is related to the utility received from the "ability or capacity" of the product and/or service to enhance the user's self-concept and worth vis-à-vis the society. Emotional value is more psychological; it is explained as the way the product or service offering meets the customers' inner feelings. The customer perceptions of functional, emotional, and social value significantly indicate the qualitative aspects borne by the product and/or service offerings in the eyes of consumers. Mathwick et al. (2001) further explained the importance of experiential value, which is based on a combination of both intrinsic values such as playfulness and aesthetics and extrinsic value such as customer return on investment and service excellence. In addition, indicated value is based on utilitarian value (which may include price savings and time savings), whereas experiential value includes entertainment, visual experience, and interaction (Lee & Overby, 2004). According to Mesich (2018), the *N-Frnds mAgri* digital platform in Rwanda to date has benefited more than 15,000 Irish potato farmers with its value-added features.

9.6 Influence on Pricing

The digitalisation of the strategy component in the McKinsey's model can partly be related to the pricing process. Its effect is seen in the form of determination of the appropriate pricing strategies, policies and actual prices. Krämer and Kalka (2017) opined that technological changes (internet availability, production digitisation, and innovation of products) usually influence the environment of a firm and can be the basis for pricing improvements and changes, a good case in example is safaricoms' *mpesa* in Kenya (Bhimani, 2021). In this process, organisations can conduct an analysis of relevant data and process information which subsequently would lead to price optimisation. However, the changes leading to price optimisation may cause unprecedented competitive responses and reactions in the entire industry. Changes in consumer behaviour as a result of easy and cheap online availability of information, numerous search engines, and several price robots always go a long way in helping find the best offers. Due to the digitalisation process, market structures become fragile, resulting in lowered market entry barriers. Cannibalisation of traditional products is also likely to happen as replicated in the Ugandan service sector (Kayemba, 2020).

In addition, Andeweg et al. (2020) find that digitalisation not only helped in establishing strong links between cooperative societies, traders, and processors but it also promoted value chain collaboration and enhanced transparency in pricing mechanisms leading to risk avoidance and reduction in Tanzania.

Pricing strategy of many firms has undergone a total rethink; this has led to changes in the types of pricing models and strategies used in the digital era. Some of these pricing models, thanks to digitalisation have made it possible to offer services and products for free to the user, for instance, google and Facebook, and further to this, new revenue streams have emerged like advertising on these platforms. Freemium models, which are very popular with start-ups, have also come up. These do not charge anything for their basic services but charge for upgrades, where they promise to offer a full range of features with no ads. Good examples of freemium models pricing models are Dropbox, Spotify, and LinkedIn. Others are like *Tigo* and *Bima* in the Tanzanian insurance sector, *Mkopa* in the Kenyan, Ugandan and Nigerian finance sector, etc. Keeping in mind that production costs generally reduce when digitisation is the basis of new business models, subscription models such as Netflix, Blue Apron, and Hellofresh have gained more traction.

9.7 Role of Digital Business Framework

Both digitisation and digitalisation of business have ushered in new synergistic value creation grids and networks such as digital business ecosystems (DBE). Digital business ecosystems can be explained as a socio-technical network of organisations, individuals, and technologies that collectively co-create value. The digital business ecosystems have become the new business frameworks; these systems are connecting the entire value chain of organisations for effectiveness and efficiency. As per Stanley and Brisco (2010), DBE has two tiers; the digital (ecosystem) and the business (ecosystem). This ecosystem stands for a virtual environment that is populated by digital concerns and entities, such as hardware, software applications, and processes (Nachira et al., 2007). The systems work on a peer-to-peer dispersed technology infrastructure that makes, disseminates, and interconnects digital services over the internet.

These business ecosystems can be considered as economic communities of organisations and individuals and that conduct their business outside their traditional industry boundaries (Moore, 1993). Therefore, DBE can be called a business framework. It entails a socio-technical environment where you find machines, equipment, and individuals, firms, and digital technologies bearing collaborative, complementary, and also competitive relationships to enhance the co-creation of value by means of shared digital platforms. For example, within the East African countries of Kenya, Uganda, Rwanda, and Tanzania, telecommunication companies, individual entrepreneurs, and other ICT-based firms have invented and provided several services in the form of mobile phone applications, which generally have formed a network of relationships easing business operations. These applications are for different stakeholders on different platforms. Some of these are; *iCow* targeting the Kenyan farmer, invented by Su Kahumbu in Kenya; *Vet Africa* by a Scotland-based tech company—Cojengo, founded by Craig Taylor and Iain Collins in partnership with Microsoft offering veterinary services in Kenya, Ethiopia, Uganda, and Tanzania; *M-Farm* for use by farmers in Kenya and Ghana ensuring to price transparency developed by Linda Kwamboka, Susan Oguya, and Jamila Abass; *Agri-wallet* offered by Dodore Kenya Ltd. founded by Ad Rietberg and Sijmen, which is a smallholder farmers purse to manage their finances; *Kilimo Salama* developed by Syngenta Foundation for Sustainable Agriculture and Safaricom Ltd., which gives up-to-date climate and weather information to farmers for sustainable agricultural practices in Kenya etc. (Emeana et al., 2020). The above is specific to the agro-business sector, and different sectors have specific applications targeted at them.

Digital business ecosystems include digital content marketing (DCM), which is aimed at fostering brand engagement and trust with consumers. The definition of DCM covers several aspects of the process of serving and understanding the consumer appropriately. It is referred to as the "management process responsible for identifying, anticipating, and satisfying customer requirements profitably" through relevant digital content (Rowley, 2008, p. 522). It is, therefore, a critical relationship marketing tool. It has been further proposed as an aid to the development of consumer interconnectivity and attachment to brands, eventually bearing a positive contribution to the firm's performance (Carranza, 2017; Kakkar, 2017).

The advantages of an organisational-based DCM include a more engaged target audience at a reduced marketing cost, which consequently may diminish the need for carrying out advertising or personal selling activity (Pulizzi, 2010). Furthermore, Bicks (2016) reveals that content marketing is likely to cost 62 per cent less than traditional marketing efforts, and likely to generate three times as many [sales] leads at the same time. For buyers and consumers, DCM is likely to improve access to the content which is most relevant to their requirement and personal needs, which may include the offering of opportunities for entertainment, brand-related learning, or heightened convenience (e.g., through time savings), leading to greater value (Lieb, 2011).

9.8 Challenges of Digital Business Framework

Some of the major challenges under this context may include systems inter-operability bottlenecks of the McKinsey model in a digital framework with its technological, semantic, and organisational facets (Chen et al., 2008). IT incompatibility, for instance, the architectural framework, the infrastructure, or the frameworks, thereof, maybe another hindrance. In East African countries, for instance, mobile connectivity index (MCI), rules for data exchange, and use in addition to digital interfaces may still be in the early stages of development and are varied (Heaphy, 2021).

Person-related challenges may also be there; for instance, individual managers, consumers, or customers may have their roles unfulfilled as a result of a dearth of required competencies or equipment. Individuals may not be in a position to cope with the dynamics, heterogeneity, opportunities, and complexity involved in value co-creation (Lenkenhoff et al., 2018).

Firms fased hurdles like having different structures and use of non-identical logics of organising in terms of responsibilities, decision-making, and autonomy. Chen et al. (2008) argued that the coherency between decision-making principles could be the main prerequisite for the evolving of ecosystems. This coherency seems to be important for a balanced exchange relationship and a minimum amount of trust between autonomous partners (Tsujimoto et al., 2017). However, this coherence may be lacking in most cases.

9.9 The Strategic Management Requirements for a Successful Digital Business

In the contemporary business environment, the success of the strategic management process in relation to digitisation and digitalisation of the process is necessary. Strategic management activities, strategy formulation, strategy implementation, strategy evaluation, and control, can be digitalised to a certain extent. Brorström (2020) has argued that, in the contemporary dynamic business scenario, both digitalisation and digitisation are core to operations. In the process of strategic management, the McKinsey 7S framework as a concept of a firm's internal business environment designing is very critical. The relationship between each of the

7Ss elements may be used to determine the strengths or the weaknesses of a firm, and the dimensions can be fused to a firm's digital transformation process (Demir & Kocauglu, 2019).

Starik et al. (2012) proposed a framework called the Strategic Environmental Management (SEM) framework through mapping the McKinsey 7Ss to identify critical characteristics of company's environmental sustainability profiles. Some scholars like Sekera and Stimel (2011) researched (eco)-sustainability and found out that the McKinsey's 7S model addresses largely operational and tactical levels, instead of strategic level. Teh (2013) posited that the McKinsey model could be a functional tool at a strategic level, where firms create and implement their (eco)-sustainability policy and strategy. As a result, in his proposal, Teh (2013) used the McKinsey 7Ss framework as a basis to build an assessment metric to measure the extent of adoption of sustainability policy and strategy and appraise an organisational eco-sustainability performance with the metrics. It is, therefore, on the basis of such a foundation that the McKinsey's 7S framework and its applicability to platformisation can be considered.

Enhanced firms' performance may be driven by several factors for such as how human resources are managed, policies, compensation, and leadership. The human resources (HR) function plays an actively critical and productive role in realising a firm's goals. The four soft Ss of the McKinsey's model tends to be skewed to the human element in an organisation. This, therefore, may mean that the entire human element can be engineered by the use of the McKinsey model (Zincir & Tunç, 2017). McKinsey's hard and soft Ss should be taken up as precedents for the optimal realisation of a firm's digitalisation process. Once these are founded appropriately on the right form of digital platformisation, then the firm's survival would be guaranteed (Adeola et al., 2021).

9.10 Discussion and Conclusion

From the accessed literature, it is evident that digitisation and digitalisation as processes guaranteeing good business performance in East Africa, are still in their infancy. The business sectors in all East African countries are at different levels of preparedness, infusion, and adoption of digital framework. Several authors and scholars have researched on digitalisation of various aspects of business, including Kaivo-Oja Roth and Westerlund (2017), who wrote on the major trends in the digital transformation across different scenarios, Shpak et al. (2016), who examined models of marketing diversification, Chaffey and Ellis-Chadwick (2016) explicated the expediency of using electronic communication technologies, Patil, (2018) on the influence of the trend of marketing digitalisation on consumers, and digital transformation technologies for large companies (Sebastian et al., 2017). In the meantime, other researchers have also concentrated on the use of digitalisation application. For instance, Reis and Melao (2019) examined the digital networkings of Portuguese companies, Holmlund et al. (2017) researched on digitalisation on banking, Hanninen et al. (2017) conducted his research on the problem of digitalisation in the retail trade. Shubham and Renu (2016) researched the change of marketing approaches to the consumer through the lens of digitalisation of marketing activity. Louw and Nieuwenhuizen (2020) opined that African firms introduce mobile-optimisation services first, then other forms of digitalisation later. This highlights the place of a 'mobile-first approach' not only to traditional brick and mortar but also digital-based firms. Few researchers have researched on digitisation of the East African business context.

As organisations seek to attain efficiencies through digitalisation of the McKinsey model, platformisation in key (Adeola et al., 2021). Robots, automation, and computers have existed in the industry for some time; however, the advancement of internet and the electronic highway have revolutionised their use. This revolution has brought up efficiencies in cost, material inputs, labour, and time. These enhanced efficiencies have made it possible to monitor the activities with ease, seamlessness in operation and processes of machines, materials, workforce, and even service and products themselves, simultaneous data collection, analysis, and utilisation of real-time decision-making.

In the contemporary business world, organisations need to survive and to successfully compete. In order to do this, they need to increasingly create a dependence on their use of information technology and their knowledge capabilities to constantly keep on innovating. Alavi and

Leidner (2001) stated that the importance of information technology (IT) in supporting knowledge management initiatives and fostering innovation cannot be discounted. IT as a component of platformisation facilitates the creation, dissemination, and utilisation of knowledge (Davenport et al., 2008), thus greatly increasing and enabling organisations' knowledge capacity and capabilities. Digitalisation has aided in the augmentation, building, and buttressing firms' knowledge capabilities. It has become a critical success factor in today's business environment (Sambamurthy & Subramani, 2004). Leonard-Barton (1995) emphasised the connection between firm innovation and the knowledge capabilities of an organisation. For digital business technologies to assist in supporting knowledge acquisition in the business environment and the assimilation and use of the same for decision-making, the concept of anchoring McKinsey's framework on platformisation is essential.

The contemporary global marketplace has become very complicated, as exemplified by the fast-changing consumer preferences, increasing competitive challenges, reduced product life cycles, and unsustainable competitive advantage. Fast response and continuous innovation are basic sources of sustainable advantage (Distanont & Khongmalai, 2018). As part of understanding their business's competitive landscape, the firms' dynamic capacity and capabilities, its agility and innovativeness will enable it to respond to unprecedented events, cope with unanticipated challenges, and raise its competitive edge. Business agility is defined as the firms' ability to operate effectively in a dynamic environment with much uncertainty and instability (Sahin, 2000). Story (2021) posits that McKinsey's 7S model is an important framework firms can use to review their marketing capabilities. It is also a business-wide construct that entails logistics processes, organisational structures, information systems, and in particular mindsets of both the management and workforce (Hartványi & Nagy, 2008). Organisations that understand their business environment can combine such understanding with their agility to better take advantage of changes in the environment since such environmental dynamism bring forth opportunities.

Braunscheidel and Suresh (2009) suggest that with mounting competitive pressures and a combination of high levels of turbulence and uncertainty, firms require agility, the use of McKinsey model can inform the organisation of its capacity. Furthermore, agility can enhance the organisations financial, non-financial, and operational performance: profitability, sales, market share, speed to market, and customer satisfaction. Research in competitive dynamics of the business environment has widely examined the patterns of competitive actions (e.g., strategic actions, responses, or a series of actions, etc.) (Ferrier, 2001) and their antecedents and consequences (Smith et al., 2001). Baum and Korn (1996) further examined specific types of competitive actions, such as market entry and exit strategies. The competitive actions, among others like patent inventions, new service and product introductions promotions, use of technology have a great potential towards the disruption of the competitive status quo within the business environment and cause dis-equilibrium within the market. As organisations seek to satisfy various customer needs, Jílková (2020) argues that the digital revolution has restructured the conventional customer behaviour model and brought some new perspectives to handle business-to-customer (B2C), business-to-business (B2B), business-to-government (B2G), and business-to-employees (B2E) in a data-driven society. Due to technological dynamism, the entire customer configuration has taken new dimensions never known before.

For the platformisation process to succeed, the presence of factors like digital technology adoption and adaptation, digital literacy, and government input in some cases cannot be discounted. It is, therefore, recommended that mechanisms to lower both digitisation and digitalisation costs, enhance adoption and adaptation, increase technology literacy have to be put in place to spur the business growth and survival.

References

Abidin, R., Osman, N. H., Zahari, F. M., & Nordin, N. (2015). Determining critical elements in strengthening the organisations: A study on the public sector. *Journal of Business Management and Accounting,* 155–169.

Adeola, O., Edeh, J., Hinson, R. E., & Netswera, F. (2021). *Digital service delivery in Africa—A platformisation perspective*. Palgrave Macmillan.

Adner, R., & Kapoor, R. (2009). Value creation in innovation ecosystems: How the structure of technological interdependence affects firm performance in new technology generations. *Strategic Management Journal*, 306–333.

Ahmad, G., & Osama, M. (2015). Value creation in digital application marketplaces: A developers' perspective. In *Thirty Sixth International Conference on Information Systems*. Association for Information Systems (AIS).

Alavi, M. D., & Leidner, E. (2001). Knowledge management and research issues. *MIS Quarterly, 25*(1), 107–136.

Andeweg, K., Lee, J. v., & Bashuna, S. D. (2020). *Youth as an asset for dairy development-What have we learned from youth-led dairy in East Africa.* Wagenigen University and Research.

Banga, K., & te Velde, W. D. (2018). *Digitalisation and the future of manufacturing in Africa.* Supporting Economic Transformation (Odi).

Baum, J. A., & Korn, H. J. (1996). Competitive dynamics of interfirm rivalry. *Academy of Management Journal,* 255–291.

Bhimani, A. (2021). *Accounting disrupted: How digitalization is changing finance*. Wiley.

Bicks, B. (2016, October 7). *All you need to know about content marketing vs traditional marketing*. https://ozcontent.com/blog/content-marketingvs-traditional-marketing.

Braunscheidel, M., & Suresh, N. (2009). The organizational antecedents of a firm's supply chain agility for risk mitigation and response. *Journal of Operations Management,* 119–140.

Bresciani, S., Ferraris, A., & Santoro, N. G. (2016). Wine sector: Companies' performance and green economy as a means of societal marketing. *Journal of Promotion Management, 22*(2), 251–267.

Briddle, F. (2017). The impact of digital marketing disruption on the localisation industry. *Multilingual,* 44–47.

Brorström, S. (2020). The strategy process as a result of learning, questioning, and performing in a city organization. *International Public Management Journal,* 611–630.

Carranza, A. (2017, October 7). *The importance of content marketing in 2017 and beyond*. Retrieved from Business 2 Community: https://www.business2community.com/content-marketing/importance-content-marketing-2017-beyond-01861200.

Chaffey, D., & Ellis-Chadwick, F. (2016). *Digital marketing*. Pearson.

Chaffey, D., Hemphill, T., & Edmundson-Bird. (2019). *Digital Business and Commerce Management.* New York: pearson.

Chen, D., Vallespir, B., & Daclin, N. (2008). An approach for enterprise interoperability measurement. *MoDISE-EUS*, 1–12.

Chuang, S., & Lin, H. (2015). Co-creating e-service innovations: Theory, practice, and impact on. *International Journal of Information Management*, 277–291.

Davenport, T. H., Prusak, L., & Strong, B. (2008, October 10). *Putting ideas to work: Knowledge management can make a difference—But it needs to be more pragmatic.* Retrieved from Wall Street Journal: https://www.wsj.com/articles/SB120468033433412107.

Demir, E., & Kocauglu, B. (2019). The use of Mckinsey's 7s framework as a strategic planning and economic assestment tool in the process of digital transformation. *PressAcademia Procedia*, 114–119.

Distanont, A., & Khongmalai, O. (2018). The role of innovation in creating a competitive advantage. *Kasetsart Journal of Social Sciences*, 15–21.

Emeana, E. M., Trenchard, L., & Dehnen-Schmutz, K. (2020). The revolution of mobile phone-enabled services for agricultural development (m-Agri Services) in Africa: The challenges for sustainability. *Sustainability*, 485–501.

Fan, P., & Zhou, G. (2011). Analysis of the business model innovation of the technology of internet of things in postal logistics. In *IEEE 18th International Conference on Industrial Engineering and Engineering Management* (pp. 532–536). IEEE.

Felix, J. C. (2018). The impact of digital marketing on business performances in online food marketing and telecommunication industries. *Business Education Journal*, 12.

Ferrier, W. J. (2001). Navigating the competitive landscape: The drivers and consequences of competitive aggressiveness. *Academy of Management Journal*, 858–877.

Goldfarb, A., & Tucker, C. (2019). Digital economics. *Journal of Economic Literature*, 3–43.

Grishikasvili, K., Dibbs, S., & Meadows, M. (2014). An investigation into big data impact on digital marketing. *Online Journal of Communication and Media Technologies*, 146–150.

Hänninen, M., Smedlund, A., & Mitronen, L. (2017). Digitalization in retailing: multi-sided platforms as drivers of industry transformation. *Baltic Journal of Management*, *13*(2), 152–168. https://doi.org/10.1108/bjm-04-2017-0109

Hartványi, T., & Nagy, Z. (2008). Agility in supply chains. *Acta Technica Jaurinensis*, 315–323.

Heaphy, E. (2021, June 8). *Mobile for development*. Retrieved from GSMA Web Site: https://www.gsma.com/mobilefordevelopment/english/reducing-divide-digital-literacy-innovators-east-africa/.

Holmlund, M., Strandvik, T., & Lähteenmäki, I. (2017). Digitalization challenging institutional logics: Top executive sensemaking of service business change. *Journal of Theory and Practice,* 219–236.

Hui, G. (2014, October 1). *How the internet of things changes business models.* Retrieved from Harvard Business Review: https://hbr.org/2014/07/how-the-internet-of-things-changes-business-models.

International Telecommunications Union. (2001). *The internet in an African LDC: Uganda case study*. International Telecommunications Union.

Jelassi, T., & Martínez-López, F. J. (2020). *Digital business transformation in Silicon Savannah: How M-PESA changed Safaricom (Kenya) in: Strategies for e-Business. Classroom companion.* Springer.

Jílková, P., & Králová, P. (2020). Digital Trends and New Payment Models in B2C E-Commerce Context. In *Proceedings of the "New silk road: Business cooperation and prospective of economic development"(NSRBCPED 2019).* Published. https://doi.org/10.2991/aebmr.k.200324.117

Kaivo-Oja, J., Roth, S., & Westerlund, L. (2017). Futures of robotics. Human work in digital transformation. *International Journal of Technology Management,* 176.

Kakkar, G. (2017, October 7). *Top 10 reasons behind growing importance of content marketing*. Retrieved from Digital Vidya: http://www.digitalvidya.com.

Kayemba, J. (2020, October 14). Retrieved from Africa Portal: https://www.africaportal.org/publications/timely-decision-businesses-uganda-adopt-modern-technology-new-world-setting/.

Kirabo, J., Namusonge, G. S., & Iravo, M. A. (2020). Strategic innovation, a contemporary management practice on. *International Journal of Social Sciences and Technology,* 81–93.

Krämer, A., & Kalka, R. (2017). How digital disruption changes pricing strategies and price models. In A. Khare, B. Stewart, & R. Schatz, *Phantom ex machina* (pp. 87–103). Springer.

Lee, E.-J., & Overby, J. (2004). Creating valiue for online shoppers: Implications for satisfaction and loyalty. *Journal of Customer Satisfaction, Dissatisfaction and Complaining Behaviour,* 54–67.

Lenkenhoff, K., Wilkens, U., Zheng, M., Süße, T., Kuhlenkötter, B., & Ming, X. (2018). Key challenges of digital business ecosystem development and how to cope with them. *Procedia CIRP,* 167–172.

Leonard-Barton, D. (1995). *Wellsprings of knowledge: Building and sustaining the source of innovation.* Harvard Business School Press.

Lieb, R. (2011). *Content marketing: Think like a publisher-how to use content to market online and in social media.* Que Publisher.

Loebbecke, C., & Picot, A. (2015). Reflections on societal and business model transformation arising from digitization and big data analytics: A research agenda. *The Journal of Strategic Information Systems,* 149–157.

Louw, C., & Nieuwenhuizen, C. (2020). Digitalisation strategies in a South African banking context: A consumer services analysis. *South African Journal of Information Management,* 8.

Maglio, P., Vargo, S., Caswell, N., & Spohrer, J. (2009). The service system is the basic abstraction of service science. *Information Systems and E-Business Management,* 395–406.

Mathwick, C., Malhotra, N., & Rigdon, E. (2001). Experiential value: Conceptualization, measurement and application in the catalog and Internet shopping environment. *Journal of Retailing,* 39–56.

Mesich, A. (2018). *Bringing value chain-based financial services to Irish potato farmers in Rwanda.* Medium.com.

Mkalama, B., & Ndemo, B. (2020, December 10). *Orchestrating smart cities, new disruptive business models and informal enterprises.* Retrieved from Intechopen: https://www.intechopen.com.

Mlay, S., Ariel, N., Mbarika, V. W., Vegah, G., Moya, Musa, B., & Balunywa, L. (2013). Global diffusion of the internet, the internet in Rwanda. *The African Journal of Information and Communication,* 45–61.

Moore, J. F. (1993, October 7). Predators and prey: A new ecology of competition. *Harvard Business Review,* 75–83.

Mpesa Foundation Academy. (2020, October 14). Retrieved from mpesa foundation academy: https://mpesafoundationacademy.ac.ke/.

Mureithi, M. (2017). The internet journey for Kenya: The interplay of disruptive innovation and entrepreneurship in fueling rapid growth. In B. Ndemo, & T. Weiss, *Digital Kenya. Palgrave Studies of Entrepreneurship in Africa* (pp. 27–53). Palgrave MacMillan.

Nachira, F., Dini, P., & Nicolai, A. (2007). *A network of digital ecosystems for Europe: Roots, processes and perspectives.* European Commission.

OECD-Development Centre. (2021). Digital transformation for youth employment and agenda 2063 in East Africa. In OECD, *Africa development dynamic: Digital transformation for quality jobs* (pp. 163–187). AUC.

Pagani, M., & Pardo, C. (2017). The impact of digital technology on relationships in a business network. *Industrial Marketing Management,* 185–192.

Patil, A. (2018). The trend of digitalization in marketing and its impact on the customers. In *International Conference on Digital Economy and its Impact on Business and Industry* (pp. 13–22). Sangli, India. International Journal of Trend in Scientific Research and Development.

Porter, M., & Heppelman, J. (2014, October 1). How smart, connected products are transforming competition. *Harvard Business Review*, 1–10. https://hbr.org/2014/11/how-smart-connected-products-are-transforming-competition.

Pulizzi, J. A. (2010). *Get content get customers: Turn prospects into buyers with content marketing*. Tata McGraw Hill Education Private Limited.

Reis, J., & Melao, N. (2019). The path to digital transformation: Overcoming prejudice in the digital era with service operations. *International Journal of Servces Operations Management,* 20–32.

Rowley, J. (2008). Understanding digital content marketing. *Journal of Marketing Management,* 517–540.

Sahin, F. (2000). Manufacturing competitiveness: Different systems to achieve the same results. *Production and Inventory Management Journal,* 56–65.

Sambamurthy, V., & Subramani, M. R. (2004). Special issue on information technologies and knowledge management. *MIS Quarterly,* 1–7.

Sebastian, I., Moloney, K., Ross, J., Fonstad, N., Beath, C., & Mocker, M. (2017). How big old companies navigate digital transformation. *MIS Quarterly Executive,* 197–213.

Sekera, L. E., & Stimel, D. (2011). How durable is sustainable enterprise? Ecological sustainability meets the reality of tough economic. *Business Horizons,* 115–124.

Shah, J. M. (2018). Impact of Digital Marketing in Business and Politics. *International Journal of Scientific & Engineering Research, 9*(12).

Sheriff, S. (2008). *Access to infrastructure*. Global Information Society Watch (GISWatch).

Shpak, N., Kyrylych, T., & Greblikaite, J. (2016). Diversification models of sales activity for steady development of an Enterprise. *Sustainability,* 393.

Shubham, S., & Renu, S. (2016). Literature review on ethical issues in digital marketing. *International Journal of Scientific & Engineering Research,* 91–93.

Siemens. (2017). *Africa digital maturity*. scribd.com.

Smith, K. G., Ferrier, W. J., & Ndofor, J. (2001). The effects of organizational differences and trust on the effectiveness of selling partner relationships. In M. A. Hitt, R. Freeman, & J. S. Harrison (Eds.), *Handbook of strategic management* (pp. 315–361). Blackwell.

Sousa, M., & Rocha, Á. (2018). Skills for disruptive digital business. *Journal of Business Research*, 257–263.

Spohrer, J., Maglio, P., Bailey, J., & Gruhl, D. (2007). Steps toward a science of service systems. *Computer*, 71–77.

Sridhar, S., & Fang, E. (2019). New vistas for marketing strategy: digital, data-rich, and developing market (D3) environments. *Journal of the Academy of Marketing Science*, 977–985.

Stanley, J., & Brisco, G. (2010). The ABC of digital business systems: Communications law. *Journal of Communcation, Media and Telecommunications Law*, 1–24.

Starik, M., Holliday, S., & Paton, B. (2012). Strategic environmental sustainability management: Highlighting the need and opportunities to recognize environmentally-hidden economic sectors. *International Journal of Business Insights and Transformation*, 8–15.

Story, J. (2021, June 8). *How to use the McKinsey 7s model in marketing*. Retrieved from Smart Insights: https://www.smartinsights.com/marketing-planning/marketing-models/mckinsey-7s-model/.

Sun, Y., Yan, H., Luc, C., Bie, R., & Thomas, P. (2012). A holistic approach to visualising business models for internet of things. *Communicatons in Mobile Computing*, 1–7.

Susenoa, Y., Laurell, C., & Sick, N. (2018). Assessing value creation in digital innovation ecosystems: A Social Media Analytics approach. *Journal of Strategic Information Systems*, 335–349.

Sweeny, J. C., & Souter, G. (2001). Consumer perceived value: The development of a multiple item scale. *Journal of Retailing*, 203–220.

Teh, D. (2013). *Strategic implementation of organizational eco-sustainability policy and strategy-a McKinsey seven S's approach*. Royal Melbourne Institute of Technology University.

The Digital Transformation Centre of Rwanda. (2020, October 14). https://digicenter.rw/.

The World Bank. (2020, October 12). *What we do -Projects and Operation*. Retrieved from The World Bank: https://projects.worldbank.org/en/projects-operations/project-detail/P171305.

Tsujimoto, M., Kajikawa, Y., Tomita, J., & Matsumoto, Y. (2017). A review of the ecosystem concept—Towards coherent ecosystem design. *Technological Forecasting and Social Change*, 49–58.

United Nations Capital Development Fund. (2020, December 10). *Better than cash alliance-research*. Retrieved from Beeter than Cash Alliance: https://www.betterthancash.org/.

Wafudu, S. J., & Kamin, B. Y. (2021). Realistic quality assurance for technical vocational education and training towards enhanced productivity: Literature review. *İlköğretim Online*, 858–869.

Yoo, Y., Henfridsson, O., & Lyytinen, K. (2010). Research commentary—The new organizing logic of digital innovation: An agenda for information systems research. *Information Systems Research,* 724–735.

Zincir, O., & Tunç, A. Ö. (2017). An imagination of organizations in the future: Rethinking McKinsey's 7S model. In R. Batko & A. Szopa (Eds.), *Strategic imperatives and core competencies in the era of robotics and artificial intelligence* (pp. 1010–1125). IGI- Global.

10

Digitalisation and Public Sector Service Delivery in Kenya

Abel Kinoti Meru and Mary Wanjiru Kinoti

10.1 Introduction

Digital service delivery is greatly influenced by the strategy (value proposition), systems (processes), structure (organisation), style (leadership), staff (employees), skills (competencies and abilities), and shared value (digital environment) adopted by an institution (Kukkamalla et al., 2020) whether private or in the wider public service sector, albeit differently. Public services, the focus for this chapter, '*are services provided by Government to its citizens directly through public service organisation or by financing private provision of services*' (GOK, 2017a). With the rapid onset of digital technology, governments have no choice but to

A. K. Meru (✉)
Riara University, Nairobi, Kenya

M. W. Kinoti
University of Nairobi, Nairobi, Kenya
e-mail: mkinoti@yahoo.co.uk

O. Adeola et al. (eds.), *Digital Service Delivery in Africa*, Palgrave Studies of Marketing in Emerging Economies,
https://doi.org/10.1007/978-3-030-83909-3_10

embrace digital processes to deliver public services. The digital public service strategy, nature of service delivery systems, and performance processes significantly impact efficiency and fairness in the provision of public goods and services (Karwan & Markland, 2006) globally. Similarly, Giest and Raaphorst (2018) suggest that the structure of public institutions, the ability to cope with digital applications and architecture, and accessibility to citizens are critical to public service delivery. The nature of the structure directly influences the public leadership style, staff competencies, and skills needed to deliver digital public services.

For a strategy to be successful, it must continuously add value to customers (Kukkamalla et al., 2020), and citizens, and this is also applicable to public service. Thus, a citizen-centric digital public service should address the specific needs and wants of the citizen, who are the key stakeholders (Tassabehji et al., 2019). Digital public service value creation is premised on efficiency, effectiveness, contribution to economy, accountability, and equity (Gil-Garcia et al., 2018; Hui & Hayllar, 2010). A digital strategy for services where the information is an asset, investments are shared and built on shared leadership and culture (collaboration) promotes digital innovations (Jones & Hooper, 2017). Criado and Gil-Garcia (2019) observe that open and collaborative digital innovation processes have resulted in the transformation of the delivery of public services. Public digital service delivery systems may be partially or fully integrated and either wholly or partially owned or subcontracted, which inhibits functionality. The existing political systems and institutions serve the service delivery structures and hamper the uptake of digital technologies (Gupta et al., 2017). Structure as applicable here, according to Brown and Toze (2017), relates to effective governance of public electronic information, use the rule of law, privacy, transparency, and accountability. The structure ought to be sensitive to changes in market trends and customer preferences, complaints, and feedback to continually improve service quality (Kukkamalla et al., 2020).

Digital public leadership styles involve either management of technology or the digital information resources as well as the diverse roles and responsibilities bestowed upon different public servants (Brown & Toze, 2017). Digital public services deploy new leadership styles, continuous decision-making processes, and better ways of organising and delivering services to cater for the needs of citizens, service users, public servants, and political leaders by integrating digital technologies in the working environment of public institutions (Gil-Garcia et al., 2018). Further, Gil-Garcia et al. (2018) posit that this digitalisation of public services challenges the traditional public administration and management styles, leading to the radical public transformation of the leadership styles and citizens' rights to access and use information and communication avenues. Thus, public service leadership ought to ensure that staff involved in digital service delivery have the right skills and shared values of transforming service delivery to the citizens. Interestingly, in many African countries, digital technology is a key enabler of reforms in public service delivery, and Kenya is no exception.

Prior to the onset of ubiquitous digital technologies, governments across the divide deployed manual and semi-automated public service delivery systems with mixed results. Today ICT plays a crucial role in the '*fourth industrial revolution*' that is heralding unprecedented growth of digital, biological, and physical technologies (GOK, 2018) in both the private and the public service sectors. Hitherto, like in Kenya, delivery of public service was centralised, non-accountable, lacked information management systems, had duplicating roles and responsibilities, and was not socially entrepreneurial (GOK, 2017a). Existing discreet service delivery systems were tedious and hugely manual prone to abuse, lengthy and inaccessible by the general public, breeding ineptitude and corruption. OECD (2014) observes that the rapidly changing digital dynamics requires governments to reorganise themselves to be more user-centric as opposed to the use of outdated internal mechanism to define the process, operations, methodologies, and frameworks for public service delivery. The six elements of digitalisation of public delivery services are discussed herein as the foundations and pillars of the digitalisation of the public service delivery process in Kenya.

10.2 Foundations and Pillars of the Digitalisation of Public Service Delivery in Kenya

To develop, maintain, and sustain rapidly changing digital technologies in public service delivery, a myriad of regional, national, and institutional measures addressing ICT policy and strategic direction came in handy for meaningful transformation at the national and county government levels in Kenya. Guided by Sustainable Development Goals (SDGs), Africa Union Agenda 2063, the Constitution of Kenya, 2010, and Kenya's Vision 2030, several measures have been put in place to aid digitisation of Public Service Delivery in Kenya. Moreover, Kenya is also a signatory and an active member of various ICT conventions and standards, such as Internet Corporation for Assigned Names and Numbers (ICANN) that have helped create a conducive environment for ICT development in the region. The Constitution of Kenya, 2010, provides the rights to access, services of reasonable quality, information, education, social security, and highest standards of health, among others. The 2010 Constitution of Kenya further articulates that all public institutions should ensure reasonable access to their services countrywide, within a devolved governing system. Key values and principles enshrined in the constitution that propagate public service delivery include: customer-centric service, efficiency and effectiveness, honesty and integrity, innovativeness and creativity, and equity and equality inter alia.

As a result, numerous digital public service delivery strategies have been adopted over the years, beginning with Vision 2030 that sought to transform Kenya into a middle-income country, globally competitive, and with high-quality life for all citizens by the year 2030. The Vision, implemented through five-year Medium-Term Plans (MTPs), envisioned an economic growth rate of 10 per cent per annum during the plan period, with equitable social development and a government that is people-centred. Kenya's Vision 2030 first MTP 2008–2012 (MTP 1), centred on '*strengthening the foundations of Knowledge based economy*', spearheaded the development of ICT strategy in the country by paving the installation of the East Africa Marine Cable Systems (TEAMS) for transmission of high-capacity bandwidth between the United Arab Emirates and Mombasa. This was then interlinked to National Terrestrial Fibre Optic Network, enabling interoperability of ministries through the Government common core network, other area networks, a data centre and integrated management information system (GOK, 2008). Similarly, other independent fibre network initiatives such as SEACOM, EASSY, and LION undersea fibre cables serve the region. The first National ICT Policy 2006, sought to ensure accessible, efficient, reliable, and affordable ICT public services by focussing on ICT infrastructure, broadcasting, telecommunications, and universal access mainly through the use of satellites for internet connection and communication, but could not address the much-needed rapid changes in the ICT sector in Kenya.

It is in light of this, through E-Government Strategy paper of 2004 (GOK, 2004) and later Public Service Transformation Framework, 2017–2022, concerted efforts were made to provide integrated ICT systems, structures, tools, and processes to hasten citizen-centred service delivery (GOK, 2017a). The framework identified five key drivers against which all public institutions were expected to adopt, namely, management of human capital (staff); transformative leadership styles, citizen-centric public institutions, effective and efficient service delivery, and productivity and innovativeness, with Information Communication and Technology (ICT), identified as a catalyst to actualise the social-economic drivers. To achieve efficient and effective citizen-centric service delivery, business process re-engineering was needed to guarantee transformative systems and processes at both national and county levels (GOK, 2017a).

With this in mind, the ICT Master Plan, 2014–2017, sought to position Kenya as a globally competitive ICT hub by developing three foundations, namely. quality ICT human resources, integrated ICT infrastructure, and information, with three pillars centred on e-government services (government information technology services to enhance productivity, governance, efficiency, and effectiveness), ICT industry, and ICT businesses. Development of ICT human capital was seen as a pre-requisite for a vibrant ICT sector, which aimed at integrating ICT in schools, colleges, and universities and develop curricula for non-ICT courses. Similarly, the presence of an elaborate ICT infrastructure was quintessential for developing an ICT-enabled economy, which called for an inclusive, reliable, secure broadband connectivity infrastructure in urban and rural areas. Finally, the foundation of integrated ICT information aimed at digitalising public information for ease of access and dissemination to promote public service delivery through a national public data hub. Thus, there was a need to build a national public data hub and develop governance structures for managing shared public data hubs, data warehouses, and data marts, with special focus on company registry database, person registry, national lands data hub, and vehicle registry database (GOK, 2014a).

Furthermore, the E-Government citizen-centric pillar was intent on automating integrated end to end Government services to actualise one-stop service models dubbed 'huduma' centres, and single window sign on (SWSO) programs to create seamless e-services for citizens, business, and investors through IT-enabled services (ITES). Subsequent adoption of ICT would spur rapid economic development as per the ambition of the second pillar, ICT as a driver of Industry. This would be beneficial to the health sector, education and security, agriculture, financial services, trade, transport, and logistics. The last pillar, developing ICT businesses through mobile software innovation and parts, was required to provide the ICT ecosystem needed to take an early lead in the ICT sector in Kenya (GOK, 2014a). Two of the Master plan's guiding principles, namely, equity and non-discrimination for enabling ICT access by all citizens and technological neutrality that sought the use of common interoperable protocols and standards, were instrumental in ensuring smooth ICT implementation in the country. However, for this to be accomplished, it requires an efficient generation, distribution, and use of energy, ICT infrastructure and platforms, and other legal frameworks.

During the Second Medium-Term Plan, 2013–2017 (MTP 11) and the Third Medium-Term Plan, 2018–2022 (MTP 111), tremendous inroads were made to support the growth of the infrastructure needed in the digitalisation process. In the energy sector, power generation capacity had by 2017 grown to 2,339.9 MW (expected to grow by 5,221 MW by 2022), national power transmission network reached 5,6767 km (expected to grow by a similar number by 2022), over 6.5

million customers were connected to electricity (an additional 5 million by 2022), 23,496 primary schools had been connected to electric, and a further 15,739 public utilities excluding primary schools were targeted by 2022.

Similarly, growth trajectory was witnessed in the ICT sector by end of 2017 with mobile penetration rate at 91.9%, mobile money transactions at 70.5% of the households and all the 47 county headquarters connected to the national optic fibre backbone infrastructure. The Government Cloud Computing infrastructure was implemented to enable sharing of big data among national and county public institutions. Besides, policy and legal frameworks were developed on national ICT policy, national communication policy, national cybersecurity master plan, and national ICT standards to support the growth of the sector (GOK, 2018). It is imperative to note that the Third Medium-Term Plan 2018–2022 (MTP 111) prioritises improvement of national ICT infrastructure, national information security (to support cloud computing), universal access to ICT (broadband connectivity to all primary and secondary schools), e-government services (open data initiative), and improve cybersecurity to enhance information flow and access to services in all the sectors in Kenya.

In terms of the governance structure of digital public service, e-government services are coordinated by ICT Authority (ICTA), a state corporation under the State Department of ICT established in 2013 after merging Government IT Services (GITS) responsible for payroll administration and integrated financial information system, Directorate of E-Government services and ICT board tasked with the responsibility of marketing Kenya as an ICT hub since 2007 (GOK, 2014a). ICTA is tasked with the responsibility of implementation of information services and ICT information in the public sector and providing oversight authority in the private sector. Online government services include health systems, social protection, national tax system, immigration information system, legal information system, integrated financial system, and education system.

The rest of the chapter delves into the implementation of selected digital public services delivery platforms in Kenya. Similar studies have been carried out; for instance, Ranerup, Henriksen, and Hedman (2016) examined types of public service platforms (PSPs) in Sweden in the healthcare, education, elder care, and pension, which supports the demand and supply side of vital public service offering with similar outcomes.

10.3 Selected Digitised Public Service Delivery Platforms in Kenya

Like in other parts of the world, significant inroads in the provision of digital public services in Kenya have been made in the deployment of technology, including e-citizen, e-social protection services, e-health, e-energy, digital learning, e-taxes, e-judiciary, and e-land, among others.

10.4 E-Citizen Services

By the end of MTP 11 (2013–2017), citizen-centric one-stop service shops (dubbed huduma centres); the Kenya integrated public service delivery model had been developed and implemented in 52 huduma centres in all the 47 counties. Under MTP 111 (2018–2022), enhancement of public service delivery systems encompassed the establishment of huduma centres in 290 sub counties with electronic services, digital record management, e-judiciary platform, and case management system. As per the GOK (2018) report, an ICT network operation centre has been established, 4G services rolled out in three cities, an e-Citizen platform and payment interface has been developed to facilitate ease of doing businesses, marriages, driving, lands, immigration, and civil registration services.

In 2014, the Kenyan Government launched e-citizen platform (https://www.ecitizen.go.ke/) with the capability of enabling access to Government to Citizen (G2C) services, including visa services (e-visa) via mobile services (Mpesa, airtel, and equitel), cards, online banking, and e-citizen agents. Similarly, businesses are able to access Government-to-Business (G2B) services such as licenses, permits, and other registrations dubbed e-business through the same portal. In addition, through the Kenya government website (http://www.mygov.go.ke/) citizens, suppliers, and investors are able to obtain the latest information on a daily basis on all government activities, including tenders, notices, and vacancies, government agendas for the central government departments and agencies and county governments. Today digital public services are readily available in far-flung market centres through the e-citizen platform.

10.5 E-Social Protection Services

Social protection in Kenya encompasses social security and social assistance programmes (GOK, 2017b), and utilises a wide range of digital payment providers, including commercial banks, microfinance institutions, savings and credit cooperatives (SACCOs), mobile network operators (such as Mpesa services), and payment service integrators (for instance, Jambopay), to serve a wide range of citizens. The social security under the oversight of Retirement Benefits Authority, boast of 20 per cent pension coverage, and an asset base in excess of ten billion dollars, made up of the National Social Security Fund (NSSF) at seven per cent, occupational retirement benefits scheme, individual retirement benefits scheme, and Civil Service Pension, a non-contributory scheme (RBA, 2019).

The social assistance, which is non-contributory Cash Transfer Programme, of approximately US$ 20 per person per month comprise five per cent for Cash Transfer for Orphans and Vulnerable children (CT–OVC) funded by GOK, UNICEF, World Bank, and DFID from 2004 and a 27% for Older Persons' Cash Transfer (OPCT) programme that began in 2018 as universal pension scheme for elderly citizens over 70 years (GOK, 2017b). Other programmes include Persons with Severe Disabilities Cash Transfer (PwSD) and the traditional General Food Distribution. The social security programme includes public schemes (civil servants pension fund) and employers' occupational and individual insurance scheme underwritten by private insurance schemes. According to Kenya Social Protection Sector Review 2017, tax-financed social protection systems stood at 0.38% of the GDP, which is an enviable level in Africa, but way below that of South Africa and Mauritius, at above three per cent, while most developed countries average 12% of GDP.

10.6 E-Health Care Services

The health sector, classified as a social pillar under Vision 2030, has gained immensely through ICT value addition since its growth cascades to other related areas such as health insurance, hospital management, pharmaceuticals, medical supply and logistics, and patients' management (GOK, 2014b). Dating back to 1966, social medical insurance cover, administered by the National Hospital Insurance Fund (NHIF), is the oldest electronic public service platform in Kenya. Initially, it catered for formal employees and their dependents, but later, it opened up voluntary contribution services to the informal sector. As of December 2016, the fund had 6.3 million paid-up members, with over 25 million beneficiaries. Payments are channelled through banks, mobile phone services or through the NHIF websites. With a monthly payment of US$ five, beneficiaries can access limited outpatient and inpatient (maternal care, renal analysis, rehabilitation, radiology, surgical procedures, cancer, and overseas treatment) cover in selected hospital countrywide and abroad. In addition, individuals and institutions obtain full medical cover from other insurance providers (NHIF, 2020).

Despite the progress made, medical insurance coverage is limited to urban dwellers and those in formal engagement (GOK, 2014b). Through, Kenya e-Health Policy 2014–2030: Towards the attainment of highest standards of health, it is envisaged, among others, that the government will be able to digitise medical records and deploy health information management system, with a view to fully implement the elusive universal health coverage for all citizens (GOK, 2014b). As per the ICT master plan (2014–2017), ICT health services could reach far-flung areas by facilitating e-health and telemedicine through an integrated national health system, linking doctor's management system, drug and supply chains system, and hospital management system, with an e-portal that provides services and information to key stakeholders (GOK, 2014b).

The GOK (2016) report notes that the main challenges in the implementation of e-health projects in Kenya include lack of infrastructure, literacy rates, skilled manpower, electric power connectivity, low funding, and government involvement. Interestingly, it is imperative to note most medical projects are funded by individuals, faith-based organisation, non–governmental organisation, and development partners. The e-health model calls for a patient-centred approach, standardised e-health solutions, integrated e-health systems, inclusive of all stakeholders with robust continuous research and development. The policy proposes a unified shared provision of e-health through a Client Registry (CR) consisting of National Unique Patient Identifier (NUPI), Master Patient Index (MPI), Terminology Service (TS), Health Information Exchange (HIE), and Personal Health Product (PHR) services, among others.

Further, the GOK (2016) report shows some of the gains made towards ensuring quality, security, interoperability, and use of ICT in healthcare in line with global trends, specifically, the Standards and Guidelines of Electronic Medical Record (EMR) Systems in Kenya (2010), Kenya Health Enterprise Architecture (2015), and Kenya Standards for E-Health Systems interoperability (2015). MTP 111 (2018–2022) envisages Universal Health Coverage by 2022 supported by a digital health programme (e-health) that encompass deployment of an electronic health information system (EHIS) interlinking health facilities to enable sharing of health data, promotion of mobile phone health care services (m-health), telemedicine, and enterprise-wide resource planning system.

Though tremendous inroads have been made, challenges abound, notably among them being the cost of health systems, rapid changes in health innovations and technologies, interoperability of diverse e-health systems in place, divergent needs and expectations of customers, incessant regulatory and legal frameworks, and the right to privacy and confidentiality of the patients (GOK, 2016).

10.7 E-Energy Services

EPRA (2020) strategic plan 2020–2023 confirms that over 70% of Kenyans (34.1 million) have access to electricity, promoting economic activities and living standards. In line with the digitisation trends, 97% of primary schools are connected to electricity to fast track the Digital Learning Programme in primary and secondary schools (EPRA, 2020), plus the adjacent communities. The plan shows that online digital platforms and applications promote energy efficiency through the use of smart metres, smart grids, smart appliances, ease in energy application, and communication. EPRA intends to develop a policy to guide upstream electricity data management by the electric firms.

Kenya Power Company customers pay their utility bills for both prepaid (tokens) and post-paid customers mainly through mobile platforms using Mpesa, Airtel, or Equitel pay bill services or through the use of m-banking applications (Kenya Power, 2020), a form of Person-to-Business (P to B) mode. Kenya Power also uses an app, MyPower (Kenya power self-service), that offers a wide range of services to consumers, including payment methods. Similarly, customer complaints, suggestions and other communications are channelled electronically. Besides, Kenya leads in Africa Solar Home System (SHS) market due to the early adoption of Pay as You Go (PAYGO) platforms that enable poor households to access cheap solar asset financing through mobile microcredits firms (Power Africa, 2019), led by Mkopa and Mobisol.

10.8 Digital Learning Programme

MOEST (2005a) sessional paper no. 1 of 2005 on policy framework for education, training, and research, singled out ICT as the backbone of Kenya's knowledge economy, given the role ICT played in the economic development of the western world. Buoyed by the policy direction the education sector support programme 2005–2010 emphasised the need for the development of a national ICT policy and strategy in education and training, an e-learning systems, provision of ICT infrastructure, and education management information system, to foster delivery of quality equitable education in Kenya (MOEST, 2005b). ICT value chain in education could trigger growth in the sector, but requires ICT devices, e-learning curricula, online learning resources, ICT trained teachers, broadband connectivity, and ultimately an e-portal to provide e-learning services and information to stakeholders (GOK, 2014a).

By the end of MTP 11 (2013–2017), the Government had provided 882,765 learners digital devices, teacher digital devices (43,777), content access points (21,133), and 19,409 projectors to primary schools in Kenya. To further strengthen the digital learning programme MTP 111 (2018–2022) sought to scale up digital learning in primary and secondary schools, incorporate Technical and vocational training (TVET), adult and continuing education (ACE), Universities, examination, and use of electronic books. The Government hopes that by developing a National ICT Strategy for Education and Training, establishing National Education Management Information (NEMIS), and by providing robust electronic data management systems (EDMS), digital learning in Kenya will be fully realised.

To foster inclusive quality education, the Government, through sessional paper no. 1 of 2019, committed to strengthen further ICT integration in education and training, by expanding ICT infrastructure, developing digital learning materials and open education resources, promote delivery of ICT-based curriculum to cover all levels including education for learners with special needs and disabilities (MOE, 2019). Since 1968, Kenya Institute of Education, which later changed to Kenya Institute of Curriculum Development (KICD) is mandated to develop curriculum and curriculum support materials mainly through mass media, distance, and electronic learning (KICD, 2020). During the 2010–2015 strategic period, KICD managed to establish a database of e-resources, an e-learning laboratory, e-learning model classroom, digital devices test centres, developed online orientation course for teachers, and trained teachers on how to integrate ICT in teaching and learning (KICD, 2020).

The KICD Strategic Plan 2015–2020 sought to enhance the use of ICT in all education programmes by establishing an Education Research Information System (ERIS), use of cloud services, streaming online digital content through EDU TV channel and radio. KICD has so far managed to prepare, approve, and disseminate interactive digital content (through Kenya education cloud), including sign language, education learning materials, from early years education, primary, secondary to technical vocational education and training (KICD, 2020). KICD uses a variety of mass media, electronic and distance learning to support education in Kenya; common among them is the Education TV channel (EDU TV), the first of its kind in Kenya, and KICD Radio, which has been in use for decades in partnership with the Kenya Broadcasting Corporation (KBC). ICTA (2020) Digischool report shows that Digital Learning Programme (DLP) covers approximately 23,951 primary schools in Kenya with over eight million pupils enabling learners to acquire twenty-first century Skills (literacy, learning, and life skills) by integrating ICT in teaching, learning and management of education and ultimately, promoting universal access to education.

10.9 E-Taxes

It is true that financial inclusivity is positively related to the level of economic development of a country, but in Africa, the penetration rate of traditional financial services over the years has been extremely slow. The rapid adoption of mobile money in Kenya, through Mpesa, a mobile phone financial service platform that facilitates money transfer, real-time retail payment, virtual savings and credit, infers that the sector has potential to transform end-user adoption of ICT services throughout the country. By end of Medium-Term Plan 11 (2013–2017), the government had made major inroads through implementation of an integrated Financial Management Information System (IFMIS) to oversee prudent use of financial resources between the national and county government, an integrated tax management system (itax), which allows the filing of online tax return and use of m-tax, an integrated customs management system (iCMS) and electronic cargo tracking system.

Since 2015, Kenya Revenue Authority (KRA) collects taxes from individuals, businesses, and rental income countrywide through the itax online portal (https://itax.kra.go.ke/), and for exercisable duty goods such as bottled water, juices, energy drinks, soda, and other non-alcoholic drinks, licensed dealers use Excisable Goods Management System online portal (https://egms.kra.go.ke) while, cargo clearance is done through Integrated Customs Management System (iCMS), while a Customer Service Management System (CSMS) is used to enhance client operational experience.

10.10 E-Judiciary Services

Successful public service delivery relies heavily on a robust judiciary, the arm of government that champion's the rights of every citizen. This hitherto has not been the case due to the lack of proper online systems and infrastructure. In Kenya, the Sustaining Judiciary Transformation report 2017–2021 emphasised the need for an efficient and effective service delivery system as opposed to struggling with institutional development and endless capacity-building efforts to expedite justice, by adopting an unparalleled Judiciary digital strategy. The Judicial digital strategy was informed by the successful implementation of Judicial Strategic Plan (2014–2018) and Judiciary Transformation Framework (2012–2016), which observed that lack of ICT facilities and innovative technological solutions hampered the delivery of justice, and singled out ICT as a key enabler of justice (Judiciary, 2017).

The judicial digital strategy focussed on five key aspects of the digitisation process, namely; judicial operations support system (citizen-centric registry and case scheduling), court management system (transcription and documentation), enterprise resource planning (administrative capabilities), document archive management, and ICT infrastructure. The judicial digital strategy was premised on a Judiciary ICT Master Plan 2018–2022 developed with the primary objective of establishing an Integrated Court Management System (ICMS) through an electronic judicial portal, interlinked with electronic court systems, enterprise resource systems, and communications and collaboration systems (Judiciary, 2018). To this end, in mid-2020 the judiciary launched an e-filing system (https://efiling.court.go.ke) enabling Litigants, Lawyers, Prosecutors, High Court, Court of Appeal, and Supreme Court to serve justice expeditiously to everyone thus, rapidly reducing bottlenecks and enhancing transparency (Business Daily, 7 July 2020). Through the online system, litigants can ascertain the cost, pay, and serve defendants with electronic court files.

10.11 E- Land Registry Services

Land resources affect the delivery of all the aforementioned, thus constitute a very critical resource as far as public delivery of services is concerned. As per the MTP 11, by 2017, the GOK had initiated a couple of projects to digitise land registries through electronic document management systems (EDMS), online search and payments in some registries and a national spatial plan. Under MTP 111 by 2022, the government hopes to fully implement a national land information management system (NLIMS) and develop Kenya national spatial data infrastructure (KNSDI) to expedite handling land-related issues.

10.12 Conclusion and Recommendations

Given the digitalisation of public service delivery in the provision of e-citizen-centric services, social protection, healthcare, energy, education, judiciary, taxes, and land registry services in Kenya, it is imperative to note that the strategies, systems, and structures adopted coupled with the leadership styles, staff and skills deployed have been instrumental in the digital public service implementation process. Also evident is the coordination of these elements from the national level to the key specific sector public institutions levels through the provision of key foundations and enablers of digital technologies combined with elaborate collaboration with the private sector digital platforms. Through national policy and legal frameworks, plus timely institutional strategic plans, key timelines and deliverables have been met and challenges addressed. The ability to timely finance the digitalisation process, though not explicitly acknowledged in the analysis, plays an equally significant role.

Despite the successes made in the digitisation of public service delivery in Kenya, challenges abound. Though internet connectivity is within reach of a sizeable population segment, the cost of internet bandwidth, smart mobile phone handsets, and laptops are very prohibitive. Although concerted efforts were made to make available locally assembled laptops and other ICT parts, most of the devices are imported, and users have to buy their own gadgets. This has slowed the adoption of digital public services against the projections. Thus, whereas the policy framework and strategic direction are in place, the provision of ICT infrastructure, especially portable devices, has slowed the momentum gained so far. There is, therefore, a need to re-examine further the foundations, pillars, and guiding principles of the adoption of ICT and mobile platforms in the provision of government services in Kenya. However, the mileage gained can be used by other countries to benchmark their public service delivery platforms. Notably, with the unprecedented degree of adoption of online platforms in Africa, its overall contribution to the social, economic, and political development of the continent will have far-reaching positive implications on the future of the continent if e-government strategies are implemented.

References

Brown, D. C. G., & Toze, S. (2017). Information governance in digitized public administration. *Canadian Public Administration, 60*(4), 581–604. https://onlinelibrary.wiley.com/doi/full/10.1111/capa.12227

Business Daily. (2020, July, 1). Judiciary role out electronic filing system. *Business Daily.* https://www.businessdailyafrica.com/economy/Judiciary-rolls-out-electronic-filing-system/3946234-5586186-104f48y/index.html

Criado, J. I., & Gil-Garcia, J. M. (2019). Creating public value through smart technologies and strategies: From digital services to artificial intelligence and beyond. *Journal of Public Sector Management.* https://www.emerald.com/insight/content/doi/10.1108/IJPSM-07-2019-0178/full/html

EPRA. (2020). *Energy and Petroleum Regulatory Authority (EPRA) strategic plan 2020–2023.* Ministry of Energy and Petroleum: Energy and Petroleum Regulatory Authority. https://www.epra.go.ke/about/our-strategic-plan/

Giest, S., & Raaphorst, N. (2018). Unraveling the hindering factors of digital public service delivery at street-level: The case of electronic health records. *Policy Design and Practice, 1*(2), 141–154. https://doi.org/10.1080/25741292.2018.1476002

Gil-Garcia, J. M., Dawes, S. S., & Pardo, T. A. (2018). Digital government and public management research: Finding the crossroads. *Public Management Review, 20*(5), 633–646. https://doi.org/10.1080/14719037.2017.1327181

GOK. (2004). *E—Government strategy: The strategic framework, administrative structure, training requirements and Standardization Framework*. https://www.ict.go.ke/wp-content/uploads/2019/05/KENYA-E-GOVERNMENT-STRATEGY-2004.pdf

GOK. (2008). *Medium Term Plan (MTP 1) 2008–2012*. Retrieved on October 8, 2020, http://vision2030.go.ke/inc/uploads/2018/06/kenya_medium_term_plan_2008-2012-1.pdf

GOK. (2014a). *The Kenya national ICT master plan 2014–2017*. Ministry of Information and Communication Technology. http://icta.go.ke/pdf/THE%20NATIONAL%20ICT%20MASTERPLAN%202017.pdf

GOK. (2014b). *Kenya health policy 2014–2030: Towards attaining the highest standards of health*. Ministry of Health. http://publications.universalhealth2030.org/uploads/kenya_health_policy_2014_to_2030.pdf

GOK. (2016). *Kenya national eHealth policy 2016–2030: Towards attainment of the highest standard of health through adoption and use of ICT (digiafya)*. File:///C:/Users/akinoti/Downloads/KENYA-NATIONAL-eHEALTH-POLICY-2016-2030.pdf.

GOK. (2017a). *Public service transformation framework: Transforming Kenya our country ourpeople our future 2017–2022*. The Presidency, Ministry of Public Service, Youth & Gender Affairs. https://uclgafrica-alga.org/wp-content/uploads/2019/05/PUBLIC-SERVICE-TRANSFORMATION-FRAMEWORK.pdf

GOK. (2017b). *Kenya social protection sector review 2017*. Ministry of Labour and Social Protection State Department for Social Protection. http://www.socialprotection.or.ke/images/downloads/KENYA-SOCIAL-PROTECTION-SECTOR-REVIEW/Kenya%20Social%20Protection%20Sep%204.pdf

GOK. (2018). *Third Medium Term Plan (MTP 111) 2018–2022*. Retrieved on October 4, 2020, https://planning.go.ke/wpcontent/uploads/2018/12/THIRD-MEDIUM-TERM-PLAN-2018-2022.pdf

Gupta, S., Keen, M., Shah, A., & Gerdier, G. (Eds.). (2017). *Digital revolutions in public finance*. Washington, DC. International Monetary Fund.

Hui, G., & Hayllar, M. K. (2010). Creating public value in e-government: A Public-Private-citizen collaboration framework in web 2.0. *The Australian Journal of Public Administration, 69*(S1), S120–S131. https://onlinelibrary.wiley.com/doi/epdf/10.1111/j.1467-8500.2009.00662.x

ICTA. (2020). *Digischool.* http://icta.go.ke/digischool/about-digischool/

Jones, S., & Hooper, T. (2017). New Zealand's ICT strategy: The respective roles of senior and middle management in promoting collaboration and innovation. *Asia and Pacific Policy Studies, 4*(3), 484–495. https://onlinelibrary.wiley.com/doi/full/10.1002/app5.199

Judiciary. (2017). *Sustaining judiciary transformation: A service delivery agenda 2017–2021.* file:///C:/Users/akinoti/Downloads/STRATEGIC%20BLUEPRINT.pdf.

Judiciary. (2018). *Judiciary ICT master plan 2018–2022.* https://www.judiciary.go.ke/download/judiciary-ict-master-plan-2018-2022/

Karwan, K. R., & Markland, R. E. (2006). Integrating service design principles and information technology to improve delivery and productivity in public sector operations: The case of the South Carolina DMV. *Journal of Operations Management, 24*(4), 347–362.

Kenya Power. (2020). *Paying your electricity bill.* https://kplc.co.ke/content/item/30/Paying-your-Electricity-Bill

KICD. (2020). *Kenya Institute of Curriculum Development (KICD). Strategic plan 2015–2020.* https://kicd.ac.ke/about-us/kicd-functions/

Kukkamalla, P. K., Bikfalvi, A., & Arbussa, A. (2020). The new BMW: Business model innovation transforms an automotive leader. *Journal of Business Strategy.* https://www.emerald.com/insight/content/doi/10.1108/JBS-02-2020-0021/full/html

MOE. (2019). *Ministry of Education (MOE). Sessional paper no. 1 of 2019: A policy framework for education and training for sustainable development in Kenya; towards realizing relevant and inclusive education and training for sustainable development.* https://www.education.go.ke/images/NESSP/SESSIONALPAPER2019.pdf

MOES&T. (2005a). *Ministry of Education Science and Technology (MOES&T). Sessional paperno. 1of 2005 on a policy framework for education, training and research: Meeting the challenges of education training and research in the 21*st *century.* http://www.knqa.go.ke/wp-content/uploads/2018/10/sessional-paper-sept.-2005-final.pdf

MOES&T. (2005b). *Ministry of Education Science and Technology (MOES&T): Kenya education sector support programme 2005–2010; delivering quality equitable education.* https://planipolis.iiep.unesco.org/sites/planipolis/files/ressources/kenya_kessp_final_2005.pdf

NHIF. (2020). *Health insurance operations.* http://www.nhif.or.ke/healthinsurance/Operations

OECD. 2014. *Recommendation of the council on digital government strategies.* http://www.oecd.org/gov/digital-government/Recommendation-digital-government-strategies.pdf

Power Africa. (2019). *Off—Grid solar market assessment Kenya.* https://sun-connect-news.org/fileadmin/DATEIEN/Dateien/New/PAOP-Kenya-MarketAssessment-Final_508.pdf

Ranerup, A., Henriksen, H. Z., & Hedman, J. (2016). An analysis of business models in public service platforms. *Government Information Quarterly, 33*(1), 6–14. ISSN 0740–624X, https://doi.org/10.1016/j.giq.2016.01.010http://www.sciencedirect.com/science/article/pii/S0740624X16300107

RBA. (2019). *Retired benefits authority's strategic plan 2019–2024.* Retirement Benefits authority. file:///C:/Users/akinoti/Downloads/RBA%20STRATEGIC%20PLAN%202019%20-%202024-compressed.pdf.

Tassabehji, R., Hackney, R., & Maruyama, T. (2019). Evaluating digital public services: A contingency value approach within three exemplar developing countries. *Information Technology and People, 32*(4), 1021–1043. https://www.emerald.com/insight/content/doi/10.1108/ITP-08-2017-0260/full/html

Part III

Recommendations for Skills Development in Digital Service Delivery

11

Digital Skills and Strategic Postures: Insights from African Digital Entrepreneurs

Nasiru Taura

11.1 Introduction

The 'ubiquitous' nature of the internet has stimulated a renewed interest in digital entrepreneurship in Africa (Ranchhod, 2019). Unlike conventional entrepreneurship, the processes of digital entrepreneurship require a high degree of ICT competencies to integrate web applications, customise market-specific online experiences, build technology infrastructure, integrate business processes, and build brand community (Ngoasong, 2018). Specifically, digital entrepreneurship encompasses the processes of production, application, and distribution of technology (digital software) by '*skilled* and *opportunity-oriented* individuals and ventures' (Bolat, 2019; Friederici, 2019: 10). The process also entails 'identifying technology-intensive opportunities, efficient gathering of

N. Taura (✉)
Bournemouth University, Poole, UK
e-mail: ntaura@bournemouth.ac.uk

O. Adeola et al. (eds.), *Digital Service Delivery in Africa*, Palgrave Studies of Marketing in Emerging Economies,
https://doi.org/10.1007/978-3-030-83909-3_11

resources, such as capital and talents, adapting to rapid growth and changes' (Siyanbola et al., 2011).

Higher digital competencies can increase the likelihood of interpreting contextual constraints as entrepreneurial opportunities (Ngoasong, 2018), as well as a more positive outlook for interpreting situated contextual challenges as an asset instead of a liability (Welter, 2011). Digital skills also enable digital entrepreneurs to shape and influence their entrepreneurial choices and post-entry strategic decisions (Autio et al., 2014). This has led to some new generation of African entrepreneurs becoming active seekers of digital skills—hence the rise of digital skills provisioning as a key aspect of Africa's digital entrepreneurial ecosystem (Sussan & Acs, 2017).

Many digital entrepreneurs in Africa embark on the journey of digital skills development without a clear strategy due to insufficient entrepreneurial digital competencies (EDC) (Ngoasong, 2018). Failure to pursue a strategic approach for digital enterprises often leads to an eclectic collection of a broad 'hodgepodge' (Shane & Vankataraman, 2000), of a mainly fragmented portfolio of digital skills, not enabling them to create and capture value locally and globally (Lepak et al., 2007). The above is not surprising since the field of entrepreneurship itself has been described as a 'broad label under which a hodgepodge of research is housed' (Shane & Vankataraman, 2000). Although the 'ubiquitous' nature of the internet has enabled numerous opportunities in the African continent, it has also escalated the need to acquire multiple digital skills (Taura & Radicic, 2019).

The above developments have led to the creation of multiple skills provision platforms in Africa, namely digital/tech hubs, innovation labs, hackerspaces, fab/maker spaces, DIY labs, among others (Atiasea et al., 2020; Friederici, 2019; Hopkins, 2015). Unfortunately, the development of such platforms has not led to commensurate creations of world-class digital ventures/solutions to come out of Africa. The average African digital enterprise has been described as entities unable to expand internationally, attract VC, disrupt traditional industries, and create local digital infrastructures (Friederici et al., 2020). Scholars argue that the internet connectivity may have even worsened instead of enabling opportunities for African regions to catch up with the rest of the world (Friederici et al., 2017; Ojanpera et al., 2017).

Contrary to above, as indicated across the continent, especially in the digital incubators (Ngoasong, 2018)—a new generation of digital entrepreneurs is on the rise (Ngoasong, 2018). The nature of their networks is characterised by: (the use of modern IT, trust, transparency, advocacy, commitment to intra-African commerce, and vision to promote regional economic integration) (McDade & Spring, 2005). They are transforming the African business landscape, particularly through a strengthened private sector economic growth (McDade & Spring, 2005). We believe that the heterogeneity of the African business landscape makes the tendency to assume their universal underperformance or non-performance to be untenable. We take a pragmatic view of the African digital landscape focusing on the variations in the performances of African digital enterprises—in which due to differences of strategic postures and practices induced by skills-sets, some African digital entrepreneurs remain stagnant, some retrogressed, but some few prosper locally or globally (Taura & Radicic, 2019; Taura & Watkins, 2014). Our quest to understand the nature of these variations in digital skills-sets and competencies in Africa, and how they create and capture value (Lepak et al., 2007) has spurred our focus on a central research question that seeks to find:

> What strategic postures and practices are deployed by successful African digital enterprises, and how do they develop their portfolio of digital skills-sets and entrepreneurial competencies?

The above central research question has led to the development of four baseline propositions taking into consideration peculiarities and hostile environment of doing digital business in Africa (Chakravorti & Chaturvedi, 2019), and the penurious resources environment (inhibited mainly lack of digital infrastructure) among others. The propositions encompass aspects of digital bricolage, passion and learning from failure, breadth and depth of digital skills, as well as co-evolution of digital competencies. This study is vital, as we believe that by understanding the strategic postures and practices of digital enterprises in Africa, we can propose theoretical advances that are quintessentially African. In so doing, the identified salient features that enable these African digital firms to succeed despite the challenges and limitations in their environments can provide a source of local narrative and aspirational capital for prospective African digital enterprises to seek to achieve (Friederici et al., 2020). Our work is influenced by theories of entrepreneurial, strategic, and organisational actions (Greenfield & Ribbins, 1993; McMullen & Shepherd, 2006).

The chapter is organised as follows: the introduction sets the stage and raises the central research question. Thereafter, the emergence, concept, and scope of African digital entrepreneurship are traced and examined to provide an overview. Before examining the strategic postures and practices, the debates in regard to the digital skills paradox are presented, taking into consideration the African experiences. Finally, and in the light of proposed theoretical advances and the African-centric narrative of digital enterprises, four baseline propositions are postulated.

Also, we summarised the propositions in the form of a practical tool/matrix, which other African digital entrepreneurs could employ while developing their digital skills and competencies portfolio. The chapter concludes with insights and potentials of skills development and digital entrepreneurship in Africa.

11.2 Digital Entrepreneurship in Africa: Emergence, Concept, and Scope

11.2.1 Emergence of Africa Digital Entrepreneurship

Although Sub Saharan Africa (SSA) is 'one of the least wired parts of the globe' (Poushter et al., 2018: 6), the arrival of undersea digital networks such as Seacom, EASSy, TEAMS, WACS, and ACE (Africa Coast Europe), among others has led to the emergence and development of a critical mass of digital enterprises in Africa (Ranchhod, 2019). Despite a late start, Africa experiences one of the fastest growth rates of internet usage globally (Gathege & Moraa, 2013). Consequently, between 2010 and 2016 alone, it was estimated that about 173–314 digital/tech hubs sprung up on the African soil to support entrepreneurs (Friederici, 2019).

The digital networks as well as support organisations such as tech hubs have enabled and supported the proliferation of newer forms of opportunities for entrepreneurs to exploit a digital space in both coastal and landlocked areas of Africa (Friederici et al., 2017; Ranchhod, 2019). Also, the new media (social media) have stimulated, and deepened interests in internet-enabled services/ventures and are shaping new practices and experiences for African digital entrepreneurs (Bolat, 2019). The ubiquitous nature of the internet has risen the aspirations of African entrepreneurs to create and capture values on a level playing space beyond traditional borders, in ways that were not thought possible (Taura et al., 2019; Friederici et al., 2020; Sussan & Acs, 2017). The aspiration of digital entrepreneurship to become a powerful driver to local economic transformation and development in Africa as well as the mobile-first mindset are leading to significant changes in the landscape (Bolat, 2019; Ndemo & Weiss, 2016; IMDs World Digital Competitiveness Index, 2017).

Today Africa is home to many digital-based ventures, including software development, digital platforms, e-commerce, and multi-media—who sell digitised products and services (Ngoasong, 2018). Particularly, the two largest economies, Nigeria and South Africa remain in the 'break out' and watch out zones, respectively, and digitally savvy Kenya has picked up an impressive level of momentum by assembling a thriving ecosystem (Chackrovarti et al., 2017). The above demonstrates how digital entrepreneurship is emerging, with variations among the African countries on digitalisation likely to generate more healthy competitions, growths, and competitiveness on the continent (Taura et al., 2019).

11.2.2 Concepts of Digital Entrepreneurship in Africa

The digital entrepreneurship concept and processes essentially involve the production and trading of '*digital artefact*'. These are 'man-made purposeful objects embodied in information and communication technology components of software and hardware' (Von Briel et al., 2018: 292). They can be re-combined, edited, and distributed, as well as offer unlimited scope to developing new digital solutions (Wim and Werner, 2019), thus, require complementary digital skill-sets. Digital skills deficiencies (technical and content-related), (Claro et al., 2012; Janssen et al., 2013) have become one of the most significant factors inhibiting Africa to realise the full potential offered by the digital revolution. As entrepreneurs can develop successful entrepreneurial ventures by delegating the technical operations in more capable hands, we follow other scholars shift towards what is considered as the higher order or content-related skills (Claro et al., 2012; Janssen et al., 2013).

We consider the entrepreneurial search process as essentially cognitive (Simon, 1969; Sarasvathy, 2001; Sarasvathy, 2003)—hence a digital entrepreneur in the twenty-first century should be fully equipped with the cognitive competencies dimension of the digital entrepreneurial process, including critical thinking, creativity, and problem-solving (Wechsler et al., 2018). Cognitive research in entrepreneurship has consistently demonstrated how cognitive mastery can lead to 'expert entrepreneurship' (Sarasvathy et al., 2008; Sarasvathy, 2001). We believe the twenty-first-century African digital entrepreneur who masters the cognitive processes to 'search for relevant information, justify their choices, generate innovative and worthwhile ideas for their fields, and find solutions to the problem in digital environments' would be the most effective to create and capture value (Şendağ & Odabaşı, 2009; Yang, 2015).

11.2.3 Scope of Digital Entrepreneurship and Skills in Africa

Regarding the scope of digital entrepreneurship and skills in Africa, the following are crucial: the higher order cognitive digital skills: '*information digital skills*' (defining the search queries, selecting a website to seek information, selecting information or in search results, and evaluating the information found); '*critical thinking digital skills*' (justification, breadth of understanding, and critical assessment); '*creative digital skills*' (fluency and originality); '*problem-solving digital skills*' (identifying the problem, providing appropriate solutions, and explaining the solutions) (Van Laar et al., 2018). Of the four higher order cognitive digital skills identified, research has shown that the most difficult ones are 'information digital skills' as well as 'problem solving digital skills' (Van Laar et al., 2018).

UNESCO Digital Skills for Life (2017) has also identified the following key digital skills: *Networked computing* (skills such as trans-media navigation, circulation of contents, and understanding of audiences); *Social and Collaborative* (collaborative problem-solving, social skills to participate in online communities); *Proprietary and open forms of technological provision* (co-production requires technical skills, collaborative design capabilities, and understanding of IP). *Participatory/Co-creation and Making* (working creatively together with others, multitasking, experimentation); *Data-based and Computational* (data literacy skills, understanding of algorithms); *Remote and Automated Systems* (interpersonal; skills to collaborate alongside machines and other automated systems. We believe the starting point for the continent of Africa is to consider developing an effective system of strategic skills development, including (re-skilling and or up-skilling) to encourage digital entrepreneurs, and intrapreneurs on the continent to develop digital competencies. In response to the needs of African digital entrepreneurs, we have proposed certain useful strategic postures that can enable them to pursue the development of digital competencies over time.

11.3 Digital Skills Deficiency: A Quintessentially African Experience

Several studies have already established that African entrepreneurs suffer from poorly developed entrepreneurial skills, lack of skilled personnel, low-level technological capabilities, and limited technical and technological human resources (Adeboye, 1997; Fick, 2002). Some even argued that such negative skills development path was inherited since independence (Adeboye, 1997; Fick, 2002; Robson et al., 2009).

A new generation of platforms, mainly in form of DIY-Tech Hubs, Fab Maker spaces, are challenging the traditional University systems in Africa—with newer approaches to knowledge and skills development for entrepreneurs (Mounde et al., 2020). These are platforms that provide enabling environment for engaging users and stakeholders in knowledge co-creation in African settings (Mounde et al., 2020). Within the last three years, the number of tech hubs in Africa doubled from 314 in 2016 to 643 in 2019 (Kelly et al., 2016). They can operate as incubators, accelerators, co-working spaces, fab/maker spaces, etc. They often use their virtual learning platforms to foster skills development through training and workshop—thus broadening and deepening the skills need of African entrepreneurs (David-West et al., 2018; International Trade Centre, 2019). They focus on Mode–2 knowledge creation (which is knowledge created in the context of application) (Mounde et al., 2020). Consequently, they provide an alternative avenue for tacking local and community solutions using below-the-radar innovations (Mounde et al., 2020).

A variation of the DIY-Tech hub, referred to as fab/maker space movement, focuses on people who engage in the creative production of artifacts in an open space—using example rapid prototyping, innovative thinking (Mounde et al., 2020). There are now over eight maker spaces in Kenya (Nairobi, Kisumu, and Mombasa) as well as one in the University of Nairobi (Baarbé & Nzomo, 2017). Often associated with tinkerers, hackers, designers, and inventors—but now found legitimacy in universities as fab labs (Vossoughi et al., 2016). They operate based on the philosophy of democratisation of knowledge and access to tools/skills normally preserved for experts (Sheridan et al., 2014).

In the light of the development of skills provision centres across Africa in the form of digital/tech hubs, Fabs and Makerspaces labs, incubators/accelerators, digital training platforms, as well as traditional University skill centre provisions among others, it is expected that there would be a fundamental rise in entrepreneurial and digital competences across the continent. Paradoxically, the dramatic explosion of skills provision centres has not translated into a commensurate entrepreneurial and digital competence across the continent. It has been quite challenging for the hubs to find and utilise experienced entrepreneurs to pass on their skills to less experienced ones, due to lack of real engagement and commitment (Friederici, 2019). A report published by Harvard Business Review on the ranking of the countries by tech, data, and business skills generates some thought-provoking results on the position of developing economies in particular Africa.

> Countries with developing economies — and with less to invest in education — see the largest skill deficiencies, with 90% ranking in the lagging or emerging categories. A country's rank across the business, technology, and data science is negatively correlated with per-capita GDP and positively correlated with automation risk, meaning more skilled countries show better economic performance and lower risk of labor market disruption from automation. (Sands & Bakthavachalam, 2019)

Of the 60 countries included in the report, Nigeria was classified as a laggard country Number 53 (business skills) and last number 60 (tech skills) (Sands & Bakthavachalam, 2019). Also, Egypt and Kenya were ranked as 57 and 58, respectively, on tech skills (Sands & Bakthavachalam, 2019). In addition to the above, the only African country that made it to the Ease of Doing Digital Business, South Africa, was not a strong performer either (Chakravorti and Chaturvedi, 2019). The Africa story of skills deficiency is not, however, a final arbiter (conclusive)—regarding Africa's skills development potentials.

Some reports focusing on the evolutionary tendencies have mapped Africa's digital skills landscape with a more positive outlook for the future. For example, Chakravorty et al. (2017), which focused on mapping the digital momentum zones in Africa, reported that 'the two largest economies, Nigeria and South Africa, remain in Break Out and Watch Out zones, respectively, digitally savvy Kenya has picked up an impressive level of momentum by assembling a thriving ecosystem'.

The African youths aspiring to become digital entrepreneurs have chosen to focus their primary question on how can they organise their entrepreneurial and digital skills search and retention more effectively, rather than worrying about the systemic challenges of corruption, market failures, political instability, and weak institutions (Adeboye, 1997; Fick,

2002; Robson et al., 2009). They realised that unlike their counterparts in more advanced economies, they must learn to handle the double burden of having to learn institutional entrepreneurship in the process of becoming effective digital entrepreneurs. They traverse the difficult and sometimes hostile terrain of doing digital business rather patiently—while building their skills. Accordingly, they are more likely to concern themselves with evaluating and assessing which of the skills provision sources are more appropriate for their skills development and prospects. Below we explore ways in which some African entrepreneurs are prospering by following certain strategic postures:

11.4 Propositions on Strategic Postures

11.4.1 Digital Bricolage as a Strategic Posture-1

African digital entrepreneurs operate in environments with penurious resources constraint, which necessitate them to become digital bricoleurs early in their start-up journey (Levi-Straus, 1996; Ruling & Duymedjian, 2014). They develop enterprises within a digital ecosystem with weak infrastructural capabilities (Susan & Acs, 2017). Their limited resources and identity forced them into a closed and finite world of inward resource seeking—hence provoking them to use 'what is at hand' and familiar (Levi-Straus, 1996). One African entrepreneur stated how 'making do' with available 'digital asset' a computer triggered him into becoming a digital media entrepreneur as stated below:

> After graduation, there were no jobs. My dad bought me this machine [pointing to a desktop computer] which is eight years old now. I sat with my computer and started learning and developing my business. I refer to it as a media business. We help institutions to communicate online, on print, brochures, letterheads and business cards. We use ICT as a vehicle to do our business. (Entrepreneur 4, cited in Ngoasong, 2018: 493)

Digitalisation and dematerialisation facilitated their ability to enact digital bricolage by 'making do' applying combinations of the digital resources at hand to new problems and opportunities (Levi-Straus, 1996; Ruling & Duymedjian, 2014). They tended to highly rely on their coordinating mechanisms to mix and recycle digital opportunities into new meaning to solve local problems (Levi-Straus, 1996; Ruling & Duymedjian, 2014). The study reported how an African entrepreneur developed an app that uploaded the packages of local tourist attractions in Cameroon, acting as an online medium coordinating between the local tourist agencies and tourists (Ngoasong, 2018).

Hence, the entrepreneur applied digital bricolage by identifying under-utilised resources (unavailable local tourist information online), mixing it with data collection by physically travelling to the tourist destinations—and thereafter, made it available for tourists at a commission (Ngoasong, 2018). Since digital resources and ubiquitous connectivity have opened up almost limitless possibilities to share, assemble, and re-combine resources online (Ruling & Duymedjian, 2014; Taura & Radicic, 2019), they often began their search for under-utilised/underrepresented digital assets to be combined, or re-mixed early in their start-up journey. Also, since they realised they do not have resource advantages available to the larger digital platforms (unicorns) operating in more favourable environments to develop legitimacy, they focus attention on the local resources available to them, including their technical knowledge owner's technical knowledge base (Cooper, 1971; Watkins, 1973), amateur local (developers, programmers, coders, etc.) and self-taught skills that would otherwise go unapplied (Vallierie & Gegenhuber, 2014), to create functional platforms with less aesthetic properties. In addition, another African entrepreneur was reported to have explained how limited access to finance has led them 'to rely on students, interns with knowledge of IT and market research, hired ad-hoc on either low pay or as volunteers to physically collect and input the travel data of local bus companies on to the digital platform' (Ngoasong, 2018).

Their main challenge often arises in designing and developing digital artefacts—by drawing from fragments of the best possible eclectic sources and sampling of available digital skills and other resources locally (Vallierie & Gegenhuber, 2014). In particular, the knowledge required for sources of digital skills supply as well as the coordinating mechanism to create, share, and exchange digital artifacts are limited in Africa (Ruling & Duymedjian, 2014). For example, a study suggests that, despite the hopes of democratisation afforded by the information revolution, the SSA is still struggling to provide an atmosphere for efficient collaborative software development/coding, and internet domain registrations (digitally mediated knowledge production) in comparison to other geographical spaces around the world (Ojanpera et al., 2017).

The above can be exacerbated by the tendency of collective bricolage (world view)—which arises due to shared socio-cognitive proximities (Bechky & Okhuysen, 2011). Consequently, this puts the digital bricoleurs under pressure to coordinate knowledge/content production and exchange on an online community-based system in digitally mediated spaces (Ojanpera et al., 2017; Ruling & Duymedjian, 2014). They have had to remain creative under pressure and apply themselves to knowing all the available digital resources/skills in their locality '*intimately*', establish coordinating mechanisms to enable digital bricolage, leading to insights from novel combinations (Ruling & Duymedjian, 2014). A new generation of African entrepreneur-bricoleurs (Ngoasong, 2018), highly educated, and professionally networked are changing the narrative of how digital bricolage is enabling them to forge new ways of digital value creation.

Some of these entrepreneurs acquired formal ICT education, but many have self-taught themselves, for example, aspects of ICT, web/mobile development, and multi-media (Ngoasong, 2018).

By utilising the power of ubiquitous internet, they identify underutilised or discarded digital resources/assets—which can be in the form of digital artifacts such as 'codes' already developed elsewhere, and then mix, and re-mix, re-combine, edit with their complementary skills-sets to develop a fully functional value-driven digital solutions (Naudé & Liebregts, 2020; Von Briel et al., 2018), but also require complementary digital skill-sets. Please see an example from the interview extract from a Maputo-based entrepreneur below:

> They asked, can you help us to sort this problem. I said now I have to think of a solution to build that, that's when I started to search and – I like to do things fast. I said, if I'm going to do this from scratch, it would take too much time, and I would be losing too much time on testing. And, clients at the end of the day, don't like to be the first users, they are the beta testers. I search everywhere; I find it in a piece of code that was already built. I gave a proposal for the owner of the code: Don't you want to sell me your code? Then I bought the code and start putting all my modifications: then adding all the needs that all other companies will need. (Founder in Maputo, cited in Friederici et al., 2020: 161)

As demonstrated above, several examples of digital bricolage abound in Africa, and this is likely to continue developing (Ngoasong, 2017), as a popular strategic posture and practice adopted by African digital entrepreneurs who prosper. Popular examples include using under-utilised pieces of codes (Friederici et al., 2020), harnessing mobile technologies and social media, online and offline bricolage (bridge) (Ngoasong, 2018). Given the above, we state the following propositions:

Proposition 1: *Entrepreneurs in Africa who adopt digital bricolage as a strategic*
Posture (Ability to coordinate under-utilised fragments of skill-sets and or digital
Artifacts) are more likely to develop a portfolio of mixed skill fragments for
Collaborative value creation and capture

11.4.2 Passion for Technology and Learning from Failure as a Strategic Posture-2

Competence includes skills as well as goal pursuit (Ngoasong, 2018). Thus, passion provides essential energy towards coherence and coordination of the goal pursuit (Cardon et al., 2009). A study of African entrepreneurs demonstrates how entrepreneurs without formal ICT education have engaged in self-study and learning by doing to develop their digital competencies driven mainly by passion and a strong desire for new technologies (Ngoasong, 2017).

Passion provides intense positive energy for entrepreneurs to engage in the search for newer digital competencies. In so doing, the entrepreneurial passion provides 'consciously accessible, intense positive feelings experienced by engagement in entrepreneurial activities associated with roles that are meaningful and salient to the self-identity of the entrepreneur' (Cardon et al., 2009: 517).

Passionate African digital entrepreneurs, in their rush to embrace new technology and or utilise it in exploiting opportunities in Africa, as well as the rush to be first trendsetters in Africa, fail early but cheaply—but frequently innovate afterwards (Sarasvathy, 2001; Taura & Radicic, 2019). Due to the hostile nature of their environment, they often encounter multiple failures along the way, but they remain undeterred, using the failure as a basis to intensify search or experimentation with newer combinations of resources—hence leading to more variety, and less uncertainty (McGrath, 1999).

While some quit after few failures, the most passionate African entrepreneurs persist, while learning from the failures and building vital digital skills to be utilised eventually (McGrath, 1999). While failure can be catastrophic, it also enables entrepreneurs to see things differently (McGrath, 1999). For example, failures enable intensified search more broadly in areas that might not have initially been intended or planned by the entrepreneurs (McGrath, 1999). It also reduces the uncertainties, should the entrepreneurs re-launch another digital enterprise after failure (McGrath, 1999).

The process of learning after a business failure for African entrepreneurs with a passion for technology enables them to learn multiple relevant digital skills from past experiences (Ucbasaran et al., 2013). Such accumulation from prior experiences, and leveraging of the human capital here in form of (digital competencies), enables entrepreneurs to develop portfolios through the subsequent launch of innovative products and services—frequently (Robson et al., 2012; Taura & Radicic, 2019). By becoming serial and portfolio entrepreneurs the negative impact of failing reduces, as the cost of failure could be spread, and also the option value available to them from their other business undertakings is high in comparison to novice entrepreneurs (McGrath, 1999).

Although the failure rate of the business is high globally, it is higher in Africa comparatively due to institutional void, weak infrastructure among others (Adeboye, 1997; Fick, 2002; Robson et al., 2009). Also, given the hostile environment of doing digital business in Africa, the high failure rate of digital entrepreneurs could be transformed into an opportunity to preserve certain selective skills learned during the failed attempt for subsequent reproduction and accumulation (Aldrich & Reuf, 2006; Gluckler, 2007).

A high failure rate can be positive, provided that the cost of failing is limited such that high rates of business founding and exiting are associated with economic vibrancy (Birch, 1979). Also, through 'optimistic martyrdom', those who failed can signal new market opportunities for other more competent entrepreneurs (Kahneman, 2011). By adopting real options reasoning, they focus on the 'downside' instead of 'upside' to minimise costs through practices of, for example, re-selling the assets and repurposing the digital skills learned in the process, and they fall forward instead of backward (McGrath, 1999).

On the one hand, while passion (intense positive feeling) enables the African digital entrepreneurs to embark on a coherent goal pursuit of developing certain digital skills and competencies (Cardon et al., 2009). On the other hand, multiple early failures lead to the repurposing of learned digital skills by applying them in newly launched ventures to create new digital solutions and or artifacts (Robson et al., 2012).

This creates a branch-like structural shape with multiple repurposed branches of originally failed ideas. Such portfolio digitally competent entrepreneurs in Africa tended to exhibit enduring and strong skills competencies root. Given the strong root, they go ahead to re-launch new digital innovations and succeed eventually (Robson et al., 2012). Examples were found in a study of Ghanaian portfolio entrepreneurs—who experienced a higher degree of success when they launch innovations in comparison to novel entrepreneurs (Robson et al., 2012). Given the above, and by extension, we suspect that the skills acquired in building the portfolio of innovative digital ventures, as well as the learnings from previous experiences of failures, can improve the likelihood of developing entrepreneurial digital competencies. Thus, we state the following propositions:

Proposition 2: *Entrepreneurs in Africa with a high degree of passion for technology*

(Ability to use intense positive feelings to pursue goals) and ability to learn from

Previous experiences of failure, are more likely to develop a

Coherent and robust digital portfolio of skills for creating and capturing value

11.4.3 Breadth and Depth of Digital Skills as Strategic Posture-3

External search strategies can give rise to the performance heterogeneity of firms (Laursen & Slater, 2006). Thus, it has become imperative for African digital entrepreneurs to develop a clear strategy of organising digital skills search through a 'depth' of (platforms) or 'breadth' across multiple (platforms) channels.

The arrival of digital technologies in Africa has transformed the environment of doing business and created newer opportunities; but at the same time have intensified the need for digital entrepreneurs to engage in active search for critical digital skills 'widely' and 'deeply' (Laursen & Slater, 2006). Previous studies on search, although insightful, have focused attention on knowledge and firm as the unit of analyses (Katila & Ahuja, 2002; Laursen & Slater, 2006). Most of such studies also focused on advanced Western economies.

We extend these studies by focusing on the search for digital skills pursued by African entrepreneurs, and how they utilised different strategies—to enable them to acquire critical digital competencies. For example, acquiring skills in fab labs or DIY Tech hub requires different pedagogic processes, compared to a University (Mounde et al., 2020). Following Laursen and Slater (2006), we focus on the external channels (in this case—suppliers of digital skills in Africa)—mainly Fab or Maker spaces, Innovation and tech hubs, incubators/accelerators, University's, etc. (Mounde et al., 2020). To understand the effectiveness of search on these platforms/channels, we see each of them as a separate search space, requiring different organisation practices (Laursen & Slater, 2006). Thus, we developed propositions that provide insights on the importance of breadth and depth to external digital skills search in the African context/setting.

While external search 'breadth' focuses on the broad number of external sources and channels, the external search 'depth' focuses on the extent drawn/acquired deeply from the aforementioned external sources and channels (Laursen & Slater, 2006). The explosion of such skills centres in Africa can confound even the providers, and to a great extent, the target entrepreneurs—hence the need for a clear strategy to develop digital skills and competencies.

Organising skills through a breadth of multiple digital platform channels (skills provision centres) can be daunting especially for digital start-ups in Africa. The resource-constrained small digital firms in Africa are often faced with the difficult problem of 'attention allocation problem' (Ocasio, 1997).

Choosing the right mix of platforms to concentrate on for skills building by digital entrepreneurs in Africa requires a certain degree of managerial attention and commitment (Taura & Radicic, 2019). In an attempt to balance between internal vs. external strategies to acquire relevant knowledge as well as skills from numerous platform channels (skills provision centres) (Grimpe & Kaiser, 2010), the constrained resource base of the digital firm suffers (Taura & Radicic, 2019).

Scholars have suggested that a clear search criterion provides opportunities to choose among the variety of paths. African entrepreneurs, without or low levels of absorptive capacity who search digital skills broadly across all platforms, channels, and sources, are unlikely to succeed in developing the digital competence required for developing world-class digital solutions (Africa Trade Report, 2019; Banga & te Velde, 2018). Alternatively, the African digital entrepreneurs with high levels of absorptive capacity are the ones who succeed in developing a portfolio of complementary digital skills to create and capture value (Africa Trade Report, 2019; Banga & te Velde, 2018).

The African entrepreneur must develop the absorptive capacity to acquire and absorb technological knowledge in the digital age (Banga & te Velde, 2018). Otherwise, the entrepreneur runs the risk of being unable to leverage digitalisation and leverage out of low value-added activities (Africa Trade Report, 2019). Value creation and capture in the digital age are increasingly shifting towards intangibles (Africa Trade Report, 2019). In the process, low value-added opportunities will be lost, giving rise to new opportunities to be pursued in the higher value-added digital environments (Africa Trade Report, 2019). For example, it was reported that

> The cost of robotics and 3D printers is declining at 5-6% annually in developed countries such as the United States, while wages in developing countries are rising…A growing number of studies finds that robot cost in the United States will become cheaper than Kenyan formal labor by 2033…". United States might find it more cost-efficient to re-shore production back to US factories World Bank, 2017; Banga & te Velde, 2018 (cited in Africa Trade Report, 2019: 18)"

Given the above, entrepreneurs in African countries like Kenya who have made business process outsourcing (BPO) a core component of its national development strategy, 'Vision 2030' Republic of Kenya, 2007—would have intensified their higher value-added digital skills to complement their current skill-sets (cited Africa Trade Report, 2019).

Such entrepreneurs that develop their complementary digital skills transitioning from low to higher value-added are the ones fuelling the popular digital business model in Africa, which is based on the premise of 'repurposing' other digital artifacts to solve African problems (Friederici et al., 2020).

Given the changing nature of the economies to knowledge-based and increasingly digital, we suspect that African entrepreneurs, who invest time in developing a search strategy in its 'breadth' and 'depth' with the required absorptive capacity, will be the ones in a position to create value by acquiring, licensing, reverse engineering, and reassign jobs that might have been lost within the African ecosystem. Consequently, entrepreneurs with absorptive capacity who adopt breadth posture, (ability to pursue digital skills development goal search from multiple digital skills provision centres), are more likely to develop a portfolio of complementary skills for creating and capturing value. On the other hand, the entrepreneurs with absorptive capacity who adopt depth posture, (ability to pursue digital skills development goal search from few digital skills provision centres), are more likely to develop a specialist skills-set for creating and capturing value. We state the following propositions for those who apply the oscillation strategy:

Proposition 3: *Entrepreneurs in Africa with absorptive capacity—who adopt oscillation*
Strategy (moving in between breadth and depth postures together) are more
Likely to develop a portfolio of balanced rounded skills for creating
And capturing value

11.4.4 Co-Evolution of Digital Skills as a Strategic Posture-4

Entrepreneurs' ability to select relevant skills, accumulate/retain, as well as replicate enables them to consciously develop relevant adaptive skills and competencies in line with current and digital futures (Breslin, 2008; Peneder, 2001). However, adaptive skills are not sufficient in a rapidly changing digital environment (Murmann, 2013). Hence, some African digital entrepreneurs adopt a co-evolutionary way of thinking to enable them to develop as a whole with the entire digital ecosystem that evolves (and grows) as well partake in shaping the total ecology of socio-technical systems (Clarke et al., 2014; Graham, 1998; Susan & Acs, 2017).

The co-evolution perspective approaches the discreteness of boundaries between agency (the entrepreneurs) and structure of the system as non-existent (Clarke et al., 2014). This allows for the relational and bi-directional digital entrepreneurial competencies growth, alongside other actors in the digital ecosystem (the suppliers of digital skills, regulators, rivals, and future generations), each continually producing the other (Clarke et al., 2014). The co-evolution perspective is vital as it promotes the ecological balance of the system (Clarke et al., 2014). In addition, it emphasises mutually shared cumulative assets/resources based on relationships at a level of total ecology (Clarke et al., 2014).

Prosperous digital entrepreneurs in Africa are the ones who utilise the network in which they are embedded, as a locus of their digital innovativeness (Nambisan & Sawhney, 2011; Pittaway et al., 2004). In so doing, they co-evolve with other agents within the same network structural equivalence or knowledge domain (Nooteboom, 1994). They take an active role in shaping their network formation and reproduction over time, of digital platforms in the ecosystem (Jack & Anderson, 2002: Susan & Acs, 2017).

They can utilise their information and critical digital skills to filter the contents of relations and exchanges in their entrepreneurial settings, taking into consideration the network of relationships in the digital ecosystem (Jack, 2010; Tidd & Bessant, 2009; Susan & Acs, 2017). This leads to the reproduction of their network structure, helping them to the accumulated social capital of digital competencies—to create and capture values in the network structural holes (Burt, 2000; Walker et al., 1997). It is within the context of these network activities (formations and reproductions) over time that African digital entrepreneurs drive the co-evolution of their digital innovations.

The average digital entrepreneurs in Africa adopt what we have termed the digital 'hoping' survival strategy in which they jump from one skill-set to another without the careful mapping of relatedness of the knowledge bases (Taura & Watkins, 2014). Such actions lead to a 'hodgepodge' of un-related digital skills, making it more difficult to coordinate a meaningful relationship between the skills in ways that enable them to create and capture values (Lepak et al., 2007; Shane & Vankataraman, 2000). Sometimes, the hodgepodge skills can be cognitively distant instead of proximate—hence creating higher level coordination costs which the entrepreneurs can barely afford (Taura & Radicic, 2019).

Hence, African digital entrepreneurs who map their key skills attributes and use them in shaping the digital ecosystem bi-directionally with other actors are more likely to succeed (Susan & Acs, 2017). By utilising certain co-evolutionary levers—such as commercial ties and exchange of personnel entrepreneurs, can develop 'foresight' (Murmann,

2013). This is vital as connecting with digital futures—enables the entrepreneur to develop the cumulative absorptive capacity now, to prepare them for digital skills of the future. Co-evolution is compatible with more recent theorising on mastering expert entrepreneurialism and effectuation focusing on shaping and controlling the future (Sarasvathy, 2001; Sarasvathy et al., 2008).

Digital entrepreneurs who are able to design organisations that can design their future environments will be the ones with the highest degree of digital competencies (Sarasvathy, 2001; Sarasvathy, 2003). Their hindsight provides the basis for developing foresight skills to prepare for digital futures. Their perspective approach to probing the future enables them to develop competent digital procedural memory of skills (Walsh & Ungson, 1991). Procedural memory is memory 'for how things are done' or memory for 'things you can do' (Walsh & Ungson, 1991). Therefore, procedural memory involves skills or routines (Walsh & Ungson, 1991). A key characteristic of procedural memory is that it becomes automatic or accessible unconsciously—hence referred to as motor memory (Walsh & Ungson, 1991). In addition to the preparedness of the future, when the opportunity arises from the digital futures, such entrepreneurs are positioned well in such a way to improvise speedy and coherent actionable decisions for creating and capturing value (Walsh & Ungson, 1991). Thus, given the above, we believe

Entrepreneurs in Africa who adopt co-evolution as a strategic posture
(Ability to bi-directionally select, accumulate, and replicate digital skills)
are
More likely to develop cumulative readiness skill to improvise
Digital solutions for creating and capturing value

The above tool/matrix (Fig. 11.1) is intended to guide African digital entrepreneurs to diagnose, monitor and plan (short and long-term) their digital skills and competencies postures. It is a practical tool developed from a constellation of entrepreneurial action and strategic option literature.

The Digital Entrepreneurs Skills Matrix

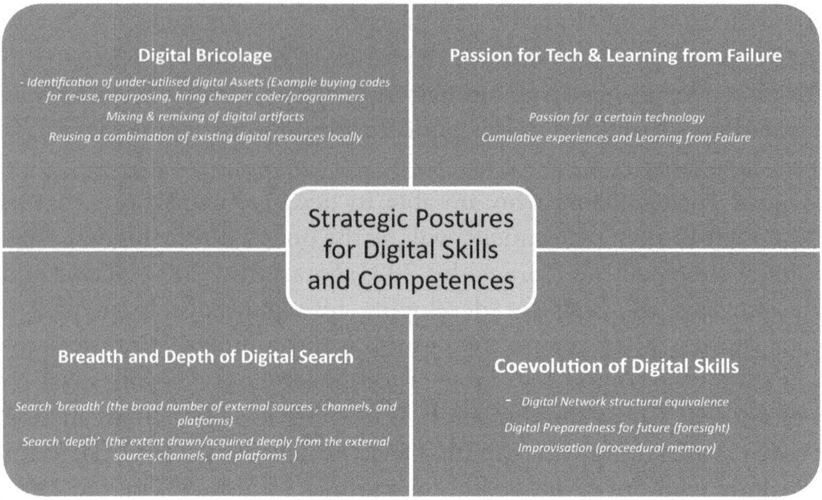

Fig. 11.1 The Digital Entrepreneurs Skills Matrix (*Source* Author's Diagram)

11.5 Conclusion and Future Research

This chapter made a vital contribution to our understanding of the digital skills deficiency in Africa within the context of digital entrepreneurship practice. Thus, the chapter examined the emergence, scope, and concept of digital entrepreneurship in Africa. The chapter concludes that, although the emergence of the concept of digital entrepreneurship has impacted the creation of new ventures and the transformation of existing businesses in Africa, the full potentials are yet to be realised. Africa has the potential to be one of the leading global digital entrepreneurial ecosystems if the digital skills deficit can be tackled effectively.

Africa should intensify efforts to strategic skills development, including (re-skilling, and or up-skilling), to encourage digital entrepreneurs, and intrapreneurs on the continent to develop digital competencies.

Given the broad scope of vital digital skills required for African entrepreneurs to thrive, including information digital skills, critical thinking digital skills, problem-solving digital skills, creative digital skills, African entrepreneurs must learn to approach digital skills development as a strategic asset. The development of digital skills is an active, not a passive process. It is also an essential element of the entrepreneurial process in the digital age.

In line with mode-2 theoretical advances (creating knowledge in the context of application), the chapter concludes with a summary of the digital skills matrix. The goal is to enable African digital entrepreneurs as well as stakeholders of skills provisioning in Africa to use the matrix as a tool to diagnose, map, and strategically plan their digital skills and competencies development. The main limitation of the study is that it is mainly conceptual—relying on available evidence of practices published. Going forward, future research should focus on testing the stated propositions as well as developing a more comprehensive matrix. The propositions can be tested using quantitative approaches or developing the propositions into a full-blown theory of digital entrepreneurship and skills in Africa by conducting interviews with digital entrepreneurs or experts.

References

Adeboye, T. (1997). Models of innovation and Sub-Saharan Africa's development strategy. *Technology Analysis & Strategic Management, 9*(2), 213–235.

Africa Trade Report (2019). *African trade in a digital world* [Online]. https://s3-eu-west-1.amazonaws.com/demo2.opus.ee/afrexim/African-Trade-Report_2019.pdf

Aldrich, H. E., & Reuf, M. (2006). *Organizations evolving* (2nd ed.). Sage.

Atiasea, V. Y., Koladea, O., & Liedong, T. A. (2020). The emergence and strategy of tech hubs in Africa: Implications for knowledge production and value creation. *Technological Forecasting & Social Change, 161*, 120–307.

Autio, E., Kenny, M., Mustar, P., Siegel, D., & Wright, M. (2014). Entrepreneurial Innovation: The Importance of Context. *Research Policy, 43*(7), 1097–1108.

Baarbé, J., & Nzomo, V. (2017). *"Making" knowledge for innovation and development: Researching Kenyan makerspaces.* Retrieved September 29,

2019 from https://www.openair.org.za/making-knowledge-for-innovation-and-development-researching-Kenyan-makerspaces/

Banga, K., & te Velde, D.W. 2018a. *Digitalisation and the future of manufacturing in Africa*. Supporting Economic Transformation (SET) report. ODI.

Bechky, B., & Okhuysen, G. (2011). Expecting the unexpected? How SWAT officers and film crews handle surprises. *Academy of Management Journal, 54*(2), 239–261.

Birch, D. (1979). *The job generation process*. MIT Program on Neighborhood and Regional Change.

Bolat, E. (2019). The African new media digital revolution (some selected cases from Nigeria). In N. Taura & N. Madichie (Eds.), *Digital entrepreneurship in Sub-Saharan Africa: Challenges, opportunities, and prospects*. Palgrave Macmillan.

Burt, R. S. (2000). The network structure of social capital. *Research in Organisational Behaviour, 22*, 345–423.

Breslin, D. (2008). A review of evolutionary approach to the study of entrepreneurship. *International Journal of Management Reviews, 10*(4), 399–423.

Cardon, M. S., Wincent, J., Singh, J., & Drnovsek, M. (2009). The nature and experience of entrepreneurial passion. *Academy of Management Review, 34*(3), 511–532.

Cooper, A. C. (1971). Technical entrepreneurship: What do we know?. In J. Curran, J. Stanworth & D. Watkins (Ed.), *The survival of the small firm: Employment growth, technology and politics*. Gower.

Clarke, J., Holt, R., & Brundel, R. (2014). Re-imagining the growth process: (Co)-evolving metaphorical representations of entrepreneurial growth. *Entrepreneurship & Regional Development, 26*(3–4), 234–256.

Chakravorti, B., & Chaturvedi, R. S. (2019). *HBR ranking 42 countries by ease of doing business*. https://hbr.org/2019/09/ranking-42-countries-by-ease-of-doing-digital-business

Chakravorti, B., Bhalla, A., & Chaturvedi, R. S. (2017). 60 countries digital competitiveness indexed. *Harvard Business Review*.

Claro, M., Preiss, D. D., San Martín, E., Jara, I., Hinostroza, J. E., Valenzuela, S., et al. (2012). Assessment of 21st century ICT skills in Chile: Test design and results from high school level students. *Computers & Education, 59*(3), 1042–1053.

David-West, O., Umukoro, I. O., & Onuoha, R. O. (2018). Platforms in Sub-Saharan Africa: Startup models and the role of business incubation. *J. Intell. Capital, 19*(3), 581–616.

Friederici. N. (2019). Innovation hubs in Africa: What do they really do for digital entrepreneurs? In N. Taura & N. Madichie (Eds.), *Digital entrepreneurship in Sub-Saharan Africa: Challenges, opportunities, and prospects*. Palgrave Macmillan.

Friederici, N., Ojanperä, S., & Graham, M. (2017). The impact of connectivity in Africa: Grand visions and the mirage of inclusive digital development. *Electronic Journal of Information Systems in Developing Countries, 79*(2), 1–20.

Friederici, N., Wahome, M., & Graham, M. (2020). *Digital entrepreneurship in Africa: How a continent is escaping silicon valley's long shadow*. The MIT Press.

Fick, S. (2002). *Entrepreneurship in Africa: A study of success*. Qourum Books.

Graham, S. (1998). The end of geography or the explosion of place?: Conceptualizing Space, place and information technology. *Progress in Human Geography, 22*(2), 165–185.

Greenfield, T., & Ribbins, P. (1993). *Greenfield on educational administration: Towards a humane science*. Routledge.

Gathege, D., & Moraa, H. (2013). *ICT hubs model: Understanding key factors of the activspaces*. In Bue Cameroon, Draft Report, Ihub Research Nairobi.

Grimpe, C., & Kaiser, U. (2010). Balancing internal and external knowledge: The gains and pains from R&D outsourcing. *Journal of Management Studies, 47*(8), 1483–1509.

Gluckler, J. (2007). Economic geography and the evolution of networks. *Journal of Economic Geography, 7*(5), 619–634.

Hopkins, C. (2015). *How Africa grew more than 200 local tech scenes*. The Daily Dot (Blog). https://www.dailydot.com/debug/africa-tech-hubs-hacker-spaces-incubators/

IMD's World Digital Competitiveness Index. (2017). [Online] file://bournemouth.ac.uk/data/staff/home/ntaura/Downloads/world_digital_competitiveness_yearbook_2017.pdf. Accessed 18 October 2018.

International Trade Centre. (2019). *Tech hubs in Africa: How can they support tech start-ups across the continent?* International Trade Centre, Geneva. http://www.intracen.org/uploadedFiles/intracenorg/Content/Publications/TechhubsAfrica_final_Low-res.pdf

Janssen, J., Stoyanov, S., Ferrari, A., Punie, Y., Pannekeet, K., & Sloep, P. (2013). Experts' views on digital competence: Commonalities and differences. *Computers & Education, 68*, 473–481.

Jack, S. (2010). Approaches to studying networks: Implications and outcomes. *Journal of Business Venturing, 25*, 12–137.

Jack, S., & Anderson, A. (2002). The effects of embeddedness on entrepreneurial process. *Journal of Business Venturing, 17*(5), 467–487.

Kahneman, D. (2011). *Thinking, fast and slow*. Penguin Books Limited.

Katila, R., & Ahuja, G. (2002). Something old, something New: A longitudinal study of search behaviour of new product introduction. *Academy of Management Journal, 45*(8), 1183–1194.

Kelly, T., John, C., & Firestone, R. S. (2016). *How tech hubs are helping to drive economic growth in Africa*. http://documents.worldbank.org/curated/en/626981468195850883/How-tech-hubs-are-helping-to-drive-economic-growth-in-Africa

Laursen, K., & K. Salter. (2006). Open for innovation: The role of openness in explaining innovation performance among UK manufacturing Firms. *Strategic Management Journal* (27), 131–150.

Lepak, D. P., Smith, K. G., & Taylor, M. S. (2007). Value creation and value capture: A multilevel perspective. *Academy of Management Review, 32*(1), 180–194.

Levi-Straus, C. (1996). *The savage mind*. University of Chicago Press.

McMullen, J. S., & Shephered, D. A. (2006). Entrepreneurial action and the role of uncertainty in the theory of the entrepreneur. *Academy of Management Review, 31*(1), 132–152.

McDade, B., & E., and Spring, A. (2005). The 'new generation of African entrepreneurs' networking to change the climate for business and private sector-led development. *Entrepreneurship and Regional Development, 17*(1), 17–42.

McGrath, R. G. (1999). Falling forward: Real options reasoning and entrepreneurial failure. *Academy of Management Review, 24*(1), 13–30.

Mounde, A. A., Amollo, A., & Munene, M. (2020). Understanding the maker in academic makerspaces. *Africa Habitat, 14*(1), 2524–1354.

Murmann, J. P. (2013). The coevolution of industries and important features of their environments. *Organization Science, 24*(1), 58–78.

Nambisan, S., & Sawhney, M. (2011). Orchestration processes in network-centric innovation: Evidence from the field. *Academy of Management Perspectives, 25*(3), 40–57.

Naudé, W., & Liebregts, W. (2020). *Digital entrepreneurship research: A concise introduction.* IZA Discussion Papers 13667, Institute of Labor Economics (IZA).

Nooteboom, B. (1994). Innovation and diffusion in small firms: Theory and evidence. *Small Business Economics, 6*, 327–347.

Ngoasong, M. Z. (2018). Digital entrepreneurship in a resource scare context. A focus on entrepreneurial digital competencies. *Journal of Small Business and Enterprise Development, 25*(3), 483–500.

Ndemo, B., & Weiss, T. (2016). *Digital Kenya: An entrepreneurial revolution in the making*. Palgrave Studies of Entrepreneurship in Africa S.l. Palgrave Macmillan.

Ndemo, B., & Weiss, T. (2017). Making sense of Africa's emerging digital transformation and its many futures. *Africa Journal of Management, 3* (3–4): 328–347. https://doi.org/10.1080/23322373.2017.1400260

Ojanpera, S., Graham, M., Straumann, R., De Sabbata, S., & Zook, M. (2017). Engagement in the knowledge economy: Regional patterns of content creation with focus on Sub Saharan Africa. *Information Technology & International Development, 13*, 19.

Ocasio, W. (1997). Towards an attention based view of the firm. *Strategic Management Journal, 18*(51), 187–206.

Peneder, M. (2001). *Entrepreneurial competition and industrial location: Investigating the structural patterns and intangible sources of competitive performance.* Cheltenham.

Pittaway, L., Robertson, M., Munir, K., Denyer, D., & Neely, A. (2004). Networking and innovation: A systematic review of the evidence. *International Journal of Management Reviews, 5/6* (3 & 4), 137–168.

Poushter, J., Bishop, C., & Chwe, H. (2018). Social media use continues to rise in developing countries but plateaus across developed ones. *Pew Research Centre*, 22.

Ranchhod, A. (2019). Foreword. In N. Taura & N. Madichie (Eds.), *Digital entrepreneurship in Sub-Saharan Africa: Challenges, opportunities, and prospects.* Palgrave Macmillan.

Robson, P. J. A., & Freel, M. (2008). Small firm exporters in developing economy context: Evidence from Ghana. *Entrepreneurship and Regional Development, 20*(5), 431–450.

Robson, P. J. A., Haugh, H. M., & Obeng, B. A. (2009). Entrepreneurship and innovation in Ghana: Enterprising Africa. *Small Business Economics* (32), 331–350.

Robson, P. J. A., Akuetteh, C., Westhead, P., & Wright, M. (2012). Innovative opportunity pursuit, human capital and business ownership experience in an emerging region: Evidence from Ghana. *Small Business Economics, 39*, 603–625.

Rüling, C. C., & Duymedjian, R. (2014). Digital bricolage: Resources and coordination in the production of digital visual effects. *Technological Forecasting and Social Change, 83*, 98–110.

Sands, E. G., & Bakthavachalam, V. (2019). *Ranking countries and industries by tech, data, and business skills*. https://hbr.org/2019/05/ranking-countries-and-industries-by-tech-data-and-business-skills

Sarasvathy, S. D. (2001). Causation and effectuation: Toward a theoretical shift from economic inevitability to entrepreneurial contingency. *Academy of Management Review, 26*(2), 243–263.

Sarasvathy, S. D. (2003). Entrepreneurship as a science of the artificial. *Journal of Economic Psychology, 24*, 203–220.

Sarasvathy, S. D., Dew, N., Read, S., & Wiltbank, R. (2008). Designing organizations that design environments: Lessons from entrepreneurial expertise. *Organization Studies, 29*, 331–350.

Şendağ, S., & Odabaşı, H. F. (2009). Effects of an online problem-based learning course on content knowledge acquisition and critical thinking skills. *Computers & Education, 53*(1), 132–141.

Shane, S., & Venkataraman, S. (2000). The promise of entrepreneurship as a field of research. *Academy of Management Review, 25*(1), 217–226.

Sheridan, K., Halverson, E. R., Litts, B., Brahms, L., Jacobs-Priebe, L. & Owens, T. (2014). Learning in the making: A comparative case study of three makerspaces. *Harvard Educational Review, 84*(4), 505–531.

Simon, H. A. (1969/1996). *The sciences of the artificial* (first edition published in 1969; third edition in 1996). MIT Press.

Siyanbola, W. O., Aderemi, H. O., Egbetokun, A. A., & Sanni, M. (2011). Framework for technological entrepreneurship development: Key issues and policy directions. *American Journal of Industrial and Business Management, 1*(10).

Sussan, F., & Acs, Z. J. (2017). The digital entrepreneurial ecosystem. *Small Business Economics, 49*(1), 55–73.

Taura, N., Bolat, E., & Madichie, N. (2019). Introduction to African digital entrepreneurship. *Digital entrepreneurship in sub-Saharan Africa: Challenges, opportunities, and prospects*. Palgrave Macmillan.

Taura, N., & Radicic, D. (2019). Intra-cluster knowledge exchange and frequency of product innovation in a digital cluster. *Journal of Small Business Management, 57*(S2), 350–373.

Taura, N., & Watkins, D. (2014). Counteracting innovative constraints: Insights from four case studies of African knowledge-intensive metalworking and automotive clusters—'The Akimacs.' *Entrepreneurship and Regional Development, 26*(3–4), 313–336.

Tidd, J., & Bessant, J. (2009). *Managing innovation: Integrating technological, market and organisational change* (4th ed.). John Wiley and Sons.

UNESCO. (2017). *UNESCO skills for life.* http://d-russia.ru/wp-content/uploads/2017/10/Digital-skills-for-life-and-work_259013e.pdf

Von, Briel, F., Recker, J., & Davidson, P. (2018). Not all business venture ideas are created equal: Implications for venture creation process. *The Journal for Strategic Information Systems, 27*(4), 278–295.

Valliere, D., & Gegenhuber, T. (2014). Entrepreneurial remixing: Bricolage and postmodern resources. *Entrepreneurship and Innovation, 15*(1), 5–15.

Van Laar, E., van Deursen, A. J. A. M., Van Dijk, J. A. G. M., & De Haan, J. (2018). 21st-century digital skills instrument aimed at working professionals: Conceptual development and empirical validation. *Telematics and Informatics, 35*(8), 2184–2200.

Vossoughi, S., Hooper, P. K., & Escudé, M. (2016). Making through the lens of culture and power: Toward transformative visions for educational equity. *Harvard Educational Review., 86*(2), 206–232.

Welter, F. (2011). Contextualising entrepreneurship—Conceptual challenges and ways forward. *Entrepreneurship, Theory, & Practice, 35*(1), 165–184.

Wim, N., & Werner, L. (2019). *Digital entrepreneurship research: A concise introduction.* IZA Discussion Paper No. 13667, Available at SSRN: https://ssrn.com/abstract=3691380

Watkins, D. (1973). Technical entrepreneurship: A cis-atlantic view. *R&D Management, 3*(2), 65–70.

Wechsler, S. M., Saiz, C., Rivas, S. F., Vendramini, C. M. M., Almeida, L. S., Mundim, M. C., et al. (2018). Creative and critical thinking: Independent or overlapping components? *Thinking Skills and Creativity, 27*, 114–122.

Walsh, J. P., & Ungson, G. R. (1991). Organisational memory. *Academy of Management: Academy of Management Review, 16*(1), 57–91.

Walker, G., Kogut, B., & Shan, W. (1997). Social capital, structural holes and formation of an industry network. *Organisation Science, 8*(2), 109–125.

Yang, Y. T. C. (2015). Virtual CEOs: A blended approach to digital gaming for enhancing higher order thinking and academic achievement among vocational high school students. *Computers & Education, 81*, 281–295.

12

Developing and Managing Skills and Competencies for Digital Business in Africa

Isaiah Adisa and Ogechi Adeola

12.1 Introduction

The impact of digitalisation across the globe cannot be over-emphasised (World Economic Forum, 2020). Currently, there is a digital revolution globally, and businesses cannot afford to be left behind (Tahvanainen & Luoma, 2018). Digital innovation has transformed the operations and strategies of industries, including telecommunication, banking, health-care, education, and manufacturing sectors (Nadeem et al., 2018). Through digital innovations, businesses are forced to change their mode of operations to remain relevant. To this end, businesses must ensure they have the internal resources to fit into the digital business space. Internal

I. Adisa (✉)
Olabisi Onabanjo University, Ago-Iwoye, Ogun State, Nigeria

O. Adeola
Lagos Business School, Pan-Atlantic University, Lagos, Nigeria
e-mail: oadeola@lbs.edu.ng

O. Adeola et al. (eds.), *Digital Service Delivery in Africa*, Palgrave Studies of Marketing in Emerging Economies,
https://doi.org/10.1007/978-3-030-83909-3_12

resources such as staff with the right skills and competencies are needed to respond to the requirements of the digital market audience (Andriole, 2018; Royle, & Laing, 2014). Electronic platforms are taking the place of traditional stores and malls, while the resultant effect is a change in marketing strategy and the skills of the workforce (Belleflamme, & Peitz, 2019; Hagberg et al., 2016; Ludike, 2018; Van Kerrebroeck et al., 2017). Marketing of products and services in the digital age for effective customer engagement will require that businesses equip their staff with the right digital competencies to meet the digital needs of the market. Additionally, job seekers who do not have the right digital skills might not fit into the labour market.

In this digital era, industries and organisations must strategically evolve if they desire to be relevant in the digital space (Royle & Laing, 2014; Tumbas et al., 2017). Though digitalisation comes with its disruptions and challenges, it is the new trajectory of the market space (Koski et al., 2016; Parviainen et al., 2017; Skog et al., 2018). Opportunities also abound in the digital space, but they will be accessible only to individuals and business organisations with the right digital skillset (Hoberg et al., 2017; Van Deursen & Van Dijk, 2014). Business organisations, often times, do not need to look outward for rare and inimitable talents to remain competitive in the digital world. The option of developing and managing these skills for organisational goals is worth adopting. Organisations can develop their workforce's skill set through the vestibule and on-the-job training to equip their staffers with adequate skills and abilities rather than recruiting new hands, thereby saving cost.

There is a growing need for digital skills in Africa with half of the jobs requiring digital skills and competencies (Fuchs & Horak, 2008; International Finance Corporation, 2019; Jenkin & Naude, 2019; Makoe, 2012). The adoption of digitisation and automation in agriculture, manufacturing, and service sectors in sub-Saharan Africa has increased the demand for digital skills and competencies among personnel (International Finance Corporation, 2019). Therefore, the demand for digital skills in the sub-Saharan region is expected to grow faster than in other regions in Africa. However, there is an observed skill gap in Africa and mostly in sub-Saharan Africa than other parts of the region in the availability of digitally skilled personnel (International Finance Corporation,

2019). Hence, it is important to increase the availability of digitally skilled personnel in the region and the rest of Africa if the continent's economy would not falter.

The implication of a digital skill gap is that businesses without the requisite Knowledge, Skills, and Abilities (KSA) might lack the capability to compete in the new business environment. Organisations must, therefore, upgrade the skill set of their workforce through training or recruitment. To do this, they must understand the workforce skills and competencies needed in this digital age. Therefore, the chapter identifies digital skills and competencies businesses should look out for in the labour market and equip their staff members with these skills. This chapter provides critical skills and competencies that organisations should equip their workforce with to add value and compete in the digital market space.

In addition, the chapter identifies how business organisations can develop digital skills required for staff members and how to manage these skills effectively for the desired outcome. The next section will focus on digital business in Africa, followed by sections on skills and competencies for digital business in Africa which are anchored on the firm's resource-based theory. The last three sections focus on how organisations can manage digital skills and competencies in Africa, recommendations, and conclusion.

12.2 Digital Businesses in Africa

Information and Communications Technology (ICT) offers enterprise management, growth, and development opportunities for businesses that necessitate the adoption of these technologies for operation (Mutula & Van Brakel, 2007). Through ICT, businesses can remove geographical barriers that limit their product/service market while also building customer engagement (Ziemba et al., 2020). Digital businesses are replacing brick-and-mortar enterprises while creating values and opportunities missing in the latter (Mahadevan, 2000; Mustaffa & Beaumont,

2004). Small- and medium-sized enterprises are leveraging the opportunities in digital innovation by adopting digital practices and techniques to create a niche for their businesses in the market (Demirkan et al., 2016; Scuotto et al., 2017). Businesses with digital practices are increasing in developing countries, though not at the same rate as digital businesses in developed countries (Ngoasong, 2018). Beyond the current growth rate of digital businesses in Africa, there is a nascent market that businesses in Africa can tap from in order to take their enterprise activities to the next level (Ngoasong, 2018). Enterprises in Africa, going digital in their practices, must understand the context-specific opportunities in Africa, which they strategically want to access. They must understand the digital landscape appropriate for their target audience and implement strategies to respond to their market needs.

Digital businesses are described in different contexts depending on the perspective of the user. It has been defined from the perspective of marketing, finance, and even operations management. To Lee and Whang (2001), a digital business is the adoption of internet-based computing and communications to execute both front-end and back-end business processes. This definition construes "digital businesses" as a system utilised to achieve business goals. For Scott (2000), digital businesses are an enterprise with a technological fusion of business processes and organisational structure needed to create value and achieve business goals. These authors suggest that digital businesses can be seen as applications and models. On the one hand, digital business is seen as an application in terms of tools and technological facilities used by an organisation to carry out its daily activities towards achieving its business goals. To Wall et al. (2007), digital business is an application when it uses information and communications technology to facilitate faster business transactions.

On the other hand, digital business is argued to be a model as it redefines the traditional business practice and strategically adopts technology to maximise customer value and profits. In the context of this chapter, we approach digital business from a holistic perspective, which positions it as an application and a model. Through technological application, organisations can strategically innovate their business process to achieve the desired outcome. The desired outcomes, in this case, are customer satisfaction, business growth, and profit maximisation.

In Africa, small-, medium-sized, and multinational organisations are utilising digital innovations to drive their business goals despite the challenges in their operating environment (Bolat & Taura, 2019). For instance, in Ghana and Nigeria, the agricultural sector is evolving through digital innovations. Agri-tech organisations in Ghana such as Farmerline, Farmable, and Esoko are reviewing traditional business models to fit into current realities by providing communication, crowd-funding, and pricing data (Bolat & Taura, 2019) while also bridging the gap between the market and the farmers. A similar result was obtained in the Nigerian agricultural sector with Prime Wave, an engineering company supplying equipment to aid rice processing. Prime Wave is also partnering with Al Wabel Trading Company—a rice miller, to invent technological solutions that will engender rice processing in Nigeria (Bolat & Taura, 2019). Such innovations are driven by the availability of technological resources and can spur the process of production, sales, and marketing of goods and services. Opportunities such as the abovementioned abound in Africa for businesses therein to take their enterprise activities to another level.

Specifically, the arts, media, and entertainment industries in Nigeria and Kenya have embedded digital technologies in carrying out their activities. Digital businesses are increasing in Africa, but digital skills to drive the next phase of business innovations are largely missing (Madden & Kanos, 2020). The current focus is on Industry 4.0, which emphasises the utilisation of smart technology and other modern technological tools in the manufacturing process, service delivery, and customer engagement (Hecklau et al., 2016). These authors recounted that sub-Saharan Africa has a skill gap for twenty-first-century business. Madden and Kanos emphasised that sub-Saharan Africa ranked lowest among other world regions on the percentage of the labour force on LinkedIn and digital skills availability. Though Kenya, Nigeria, and South Africa has a higher level of digital skills than the rest of sub-Saharan Africa's total average, there is evidence that digital skills and competencies are needed in Africa for the development of businesses and the actualisation of goals (Madden & Kanos, 2020).

12.3 Skills and Competencies for Digital Businesses in Africa

Technological innovation is the game-changer for entrepreneurs and enterprises globally as it provides opportunities to meet the need of the market and enhance business success. Technological innovations have changed the face of businesses by transforming the processes of productions and service delivery (Craffert et al., 2014). These changes are not limited to organisational structures; people must also upskill to create the needed market value. As digital businesses increase in Africa, the continent must have a labour force with the right digital skills to compete globally. Competency and skills are closely related, with minor differences. Competency is a broader categorisation of skills. Therefore, a skill is limited in the application, while competencies cover what a skill is and extends the definition. Cedefop (2008) defines a skill as the ability to perform tasks, solve problems, while competence is the adequate application of learning outcomes within a defined context. According to Ananiadou and Claro (2009), skills and competencies in the twenty-first century are different from the requirement of the nineteenth century; for this purpose, organisations must be aware of the primary digital skills and competencies required in their contemporary business space.

Digital skills and competencies are described in this chapter as the primary technological knowledge, skills, and abilities applied to the work process to achieve the desired outcomes. Staff members are expected to possess the skills and competencies the organisation needs to survive and create a niche in the digital market. Digital transformation is an essential aspect of today's business strategy, and technological skills rank among the top skills businesses seek from the labour market (Hoberg et al., 2017). Different roles are evolving, requiring digital skills and competencies that will influence an organisation's structural and cultural changes. In a survey conducted by Hoberg et al. (2017), 14 digital skills and competencies required for digital business transformation were identified, as shown in Table 12.1.

The skills are ranked in their order of importance and priority. It is essential that as businesses adopt digital practices, they must emphasise digital security strategies to protect their data and businesses. For

Table 12.1 Skills needed for digital businesses transformation

S/N	Skills	Percentage showing ranking (%)
1	Digital Security	88
2	Mobile Technologies	87
3	Business Change Management	84
4	Big Data Analytics	84
5	Cloud Computing	76
6	Internet of Things	75
7	Business Networks	71
8	Product/Service Integration	66
9	In-Memory Databases	6
10	Entrepreneurship	65
11	Social Media	63
12	Artificial Intelligence	56
13	Novel Interfaces	50
14	Blockchain	36

Source Hoberg et al. (2017)

instance, organisations providing electronic payment services in this digital age must invest in digital security to protect their customers' financial data. As businesses have more online visibility, there is also an increase in online threats. Michota (2013) examined digital security concerns and threats facing women entrepreneurs in developing nations and identified issues such as security, privacy, social networking worms, digital threats, digital leaks, impersonation, and trust issues as key threats and concerns for women entrepreneurs seeking to put their business on the digital space. The availability of personnel with digital security skills will, if not solve, reduce the threats to digital insecurity and fears. Personnel with digital security skills are, therefore, crucial to the performance of today's digital business.

Mobile technologies provide countless opportunities for businesses, goods, and services to be offered to individuals wherever they are. Studies have shown that convenience and comfort are key factors that attract consumers' patronage (Collier & Kimes, 2013; Spake et al., 2003). Organisations must make services or products available on mobile technologies to enhance business growth. Business change management is also an important skill and competence needed in an organisation willing to adopt digital innovation. Going digital will have its structural disruption in the organisation, and it will take managers with the requisite change management skills to coordinate the process and manage the effects on workers and the organisation. Therefore, businesses must ensure that those at the managerial level are groomed on change management strategies because the adoption of digital innovations will bring structural and product/service changes to the organisation. Developing an intent to have your business in the digital space is not sufficient as all related business activities must be aligned to digital procedures. The corporate strategy which other business activities lean on should be premised on innovative approaches which will require innovative skills and competencies. Also, digital skills and competencies are expected of operational staff and those at the helms of business management. Staff with innovative skills will be needed from top to bottom.

Big data analytics is also an important skill and competency needed for digital business in this era. Businesses are driven by information, and it is important that accurate information is used to predict the market, understand the current need of the market, and what the direction would be in the next few years. With big data, organisations can make precise and accurate decisions that will drive business growth (Hoberg et al., 2017). Therefore, big data analytics is a crucial personnel skill and competency needed by businesses in this era. Cloud computing and the Internet of Things (IoT) offer businesses the opportunity to collect important data in real-time about how, when, and where a consumer uses a product or service (Hoberg et al., 2017). It allows organisations to store, process, and make logical sense from data towards making and implementing customer-centred decisions. IoT is an essential aspect of technological revolution, which allows technological tools to communicate through the internet. It consists of physical and virtual "things", with identities, physical attributes, and virtual personalities (Psannis et al., 2014). IoT is crucial in computing information and communication systems, which describe a world of digital elements where everything is interconnected. In business, it can be utilised to develop new products and services that meet the needs of the African market. To achieve this, the organisation will surely need personnel with such skill. Cloud computing is a technological revolution that businesses need to leverage on with skilled personnel. Cloud computing engenders communication between organisations with the potential to provide financial and operational benefits to small businesses (Attaran & Woods, 2019).

Businesses require personnel with business network skills, such as building relationships, and leveraging influential connections in today's business space. Product/service integration competency and in-memory database skills were also identified. Furthermore, entrepreneurship, social media, artificial intelligence, novel interfaces, and blockchain skills are sacrosanct to the growth and development of businesses in this era. A key observation from the identified skillset is that despite the emphasis on digitalisation, skills such as entrepreneurship and business networks are still needed in the digital business space because it takes an employee with an entrepreneurial mindset to create something unique from the digital tools (Scheepers, 2008). Without appropriate business networking skills, the business may have a limited market share. As businesses in Africa tap into the opportunities in the digital space, appropriate digital hard and soft skills must be developed.

12.4 Developing Digital Skills and Competencies in Africa: A Resource-Based Perspective

The Resource-Based Theory (RBT) of the firm by Barney (1991) contends that for businesses to enhance their competitive advantage and remain relevant in their sector, they must possess rare, valuable, difficult to imitate non-substitutable resources. There are numerous resources in the organisation, which range from cash, technology, buildings, etc. The resources we are most concerned with here are the human resources in the organisation. Given Barney's position on the business resource as her primary strength for creating a niche in the market, and rightly positioning itself for business performance. We propose that businesses in Africa can develop the digital skills and competencies of their workforce through recruitment, personnel training, and retention.

Evidence shows a substantial digital skill gap in Africa that businesses need to compete in the digital market (James, 2019; Mutula & Van Brakel, 2007). From the perspective of the resource-based theory, to create digital business values that will be rare, non-substitutable, and inimitable, the businesses in Africa must develop their internal human digital capacities to fit the demands of their market. To achieve this, businesses in Africa should either train or recruit personnel with these digital skills. Sousa and Rocha (2019) observed that digital learning through an organisation is the right step in the right direction towards bridging the gap between the current market skill need and what the employees possess.

We propose in this chapter that: organisations must first identify the digital skills needed in their sector; examine the current stock of manpower available; access the resource base of the business; and decide on the training of internal employees or recruit new hands. We discuss this argument further.

a. Top Management Support

Transforming a business into a digital space is not just about adopting technology and recruiting personnel with digital skills into the organisation. It requires the understanding and support of top management to address the change within their business space and respond quickly with competitive solutions (Baculard, 2017). The management must be working with a strategic blueprint that might inform decisions such as creating new departments, empowering workers, or developing new products or services. The current trend of the market would determine the actions and steps to be taken by the organisation. There must be a clear focus on digital opportunities, which will require top management support. Companies should have "holistic view of digital threats and opportunities facing key parts of the business and develop a strategy to harness the opportunities and manage the threats". Management support for digital business innovation in Africa must not be contingent on submitting to market pressure but filling a gap and meeting consumers' needs. Besides providing financial and human resources for going digital, the management must have the strategic willpower and vision to respond to the need of the society. The top management must be passionate about going digital (El-Haddadeh, 2020; Smith & Tushman, 2005).

b. Evaluate Manpower Skill Inventory

Top management support provides the needed environment for the adoption and implementation of strategies geared towards digital business innovation. To have the required stock of manpower with the right digital skill, the management must do a manpower skill inventory to analyse the current workforce skill. Managers must provide answers to questions such as "what is the quantitative and qualitative nature of the human resource in the organisation"? Do they have the needed skill to compete in this sector? Do we need to recruit or train our workforce with the needed skills to compete in this sector? To arrive at the right answer, the organisation might conduct a workforce skill inventory analysis to evaluate if their current workforce skills meet their sectorial market needs.

c. Identify the Digital Skill Requirement in Your Sector

The next step is to identify the specific digital skills relevant in the sector in which the business operates as different sectors have digital skills peculiar to them. An organisation must understand the digital skill and competency required to meet customers' needs before they can effectively develop the digital skills and competencies of their workforce. For instance, Ngoasong (2018), from an entrepreneur perspective, examined how the digital competencies of entrepreneur's can be developed in Africa. Ngoasong suggests that there must be policy intervention for the development of information and communications technology infrastructure, transport, local distribution, and training opportunities to develop an entrepreneur's digital competencies. Royle and Laing (2014) conducted a study to understand the digital marketing skill gap and observed that focusing on evaluation metrics, guidance on best practices, future-proofing, and strategic integration are skills needed for the communication industry. Similarly, Baro et al. (2019) examined digital literacy skills and knowledge-based competencies among librarians in

Africa and observed that librarians in Africa require digital skills such as uploading documents to online platforms, search skills, sending and receiving e-mails skill, and usage of different social media. Baro et al. added that digital library development skills, applying new technologies into library services, ability to create separate file formats, and usage of open-source software skills were also required. Library website development skills were discovered as the most in-demand skills among librarians.

Generally, three core competencies were reported by AON'S Assessment Solutions (ASN) (2020) for organisations trying to create a niche for their business in the digital space. The first is Learnability: an individual's desire to develop and improve; Agility: an individual's capability to adapt quickly and effectively; and Curiosity: having an inquisitive and enthusiastic approach and open to change. AON'S proposed that when employees score low on these core competencies, they are likely to be uncomfortable and less effective in a digital space. It is important for organisations to assess the digital readiness of the workforce before instituting a digital innovation in a unit, department, or the whole business. Besides, these three core competencies are needed in businesses irrespective of organisation, region, or nation. Other personnel skills that are also important, according to AON'S (2018), are:

i. Drive to succeed: This is taking initiatives and following the path to achieving objectives
ii. Handling data: This involves analysing information and evaluating the situation and making decisions utilising data.
iii. Strategic solution: This is providing creative solutions to stakeholder's problems
iv. Business acumen: This is understanding the need of the consumers and creating, developing business opportunities through them.
v. Virtual collaboration: Individuals in a contemporary organisation should have this ability, especially in the light of the covid-19[1] pandemic. It is the ability to interact with others remotely while working together to achieve common goals.

---

[1] https://africacdc.org/covid-19/.

vi. Digital communication: It is the ability to communicate and interact with others via technological application. This is highly crucial in today's organisation considering the changes Covid-19 has brought forth.
vii. Mental endurance: Individuals must have the mental resilience and ability to cope with pressure and setbacks
viii. Coaching mindset: Supporting the development of one another is an important factor for feedbacks and engagement

Identifying a digital need is important before making any other decision on digital transformation. It is a crucial step towards creating a niche in the digital space.

d. Make a decision

At this stage, the organisation decides to either train the workers or recruit new workers, taking into consideration the cost implication. The two options have both advantages and disadvantages. Training the workforce at the expense of recruiting has its advantage and disadvantages. The choice of training allows the organisation to retain its workforce and continue to work with individuals who understand the nature and process of work in the organisation. Bringing in a new employee might mean the organisation will incur the cost of recruitment and the new staff orientation process on the job, which might cost time and money (Tapia & Kvasny, 2004). On the other hand, the organisation will benefit from recruiting a new employee that will offer fresh ideas and proffer new methodologies to how things are done within the organisation. The organisation has to decide which of the two options harnesses its comparative advantage and, thereafter, make a decision.

Training or recruiting staff with digital skills and competencies needed in an organisation to create value for businesses in Africa should not be the end to the quest for digital innovation that meets consumer needs. Therefore, the training process, goals, and methodologies must be designed to fit the organisation's market needs. Recruitment and training will require a financial investment which the business must ensure they can fund. The financial demand must be compared to the proposed value benefits in the investment; this is crucial in making a decision.

Effective training helps to bridge the gap between the skills and competencies an individual has for a job and the requirement of the job (Chetty, Aneja et al., 2018a; Chetty, Qigui et al., 2018b). The organisation must design training goals and objectives in line with the training need of the job. This would inform the training methods and conduct. For instance, The International Finance Corporation (2019) suggested that short courses between 3 and 12 months are ideal, with the integration of instructional methods which are centred on practical learning than theoretical knowledge, is crucial to bridging the digital skill gap among employees in sub-Saharan Africa. Digital skills are more concerned with practical knowledge than theories; organisations must, therefore, ensure that the training method is practical. Off the job training should be adopted so that the individual can spend time learning the skill practically.

g. Assess progress and evaluate competencies

The management must constantly evaluate the success and otherwise of the decision made to provide interventions where needed. The organisation must determine if they have been able to achieve their goal of having a stock of manpower with the needed digital skills. Evaluating the progress made will help make informed decisions on how to sustain the success achieved or initiate a new strategy towards achieving the desired goals. Initiating a new direction or managing the current trajectory will be determined by the management.

12.5 Managing Digital Skills and Competencies in Africa

Developing digital skills and competencies among staff is important, but managing these skills and competencies is crucial. This is because poor management of the investment in digital skills of employees will waste resources and time without achieving the intended value proposition. Hence, businesses in Africa must manage their investment in digital skills appropriately. Figure 12.2 provides recommended steps that can be adopted to manage digital skills and competencies by organisations in Africa.

i. **Avoid a person-job fit gap:** To ensure that human capacity is adequately put to use, businesses must avoid a gap between the person (personality, skills and competencies) and the job (task, responsibilities and roles). A gap in the person-job occurs when there is no fit between the job and the person. When the digital skill an individual has is not channeled towards the right job, and the individual performs below capacity, a person-job fit gap has occurred. Also, when an employee is digitally unskilled and placed on a job that requires digital savvy, a gap has occurred in the person and the

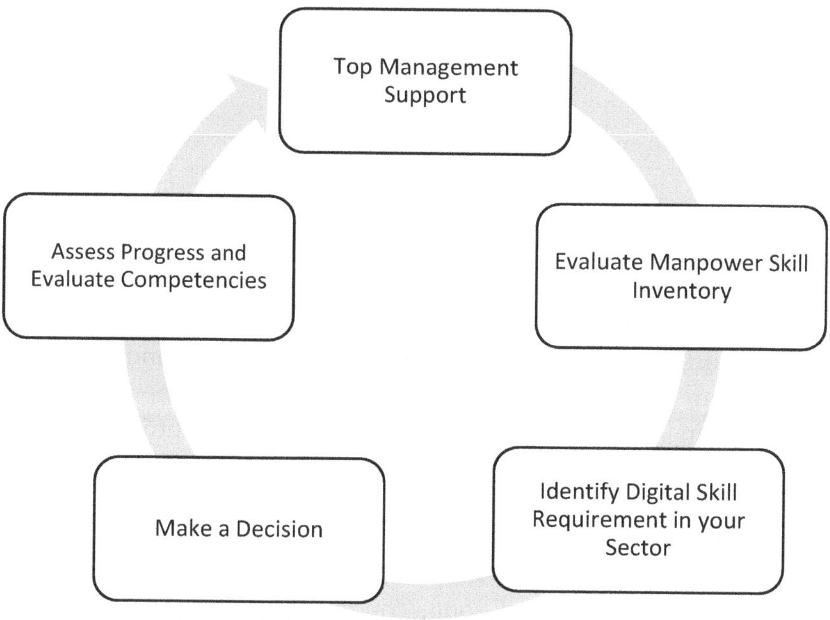

Fig. 12.1 Process of developing digital skills and competencies (*Source* Authors)

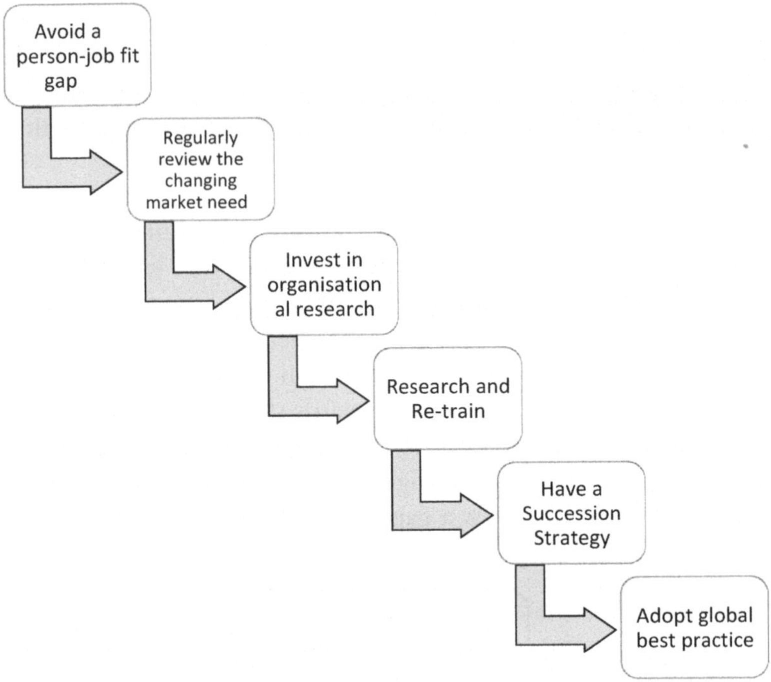

Fig. 12.2 Steps to managing digital skills and competencies in Africa (*Source* Authors)

job. Organisations must prevent such occurrences to avoid workplace redundancy and wastage of human resources.

ii. **Regularly review the changing market need:** Organisations must also constantly review the market changes to understand the market direction, new products, and services required, and how the organisation fits in. Businesses in Africa must be able to project the skills and competencies required of the market and make an appropriate plan not to be caught off guard. This is crucial because the market in Africa is vulnerable to changing market dynamics, which can alter consumer demand. For instance, International Finance Corporation (2019), a World Bank Group, conducted a study in sub-Saharan Africa to explore the digital skills needed in the region now and in the coming years and discovered that skills such as web research, basic software use, digital marketing, and artificial intelligence are in high demand in sub-Saharan Africa. Therefore, organisations must continuously review the changing market need to be abreast and ensure they are not left behind in the digital revolution.

iii. **Invest in organisational research:** For an organisation to be abreast of the changing market trends, it must invest in market research. Market research is vital as it provides businesses with the needed market information and insights needed to make the right decisions. Investment in research will update the management of the current enterprise skills required for market performance as consumer demand changes. Therefore, to manage available skills and competencies within the organisation to ensure that the business has rare, inimitable, and non-substitutable skills and competencies needed to drive and sustain business performance, organisations in Africa must invest in market research.

iv. **Research and Re-train:** Assess and upgrade competencies in line with the changing trends in the digital world to avoid being left behind in the development of innovative products or services. The organisation should be able to identify the consumers' future needs within its market and begin to put in place an appropriate structure, attract the needed skill, and initiate the expected innovation to be ahead of the consumers. Investment in market research will give information on the market's current situation and the necessary steps the organisation should take to remain competitive. A notice of a skill gap, showing a need in the market with a lack of human capacity to respond to this change, should result in the re-training of the concerned department and staff. Training is a continuous process, and the organisation cannot rely on its workforce skillset for a long time. There will always be a change in taste, product, and service desirability of the consumers in a market. For this reason, the organisation must continuously research, orientate, train, and re-train its workforce on the new skill required for product and service delivery.

v. **Have a succession strategy:** Having a sustainable pipeline of human capital with digital skills is vital for managing skills and competencies in an organisation. Businesses in Africa must ensure a talent succession pipeline that does not allow the organisation to be deficient in having the right person doing the right job at the right time. In an era where digital skills are scarce and rare in Africa, businesses must ensure that they have a system that mentors young employees, ensuring the transfer of knowledge, skills, and abilities from the older workers to the younger ones. By doing this, the business will not be deficient in a digitally trained workforce ready for the current and future needs of the market.

vi. **Adopt global best practice:** Businesses in Africa must ensure that their practice is in line with global best practices because this is important for business competition. Questions such as: does our mode of operation conform to global best practice in this sector? Does our product/service meet up with the global standard? How can we improve our business process and outcome? These questions are important for the organisation to continually evolve and not be left behind in their sector or industry. It is important that businesses in Africa realise that they are competing in a global business space that is engendered by digital technology. Hence, the need for a constant review of their business practices in line with global standards.

12.6 Recommendations for Government and Businesses in Africa

The digital skill gap in Africa is of great concern as this might slow the digital business transformation drive agenda in Africa. However, the government and business organisations in Africa can respond to this challenge and turn the table in her favour.

First, businesses in Africa must understand the market's product and service needs before deciding on the digital innovation that fits their businesses type. This is vital as the digital transformation endeavour of the businesses must be driven by the need of the consumers in the market; digital innovation not focused on meeting the need of the consumers will not achieve the desired business outcomes. Businesses in Africa must ensure that the digital design they seek to adopt meets the need or responds to consumers' need in the market.

Second, there are generic and specific digital skills. Generic digital skills are contingent on the essentials of digital skills, which allow the citizens to harness the opportunities in technology. However, there are professional skills which this chapter has focused mostly on that are specific to occupations and professions that employees must be empowered with. The digital skills and competencies required in the banking sector are not the same as in the agricultural sector, and it also differs from the requirements in the educational sector. Businesses in Africa must understand the kind and nature of skills and competencies needed in their sector to enhance and sustain business performance and competitive advantage. What works in business "A" rendering logistic service is not necessary the digital innovation required for the farmer trying to predict rainfall and harvest seasons correctly. Businesses should understand their sector's skill and competency and adopt necessary steps identified in this chapter to meet them.

Third, the opportunities are there for businesses in Africa to tap into the market created through digital innovation; however, businesses must ensure they rightly position themselves with the right skills and competencies to attract and retain customers and enjoy a competitive advantage. Businesses must also understand that to create a rare, non-substitutable, and inimitable workforce with the right skills and competencies, they should train their internal workforce to fit into their digital needs or recruit expatriates. However, appropriate management of human resource capitals is key to remaining relevant and competitive in the African market.

Lastly, the government has a role to play in bridging the digital literacy gap among its citizenry and improving the digital skills and competencies needed for business performance. The government must make a conscientious effort to include essential digital skills in schools' curriculum from primary, secondary, and tertiary institutions. Formal education provides a good platform for embedding digital skills in the citizens. Universities will have to revisit their curriculum and make necessary changes. Otherwise, many graduates in Africa will not fit into the labour market need. The privately owned businesses in Africa must begin to take measures to develop and maintain digital skills in their human capital.

12.7 Conclusion

Digital business has come to stay, and Africa must prepare its human capital for the current and future business needs. The best approach to developing digital skills and competencies in an organisation is contingent on the financial and human resources available to the organisation and the consumers' needs. Organisations will only create a rare, inimitable, and non-substitutable workforce with the right digital skills when the organisation aligns its resources to the need of the market. Digital business is not just about the people but also the structure and process of the organisation. The government and private-owned organisations have a role to play in ensuring that the demand and supply of digitally skilled personnel are at equilibrium.

References

Ananiadou, K., & Claro, M. (2009). *21st century skills and competences for new millennium learners in OECD countries.* OECD Education Working Papers, No. 41. OECD Publishing (NJ1).

Andriole, S. J. (2018). Skills and competencies for digital transformation. *IT Professional, 20*(6), 78–81.

AON'S Assessment Solution. (2018). Future-Proofing Your Talent. Retrieved from: https://mclagan.aon.com/aon.mclagan/media/files/2019/future-proofing-your-talent.pdf

AON'S Assessment Solution. (2020). *Essential competencies for digital future.* Retrieved from https://insights.humancapital.aon.com/talent-assessment-media-articles/the-essential-competencies-for-digital-transformation

Attaran, M., & Woods, J. (2019). Cloud computing technology: Improving small business performance using the Internet. *Journal of Small Business & Entrepreneurship, 31*(6), 495–519.

Baculard, L. P. (2017). *To lead a digital transformation, CEOs must prioritise.* https://hbr.org/2017/01/to-lead-a-digital-transformation-ceos-must-prioritize

Barney, J. (1991). Firm resources and sustained competitive advantage. *Journal of Management, 17*(1), 99–120.

Baro, E. E., Obaro, O. G., & Aduba, E. D. (2019). An assessment of digital literacy skills and knowledge-based competencies among librarians working in university libraries in Africa. *Digital Library Perspectives, 35*(3/4), 172–192.

Belleflamme, P., & Peitz, M. (2019). Managing competition on a two-sided platform. *Journal of Economics & Management Strategy, 28*(1), 5–22.

Bolat, E., & Taura, N. (2019). *The conversation-digital technologies are transforming African businesses, but obstacles remain.* https://theconversation.com/digital-technologies-are-transforming-african-businesses-but-obstacles-remain-120005

Cedefop. (2008). *Terminology of European education and training policy. A selection of 100 key terms.* Office for Official Publications of the European Communities. https://www.cedefop.europa.eu/files/4064_en.pdf

Chetty, K., Aneja, U., Mishra, V., Gcora, N., & Josie, J. (2018a). Bridging the digital divide in the G20: Skills for the new age. *Economics: The Open-Access, Open-Assessment E-Journal, 12*(2018–24), 1–20.

Chetty, K., Qigui, L., Gcora, N., Josie, J., Wenwei, L., & Fang, C. (2018b). Bridging the digital divide: measuring digital literacy. *Economics: The Open-Access, Open-Assessment E-Journal, 12*(2018–23), 1–20.

Collier, J. E., & Kimes, S. E. (2013). Only if it is convenient: Understanding how convenience influences self-service technology evaluation. *Journal of Service Research, 16*(1), 39–51.

Craffert, L., Ungerer, M., Visser, K., Morrison, J., & Claassen, W. (2014). *Strategies, practices and skills for competitiveness in the digital economy: A perspective on large companies in South Africa.* University of the Western Cape.

Demirkan, H., Spohrer, J. C., & Welser, J. J. (2016). Digital innovation and strategic transformation. *IT Professional, 18*(6), 14–18.

El-Haddadeh, R. (2020). Digital innovation dynamics influence on organisational adoption: The case of cloud computing services. *Information Systems Frontiers, 22*(4), 985–999.

Fuchs, C., & Horak, E. (2008). Africa and the digital divide. *Telematics and Informatics, 25*(2), 99–116.

Hagberg, J., Sundström, M., & Nicklas, E. Z. (2016). The digitalisation of retailing: An exploratory framework. *International Journal of Retail & Distribution Management, 44*(7), 694–712.

Hecklau, F., Galeitzke, M., Flachs, S., & Kohl, H. (2016). Holistic approach for human resource management in Industry 4.0. *Procedia Cirp, 54*(1), 1–6.

Hoberg, P., Krcmar, H., & Welz, B. (2017). Skills for digital transformation. Technical University of Munich, chair for information systems, Study. Retrieved from https://www.scribd.com/document/496673897/Sap-Skills-for-Digital-Transformation.

International Finance Corporation (IFC) LEK Consulting. (2019). *Digital skills in Sub-Saharan Africa: spotlight on Ghana.*

James, J. (2019). Confronting the scarcity of digital skills among the poor in developing countries. *Development Policy Review.*

Jenkin, N., & Naude, R. (2019). *Developing competencies for a just transition of the South African banking sector: Digitalisation.* University of Witwatersrand, Johannesburg, South Africa.

Koski, H., Melkas, H., Mäntylä, M., Pieters, R., Svento, R., Särkikoski, T., ... & Matikainen, L. (2016). *Technology disruptions as enablers of organisational and social innovation in digitalised environment* (No. 45). ETLA Working Papers.

Lee, H. L., & Whang, S. (2001, November). E-business and supply chain integration. In *Standford global supply chain management forum* (Vol. 2), pp. 1–20.

Ludike J. (2018). Digital employee experience engagement paradox: Future-proofing retention practice. In M. Coetzee, I. Potgieter, & N. Ferreira (Eds.), *Psychology of retention.* Springer.

Madden, P., & Kanos, D. (2020). *Figures of the week: Digital skills and the future of work in Africa.* https://www.brookings.edu/blog/africa-in-focus/2020/07/22/figures-of-the-week-digital-skills-and-the-future-of-work-in-africa/

Mahadevan, B. (2000). Business models for Internet-based e-commerce: An anatomy. *California Management Review, 42*(4), 55–69.

Makoe, M. (2012). Teaching digital natives: Identifying competencies for mobile learning facilitators in distance education. *South African Journal of Higher Education, 26*(1), 91–104.

Michota, A. (2013). Digital security concerns and threats facing women entrepreneurs. *Journal of Innovation and Entrepreneurship, 2*(1), 1–11.

Mustaffa, S., & Beaumont, N. (2004). The effect of electronic commerce on small Australian enterprises. *Technovation, 24*(2), 85–95.

Mutula, S. M., & Van Brakel, P. (2007). ICT skills readiness for the emerging global digital economy among small businesses in developing countries: Case study of Botswana. *Library Hi Tech, 25*(2), 231–245.

Nadeem, A., Abedin, B., Cerpa, N., & Chew, E. (2018). Digital transformation & digital business strategy in electronic commerce-the role of organisational capabilities. *Journal of Theoretical and Applied Electronic Commerce Research, 13*(2), 1–8.

Ngoasong, M. Z. (2018). Digital entrepreneurship in a resource-scarce context: A focus on entrepreneurial digital competencies. *Journal of Small Business and Enterprise Development, 25*(3), 483–500.

Parviainen, P., Tihinen, M., Kääriäinen, J., & Teppola, S. (2017). Tackling the digitalisation challenge: How to benefit from digitalisation in practice. *International Journal of Information Systems and Project Management, 5*(1), 63–77.

Psannis, K. E., Xinogalos, S., & Sifaleras, A. (2014). Convergence of Internet of Things and mobile cloud computing. *Systems Science & Control Engineering: An Open Access Journal, 2*(1), 476–483.

Royle, J., & Laing, A. (2014). The digital marketing skills gap: Developing a digital marketer model for the communication industries. *International Journal of Information Management, 34*(2), 65–73.

Scheepers, M. J. (2008). Entrepreneurial mindset of information and communication technology firms. *South African Journal of Information Management, 10*(4), 2–11.

Scott, K. V. (2000, September). The technical writer as software process catalyst. In *18th Annual conference on computer documentation. Ipcc sigdoc 2000. Technology and teamwork. Proceedings.* IEEE Professional Communication Society International Professional Communication Conference an (pp. 269–280). IEEE.

Scuotto, V., Del Giudice, M., Della Peruta, M. R., & Tarba, S. (2017). The performance implications of leveraging internal innovation through social media networks: An empirical verification of the smart fashion industry. *Technological Forecasting and Social Change, 120*, 184–194.

Skog, D. A., Wimelius, H., & Sandberg, J. (2018). Digital disruption. *Business & Information Systems Engineering, 60*(5), 431–437.

Smith, W. K., & Tushman, M. L. (2005). Managing strategic contradictions: A top management model for managing innovation streams. *Organisation Science, 16*(5), 522–536.

Sousa, M. J., & Rocha, Á. (2019). Digital learning: Developing skills for digital transformation of organisations. *Future Generation Computer Systems, 91*, 327–334.

Spake, D. F., Beatty, S. E., Brockman, B. K., & Crutchfield, T. N. (2003). Consumer comfort in service relationships: Measurement and importance. *Journal of Service Research, 5*(4), 316–332.

Tahvanainen, S., & Luoma, E. (2018). Examining the competencies of the chief digital officer. In *AMCIS 2018: Proceedings of the 24th Americas Conference on Information Systems*. Association for Information Systems. https://aisel.aisnet.org/amcis2018/OrgTrasfm/Presentations/16/

Tapia, A. H., & Kvasny, L. (2004, April). Recruitment is never enough: retention of women and minorities in the IT workplace. In *Proceedings of the 2004 SIGMIS conference on Computer personnel research: Careers, culture, and ethics in a networked environment* (pp. 84–91).

The Economic Forum. (2020). *Understanding the impact of digitalisation on society*. https://reports.weforum.org/digital-transformation/understanding-the-impact-of-digitalization-on-society/

Tumbas, S., Berente, N., & vom Brocke, J. (2017). Three types of chief digital officers and the reasons organisations adopt the role. *MIS Quarterly Executive, 16*(2).

Van Deursen, A. J., & Van Dijk, J. A. (2014). *Digital skills: Unlocking the information society*. Springer.

Van Kerrebroeck, H., Brengman, M., & Willems, K. (2017). Escaping the crowd: An experimental study on the impact of a virtual reality experience in a shopping mall. *Computers in Human Behavior, 77*, 437–450.

Wall, B., Jagdey, H., & Browne, J. (2007). A review of eBusiness and digital business—Applications, models and trends. *Production Planning and Control, 18*(3), 239–260.

Ziemba, E., Eisenbardt, M., Mullins, R., & Dettmer, S. (2020). Consumer engagement in business process innovation–ICT companies cases from Poland and UK. *Journal of Computer Information Systems*, 1–14.

13

Virtual Teams: The New Work Norm for the Post Covid-19 Era

Abdullah Promise Opute

13.1 Introduction

Marketing literature notes that digital evolution is massively shaping marketing dynamics and indeed defining the marketing norm (e.g., Opute, 2017). For a couple of decades now, we have entered the digital era, and digital mechanics such as Internet, Internet of things (IoT), social media, digital communication, and digitisation are constituent parts of daily life (e.g., Spencer & Sutton-Brady, 2020; Opute et al., 2020b). Within that marketing discourse, it has been emphasised that digital technologies form a significant tool that companies use to respond to consumers' stimuli (Opute et al., 2020a; Belk, 2013; Opute, 2017) and also for marketing strategy delivery and consumer behaviour tracking (Opute, 2020a; Enyinda et al., 2020; Ozuem et al, 2008).

A. P. Opute (✉)
GPROM Academic and Management Solutions, Salzk, Germany
e-mail: promise.opute@gpromsolutions.org

O. Adeola et al. (eds.), *Digital Service Delivery in Africa*, Palgrave Studies of Marketing in Emerging Economies,
https://doi.org/10.1007/978-3-030-83909-3_13

Furthermore, it has been noted that businesses are increasingly leveraging digital technologies for marketing implementation and in securing competitive advantage, both in local (e.g., Opute, 2020a) and also in global markets (e.g., Rachinger et al., 2019; Opute, 2020a).

Within that target of implementing marketing and securing competitive advantage, a typical operational strategy used in organisations relates to team working. Whilst team working as a useful tool towards achieving organisational deliverables is by no means a new trend (see Table 1), the trend of virtual team working has gained significant importance over the last two decades. In addition to the influence of technological evolution on virtual team working, another force driving virtual team working endorsement is growing globalisation of markets and increased organisational dispersion across geographical settings (e.g., Kimble, 2011; Schouten et al., 2016). Given the internationalisation of trade and increased networks amongst organisations, virtual team working has become a strategic operational tool. Consequently, there has been an increasing academic and management attention on improving the understanding of virtual team working (e.g., Schouten et al., 2016; Strohmeier, 2020; Kuusisto, 2017; Strohmeier, 2018).

The Covid-19 pandemic has exerted unprecedented global implications, compelling organisations to resort to virtual team working to curtail the economic damage. Given the severe implications of the Covid-19 pandemic on the global business community, leading to a huge economic downturn precipitated by the lockdown containment measure, virtual team working would not only become a more competitive strategy but also an operational norm. In the Special Issue Call for Papers of the Journal of Business and Industrial Marketing (2020)—"Interactions, Relationships and Networks in a digital era," Guest Editors Spencer and Sutton-Brady comment thus: "recent events linked to Covid and associated phenomena such as social distancing have accentuated the digital effect" (p. 1). The various industrial sectors are all upgrading their practices to fit the new dispensation. As succinctly captured by Hacker et al. (2019) not only is the changing workplace increasing the utility of the virtual teams' strategy in responding to the complex dynamics of contemporary organisational issues, but also the pertinence for addressing the associated management challenges cannot be overlooked. This management challenge premise is a critical space for knowledge development (e.g., Hacker et al., 2019; Chatfield et al., 2014; Jimenez et al., 2017; Lukić & Vračar, 2018). Furthermore, literature underlines the need to incorporate information systems (e.g., Munkvold & Zigurs, 2007; Schouten et al., 2016), human resource management (e.g., Strohmeier, 2020; Kuusisto, 2017; Strohmeier, 2018), and psychology (e.g., Kimble et al., 2010; Hacker et al., 2019; Mocktinis et al., 2012; Gilson et al., 2014) viewpoints in the understanding of virtual teams.

Inspired by domain discourse, this chapter aims to contribute to filling a research gap in the area of virtual teams. To do that, this chapter draws its foundation from the management logic that a leadership fit is strategic to effectively steering team working towards optimising symbiotic interrelation and organisational performance (Opute, 2014). Founded in that thinking, this chapter forwards a conceptual perspective that is aimed at ensuring effective virtual team working, taking into consideration interdependence as a critical feature in team working, human resource management theory, psychological factors, and infrastructural features. The conceptual framing of this chapter is important because limited attention has been given to understanding how to optimise team collaboration and task performance in virtual team working (Schouten et al., 2016).

Next, digital technologies and team working is presented as a theme, explaining clearly team work, virtual team working, and how digital technologies are becoming a central part of modern society and team working. Following that, the benefits of virtual team working are explained. Thereafter, typical challenges that may impede the effectiveness of virtual teams are considered. In that regard, this chapter draws from the psychological foundation, HRM, and infrastructural theories to flag management initiatives that organisations can take towards ensuring effective interdependence and optimal alignment amongst virtual team members. In the concluding part of this chapter, recommendations for organisations in the African setting are offered, and the core conclusions underlined. Also, directions for future research are flagged.

13.2 Digital Technologies and Team Working

Daily life dynamics are becoming increasingly digital technologies enabled (Opute, 2017). By implication, therefore, life activities have become increasingly virtual based in contrast to the conventional trend of face-to-face interactions. Hence, marketing literature notes that there is a glaring paradigm shift in the way marketing is practised from the conventional practice to internet and digital technologies-based marketing (e.g., Opute, 2017). That marketing implication is further underlined by recent observation that the "place" marketing mix feature no longer being only physical, but also digital based (Opute et al., 2020b). In marketing literature, digitalised technologies-based marketing (also called e-commerce) has been defined as "the process of buying, selling, transferring, or exchanging products, services and/or information via computer networks, mostly internet and intranet" (Turban et al., 2010: 48). In other words, selling activity is no longer domain-specific but rather transpires through digital technologies.

From the point of team working, there is an increasing trend of digital technology-based working. Whilst team working has been an established organisational structure since the 1970s, modern team working has shifted significantly to the virtual form (Kimble, 2011). Three critical factors have facilitated the virtual team working significance:

1. Evolving digital technology,
2. Internationalisation of trade and global networks, and
3. Virtual team working as a response mechanism to the containment implications of Covid-19.

A team—a group of "*individuals interacting adaptively, interdependently, and dynamically towards a common and valued goal*" (Salas et al., 2000: 341), and may be of diverse dimensions (e.g., task interdependence, role structure, lifespan) (Wildman et al., 2012). Virtual team is a particular type of team and implies "*groups of geographically and/organisationally dispersed co-workers that are assembled using a combination of telecommunications and information technologies to accomplish an organisational task*" (Townsend et al., 1998: 18). In a virtual team, membership could take any of two forms (Kimble, 2011): (1) relatively stable (for example, an established sales team), or (2) change regularly (for example, project teams). Thus, virtual teams could be ad hoc or permanent. Membership of a virtual team could be composed of people from the same organisation or a number of different organisations. Also, team members may work within a not spatially significant space (for example, they could work in the same building) or could be significantly spatially distant (for example, work in different cities or countries). Finally, virtual team members may work at the same or at different times. The framing of virtual team working in this chapter relates to any form of virtual working where membership could be composed of people either from the same organisation, different organisations, or even of a global form (across countries).

13.3 Benefits of Virtual Team Working

Virtual team working is a strategic operational tool that organisations embrace to compete effectively in the marketplace. Within that goal of staying competitive, the central target is to leverage virtual team working to enable team members to work virtually to achieve organisational goal—offer deliverables to customers at a profit. One major benefit of virtual team working for organisations is that it offers flexibility, i.e., reducing relocation time and cost of agile virtual teams (Anderson et al., 2007). Beyond that, virtual team working can be utilised as a tool to enable innovative marketing strategy:

Enables Network and Cooperation: As a strategic operational tool, virtual teams enable organisations to leverage scarce resources across geographic and other boundaries (Munkvold & Zigurs, 2007: 287). As noted by Chatfield et al. (2014), organisations utilise virtual team working to capture diverse knowledge resources towards business value creation. Virtual team working allows organisations to strategically build networks and forge forces with competitors towards gaining entry to market segments that were prior to beyond their reach. Thus, virtual team working can be used as a tool towards enabling innovative marketing. Also, virtual team working can be leveraged to enable competitors to cooperate with each other and their customers towards building a customer relationship management system for their mutual benefits (Kimble et al., 2010).

Enables Globalisation: Virtual team working is also a strategic tool for internationalisation of businesses. Businesses could leverage virtual team working to globalise business operations. For innovative organisations, virtual team is a highly useful option towards penetrating global markets (Chatfield et al., 2014). Furthermore, on the point of innovativeness and market penetration, it has been documented that technology-enabled virtual team working enables not only better team performance but also swift entry to markets (e.g., May & Carter, 2001).

Further details on the benefits of virtual team working are captured in Table 13.1.

Table 13.1 Level of Use of Virtual Working Teams in Organisations (including Estimates of Use)

Authors	Insights (including estimates)
Gartner (2003)	This study estimated that 60% of all major corporations used virtual teams (see Gibson & Gibbs, 2006; Martins et al., 2004)
Gartner (2012)	It was estimated that 80% of major corporations would be using virtual teams by 2016
Gartner (2016)	In a survey of virtual teams, it was found that 85% of respondents in corporations work on virtual teams
Hoch & Dulebohn, 2017	In a study involving 3000 managers from 100 countries, it was found that 40% of employees in their individual organisations spent at least half their work time on work involving virtual teams
RW3 Culture Wizard, 2016	This study notes that 48% of the virtual teams were global compared to 41% and 33% for 2014 and 2012, respectively

Source Author. Facts collated fromHacker et al., 2019

13.4 Managing Virtual Teams: Critical Factors

Workgroups form critical organisational trends in responding effectively to contemporary marketplace dispensation (e.g., Kimble, 2011; Opute, 2014). Teams are organisational units constituted by organisational personnel who pursue a common goal, and members have a mutual responsibility for the outcome of the team effort. Whilst teams and team working enable organisations to work flexibly and effectively towards achieving organisational targets—which could be tangible products or services or even sub-product or other organisation's value chain units (Kimble, 2011), the implementation strategy may vary from one organisation to another. The implementation diversity is not a core theme in this chapter, rather the premise in this chapter relates to virtual team working. Therefore, this section aims to highlight critical factors upon which the effectiveness of virtual teams hinge in organisations. As evidenced in Table 13.1, virtual teams have been used in organisation since about twenty years.

Team Management: The Role of Leadership—Achieving effective teams is a huge challenge (e.g., Opute, 2012, 2014) and even more for a virtual team (e.g., Hacker et al., 2019). Critical to ensuring harmonious team working is a fit leadership strategy that enables optimal symbiotic interrelation (Opute, 2014). In a recent publication that offered a retail marketing perspective for effectively absorbing the lockdown impact associated with crises situations such as Covid-19, Opute et al. (2020b) re-echo the leadership fit importance. Virtual team leadership literature sensitises two central themes (Gilson et al., 2014): leadership behaviours and leadership traits. The focus in this chapter is not to engage intensively with the behaviour and traits themes, but rather on the transformational leadership foundation, which, as documented in virtual team literature, is grounded on personality and communication factors (Balthazard et al., 2009) and can enable performance, satisfaction (Purvanova & Bono, 2009), and motivation (Andressen et al., 2012).

Leadership is important in virtual team functioning (Gilson et al., 2014): it influences how teams deal with obstacles, and how teams adapt in challenging situations. Underpinned by this leadership logic, the conceptualisation of this chapter aligns with the foundation that ensuring a fit leadership strategy is primary to ensuring effective virtual teams. A fit and effective leadership would ensure that the infrastructural, human resource and development, and psychological components associated with virtual team working are adequately taken care of.

Psychological Factors—It is important to commence with this factor because interdependence is a critical feature in team working and the extent to which symbiotic interrelation is achieved hinges largely on the extent to which interdependence is optimised (e.g. Opute, 2014; Opute & Madichie, 2016). As stated earlier, the conceptual framing of virtual teams in this chapter reflects a membership from within one organisation, across several organisations, and across geographical and continental levels. Founded on the criticality of trust in the formation and sustenance of virtual teams (e.g., Hacker et al., 2019) and recognising that "trusting a stranger with whom there is no prior relationship or a physical encounter is risky" (Owonikoko, 2016: 26), the psychological framing in this chapter embodies cognition-based and affect-based trust theories of interpersonal relationships (McAllister, 1995). This theoretical framing is further rationalised on the logic that culture significantly conditions the mindset of individuals and thus lack of trust may be a rational response in relationships involving heterogeneous cultures (Opute et al., 2020c; Hagos et al., 2018), a cultural contention that resonates with German norm—*Vertrauen ist gut, Kontrolle ist besser*, which means who you do not know, do not trust.

Ensuring unity in thoughts and perceptions is critical towards ensuring essential cognition-based trust for effective working relationships (e.g., Opute, 2014; Opute & Madichie, 2016). High levels of cognitive trust enable a conducive team climate where members feel relaxed and freely share information and build interpersonal relationships (Owonikoko, 2016). From the point of task performance, when such level of cognitive trust obtains, team members leverage their thoughts and intuition to accept team members, as well as show faith in their effectively implementing their tasks (Kanawattanachai & Yoo, 2002).

Organisations would need to give due attention to *cultural* heterogeneity amongst virtual team members and take necessary steps to ensure that there is a harmonious climate that thrives on trust amongst team members (e.g., Opute, 2012, 2014). Cultural diversity negatively affects relationship amongst personnel in intra-organisational (e.g., Opute, 2014; Opute & Madichie, 2016) and inter-organisational (e.g., Shao et al., 2020) settings. Further culture-based literature contends that in global virtual teams, collectivistic oriented members favour team processes than individualistic oriented members (Mockaitis et al., 2012). Literature also documents that whilst team members from certain countries (e.g., the United States) favour the inclusion of team members in discussions and decisions, members from other locations (e.g., Belgium, India, and The Netherlands) do not support such practice (Dekker et al., 2008). Failure to manage culture-based challenges in a virtual team working space would lead to frustration amongst team members and that would impair interdependence and alignment between team members. *Trust and Identity* are critical features for achieving effective virtual working (Hacker et al., 2019). Virtual team working is highly technology reliant, and a typical challenge of technology is its capacity to disrupt trust in virtual team working (Hacker et al., 2019). Securing trust amongst virtual team members is a critical step towards overcoming the diverse problems in virtual team working (Hacker et al., 2019).

Virtual team leaders must ensure mechanisms that build and maintain trust amongst virtual team members. In a digitally enhanced environment, trust amongst virtual team members is critical to achieving one identity behaviour in organisations, therefore organisations must ensure processes that facilitate and sustain trust amongst virtual team members. To share timely and accurate information, and work amicably and effectively and display transparent unified effort behaviour, a good measure of trust must exist amongst team members. To adequately ensure amicable work climate, the leadership must also ensure affect-based trust amongst virtual team members. Humans are a bundle of emotions, and the emotional frame of individuals may influence the level of trust they may have in other people, especially when the interaction between individuals is virtual based. According to Webber (2008), affect-based trust is borne out of emotions, care, concern, and empathy that team members display in implementing their individual tasks. When team members experience high affect-based trust, they would freely share task-related as well as personal information regardless of nationality, geographical disparity, level or means of communication (Sarker et al., 2011). To steer virtual team working in the right direction, the leadership approach must incorporate mechanisms that give due attention to the aforementioned psychological features.

13.4.1 Human Resource and Development (Training)

Technology is a critical factor in virtual team working; consequently, adequate attention must be given to this factor to ensure optimal virtual team working (e.g., Hacker et al., 2019; Gilson et al., 2014). In doing that, it is very important that organisations bear in mind the challenges associated with technology-based team working, one of which is that team members may not be very familiar with the technological features of the new work norm (e.g., Opute et al., 2020b; Jarvenpaa & Leidner, 1999). The leadership must therefore ensure appropriate human resource management plan to enable effective virtual team working.

Within that point of human resource management, a critical point relates to the training of virtual team members to uplift their skills levels to enable them effectively work with technology-based processes. Team members need to understand how to navigate through the digitised work processes using the operational platforms, such as MS Teams, Zoom, etc. Familiarising themselves with these platforms could be very challenging for some team members, so the organisational leadership must invest in resources that would aid that transition process.

A core pre-requisite for effective team interdependence and decision-making performance is a shared understanding of performance (Schouten et al., 2016; Opute, 2008). Achieving shared understanding—a common understanding of a task as well as an understanding of each other's viewpoint (Weick, 1985), should be a core human resource management focus towards effective virtual team working. For example, for a decision task in a virtual team, team members would need to share their understanding of the decision process and decisions to be made, and a common understanding must be reached. Thus, social interactive skills would be required for optimal team interaction (Schouten et al., 2016), and for effective virtual team working, the human resource management mechanisms must ensure that team members acquire relevant social interactive skills to ensure a common understanding.

A central target for organisations is to ensure effective virtual team working that would enable organisations to profitably satisfy customers. With regard to managing virtual team-related challenges, the leadership should also focus on HRM training that would enable team members engage effectively with customers. A virtually based operational process will bring obvious challenges for team members as well as customers who may not be familiar with technology-based retail as well as relationship processes of the firm. The leadership must ensure that the virtual team is not only adequately skilled to engage effectively with the technology-based platforms but also in achieving customer orientation. In the particular case of team members that have direct contact with customers, the leadership must ensure that these are well skilled in ensuring strategic engagement with customers and also helping customers to effectively navigate the associated technology-induced challenges of the new marketing norms.

13.4.2 Infrastructure

Digital technologies are critical for effective virtual team working (Chatfield et al., 2014). To achieve optimal symbiotic interrelation (effective information sharing, involvement and unified effort [e.g., Opute & Madichie, 2016; Opute et al., 2013]) for corporate success, the organisation must ensure appropriate digital infrastructure to aid virtual team working. The organisation must invest in technological devices and packages that aid virtual team working. Typical virtual team working platforms include Microsoft Teams, Zoom, Webex, Skype. Whilst these platforms enable virtual team working, they may differ in their designs and the extent of what is doable and how. Therefore, organisations must ensure a suitable option that enables virtual team members to effectively navigate through their work challenges.

Towards ensuring effectiveness in virtual team working, the leadership must also focus on managing team priorities, tracking progress levels, and managing failures in the operational dynamics in the team working infrastructure. This will involve tactically organising the virtual working platform to ensure a clear definition and allocation of tasks. Equally, the platform must be structured not only to allow for easy and timely sharing of information but also cross alignment between the team members. The virtual team working platform should be structured to allow for effective chatting, and relevant documentation to be uploaded onto the platform for members to access and effectively carry out their tasks. Members should also be able to interact one on one amongst themselves and effectively interrelate symbiotically to achieve organisational objectives.

Towards achieving effective virtual team working and organisational targets, the virtual team working platform should also integrate software that enables video conferencing, archiving of such video conferences for future accessing by team members. Also, virtual whiteboard tools should be integrated to enable team members to brainstorm and pull ideas together and review their past processes. Integrating such tools would enable team members to effectively organise their thoughts as whiteboard tools contain collaborative features such as a comment section and cloud sharing (syncing). Effective communication and sharing of ideas are essential for effective virtual team working (Chatfield et al., 2014). To optimise team working, the virtual platforms should be structured to enable:

1. Screen sharing
2. Instant messaging
3. Note taking
4. Group chat
5. Team building activities
6. Reviews and check-ins

13.5 Recommendations for Organisations in the African Setting

Firstly, the conceptual framework forwarded in this chapter is summarised in Fig. 13.1. The conceptual framework suggests a leadership strategy viewpoint for ensuring optimal symbiotic interrelation in

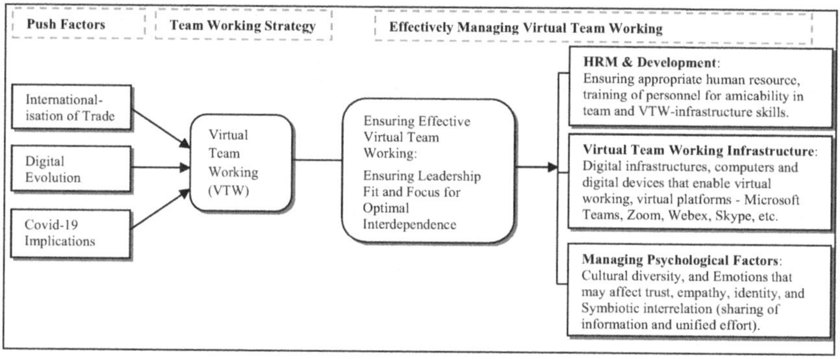

Fig. 13.1 Optimising Virtual Team Working: A Leadership Strategy underpinned on HRM, Infrastructural and Psychological Foundations (*Source* Author)

virtual-based team working towards corporate success. The framework underlines the pertinence for organisational leadership to ensure not only adequate infrastructural and human resource management and development, but also the criticality of giving due attention to the numerous psychological factors that may undermine the effectiveness of virtual team working.

The after-effects of the Covid-19 pandemic on organisations and consumers have awakened a focus for staying agile, thinking creatively, and responding pro-actively to change circumstances, as well as staying future focused. In responding to the Covid-19 pandemic, businesses have resorted to virtual team working as a rational strategy for overcoming the lockdown containment impact. Whilst virtual team working, in itself, is not a new operational tool, the aftermath of Covid-19 does underscore the pertinence for organisations to endorse that working strategy. In a not too distant future, virtual team working would be the established norm, and organisations that fail to embrace the new norm would perish. Two critical developments rationalise that conclusion. First, digital technologies have not only evolved significantly but have also become a core part of daily life, and as a matter of fact, human attitude has shifted significantly from conventional face-to-face interaction to virtual modes (e.g., Opute et al., 2020a, 2020b). Second, natural (including health) crises do occur, and the Covid-19 pandemic has exposed the business operational frailties of physical face-to-face interactions. In situations where movement restriction may be a containment strategy, virtual team working strategy would enable organisations to effectively navigate the operational challenges they face towards effectively ensuring deliverables to customers, and keeping the economy active.

The world in which we live is becoming increasingly dynamic, and only organisations that are armed with adequate operational strategy would survive in the constantly evolving marketplace. For organisations in the African setting, entrepreneurship activity has been documented to be relatively less productive (e.g., Opute, 2020a; Iwu & Opute, 2019), hence high levels of unemployment and poverty (e.g., Du Toit et al., 2018; Iwu et al., 2020), recognising that virtual team working would become the new operational norm in no distant future is critical.

No doubt, the virtual team working trend is one with dual implications for the African setting. First, endorsing the virtual team working strategy is unavoidable and would enable businesses in that setting to remain economically active. To attain the entrepreneurship capacity to be productive and enable economic growth, organisations in the African setting would need to embrace the emerging norm—virtual team working. Doing that would enable organisations in that setting to effectively explore innovative entrepreneurship marketing targets (see Opute, 2020a). Utilising virtual team working would facilitate an organisation's ability to leverage networking outlets and gain access to new markets. locally and internationally.

The second implication, however, is the associated challenge in how the new norm is endorsed. Here, African businesses would need to ensure leadership that is pro-active, committed, and armed with a clear strategy to effectively implement the transition. Organisations in this setting must ensure adequate investment in technological infrastructure, human resource management (including training and development), as well as ensuring that typical psychological factors that may impede effective symbiotic interrelation in the virtual team working space are eliminated. Thus, businesses must ensure that they acquire the service of a relevant virtual working platform that offers adequate features required for their team working. Also, members of the virtual team must be adequately trained to understand how to use the platform features to communicate effectively and share relevant information for effective inter-dependence. This will also require skills for achieving shared understanding and social interactive behaviour. Finally, effectively implementing virtual team working requires the psychological factors (e.g., culture differences) that may undermine mutual understanding, harmony, trust, and identity, and extendedly symbiotic interrelation are effectively managed.

Organisations in the African setting should ensure appropriate operational mechanisms for monitoring, evaluating, and ensuring that necessary corrective measures are taken towards ensuring effective and goal congruity virtual team working. Equally important in that regard is that organisations in the African setting must keep an eye on emotions-related features (Opute, 2020b) that undermine virtual team working. Intensive emotion-based relationship conflict has been noted to be a common plague of virtual team working (e.g., Ayoko et al., 2012; Connelly & Turel, 2016). To maximise symbiotic interrelation in virtual team working and performance synergy, effective measures to address such conflict features must be ensured. Finally, organisations in the African setting must give due attention to the numerous stress-related features that team members may face due to working virtually, for example, coping with family-related stress factors whilst working virtually from home.

13.6 Conclusion and Future Research Directions

Daily life routine has become increasingly digital technology enabled, both for the individual as well as organisations. For marketers, a direct consequence is the marketing paradigm shift from the conventional physical-based place to virtual-based place marketing premise. Another consequence of the digital technology evolution is the team working enablement influence. Virtual team working is a further consequence of digital technology evolution. However, besides the technological inducement, virtual team working is gaining increasing endorsement due to its flexibility and market penetration (innovative and globalisation) benefits. As a consequence of the Covid-19 pandemic that paralysed the global economy, virtual team working has not only gained further endorsement as a strategy for organisations to offer deliverables to customers but would, in the future, become the norm, as the global effort intensifies to avoid the global paralytic damage of the Covid-19 pandemic. As warned by Opute et al. (2020b: 84), "human nature has witnessed different forms of health crises, and to believe that Covid-19 may be the last of such health crises would be unimaginable."

In the post COVID-19 economic landscape, businesses must find new ways of offering deliverables to customers. Businesses would need to start visualising and planning for the post COVID-19 era. Thriving in the post Covid-19 would require businesses that are not short-term "fire fighting" oriented but rather businesses that display sustainable long-term philosophy and offer business models that are robust and withstand shocks and uncertainties.

In their study that forwards innovative retail marketing response strategy for overcoming the unprecedented implications of Covid-19 pandemic, Opute et al. (2020b) noted that the Covid-19-induced challenges should be a wake-up call for businesses to endorse pro-active, agile, and innovative strategies for effectively responding to natural disaster-related crises and challenges where restriction of movement may be enforced. Businesses are indeed responding effectively to the Covid-19-induced movement impairment challenge through virtual working strategy. Indeed, for numerous associated benefits, businesses may continue with the virtual strategy even post Covid-19. Virtual team working is the new norm for businesses to compete in the digital era. Whilst the endorsement of virtual team working is undoubtedly important, and indeed would become the norm post Covid-19, ensuring effective virtual team working is a huge challenge that requires a fit leadership strategy that is agile and contingency driven and gives due consideration to infrastructure, HRM, and interdependent and social interactive factors. Such a leadership focus is of critical importance towards achieving effective symbiotic interrelation in virtual team working.

Virtual team working would be a theoretical premise that would gain tremendous importance in the post Covid-19 era as the effort not only to absorb the pandemic-induced shocks but also to ensure future-oriented practices for sustaining the operational flow of organisations even in times of lockdown would increase. It would be rational to expect a surge in knowledge development in this area in the near future. Future research should aim to shed light on how effective organisational initiatives have been in the use of virtual team working in responding to the Covid-19-induced mobility restriction challenges. Critical questions in this regard include (but are not limited to): what modus operandi are organisations prioritising and why? What are the core challenges that organisations are facing and how are they overcoming them? Finally, what future-oriented strategies are organisations focusing on towards mitigating mobility restriction challenges in the future?

References

Anderson, A. H., Mcewan, R., Bal, J., & Carletta, J. (2007). Virtual team meetings: An analysis of communication and context. *Computers in Human Behavior, 23*(5), 2558–2580.

Andressen, P., Konradt, U., & Neck, C. P. (2012). The relation between self-leadership and transformational leadership: Competing models and the moderating role of virtuality. *Journal of Leadership & Organizational Studies, 19*, 68–82.

Ayoko, O. B., Konrad, A. M., & Boyle, V. (2012). Online work: Managing conflict and emotions for performance in virtual teams. *European Management Journal, 30*(2), 156–174.

Balthazard, P. A., Waldman, D. A., & Warren, J. E. (2009). Predictors of the emergence of transformational leadership in virtual decision teams. *The Leadership Quarterly, 20*, 651–663.

Belk, R. W. (2013). Extended self in a digital world. *Journal of Consumer Research, 40*(3), 477–500.

Chatfield, A. T., Shlemoon, V. N., Redublado, W., & Darbyshire, G. (2014). Creating value through virtual teams: A current literature review. *Australasian Journal of Information Systems, 18*(3), 257–269.

Connelly, C. E., & Turel, O. (2016). Effects of team emotional authenticity on virtual team performance. *Frontiers in Psychology., 7*, 1336. https://doi.org/10.3389/fpsyg.2016.01336

Dekker, D. M., Rutte, C. G., & Van den Berg, P. T. (2008). Cultural differences in the perception of critical interaction behaviors in global virtual teams. *International Journal of Intercultural Relations, 32*, 441–452.

Du Toit, M., De Witte, H., Rothmann, S., & Van den Broeck, A. (2018). Unemployment experiences in context: A phenomenological study in two townships in South Africa. *Journal of Psychology in Africa, 28*(2), 122–127.

Enyinda, C. I., Opute, A. P., Fadahunsi, A., & Mbah, C. H. (2020). Marketing-sales-service interface and social media marketing influence on B2B sales process. *Journal of Business & Industrial Marketing*, Vol. ahead-of-print No. ahead-of-print. https://doi.org/10.1108/JBIM-01-2019-0053

Gartner. (2003). *Hype cycle for emerging technologies*. Published 2nd July 2003. Accessed at: https://www.gartner.com/en/documents/399359/hype-cycle-for-emerging-technologies-2003

Gartner. (2012). *PPM & IT governance summit [Brochure]*. Retrieved January 13, 2017, from http://imagesrv.gartner.com/summits/docs/na/program-management/PPMIT4_Brochure.pdf

Gartner. (2016). *Virtual teams*. Accessed at: https://www.gartner.com/en/information-technology/glossary/virtualteam

Gibson, C. B., & Gibbs, J. L. (2006). Unpacking the concept of virtuality: The effects of geographic dispersion, electronic dependence, dynamic structure, and national diversity on team innovation. *Administrative Science Quarterly, 51*(3), 451–495. https://doi.org/10.2189/asqu.51.3.451

Gilson, L. L., Maynard, M. T., Young, N. C., Vartiainen, M., & Hakonen, M. (2014). Virtual Teams research: 10 years, 10 themes, and 10 opprtunities. *Journal of Management, 41*(5), 1313–1337.

Hacker, J., Johnson, M., Saunders, C., & Thayer, A. L. (2019). Trust in virtual teams: A multidisciplinary review and integration. *Australasian Journal of Information Systems, 23*, 1–36.

Hagos, S., Izak, M., & Scott, J. M. (2018). Objective institutionalized barriers and subjective performance factors of new migrant entrepreneurs. *International Journal of Entrepreneurship Behaviour & Research*. https://doi.org/10.1108/IJEBR-06-2018-0405

Hoch, J. E., & Dulebohn, J. H. (2017). Team personality composition, emergent leadership and shared leadership in virtual teams: A theoretical framework. *Human Resource Management Review, 27*(4), 678–693.

Iwu, C. G., & Opute, A. P. (2019). Eradicating poverty and unemployment: Narratives of survivalist entrepreneurs. *Journal of Reviews on Global Economics*. pp. 1438–1451. https://doi.org/10.6000/1929-7092.2019.08.127

Iwu, C. G., Eze, I., Opute, A. P., Dongo, G., & Dongo, O. W. (2020). Scavenging for survival and its health implications. The Nexus between Unemployment and Ill-health. *WSEAS Transactions on Environment and Development, 17*(1), 1–18.

Jarvenpaa, S. L., & Leidner, D. E. (1999). Communication and trust in global virtual teams. *Organisation Science, 10*(6), 791–815.

Jimenez, A., Boehe, D. M., Taras, V., & Caprar, D. V. (2017). Working across boundaries: Current and future perspectives on global virtual teams. *Journal of International Management, 23*(4), 341–349.

Kanawattanachai, P., & Yoo, Y. (2002). Dynamic nature of trust in virtual teams. *Journal of Strategic Information Systems, 11*, 187–213. https://doi.org/10.1016/S0963-8687(02)00019-7

Kimble, C. (2011). Building effective virtual teams: How to overcome the problems of trust and identity in virtual teams. *Global Business and Organizational Excellence, 30*(2), 6–15.

Kimble, C., Grenier, C., & Goglio-Primard, K. (2010). Innovation and knowledge sharing across professional boundaries: Political interplay between boundary objects and brokers. *International Journal of Information Management, 30*, 437–444.

Kuusisto, M. (2017). Organisational effects of digitalisation: A literature review. *International Journal of Organization Theory & Behaviour, 20*(3), 341–362.

Lukić, J., & Vračar, M. (2018). Building and nurturing trust among members in virtual project teams. *Strategic Management, 23*(3), 10–16.

Martins, L. L., Gilson, L. L., & Maynard, M. T. (2004). Virtual teams: What do we know and where do we go from here? *Journal of Management, 30*(6), 805–835.

May, A., & Carter, C. (2001). A case study of virtual team working in the European automotive industry. *International Journal of Industrial Ergonomics, 27*(3), 171–186.

McAllister, D. J. (1995). Affect- and cognition-based trust as foundations for interpersonal cooperation in organisations. *Academy of Management Journal, 38*, 24–59. https://doi.org/10.2307/256727

Mockaitis, A. I., Rose, E. L., & Zettinig, P. (2012). The power of individual cultural values in global virtual teams. *International Journal of Cross Cultural Management, 12*, 193–210.

Munkvold, B. E., & Zigurs, I. (2007). Process and technology challenges in swift-starting virtual teams. *Information and Management, 44*, 287–299.

Opute, A. P. (2008). The antecedents of accounting-marketing integration during the strategic marketing process. Proceedings of the 22nd Annual

Conference of the Academy of Marketing, November 6–8, The Royal Automobile Club, Pall Mall, Westminster. ISBN: 978-0 9552685-5-7.

Opute, A. P. (2014). Cross-functional bridge in dyadic relationship: Conflict management and performance implications. *Team Performance Management, 20*(3–4), 121–147.

Opute, A. P. (2012). Maximizing effectiveness in team sports: The personal audit tool. *Team Performance Management, 18*(1 & 2), 78–101.

Opute, A. P. (2017). Exploring personality, identity and self-concept among young consumers (Chapter Five). In *Young Consumer Behaviour: A Research Companion*. Taylor and Francis. ISBN: 978-0-415-79008-6 (hbk).

Opute, A. P. (2020a). Small and medium enterprises marketing: Innovation and sustainable economic growth perspective. In *Entrepreneurship Marketing: Principles and practice of SME Marketing*. Routledge Publishers.

Opute, A. P. (2020b). Teamwork and customer service (Chapter 14). In *Customer Service Management: A Strategic and Operational Perspective*. Taylor and Francis.

Opute, A. P., & Madichie, N. (2016). An interrogation of Accounting-Marketing Interface in UK financial services organisations: Mixing Cats with Dogs? *Australasian Marketing Journal, 24*(3), 214–225.

Opute, A. P., Dedoussis, E., & Tzokas, N. (2013). Building blocks of Accounting-Marketing integration in UK financial services organizations. *Journal of Marketing and Operations Management Research, 1*(4), 323–336.

Opute, A. P., Irene, B. N., & Iwu, C. G. (2020a). Tourism service and digital technologies: A value creation perspective. *African Journal of Hospitality, Tourism and Leisure, 9*(2). ISSN: 223-814X.

Opute, A. P., Iwu, C. G., Adeola, O., Mugobo, V., Okeke-Uzodike, O. E., Fagbola, S., & Jaiyeoba, O. (2020b). The covid-19-pandemic and implications for businesses: Innovative retail marketing viewpoint. *Retail Marketing Review*, 16, SE.

Opute, A. P., Madichie, N. O., Hagos, S. B., & Ojra, J. (2020c). Entrepreneurship behaviour of African minorities in the UK: 'Demystifying cultural influence'. *International Journal of Entrepreneurship and Small Business*.

Owonikoko, E. A. (2016). Building and maintaining trust in virtual teams as a competitive strategy. Doctoral thesis submitted at Walden University.

Ozuem, W., Howell, K. E., & Lancaster, G. (2008). Communicating in the new interactive marketspace. *European Journal of Marketing, 42*(9/10), 1059–1083.

Purvanova, R. K., & Bono, J. E. (2009). Transformational leadership in context: Face-to-face and virtual teams. *The Leadership Quarterly, 20*, 343–357.

Rachinger, M., Rauter, R., Müller, C., Vorraber, W., & Schirgi, E. (2019). Digitalisation and its influence on business model innovation. *Journal of Manufacturing Technology Management, 30*(8), 1143–1160.

RW3 CultureWizard. (2016). Trends in Global Virtual Teams: Virtual teams survey report - 2016. Retrieved December 10, 2020, accessed at: http://cdn.culturewizard.com/PDF/Trends_in_VT_Report_4-17-2016.pdf

Salas, E., Burke, C. S., & Cannon-Bowers, J. A. (2000). Teamwork: Emerging principles. *International Journal of Management Reviews, 2*(4), 339–356.

Sarker, S., Ahuja, M., Sarker, S., & Kirkeby, S. (2011). The role of communication and trust in global virtual teams: A social network perspective. *Journal of Management Information Systems, 8*, 273–309. https://doi.org/10.2753/MIS0742-1222280109

Schouten, A. P., van den Hooff, B., & Feldberg, F. (2016). Virtual Team work: Group decision making in 3D virtual environments. *Communication Research, 43*(2), 180–210.

Shao, L. H., Bouzdine-Chameeva, T., & Lunardo, R. (2020). The interacting effect of business and cultural distances on relationship management and export performance: The case of wine export between France and China. *Journal of Business & Industrial Marketing, 35*(11), 1659–1672. https://doi.org/10.1108/JBIM-04-2019-0142

Spencer, R., & Sutton-Brady, C. (2020). Interactions, relationships and networks in a digital era. Special issue call for papers from *Journal of Business & Industrial Marketing*.

Strohmeier, S. (2018). Smart HRM—A Delphi study on the application and consequences of the Internet of Things in Human Resource Management. *The International Journal of Human Resource Management, 20*(3), 528–543.

Strohmeier, S. (2020). Digital human resource management: A conceptual clarification. *German Journal of Human Resource Management, 34*(3), 345–356.

Townsend, A. M., DeMarie, S. M., & Hendrickson, A. R. (1998). Virtual teams: Technology and the workplace of the future. *The Academy of Management Executive, 12*(3), 17–29.

Turban, E., King, D., Liang, T. P., & Turban, D. (2010). Electronic commerce 2010: A managerial perspective. Pearson Education.

Webber, S. S. (2008). Development of cognitive and affective trust in teams: A longitudinal study. *Small Group Research, 39*, 746–769. https://doi.org/10.1177/1046496408323569

Weick, K. E. (1985). Cosmos vs. chaos: Sense and nonsense in electronic contexts. *Organizational Dynamics, 14*, 51–64.
Wildman, J. L., Thayer, A. L., Pavlas, D., Salas, E., Stewart, J. E., & Howse, W. R. (2012). Team knowledge research: Emerging trends and critical needs. *Human Factors: THe Journal of the Human Factors and Ergonomics Society, 54*(1), 84–111.

14

NETIQUETTE: Towards Digital Etiquette in Africa

J. N. Halm

14.1 Introduction

To refer to the advancement of information technology (IT) as a revolution would be to give it the best description available. There is rarely an aspect of human existence that the IT revolution has not touched—and at the core of this movement is technology so powerful, it just cannot be dismissed. The Internet, together with all its components and various aspects, has such power over humanity that its influence cannot be overstated.

According to Kemp (2021), as of January 2021, 59.5% of the global population of 7.83 billion, approximately 4.66 billion, use the Internet in one way or another. Nearly two-thirds of the global population will have Internet access by 2023. There will be 5.3 billion total Internet users (66% of the global population) by 2023 (Cisco, 2020). With almost six

J. N. Halm (✉)
Grit Business Group, Accra, Ghana

O. Adeola et al. (eds.), *Digital Service Delivery in Africa*, Palgrave Studies of Marketing in Emerging Economies,
https://doi.org/10.1007/978-3-030-83909-3_14

out of every ten people making use of the Internet, it is no wonder that the Internet has such a strong influence globally. There are many who spend a greater portion of their waking hours on the Internet.

Even the African continent, where it is estimated that 23% of its population has no access to a mobile-broadband network, was still able to achieve 21% growth in 4G rollout in 2020. This was during a time when growth in access to broadband was negligible in all the other regions (ITU, 2020). Virtually, all urban areas in the world are covered by a mobile-broadband network, although there are still significant gaps in rural areas. In essence, however, it is only a matter of time before the entire world is covered with Internet access.

Shea (1994) asserts that the two main purposes why people employ the Internet are to communicate with other people and to retrieve information. Among the uses of the Internet, communicating and socialising with others ranks among the top reasons people log on to the Internet. Hofstetter (2004) states that communicating with others is the most powerful use of the Internet.

The pervasive use of the Internet to communicate is not surprising since social interactions have always been a part of the human experience. Human beings are wired to be social, with our deep motivations to stay connected as basic as our need to seek pleasure and avoid pain (Lieberman, 2013). However, with the new tools and technology at the disposal of humanity especially the Internet, humankind has, to date, its great opportunity for socialising. Ours has become a world that looks and feels a lot closer socially. Technology has all but erased the great distances, physical and otherwise, that existed between individuals.

14.2 Digital Citizenship

With the Internet and other forms of digital technologies taking over the lives of individuals, there has arisen a need for the proper and codified behaviours around the use of these technologies. All users of digital technologies have rights to the use of the digital technologies available, but it is important that they act responsibly in making use of new technologies.

It is these rights and responsibilities of digital technology users that have given rise to the concept of Digital Citizenship—the norms of appropriate, responsible behaviour concerning digital technology use (Ribble & Bailey, 2007). Frau-Meigs et al. (2017) summarised the concept of Digital Citizenship as creating, working, sharing, socialising, investigating, playing, communicating, and learning with using digital technology in a competent and positive manner.

Embedded within the concept of digital citizenship is the idea of digital natives—individuals who by virtue of being birthed in the digital age tend to take the Internet for granted. The digital native is so immersed in the digital world that he or she does not see it as anything out of the ordinary. For these individuals, the Internet is very much a natural part of their daily lives, fully integrated into their daily routines (Mossberger et al., 2008). Dingli and Seychell (2015) define *digital natives* as "individuals who do not find the complexity of the digital era and constant updates in the field of technology problematic" (p. 9).

Ribble and Bailey (2007) identified nine elements that together make up digital citizenship. These are:

i. *"Digital Access: full electronic participation all society;*
ii. *Digital Commerce: the buying and selling of goods online;*
iii. *Digital Communication: the electronic exchange of information;*
iv. *Digital Literacy: the capability to use digital technology and knowing when and how to use it;*
v. *Digital Etiquette: the standards of conduct expected by other digital technology users;*
vi. *Digital Law: the legal rights and restrictions governing technology use;*
vii. *Digital Rights and Responsibilities: the privileges and freedoms extended to all digital technology users, and the behavioural expectations that come with them;*
viii. *Digital Health and Wellness: the elements of physical and psychological well-being related to digital technology use;*
ix. *Digital Security: the precautions that all technology users must take to guarantee their personal safety and the security of their network"* (p. 10).

It is important to note that the concept of digital citizenship is not restricted to only the activities of the individual when it comes to engaging with digital technology. Richardson and Milividov (2019) defined a digital citizen as someone who—through the acquisition of the right competencies— can engage in an active, positive, and responsible manner with both online and offline communities. It is the expectation of positivity and responsibility on users of digital technology, viz. the Internet that forms the basis of this chapter.

14.3 Netiquette

As implied, every society has expectations of its citizens. These expectations are what keeps society functioning with civility. In African traditional culture, etiquettes, as well as social formalities, differences in individual status, procedures, and roles of institutions are held in very high regard because they provide the foundation of community life (Chernoff, 1979). According to Idang (2015), inspite of the various different ethnic nationalities that inhabit the continent, there are always shared values among the various tribes. Any deviation from these expectations could result in interpersonal chaos that would eventually destroy society.

According to Ohler (2010), "citizenship represents doing what is right and responsible within a given social context" (p. 2). Everywhere people congregate, and there is always a need for some rules to govern behaviour. These rules are the etiquette of that society. Strawbridge (2006) defines Etiquette as a "framework of formal rules and customs governing how people behave: a description of what constitutes good manners" (p. 1). Smith (2011), however, argues that to define etiquette as rules is not accurate because although they are rooted in precedents, etiquette is also flexible and perpetually morphing.

Different rules of behaviour apply to different situations. The rules that apply in a typical African marketplace would not apply to a theatre. The rules that apply at home would not apply to a classroom. The rules that govern the behaviour of students in a classroom would not apply to the same students in a library. There is etiquette for places of worship, etiquette for places of business, and there is etiquette for social gatherings. As a new social setting, the Internet comes with its unique characteristics. It is entirely possible for one to master traditional etiquette but still be found wanting on the Internet, and thus the need for a unique set of rules to govern behaviour on the Net.

It is, however, important to note that though the rules might differ, the objectives of etiquette, whether offline and online, are largely the same—to provide an orderly and civil environment for people to interact and communicate safely. Furgang (2018) states that the goals of online etiquette and traditional etiquette are the same, i.e., to provide a safe, pleasant, and civil environment for individuals to interact. As stated earlier manners are generally fluid but according to (Post et al., 2011), they all rest on the same fundamental principles of respect, consideration, and honesty. Furgang (2018) avers that online etiquette is rooted in traditional etiquette.

As identified by Ribble and Bailey (2007), Digital Etiquette is that element of digital citizenship that has to do with the standards of conduct expected by and of digital technology users. The concept goes by several terminologies. Originally meant for e-mails as one of the earliest forms of online communication, *e-etiquette (electronic etiquette)* has been used to refer to digital etiquette. Although the term now broadly refers to all kinds of electronic etiquette. For Internet use in particular specifically though, the term adopted by many is *Netiquette*.

The jury is still out on what two words contract to make up the term, *Netiquette*. For one group, it is a contraction of "network" and "etiquette" (Doyle, 2011; Shea, 1994). For others, *Netiquette* is a combination of "Internet" and "etiquette" (Chiles, 2014; Dhingra, 2018; Grobman, 2002; Sperling, 1998).

A careful observation of the term, *Internet* itself, however, reveals that both schools of thought might be right. Cerf et al. (1974) used the term "*internetwork*" to refer to the earliest workings of what was to be later known as the Internet. In effect, *Netiquette* could therefore stand for "Internetwork etiquette".

Regardless of the source of the term, however, it is generally agreed that *Netiquette* is a set of rules for behaving appropriately online. Shea (1994) noted that the word *etiquette* was from the French word for "ticket"—an indication that without the proper behaviour, one was at risk of being prevented from gaining access to a social group. Chiles (2014) defines *Netiquette* as "the social code of the Internet". Shea (1994) refers to the term as "the etiquette of cyberspace". Kallos (2004) defines *Netiquette* as the personal or professional use of technology to communicate with "knowledge, understanding and courtesy".

Kayany (2004) asserts that *Netiquette* is an informal set of rules developed by users of the Net and developed over time to guide online behaviour. To stress the informal nature of *Netiquette*, Vassos (1996) uses the term "a loose code of ethics". Doyle (2011), on the other hand, uses the term "an unwritten code of conduct". This is to say that these are not legally binding rules but are deemed as the proper way to act on the Net. In a way, one can therefore say that *Netiquette* is simply communicating properly on the Net.

14.4 Social Media

In the late 1990s and early 2000s, a change in the nature of websites led to the second revolution of the Internet. The term Web 2.0 was used to define this gradual shift (DiNucci, 1999). Web 2.0 is a term used to refer to relatively newer websites that are highly interactive and are characterised by content that is generated by interconnected user communities (Shrivastava, 2013). Slowly, the more static, one-way model of websites began to give way to more participatory, interactive websites where content was more user generated than organisation generated. This shift gave birth to what has now become arguably the most defining feature of the Internet to date–Social Media.

The delineation of what even qualifies as *Social Media,* and what does not, is not a straightforward exercise. It is debatable. There is an argument that media by its very nature is social. However, not all media are classified as social media. The term is used by some to refer strictly to only those person-to-person interactions on sites such as Facebook and Twitter. Others, however, use the term to refer to the socialisation characteristics of Web 2.0 sites (Hunsinger & Senft, 2014). Manning (2014) used the term to refer to all newer forms of media that involve interactive participation. This definition, therefore, makes room for e-mails (short for electronic mail) to be classified as social media.

Meikle (2016) argues that web-based media and technology platforms qualify as social media platforms when they combine public media with personal communication. Before the advent of social media, communication was either private or public. With social media, the line of differentiation has been erased. Individuals are sharing private information—in some cases, too private—for public consumption. By definition, therefore, *Social Media* refers to "networked database platforms that combine public with personal communication" (Meikle, 2016: 6).

This categorisation includes platforms such as Facebook, Twitter, Reddit, Tumblr, Instagram, Blogger, and YouTube, among others. The private–public criterion, however, eliminates an important platform such as Wikipedia from social media platforms. This is because, although Wikipedia is a public-directed venture, it lacks the personal dimension that makes a media social or not. Although individuals can open accounts to get editing rights into a Wikipedia page, the inability to link those accounts with accounts of other users and friends means Wikipedia is not social media (Meikle, 2016).

Kaplan and Haenlein (2012), however, in categorising the different types of social media, add collaborative projects such as Wikipedia as social media. The 2001-founded collaboration between individuals from all over the world and from all walks of life has turned Wikipedia into the de facto key information provider on the Internet. Nguyen (2010) also added 'wikis" as forms of social media since, by definition, social media are media forms that allow for social interaction, exchanging of information, experiences as well as opinions.

Aside from collaboration projects, the other categories of social media, according to Kaplan and Haenlein (2012) include:

- blogs and micro-blogs (e.g., Twitter),
- content communities (e.g., YouTube, Daily Motion, Flickr, and Imagr),
- social networking sites (e.g., Facebook),
- virtual game worlds (e.g., World of Warcraft), and
- virtual social worlds (e.g., Second Life).

Zarrella (2010) states that there are about eight types of social media. These are blogs, micro-blogs (Twitter), social networks (Facebook, LinkedIn), media sharing sites (YouTube, Flickr), social bookmarking and voting sites (Digg, Reddit), review sites (Yelp), forums, and virtual worlds (Second Life).

Jue et al. (2010) add that various electronic tools available to help individuals connect, communicate, and collaborate should all be classified as *Social Media*. Broadly, any Internet-based website that allows users to network and connects with friends, share contents[, send messages, collaborate in real time, gather news, information, feedback, or just upload or download media files much as videos, music, photos can be classified as a social media site (Taprial & Kanwar, 2012).

With the availability of a variety of social media, it is not surprising that a vast number of people log on to one site or another daily. The number of individuals sharing their private information on social media is staggering. More than half of the global population, approximately 4.33 billion individuals, are active social media users (Kemp, 2021). As a percentage of the entire global population, active social media users constitute 55.1%. There was a 13.7% annual rise from the year 2020, an increase that was attributed to the onset of the COVID-19 pandemic. As more countries went into lockdown to curb the spread of the coronavirus, people had to turn to social media to interact with family, friends, acquaintances, and customers. In the first quarter of 2020, at the peak of the pandemic, the use of the Internet was said to have increased by 35% (Austin, 2020).

According to Tankovska (2021), as of January 2021, globally, the following were the number of users for the most popular social media platforms:

- Facebook (2.74 billion),
- YouTube (2.29 billion),
- WhatsApp (2 billion),
- Facebook Messenger (1.3 billion),
- Instagram (1.22 billion),
- Weixin/WeChat (1.21 billion),
- TikTok (689 million),

- QQ (617 million),
- Douyin (600 million),
- Sino Weibo (511 million).

The number of people using social media worldwide is projected to increase to almost 4.41 billion in 2025 (Tankovska, 2021). The exact number of social media users at any point in time is difficult to ascertain since users usually have multiple social media accounts. For instance, in China, a nation with the largest social media market, 80% of social media users had multiple social media accounts (Chiu et al., 2012).

The staggering number of daily usage is a clear indication that social media has become such a pervasive presence in the lives of people. As a matter of fact, the reach of social media has led to some arguments that it has led to a blurring of the line between what is online and what is offline. Just as a normal telephone conversation would not be regarded as anything but a part of everyday life, so has social media become a part of an individual's everyday existence (Miller et al., 2016).

14.5 Communicating on Social Media

One of the unique characteristics of social media is the ability it gives individuals to interact in real time. Instant communication is, without a doubt, one of the several benefits of social media (Dalal, 2019; Gulzar, 2020). Unlike traditional media forms, which did not give receivers the opportunity to contribute to the content being produced, social media allows receivers to express their views instantly. The instantaneous response to any message posted is, however, a recipe for disaster. Users of social media must be wary of whatever they post in the heat of the moment.

Another reason why social media communication must be treated with all seriousness is that once the message is sent, it becomes next to impossible to completely delete it. Messages that are deleted at the sender's end can still be accessed by other users. Wilbanks (2020) touches on the difficulty of removing videos, tags, and posts that are put on social media. This means that a badly communicated message would begin to cause havoc the second it is sent. The potential for social media information permanence should cause users to give every post a second thought before sending. Many reputations have been ruined on social media by ill-crafted messages.

A third reason why communication on social media must be carried out with seriousness is because of the record it leaves behind, sometimes for good. Social media communication leaves a trail, which, unlike paper, cannot be easily retrieved and burnt. Social media posts, blogs, comments on other posts, tweets, Flickr photos, YouTube videos, Facebook, and LinkedIn profiles, etc., all leave behind what Flynn (2012) refers to as the "electronic equivalent of DNA evidence".

It is common knowledge that in many organisations, when recruiting for new employees, human resource executives would first take a look at an applicant's social media footprints. This investigative work tends to provide the interviewer with information about the prospective employee—information that would not be found on the one's curriculum vitae or resume. College Admissions Officers have also been known to turn down applications from prospective applicants because of something the applicant posted on social media. Flynn (2012) quoting a CareerBuilder survey states that 45% of organisations appraise a job applicant's Facebook profile as part of the recruitment process. 35% of organisations are said to have rejected an applicant's offer because of something posted on Facebook.

Evidently, the need for a code of conduct, albeit informal, to guide the use of the Internet has been made more pronounced with the advent of social media. In its early stages, when the Internet was mainly for the sharing of research information between researchers, scientists, and academics, the need was not as great as when the Internet became a social playing field. With the floodgates opened, there was a need for some sort of code of behaviour.

14.6 The Netiquette of Social Media

It is for these reasons that individuals must take their communication via social media with all gravity. This is also why it is critical for there to be some rules to help individuals communicate on the Net. *Netiquette* is therefore for the protection of those sending messages on the Net as it is for the consideration of those receiving the messages.

According to Kemp (2021), of the many reasons for using social media, staying in touch with friends and family was the overwhelming reason (49.7%) cited by global internet users aged 16 to 64 years of age. This was followed by "filling spare time" (36.9%), "reading news stories" (36.1%), and "finding funny or entertaining content" (31.5%). Other reasons given by social media users include "seeing what is being talked about" and "finding inspiration for things to do and buy". In short, social media is predominantly a medium of communication.

Because the Internet is primarily a text-based communication medium, many of the rules that govern written communication also apply on the Internet. Many people seem to forget that the Internet is just another medium for communication and thus deserves all the decorum that is attached to other media for communication. Hickey (2015) asserts that the use of good manners and common sense are casualties of social media.

Social media indeed gives users the chance to hide behind false identities to engage in all manner of unethical and, sometimes, criminal acts. Although, with the Internet, there is nothing like absolute anonymity (Lipschultz, 2015). Even absolute anonymity in no way absolves the social media user from acting appropriately. As Shea (1994) puts it, "standards of behaviour may be different in some areas of cyberspace, but they are not lower than in real life" (p. 4).

Netiquette can be broken up into general rules those that apply to all social media and those rules that apply to specific social media.

14.7 General Etiquette

Despite the differences in social media platforms, certain rules apply to all users, regardless of the platform in question. The following are some of the general *Netiquette* that social media users must consider.

14.8 Viewers Are Human, Generally

One of the core rules of *Netiquette* is to always remember that the receiver of the message is another human being with feelings. Therefore, what one will not dare to say or will even hesitate to say to someone's face should not be sent to the one over the Net. To deliberately set out to hurt another person over the Net is inappropriate. When one considers the feelings of viewers or readers, it helps to guide the kind of content that is placed on these media. The Golden Rule should be a cardinal consideration in the use of social media. Every communication must be done with the utmost respect and decorum.

14.9 Misinformation (and Disinformation)

A lie is a lie—whether offline or online. Society frowns on individuals who are known as liars. One of the challenges of social media is the potential for untruths to be peddled easily and spread rapidly. By the time the untruth is detected for what it is, it might have travelled so far that retrieving it is next to impossible. Chen et al. (2021) assert that attempting a definition of misinformation can be complex of the many similar concepts or sub-concepts associated with the term, such as disinformation, rumours, and fake news. Misinformation is simply false or inaccurate information. However, in the area of social media, there are other terms that are related to misinformation.

Wu et al. (2019) distinguishes between misinformation and

- disinformation, which is the deliberate creation and intentional sharing of misinformation.
- fake news, which is misinformation in the form of news
- rumour, which is unverified information that can be either true or false,
- urban legend, which is disinformation related to fictional stories about local events, and
- spam, which is irrelevant information that is sent to a large number of users.

In whatever shape it comes, misinformation can have disastrous consequences for the sender, receivers, and the subject.

14.10 Social Spamming

Spamming is another breach of *Netiquette*. Originally restricted to the sending of e-mails, spamming has gradually become a problem on all social media sites (Ferrara, 2019). The term used is “social spamming” (Chakraborty et al., 2016). Social spams are even more difficult to deal than e-mails spams. This is because social spams can occur in a variety of ways that make detecting quite difficult. For instance, social spam can take the form of secretly-sponsored textual posts aimed at swaying the opinion of readers. It can also take the form of an altered photo-image shared multiple times on a site (or sites) with the sole purpose of causing dissatisfaction with a particular individual, organisation, or cause. Social spam can also be used to attempt to artificially manipulate the popularity of products or views.

14.11 Posting Private Personal Information

It is almost inevitable that social media users would get personal information out into the open. Giving out personal information is a requirement to get on to most sites. However, there is some information that should be kept off social media. The rule of thumb is that if you would not be comfortable seeing whatever you are about to post on a huge billboard in the centre of your community, do not post it.

Gupta and Brooks (2013) advise against posting information regarding birthdates and addresses. Private locations should also be kept off social media. Personal Identification Numbers (PINs) and passwords must also be kept off social media. Sharing of such personalised information can lead to identity theft, digital stalking and personalised spamming (Zheleva et al., 2012). Golden (2011), however, argues that the benefits of social media far outweigh the risks of divulging sensitive information.

14.12 Posting Sensitive Information About Another

It goes against every *Netiquette* to share sensitive and inappropriate information about someone on any social media platform. This is one of the *Netiquette* that has both ethical and legal ramifications. As stated earlier, the same standards of ethical behaviour offline should guide one's behaviour on the Net. People have been cyberbullied and targeted with hate mail simply because of information about them that was shared by someone else. If the information is of a sexual kind, the sender can be prosecuted in a court of law. Another variant of this breach is the selling of private information about others to third parties for monetary gains, without the expressed consent of the one whose information is being peddled. This is common practice with some unscrupulous businesses.

14.13 Hate Speech

Posting of any content that abuses or threatens, or expresses prejudice against a particular group, based on race, religion, or sexual orientation is deemed hate speech. Many social media sites have policies against hate speech and would remove such content immediately it is flagged up. Malmasi and Zampieri (2017) distinguish between (1) hate speech; (2) offensive language but no hate speech; and (3) no offensive content.

14.14 Proofreading Before Clicking "Send"

It is important to proofread and check for errors before sending any message, regardless of the social media platform. It is true that emoticons, acronyms, and abbreviations have become a norm in digital communication. However, the standards of effective communication remain the same. Until the receiver decodes and makes meaning of the message as intended by the sender, effective communication has not taken place. Shea (1994) affirms that checking the grammar and spelling makes the sender look good online. In reverse, a poorly crafted message might be construed as proof of a poor mind.

14.15 Accompanying the Message with the Right Emotion, When Necessary

One of the main challenges that social media users face in communicating with each other is the lack of emotion that goes with written communication. In typical face-to-face communication, the receiver can see and evaluate the verbal and non-verbal cues that accompany the message being transmitted. This enables the receiver to make a better judgment about the message. However, with the predominantly text-based nature of Internet communication, the receiver is deprived of these emotional cues. Therefore, the sender is forced to rely only on the ability of the receiver to take from the message the meaning intended by the sender.

One way to go around this is to use emotion icons (emoticons) or "smilies" to indicate the emotion that is supposed to accompany the written message. In more recent times, there has been the invention of emojis (from the Japanese e, "picture", and moji, "character"). Seargeant (2019) places the widespread adopting of emojis in 2011. Even without the use of emojis, it is important that when sending messages via social media, an individual uses the appropriate words and phrases to capture the right tone.

14.16 Respond as Soon as Possible

Social media communication is such that there is an unwritten expectation of everything happening in real time. One reason for this is because a vast majority of individuals access their social media pages via their smart mobile devices, which, as the name goes, is supposed to be with the individual at any point in time. When the response to a message is delayed, there is an assumption that the receiver has received the message and is refusing to respond. This can cause a misunderstanding between the sender and receiver, if not handled well. If the communication is conducted in a business setting, then a lack of an immediate, or at worst a quick, response can result in the business losing a client.

14.17 When Others Make Mistakes

Even the best of communicators occasionally falter. Wrong syntax, misspellings, typographical errors, etc. are all to be expected on social media. This is why it is imperative that people are measured in their response when others make mistakes on social media. Shea (1994) advises that if the correction is minor, it should be ignored. There is nothing more irritating to other users than an individual with a know-it-all attitude. If there is a need for correction of a mistake that cannot be ignored, it is best to do so in private, such as via a Messenger message or a private email.

14.18 Content Ownership

It is proper *Netiquette* to seek permission to use any content that is not one's original work and give a reference for any content owners such as photo credits. This is another of the *Netiquette* that can get one into trouble with the law. Even without the threat of criminal prosecution, it is not proper for one to use another person's creation without acknowledging the source. It is akin to stealing.

14.19 Knowing Where You Are

As much as there is *Netiquette* that governs behaviour generally on the Internet, different social media platforms also require specific etiquette. Knowing the rules that govern any particular social media that one wants to use is also *Netiquette*. Just as different social settings require different etiquette, so do different social media require different *Netiquette*. The rules that apply to Facebook would not apply to LinkedIn and vice versa.

14.20 Specific Etiquette

Vaynerchuk (2013) refers to the unique content on different social media as "native content"– "native" because the content in question is indigenous or designed specifically with that platform in mind. One of the first things users need to know is what content is native to specific social media. Relatively lengthy videos are native on YouTube but might not sit too well on LinkedIn. Casual fun-looking images are native to Facebook and Instagram, but those same images are not native to LinkedIn. Knowing what is native helps the user post content that will be readily accepted on the social media site in question.

14.21 Facebook

Treadaway and Smith (2012) describe Facebook as the "digital cooler" of our days—a place we gather around to discuss the affairs of the day. One of *Netiquette* of Facebook is to desist from spamming, i.e., frequently contacting people with unsolicited and unwanted friend requests. Fortunately, Facebook is able to detect what messages qualify as spam. The company would then warn targeted users. In some cases, Facebook is able to deactivate the account of the spammer. Gunther (2012) advises users not to see friends list as a competition to see who has the most. Quality should be the consideration and not quantity when it comes Facebook friends.

14.22 Twitter

Since its inception in 2006, Twitter has grown to become an international social media phenomenon. The etiquette that apply to Twitter specifically is referred to by many as *Twittequettes* (Kent, 2015). One of the first has to do with the limit on the number of characters permissible on a Twitter post. This calls for the use of short, effective phrases, statistics, links, and quotes (CMI, 2014). Twitter is not a place for long posts. If Twitter is the social media of choice, then the individual must be ready to tweet regularly.

14.23 Instagram

According to Amaral (2015), Instagram is a combination of "instant camera" and "telegram". Although Instagram is listed as a photo and video-sharing social networking site, it is mainly known for its photos. Therefore, it is expected that individuals will be wary of the quality of photos they post on the site. Holmes (2015) advises users not to post too much too often, suggesting users restrict themselves to no more than two posts a day. Failure to heed to abode by this *Netiquette* can result in other users unfollowing the individual.

14.24 LinkedIn

Because of its core mandate of being a professionals-only social media site, it is expected of LinkedIn users to always behave professionally on the site. Profile photos must be professional headshots. It is proper *Netiquette* to complete one's profile on LinkedIn. An incomplete profile does not speak well of the individual. When sending requests for links, it is appropriate to not spam the requests. Requests should be sent to individuals personally. It is good to have a large network of contacts. However, the desire for large contacts should not mean invading the privacy of others with incessant requests. A key etiquette to observe on LinkedIn is to offer help to other professionals on the platform by providing useful information that would help them succeed (McCormick, 2016).

14.25 YouTube

The one difference between YouTube and other social media platforms is that it is a strictly online video platform. Therefore, one of its main etiquette is the posting of decent videos. Videos must also be of high quality. Low-quality videos are not only frustrating for customers, but they are an indictment on the individual or organisation posting them. It is also important to keep YouTube videos quite short, due to the short attention of most viewers. YouTube allows for comments under posts. It is therefore important for those comments to be monitored by the individual posting the videos. Where necessary, it is polite to respond to comments. To ensure that others outside of your domain get to make sense of a video, uploading the transcript is a must (Atwood, 2018).

Hickey (2015) asserts that good manners are made up of three important components. These are kindness, respect, and consideration of others. These three form the basis of the etiquette of the Internet and, by extension, on social media. It is interesting to note that these form the basis of African traditional family values. Bailey (2005) provides a dozen specific family values including respect, manners, compassion, kindness, empathy, sympathy, patience, tolerance, humility, meekness, helpfulness, and imagination skills. As more and more Africans get connected to the Internet, they must come onto the platform imbibed with these traditional values that have held for centuries on the continent.

14.26 Conclusion

The Internet and by extension, social media have changed the communications landscape. Businesses and individuals alike are logging on and spending more time on the Internet regularly. As the number of users of social media increases, and Africa makes more of its presence felt on social media, the need for adherence to *Netiquette* would become more important. This compilation of informal etiquette is meant to bring some sanity to communication on the Net. Those who will flout these rules might not get prosecuted in a court of law, but the repercussions might not be any less detrimental.

References

Amaral, I. (2015). Instagram. In F. F. Wherry & J. B. Schor (Eds.), *The SAGE encyclopedia of economics and society* (pp. 943–944). Sage.

Atwood, F. (2018). *Views, subscribers, likes & shares!": How to rank & bank your YouTube videos*. Atwood Publishing.

Austin, P. L. (2020, March). We're online more than ever right now. Can the internet itself keep up? *TIME*. Retrieved May 28 from https://time.com/5810991/internet-coronavirus/

Bailey, J. A. (2005). *Echoes of ancient African values*. Authorhouse.

Cerf, V., Dalal, Y., & Sunshine, C. (1974). Specification of internet transmission control program. *Request for Comments (RFC)* 675. Retrieved May 18, 2021 from https://datatracker.ietf.org/doc/html/rfc675

Chakraborty, M., Pal, S., Pramanik, R., & Chowdary, C. R. (2016). Recent developments in social spam detection and combating techniques: A survey. *Information Processing & Management, 52*(6), 1053–1073. https://doi.org/10.1016/j.ipm.2016.04.009

Chen, K., Luo, Y., Hu, A., Zhao, J., & Zhang, L. (2021). Characteristics of misinformation spreading on social media during the COVID-19 outbreak in China: A descriptive analysis. *Risk Management and Healthcare Policy, 14*, 1869–1879. https://doi.org/10.2147/RMHP.S312327

Chernoff, J. M. (1979). *African rhythm and African sensibility: Aesthetics, and social action in African musician idioms*. University of Chicago Press.

Chiles, D. (2014). *Internet etiquette: Netiquette fundamentals, rules, & optimization*. (n. p.)

Chiu, C., Ip, C., & Silverman, A. (2012). Understanding social media in China. *McKinsey Quarterly, 2*, 78–81.

Cisco. (2020). *Cisco annual internet report (2018–2023)* [White paper]. https://www.cisco.com/c/en/us/solutions/collateral/executive-perspectives/annual-internet-report/white-paper-c11-741490.pdf

CMI. (2014). *Online etiquette: A manager's guide to using social media*. Chartered Management Institute.

Dalal, M. (2019). *Modern communication with social media: A simplified primer to communication and social media.* BPB Publications.
Dhingra, N. (2018). *Gateway to computer studies class 05*. V-Connect Education.
Dingli, A., & Seychell, D. (2015). *The new digital natives: Cutting the chord.* Springer-Verlag, Berlin Heidelberg.
DiNucci, D. (1999). Fragmented Future. *Print, 53*(4): 32, 221–222.
Doyle, C. (2011). *A dictionary of marketing* (3rd edition). Oxford University Press.
Ferrara, E. (2019). The history of digital spam. *Communications of the ACM, 62*(8), 82–91. https://doi.org/10.1145/3299768
Flynn, N. (2012). *The social media handbook: Rules, policies, and best practices to effectively manage your organisation's social media presence, posts and potential risks.* Pfeiffer.
Frau-Meigs, D., O'Neill, B., Soriani, A., & Tomé, V. (2017). *Digital citizenship education: Overview and new perspectives (Vol. 1).* Council of Europe.
Furgang, K. (2018). *Netiquette: A student's guide to digital etiquette.* The Rosen Publishing Group.
Golden, M. (2011). *Social media strategies for professionals and their firms: The guide to establishing credibility and accelerating relationships.* John Wiley & Sons.
Grobman, G. M. (2002). *The Pennsylvania nonprofit handbook.* White Hat Communications.
Gulzar, U. (2020). A critical appraisal of crime over social networking sites in the context of India: Social Networking Sites. In K. Serpil (Ed.), *New Media and Visual Communication in Social Networks* (pp. 93–112). IGI Global.
Gunther, S. K. (2012). *Sams teach yourself Facebook in 10 minutes* (3rd ed.). SAMS.
Gupta, R., & Brooks, H. (2013). *Using social media for global security.* John Wiley & Sons.
Hickey, J. P. (2015). *Oops! Did I really post that? Online etiquette in the new digital age*. Motivational Press.
Hofstetter, F. T. (2004). *Internet technologies at work.* McGraw-Hill Technology Education.
Holmes, J. (2015). *Instagram blackbook: Everything you need to know about Instagram for business and personal*. (n. p.)
Hunsinger, J., & Senft, T. M. (Eds.). (2014). *The social media handbook.* Routledge.
Idang, G. E. (2015). African culture and values. *Phronimon, 16*(2), 97–111.

ITU. (2020). *Measuring digital development: Facts and figures 2020*. International Telecommunication Union

Jue, A. L., Marr, J. A., & Kassotakis, M. E. (2010). *Social media at work: How networking tools propel organizational performance*. Jossey-Bass.

Kallos, J. (2004). *Because netiquette matters! Your comprehensive reference guide to email etiquette and proper technology use*. Xlibris.

Kaplan, A., & Haenlein, M. (2012). Social media: Back to the roots and back to the future. *Journal of Systems and Information Technology, 14*(2), 101–104. https://doi.org/10.1108/13287261211232126

Kayany, J. M. (2004). Internet etiquette (Netiquette). G - OIn H. Bidgoli (Ed.), *The internet encyclopedia* (Vol. 2, pp. 275–284). John Wiley & Sons.

Kemp, S. (2021). *Digital 2021: Global overview report*. We Are Social Inc. https://wearesocial.com/digital-2021

Kent, G. (2015). *You are what you tweet: Harness the power of twitter to create a happier, healthier life*. Star Stone Press.

Lieberman, M. D. (2013). *Social: Why our brains are wired to connect*. Oxford University Press.

Lipschultz, J. H. (2015). *Social media communication: Concepts, practices, data, law and ethics*. Routledge.

Malmasi, S., & Zampieri, M. (2017). Detecting Hate Speech in Social Media. *Proceedings of the international conference, recent advances in natural language processing, RANLP 2017*, 467–472. https://doi.org/10.26615/978-954-452-049-6_062

Manning, J. (2014). Social media, definition and classes of. In K. Harvey (Ed.), *Encyclopedia of social media and politics* (pp. 1158–1162). Sage.

McCormick, D. (2016). *The LinkedIn manual for rookies: Answering the age-old question, "Okay, I'm on LinkedIn, now what do I do?"* Duswalt Press.

Meikle, G. (2016). *Social media: Communication, sharing and visibility*. Routledge.

Miller, D., Costa, E., Haynes, N., McDonald, T., Nicolescu, R., Sinanan, J., Spyer, J., Venkatraman, S., & Wang, X. (2016). *How the world changed social media*. UCL.

Mossberger, K., Tolbert, C. J., & McNeal, R. S. (2008). *Digital citizenship: The internet, society, and participation*. Massachusetts Institute of Technology.

Nguyen, L. (2010). *Providing customer service by use of social media channels: Best practices*. GRIN Verlag, https://www.grin.com/document/183360

Ohler, J. B. (2010). *Digital community, digital citizen*. Corwin.

Post, P., Post, A. L., Post, L., & Senning, D. O. (2011). *Emily Post's etiquette: Manners for a new world*. William Morrow.

Ribble, M., & Bailey, G. (2007). *Digital citizenship in schools*. International Society for Technology. in Education.

Richardson, J., & Milividov, E. (2019). *Digital citizenship education handbook: Being online, well-being online, and rights online*. Council of Europe.

Seargeant, P. (2019). *The emoji revolution: How technology is shaping the future of communication*. Cambridge University Press.

Shea, V. (1994). *Netiquette*. Albion Books.

Shrivastava, K. M. (2013). *Social media in business and governance*. Sterling Publishers.

Smith, J. R. R. (2011). *The etiquette book: A complete guide to modern manners*. Sterling

Sperling, D. (1998). *Dave Sperling's internet guide*. Prentice Hall.

Strawbridge, M. (2006). *Netiquette: Internet etiquette in the age of the blog*. Software Reference Ltd.

Tankovska, H. (2021). Most popular social networks worldwide as of January 2021, ranked by number of active users. *Statista.com*. Retrieved May 18, 2021 from https://www.statista.com/statistics/272014/global-social-networks-ranked-by-number-of-users/

Taprial, V., & Kanwar, P. (2012). *Understanding social media*. Bookboon.

Treadaway, C., & Smith, M. (2012). *Facebook marketing: An hour a day* (2nd ed.). John Wiley & Sons.

Vassos, T. (1996). *Strategic internet marketing*. Que.

Vaynerchuk, G. (2013). *Jab, jab, jab, right hook: How to tell your story in a noisy social world*. Harper Business

Wilbanks, L. R. (2020). Cyber Risks in Social Media. In G. H. Meiselwitz (Ed.), *Social computing and social media. Design, ethics, user behavior and social network analysis*, (Part 1, pp. 393–406). Springer Nature Switzerland.

Wu, L., Morstatter, F., Carley, K., & Liu, H. (2019). Misinformation in social media: Definition, manipulation, and detection. *ACM SIGKDD Explorations Newsletter., 21*, 80–90. https://doi.org/10.1145/3373464.3373475

Zarrella, D. (2010). *The social media marketing book*. O'Reilly Media.

Zheleva, E., Terzi, E., & Getoor, L. (2012). *Privacy in social networks*. Morgan & Claypool.

Index

A

Accountable 33
Accumulating Savings and Credit Associations (ACSAs) 163
Africa 158, 159
Africa's digital economy 59, 60
African Founded Firms 54, 55
AI-approach 168
Alibaba 54
Alphabet 4
Amazon 4, 57
Artificial Intelligence 287
Axial coding 28

B

Big Data Analytics 287
Blockchain 143, 287
Blogs and micro-blogs 333, 334
Business Change Management 287
Business Networks 287

C

Cloud Computing 143, 287
Cocoa Farmer Access to Mobile Banking Technology Benefit (CFAMBTB) Model 192
"CocoaLink" 191
Computer-based technology 21
Consumer behaviour tracking 305
Contemporary technology 188
Content communities 333
COVID-19 pandemic 6, 53, 306
Cultural barrier 120
Customer relationship management 82
Cyberspace 332

O. Adeola et al. (eds.), *Digital Service Delivery in Africa*, Palgrave Studies of Marketing in Emerging Economies,
https://doi.org/10.1007/978-3-030-83909-3

D

Data analytics 20
Developed countries 53
Dialogical interactions 28
Digital Access 329
Digital age 282, 283
Digital applications 230
Digital bricolage 260, 261
Digital business 205, 206
Digital business ecosystems (DBE) 215, 216
Digital Channels 8
Digital Citizenship 328, 329
Digital Commerce 329
Digital communication 305, 327, 329
Digital context 136
Digital conversations 27
Digital-driven stokvel 166
Digital economy 54, 55, 113
Digital economy value chain 56, 60
Digital enabler 136
Digital entrepreneurship 9, 10, 158, 164, 251
Digital environment 144
Digital era 282
Digital Etiquette 329
Digital evolution 305
Digital financial services 18, 187
Digital Health and Wellness 329
Digital infrastructure 59
Digital innovation 281
Digitalisation 4, 206
Digital Law 329
Digital Literacy 329
Digitally savvy 255
Digital market space 283
Digital mechanics 305
Digital organisations 144
Digital outcome 136
Digital payments 18
Digital platform capability 83
Digital platforms 144
Digital public services 230
Digital revolution 281
Digital Rights and Responsibilities 329
Digital security 286, 287, 329
Digital service delivery (DSD) 7, 229
Digital Services in Africa 64
Digital skill gap 283
Digital skills 57, 282, 283
Digital skills and competencies 286
Digital space 282
Digital supply chain management 9
Digital supply chains 107
Digital supply chain transformation 111
Digital technology(ies) 4, 56, 81, 230, 231, 305, 306, 328
Digital threats 287
Digital transformation 4, 81
Digitisation 17, 107, 305
Digitisation capability 20
Douyin 335
Dynamic capabilities (DC) 143

E

East African marketing 207, 208
E-Citizen Services 236
Economic transactions 56
E-Energy Services 240
E-government services 235
E-Health Care Services 238
Electronic communication technologies 219

Electronic data management systems (EDMS) 241
Emerging economies 158
Emotional value 213
Entrepreneurial digital competencies (EDC) 252
Entrepreneurship 287
Environmental barrier 119
E-Social Protection Services 237
E-stokvel 180

F

Fab/maker space movement 258
Facebook 57, 334
Facebook Messenger 334
Fastest-growing economies 5
Fast-expanding markets 22
Financial barrier 117
Financial services providers (FSPs) 19, 20, 23
Financial system 188
FinTechs 69, 70
Flutterwave 4
Fourth-generation (4G) 207
'Fourth industrial revolution' 231

G

Ghana 17
Global business community 306
Global markets 306
Greenage Energy 7

H

Healthcare and healthtech 65
Hierarchical relations 21

I

Informal credit systems 163
Information Communication Technology (ICT) 283, 284
Information technology systems 229
Infrastructural barrier 119
In-Memory Databases 287
Innovative digital technologies 107
Instagram 334
Internet Corporation for Assigned Names and Numbers (ICANN) 232
Internet, Internet of things (IoT) 305
Internet of Things (IoT) 143, 287
Intra-African commerce 253

J

Jumia 4
JumiaPay 70

K

Kenya 17
Knowledge and skills barrier 118

L

Licensed buying companies (LBCs) 197, 198
Logistics 66, 67
Lori Systems 67

M

Marketing dynamics 305
Marketplace 4
Market relations 21
Mckinsey 7S model 205

Microenterprise customers (CMEs) 19
Microenterprises 22
Microsoft Teams 315
Mobile banking technology 187, 188
Mobile money 67
Mobile Network Operators (MNOs) 194
Mobile Technologies 287
Mpesa 4

N
National Education Management Information (NEMIS) 241
Netflix 57
Netiquette 327
Network *Animation* 28
Novel Interfaces 287

O
Online business development resources 147
Organisational barrier 119, 120

P
PayPal 57
Platformisation 218
Platforms 64, 65
Product/service integration 287
Professional 22
Psychological Factors 312
Purchasing clerks (PCs) 198

Q
QQ 335

R
Regulatory barrier 118
Resource-based theory 281
Resource-based view (RBV) 84
Retail and ecommerce 65
Rotating Savings and Credit Associations (ROSCAs) 163

S
Seizing capabilities 85
Sino Weibo 335
Skill gap 282
Skype 315
Smart agriculture 189
Social ecosystem(s) 18, 19, 32, 33
Social media 21, 22, 287, 305
Social network animation 32
Social Network *Construction* 28, 29
Social networking sites 333
Social networks 17, 18
Social networks reinvention 36
Social relations 21
Social spamming 339
Social sustainability 17
Social ties 21
Stokvel 163–165
Strategic Environmental Management (SEM) 218
Strategic postures 11
Structural equation modelling (SEM-PLS) 81
Sub-Saharan African (SSA) 8, 187
Sustainable digital supply chains (DSC) 111

T

Technical and vocational training (TVET) 241
Telecommunications operators 187
Tesla 4
TikTok 334
Traditional stokvel 178, 179

U

United Nations Sustainable Development Goals (SDGs) 56

V

Virtual game worlds 333
Virtually 328
Virtual social worlds 333
Virtual team leaders 315
Virtual Teams 12
Virtual team working 306

W

Webex 315
Weixin/WeChat 334
WhatsApp 334
WhatsApp-Operated informal credit 166
Workgroups 311
World Cocoa Foundation 193

Y

YouTube 334

Z

Zoom 314, 315

The manufacturer's authorised representative in the EU is Springer Nature Customer Service Centre GmbH, Europaplatz 3, 69115 Heidelberg, Germany. If you have any concerns regarding our products, please contact ProductSafety@springernature.com

Printed and bound by CPI Group (UK) Ltd, Croydon, CR0 4YY
22/09/2026
02221063-0007